"This ambitious book represents an outstanding contribution that bridges psycho-analytic thought, contemporary neuroscience, developmental psychology, and the cultural context, creating a cohesive and unique dialogue across these essential disciplines. The approach and language are exceptionally clear ensuring that this book will appeal to readers from diverse professional backgrounds—clinicians, researchers, as well as academics—helping them think deeply about complex inter-disciplinary approaches. By thoughtfully integrating diverse perspectives this book not only enriches our theoretical understanding but also provides practical tools for clinicians. It is an indispensable resource, expertly crafted to advance both clinical intervention and scholarly inquiry."

Eamon McCrory, *CEO of Anna Freud and Professor of Developmental Neuroscience and Psychopathology at UCL, London, UK.*

"A marvellous resource book for clinicians, researchers, policy makers, as well as parents themselves, which brings together the varied disciplines within the peri-natal field. This much-needed book takes the reader on a dazzling journey through the prism of psychoanalytic, developmental, psychosocial, neuroscientific, cross-cultural, and empirical lenses. In linking the diverse disciplines in the field, the authors encompass the internal and external dimensions that shape our understand-ing of conception, pregnancy, and birth, the transition to parenthood, infant devel-opment, and the parent-infant relationship. This creative synergy provides the most comprehensive account of human development for the twenty-first century, tack-ling issues such as new reproductive technologies, socio-cultural developments, and cutting-edge research. These varied perspectives are in a constant dialogue throughout, helping to build an understanding of the complexity of early parent-hood and infancy, and of the foundations of human development. Not only this, but the book also achieves a remarkable synthesis, with a unique way of inte-grating the different approaches it explores and formulating their implications for our understanding of the developing infant's needs, and the emotional challenges of parenthood. This unique book will stimulate wider explorations, new jumping off points for research, and engender the birth of many developments clinically, and theoretically. Above all it is rich with informed and practical guidance for practitioners and parents alike. Beautifully written, with vivid and compelling clin-ical vignettes, it is a book that is full of life. A must read, this is set to be a game changer for clinicians, researchers and policy makers in perinatal health and social care—and beyond."

Andrew Balfour, *PhD, CEO Tavistock Relationships.*

"This book provides an innovative and contemporary perspective on infancy and parenthood, through socio-cultural, neurobiological, developmental and psycho-analytic writing. The centrality of the parent-infant relationship is woven throughout the book in lively examples as well as by masterful introductions and summaries by the editors. The combination of psychoanalytic theory, with the twenty-first century world of assisted ways to become a parent, while also addressing the inter-sectional issues of social, economic, cultural, and racial aspects of infancy and parenthood is unique and a hugely welcome addition to the modern field of parent-infant psychotherapy."

Michela Biseo, *ACP, BPC. Child & Adolescent Psychotherapist, Psychoanalytic Parent-Infant Psychotherapist, Course Director of the Specialist training in Parent-Infant Psychotherapy at the British Psychotherapy Foundation, London, UK.*

"This book takes the reader where no other book has taken them before; at that crit-ical time in the human life span when the relational and cultural history of one gen-eration becomes embodied in the minds and brains of the next. In this pathbreaking synthesis, the reader learns from state-of-the-art research, as well as from mature, clinical wisdom, but, most importantly, the reader is given for the first time the tools to finally understand how to fill in the knowledge gaps between the fields."

Katerina Fotopoulou, *Professor of Psychodynamic Neuroscience at University College London (UCL) and chartered psychologist and psychotherapist.*

"This lively, engaging and thought-provoking book achieves the remarkable feat of bringing multiple disciplinary perspectives into meaningful dialogue around the vital experiences of infancy and early parenthood, which should be of interest to us all given the enormous significance of this critical period of life for later develop-ment. Importantly, alongside the psychoanalytic and developmental perspectives the authors have included both neuroscientific research and a consideration of the ways in which families' varying cultural contexts can challenge our theoretical assumptions about what 'good enough' looks like, resulting in a thoroughly up-to-date contribution. Essential reading for everyone with an interest in the early years."

Liz Allison, *Director of the UCL Psychoanalysis Unit.*

"This impressive book spans the disciplines of psychoanalysis, developmental and neurobiological research, socio-cultural and attachment theory and their appli-cations in the broad field of early life. It is thoroughly contemporary in what it encompasses without neglecting the wisdom of earlier contributions; a pleasure to read across its complexity where experiences of conception, pregnancy, birth, and early life are presented in the round, enriching our understanding."

Angela Joyce, *Training and Supervising Analyst of the British Psychoanalytical Society and pioneered work with parents and infants at the Anna Freud.*

"This volume offers the most comprehensive and up-to-date exploration of psychoanalytic perspectives on early development, weaving together insights from psychoanalysis, neuroscience, and developmental research. It provides a landmark synthesis of contemporary thought on infancy and early parenthood. With its clear and accessible style, it invites seasoned researchers and clinicians as well as curious newcomers to engage deeply with the latest thinking in the field. Essential reading for anyone interested in the emotional foundations of early life, this book promises to be a lasting resource for years to come."

Patrick Luyten, *Professor of Psychodynamic Psychology at the Research Department of Clinical, Educational and Psychology and Director of the PhD in Psychoanalysis programme in UCL, London, UK.*

Perspectives on Early Parenthood and Infancy

Perspectives on Early Parenthood and Infancy offers a comprehensive exploration of these vital life stages through the lenses of psychoanalysis, neuroscience, developmental psychology, and diverse socio-cultural contexts.

Chronologically structured, this edited collection traces key stages of development through a rich collection of contributions from clinicians, researchers, and academics across a wide range of backgrounds and disciplines. The contributors look in turn at the milestones of conception and pregnancy to birth and the transition to parenthood, paying close attention to infancy and the early parent-infant relationship. The chapters explore pivotal themes, including the rapidly evolving landscape of assisted conception; the physical changes and psychological vulnerability experienced during pregnancy, birth, and early parenthood; parents' unconscious defence mechanisms; experiences of weaning, feeding, and sleeping; the perspectives of marginalised parents; and the vital role of cultural awareness in clinical practice. These topics are brought to life through clinical vignettes and current research findings woven throughout the book.

Presenting complex and meaningful information in an accessible way, each section of the book features integrative discussion chapters written by the editors, which deepen theoretical understanding, while providing practical tools for clinical application and academic research, making this volume a valuable resource for both practitioners and researchers, as well as parents.

Alejandra Perez is a psychoanalyst, Fellow of the British Psychoanalytical Society, and Psychoanalytic Parent-Infant Psychotherapist. Former Director of the MSc Early Child Development and Clinical Applications at UCL/Anna Freud (2012–2024), she now directs the Lab of Experiences and Adjustments in Parenthood in London, UK.

Elena Panagiotopoulou is a psychodynamic psychotherapist working with couples and individuals, as well as a mixed-methods researcher. She currently serves as Director of the MSc Early Child Development and Clinical Applications at UCL/Anna Freud, London, UK.

Ruth Roberts is an academic and mixed-methods researcher. She is a Senior Researcher in the Lab of Experiences and Adjustments in Parenthood at the Anna Freud, London, UK.

Perspectives on Early Parenthood and Infancy

A Psychoanalytic, Neuroscientific, Developmental and Cultural Dialogue

Edited by Alejandra Perez,
Elena Panagiotopoulou and
Ruth Roberts

Routledge
Taylor & Francis Group

LONDON AND NEW YORK

Designed cover image: Getty Image © ivetavaicule

First published 2026
by Routledge
4 Park Square, Milton Park, Abingdon, Oxon OX14 4RN

and by Routledge
605 Third Avenue, New York, NY 10158

Routledge is an imprint of the Taylor & Francis Group, an informa business

For Product Safety Concerns and Information please contact our EU representative GPSR@taylorandfrancis.com. Taylor & Francis Verlag GmbH, Kaufingerstraße 24, 80331 München, Germany.

Trademark notice: Product or corporate names may be trademarks or registered trademarks, and are used only for identification and explanation without intent to infringe.

British Library Cataloguing-in-Publication Data
A catalogue record for this book is available from the British Library

ISBN: 978-1-032-87017-5 (hbk)
ISBN: 978-1-032-86438-9 (pbk)
ISBN: 978-1-003-53047-3 (ebk)

DOI: 10.4324/9781003530473

Typeset in Times New Roman
by Newgen Publishing UK

To parents,
in their own, varied, and ever-changing parenthood
journey

Contents

Contributors

Editors' bios

Alejandra Perez is a London-based psychoanalyst, Fellow of the British Psychoanalytical Society and Psychoanalytic Parent-Infant Psychotherapist, member of the British Psychotherapy Foundation and the Anna Freud. She is part of the Executive Committee of the Psychoanalytic Parent-Infant Psychotherapy training at the British Psychotherapy Foundation. She was Programme Director of the MSc Early Child Development and Clinical Applications at University College London/Anna Freud (from 2012 to 2024). There she led the restructure of the programme, introducing clinical placements and bringing psychoanalytic theory and practice into dialogue with current research in neuroscience and developmental psychology, as well as including cultural perspectives in the teaching.

Perez supervises psychoanalytic clinical work and gives talks in the UK and internationally on clinical work with parents and infants, psychoanalysis, psychic development, and parenthood. She is currently director of LEAP (Lab of Experiences and Adjustments in Parenthood), which explores the parent-child relationship and parents' subjective experiences during the early years. She holds a PhD in Psychology from University College London, with a focus on intergenerational attachment representations. Her previous research work includes mixed-methods research on psychoanalysts' styles of working, qualitative research on mothers' experiences, and systematic reviews for the NICE mental health guidelines. She has published on her clinical and research work in international journals.

Elena Panagiotopoulou is an academic, mixed-methods researcher, and qualified couple and individual psychodynamic psychotherapist. She is currently the Programme Director of the MSc in Early Child Development and Clinical Applications at University College London (UCL)/Anna Freud, and a Senior Researcher in the Lab of Experiences and Adjustments in Parenthood (LEAP) at the Anna Freud. Clinically, she works with individuals and couples at Tavistock Relationships. Elena has an interdisciplinary academic background in psychoanalytic developmental psychology and cognitive neuroscience. She holds a PhD in Psychodynamic Neuroscience from UCL and has completed a psychodynamic psychotherapy training at Tavistock Relationships, accredited by the British Association for Counselling and Psychotherapy (BACP). Her research focuses on the bodily self, particularly during the perinatal period. Her work has been funded by the Economic and Social Research Council (ESRC) and the Neuropsychoanalysis Association (NPSA) and has been published in a range of high-impact international journals.

Ruth Roberts is an academic, mixed-methods researcher. She is currently a Senior Researcher in the Lab of Experiences and Adjustments in Parenthood (LEAP) at the Anna Freud. Ruth holds a PhD in Clinical, Educational and Health Psychology from University College London, with a focus on families with a child with conduct disorder. Her research work has focused on parenting, family functioning, child mentalising, child development, schools-based research, and longitudinal studies. She has presented her work internationally and has published her research in a range of high-impact international journals.

Authors' bios

Rachel Abedi is a Child & Adolescent Psychotherapist with experience in CAMHS, schools and research. Passionate about bridging the gap in faith-sensitive mental health provision for Muslim children, Rachel's clinical focus is on developing accessible psychotherapy services for Muslim children and families, in collaboration with community groups.

Erika Barba-Müller PhD, is a neuroscientist, psychotherapist, and psychoanalyst specialising in motherhood's neurobiology. Her research on maternal brain changes was recognised among 2016's top scientific discoveries. Based in Barcelona, she teaches, conducts research, and integrates neuroscience with psychoanalysis to improve mental health care and psychological treatments.

Andrew J. Bremner specialises in multisensory development in infancy. He completed his DPhil Psychology with Professor Peter Bryant FRS at the University of Oxford taking up an academic post at Goldsmiths, University of London, 2005–2018, latterly as Head of Psychology. Since 2018, he has been at the University of Birmingham.

Orli Dahan is a philosopher and Head of the Multidisciplinary Studies Department at Tel-Hai College, Israel. Her research encompasses the philosophy of science, consciousness studies, sexuality, and evolutionary psychology. In recent years, she has explored altered states during childbirth, coining the term 'birthing consciousness' to describe the unique state women experience during physiological birth. Dahan bridges academic research with public engagement, lecturing midwives and doctors, collaborating with healthcare professionals, delivering public talks and interviews, and advocating for optimal birthing practices. Her work aims to raise awareness and enhance women's physical and mental well-being through evidence-based childbirth insights.

Ken Daniels is an Adjunct Professor at the University of Canterbury in New Zealand. His involvement as a researcher, policy analyst, counsellor, and educator spans 50 years both in New Zealand and internationally. He has published widely in this field.

Tisha Dasgupta is an Academic Researcher specialising in inequalities in maternal and child health. Her work focuses on health systems research and service engagement for those from minoritised and marginalised groups.

Alexandra de Rementeria is Principal Child and Adolescent Psychotherapist at Lambeth CAMHS, Co-Course Lead for the Masters in Psychoanalytic Observation at the Tavistock (M7) and former Editor in Chief of the Journal of Child Psychotherapy. She is also a tutor, supervisor, and doctoral examiner on the Child Psychotherapy Training at the Tavistock (M80) and lectures nationally and internationally. She has published numerous papers and co-authored 'Finding Your Way With Your Baby' a BMA award winning book, with Dilys Daws.

Dan Erickson PhD, CFLE, is an Assistant Teaching Professor at Arizona State University where he directs the Certified Family Life Educator programme. He earned a doctorate in human development and family science from The University of Arizona. His research focuses on sibling relationships across the lifespan and the intersection of queer and religious identities. He loves mentoring students and teaching courses related to family diversity, theory, and intimate relationships. He is a father to two phenomenal humans and two exceptional white fluffy dogs. Dr Erickson constantly yearns to be near the ocean, mountains, and forest, and cherishes spending time with his family.

Katherine Fine is a psychoanalytic psychotherapist with the British Psychotherapy Foundation, working in private practice in London. She is a Clinical Associate of the Independent Psychology Service. A member of the Donor Conception Network since its inception in 1993, she has facilitated both 'Preparation for (donor conception) Parenthood' and 'Talking and Telling' workshops. She is a visiting lecturer and supervisor. She is editor of *Donor Conception for Life* (Karnac Books, 2015).

Bola Grace has extensive experience in women's health and reproductive health across multiple sectors. She has published widely, and values collaborative research in this area. She holds a PhD in Population Health & Epidemiology from University College London and an Executive MBA from the University of Cambridge Judge Business School.

Claudia Goulder is a Child and Adolescent Psychotherapist (ACP) and facilitator of postnatal 'birth reflections' classes for the charity Pregnant in West London. She previously worked with new and expectant parents in the perinatal mental health team at Chelsea & Westminster Hospital.

Vasanti Jadva is Professor of Family Psychology at City St Georges, University of London. She holds honorary positions at the Centre for Child, Adolescent and Family Research, University of Cambridge and the Institute for Women's Health, UCL. Her research focuses on the psychological outcomes for parents and children in families created by assisted reproduction including IVF, egg donation, sperm donation, and surrogacy.

Dominic Jones is a Course Tutor at Anna Freud, developing seminars and workshops on various domains of child development, including language, attachment, play, affect regulation, parenthood and so on. He has worked in education and mental health settings (Under 5s Child Psychotherapy), conducted research with non-traditional families (LEAPS), and has a background in social sciences (London School of Economics). His research and scholarly interests extend to anthropology, history, and psychoanalysis.

Akira Kanazawa is an associate professor at Kobe city university of foreign studies and has a PhD in Human Science from Osaka University. His main research interest includes low birth rate issue in Japan and creating parenthood education programme for young people. He is also a clinical psychologist and had training for child psychotherapist in Japan and worked with severely deprived children and children with autism at orphanage and paediatric hospital. Currently, he has been working with children and parents at preschools and middle schools.

Amanda Lucas is the founding director of UK parent-infant charity, Babygro, based in Cornwall. Babygro aims to inform and empower parents, and those that work with families, by communicating leading-edge research on parent-infant communication, brain development, and links to later-life (mental) health, and well-being.

Letitia Meadows is a Lecturer with the Department of Social Work at the University of Canterbury in Aotearoa New Zealand. Her research interests are primarily orientated to reproductive health and reproductive justice. She has a social work practice background in Women's Health.

Ana Mesquita is a biologist and researcher at ProChild CoLAB and Coordinator of the Biology and Development area. She holds a PhD in Biological and Biomedical Sciences from the University of Minho and conducts interdisciplinary research on early adversity and child development, with a focus on epigenetic and neurobiological mechanisms.

Lydia B. Munns is a Postdoctoral Researcher at the University of Oxford with a background in perinatal mental health and bodily experiences. She completed her PhD in Psychology at the University of York in 2024, researching how bodily changes during pregnancy influence maternal well-being, infant outcomes, attachment, and breastfeeding. She has published multiple articles in this area, exploring how perinatal bodily experiences shape psychological well-being and mother-infant relationships, and is particularly interested in using this research to inform policy change in perinatal healthcare.

Coretta Ogbuagu is a consultant child and adolescent psychoanalytic psychotherapist who has worked in the NHS with children and families for nearly 20 years. She is currently Interim Deputy Associate Clinical Director in a CAMH Service in east London. Alongside this work, she provides clinical supervision to individuals and teams from a range of mental health professional disciplines. She also enjoys writing and teaching on various child and adolescent psychotherapy courses and perinatal and infant mental health courses in the UK and abroad.

Paula Oliveira is a clinical psychologist and researcher at ProChild CoLAB, Portugal, where she integrates clinical practice and research to support professionals and promote child well-being. She holds a PhD in Psychology from UCL, and her research focuses on attachment and interventions with vulnerable families in child protection contexts.

Catherine E.J. Preston is an Associate Professor at the University of York, specialising in body representation. Her current research focuses on perinatal bodily changes and their impact on neural processes and mental well-being. Dr. Preston completed her PhD at the University of Nottingham in 2008, following which she held both a Wenner-Gren and a Marie Curie Fellowship at the Karolinska Institutet, Stockholm, before joining the department at York as a faculty member in 2016. She is also the co-chair of the Body Representation Network, where she contributes to broader discussions in the field, including tactile perception, fundamental principles of body ownership and the emotional experience of the body and body image.

Helena Rutherford is an Associate Professor at Yale Child Study Center. In her work in the Before and After Baby Lab, Dr Rutherford studies the neurobiology and psychology of parenting and mental health, with a specific focus on the perinatal period.

Björn Salomonsson is a psychiatrist and member of the Swedish Psychoanalytical Association, working in private practice. Associate Professor at the Department of Women's and Children's Health, Karolinska Institute, his research and publications focus on psychoanalytical parent-infant therapies (theory, practice, and quantitative outcomes), analysis with children and adults, and the 'weaving thoughts' presentation method. He is a member of the Layered Analysis group (Anna Freud, London) and the Immediate Parent-Infant Skin-To-Skin Study, Karolinska Institute, Stockholm. His publications have been published in many languages. In 2024, he received the Sigourney award for his contributions in the field of psychoanalytic parent-infant psychotherapy.

Sue Schraer is a psychoanalytically-informed adult psychotherapist and a psychoanalytic parent-infant psychotherapist. She is a full registrant of the BPC and UKCP. She has been a visiting lecturer at the Tavistock and Portman Clinic and at the Anna Freud Centre for Children and Families. She has worked in a Mother and Baby Unit (MBU) with acute cases and has facilitated infant observation groups on the Masters in Analytic Psychology and on the CYP-IAPT at the Anna Freud and on the Sino-British Project. She works in a perinatal mental health charity and with individual adults both for the NHS and privately.

Sergio A. Silverio is a Chartered Psychologist, Anthropologist, and Qualitative Research Expert specialising in women's mental health over the lifecourse. His work centres on understanding women's key life transitions; particularly where these present as ruptures, through bereavement, trauma, or loss—be that loss through death, loss of identity, or perceived loss of sanity.

Victoria Southgate is a Professor of Developmental Cognitive Neuroscience at the University of Copenhagen with a research focus on social cognitive development in infancy. Her research explores how infants develop an understanding of self and other, and the developmental interplay between them.

Jodi Swanson an associate teaching professor in The Sanford School of Social and Family Dynamics at Arizona State University, researches children's healthy emotional and social development and their supportive relationships and learning contexts. Her specialisation lies in self-regulatory competencies (e.g., effortful control, emotion management) and how parents and teachers can foster these. She regularly teaches courses in social science research and statistical methods, human development and relationships across the lifespan, and family processes. She lives in Louisville, Kentucky, with her family, where she practices yoga, pushes the limits in HIIT and dance classes, quilts, and paints watercolour in free moments.

Lisa Thackeray is a postgraduate research tutor at the Anna Freud Centre where she teaches and supervises MSc and doctoral students. She specialises in qualitative research methods, particularly Interpretative Phenomenological Analysis, working in the field of child, adolescent, and family mental health.

Kate Thompson is a couple psychoanalytic psychotherapist, supervisor, and lecturer with over 25 years of experience working with couples and individuals. Kate has a special interest in work with parents and has taught for over 10 years in the NHS, specialising in couples and depression. Kate is co-Editor in Chief of the *Journal of Couple and Family Psychoanalysis*, co-edited and co-authored '*Couples as Parents*' (Routledge, 2024); '*Engaging Couples: New Directions in Therapeutic Work with Families*', (Routledge, 2018) and a special edition of the *Journal of Couple and Family Psychoanalysis* on *Divorce and Separation,* (Phoenix, 2021).

Sarah E. Veale is a Doctoral Researcher in Health Sciences at the University of York, where her research examines how intersecting inequalities influence what mother-baby dyads eat in the first 1,000 days of life in the UK. Using qualitative research, socioecological frameworks, and systems thinking, she explores the structural, social, and cultural factors shaping maternal and infant nutrition. Her broader academic interests include maternal health, food choice, sustainability, and health inequalities. She has contributed to research on hospital food waste and climate adaptation in healthcare settings and serves as an Early Career Researcher (ECR) Board Member for UKRI AgriFood4NetZero, where she collaborates on policy-driven research to advance sustainable and equitable food systems.

Pascal Vrticka is an Associate Professor / Senior Lecturer in Psychology at the University of Essex (Colchester, UK) and Principal Investigator of the Social Neuroscience of Human Attachment (SoNeAt) Lab. His work focuses on the neurobiology of human relationships, caregiving and attachment, including parent-child interpersonal neural synchrony.

Foreword

The study of early parenthood and infancy lies at the intersection of several disciplines, each offering unique insights into how we come to understand ourselves, others, and our shared social world. Alejandra Perez, Elena Panagiotopoulou, and Ruth Roberts, through this remarkable volume, *Perspectives on Early Parenthood and Infancy: A Psychoanalytic, Neuroscientific, Developmental and Cultural Dialogue*, bring together a diverse array of voices to illuminate the intricate interplay between psychoanalysis, neuroscience, developmental psychology, and sociocultural contexts.

At the heart of this interdisciplinary dialogue lies a fundamental truth deeply embedded in psychoanalytic thinking: the human brain develops not in isolation but through its vital engagement with other minds. The infant's emerging capacity to understand itself—indeed, to form an identity, to see its place in the world—is profoundly shaped by the adult caregivers who interpret, reflect, and respond to its nascent emotional states. Through processes of mirroring, mentalising, and enabling emotional containment, caregivers offer the infant a coherent sense of self, enabling the child's mind to crystallise its experience into meaningful psychological realities. As this book wonderfully illustrates, developmental neuroscience has further elucidated this process, demonstrating with increasing clarity how these interpersonal interactions directly shape the neural architecture underpinning self-regulation, emotion understanding, and social cognition.

As the contributions within this book evidence, the integration of psychoanalytic insights with neuroscientific findings enhances clinical practice by offering clinicians more nuanced tools to support early parent-child relationships. Beyond this, the developmental perspective enables us to see with greater clarity the vulnerable infant in adult minds when challenged by internal or external pressures. The capacity for secure attachment, fostered through sensitive, attuned caregiving, underpins not only emotional and psychological health but also the basis for interpersonal trust and social understanding essential for learning and cultural engagement. Indeed, secure attachment through more robust interpersonal understanding fortifies social trust, a vital ingredient in the transmission of knowledge across generations, forming the very basis of human culture.

Befitting a psychoanalytic text, this book is a historical narration, taking its reader through early human development, addressing critical developmental stages beginning with conception and the complex contemporary psychological, emotional, and social dynamics that surround fertility, donor conception, and surrogacy. Much has changed, yet the basic human desires for a continuous identity across time continues to guide our attitude to reproduction and early human life.

The book explores pregnancy, offering deep insights into the impact of physical and psychological transformations, the bodily self, and socio-cultural contexts including marginalised contemporary experiences such as transgender pregnancy. Bodily awareness is indeed archaic and modern science places it fairly and squarely in the foetus. If bodily self-awareness starts in the womb perhaps its vicissitudes in later development should be easier to understand.

Birth, another transformative and often challenging process, is explored through a series of psychoanalytic narratives, encompassing both neurobiology and the impact of traumatic experiences. This work highlights the importance of creating supportive and psychologically safe environments for parents and infants alike.

The chapters dedicated to the transition to parenthood provide compelling explorations of the psychological, neurobiological, and relational shifts parents undergo, emphasising the profound implications of these changes on family systems, couple relationships, and parental identities. Additionally, the book extensively examines infancy, providing a sophisticated and sensitive perspective on infant mental health, the internal world of the baby, and how developmental contexts shape emerging self-awareness and attachment patterns.

A particularly valuable aspect of this volume is its detailed attention to early parent-infant interactions. These relationships are the basis of forming affect regulation, emotional resilience, and mentalising abilities, critical for the child's long-term development. Several contributions carefully examine culturally specific practices, emphasising how cultural competence can profoundly improve mental health interventions and engagement in diverse communities, thus broadening the scope of effective preventative and clinical practices.

One of the critical contributions of this volume lies in its recognition that our understanding of infancy and parenthood must be situated within a broader socio-cultural context. Cultural narratives shape parental expectations, practices, and anxieties, influencing the developmental trajectory from conception through infancy. By integrating cultural perspectives alongside psychoanalytic and neuroscientific insights, the authors provide a richly textured account that enhances our capacity for empathy and effectiveness in clinical settings, ultimately fostering more inclusive and responsive mental health practices.

This remarkable integration is particularly relevant to the clinical realm, where effective interventions hinge upon understanding not merely of individual pathology, but the dynamic interplay between individual minds and their interpersonal contexts. By bridging disciplines, this book enables clinicians, researchers, and educators to transcend professional silos, ensuring more comprehensive and compassionate approaches to early interventions and prevention.

In bringing together these vital insights, Perez, Panagiotopoulou, and Roberts offer us not merely a synthesis of existing knowledge, but an invitation to engage deeply with the profound complexities of early human development. Their work represents a significant step forward in the ongoing dialogue between psychoanalysis and developmental neuroscience, offering both academic enrichment and tangible clinical guidance. It is an essential read for all who seek to nurture the developing minds that will shape the generations yet to come.

Peter Fonagy

Acknowledgements

First, our deepest gratitude to the many expectant parents, parents, babies, and families that have been our patients or research participants who have taught us so much.

We extend our sincere thanks to our contributors for their expertise and commitment, which has made this book far richer than we could have imagined. We are also appreciative of their goodwill and flexibility in navigating the limitations of word count and a demanding timeline.

We are also indebted to the Anna Freud and University College London, true multidisciplinary institutions that we have all been fortunate to form part of. We have greatly benefitted from the intellectual companionship and exposure to various and innovative ways of thinking, as well as developing long-lasting friendships. A special thanks to Peter Fonagy, who has been an inspiration for his capacity to be at the forefront of developmental research, deep knowledge of different psychoanalytic schools, and for his creativity and clinical insight in developing new forms of treatment. We are also grateful to Peter, together with Anne Marie Sandler, for setting up the MSc programme (then named Psychoanalytic Developmental Psychology) and establishing an enduring collaboration between the Anna Freud and University College London. Another important thanks is to Eamon McCrory for his exceptional leadership of the MSc courses, and for the energy and wisdom he brings to academic development.

A special thanks to all the researchers who have been involved in LEAP. We are especially grateful to our Research Officer, Maria Christina Vourda, for her invaluable assistance and dedication in conducting and keeping the various projects organised and on track.

Individually, we also wish to express personal thanks:
Alejandra Perez would like to acknowledge the many individuals, experiences, and reflective dialogues that have shaped her professional journey as a psychoanalyst, Psychoanalytic Parent-Infant Psychotherapist, and academic. These influences have been a vital source of inspiration for this book. First and foremost, with deepest gratitude to the British Psychoanalytical Society for its unwavering commitment to the advancement of psychoanalysis. Its ability to embrace passionate

debate and the richness of diverse professional, cultural, and theoretical perspectives has been a powerful example of how such plurality can foster truly original and creative thinking. She would like to extend her thanks to her supervisors: Leon Kleimberg, Angela Joyce, Stephen Grosz, Don Campbell, Marie-Zaphiriou-Woods, Michael Feldman, and Ron Britton, for their invaluable insight and support at different stages of her psychoanalytic career. To the pioneering figures of the Parent-Infant Project at Anna Freud: Tessa Baradon, Michela Biseo, Angela Joyce, Jessica James, and Carol Broughton, whose vision and early guidance introduced her to the world of Parent-Infant Psychotherapy. And a special recognition to Michela Biseo, Amanda Jones, and Jane Turner, for their determination to continue this important training. With gratitude to the Postgraduate Studies team–especially to Eamon McCrory, for his support, and to Nick Midgley, whose deep knowledge and passion for Anna Freud's work and qualitative research ignited her own journey into these fields. To Howard Steele and Pasco Fearon, for their steady guidance on the rigour and patience that longitudinal research demands. Warm thanks to her psychoanalytic colleagues and friends at 19 Bloomsbury Square, for the brief but enriching coffee-break dialogues. To the staff and students of the MSc in Early Child Development and Clinical Applications, past and present–thank you for fostering a vital space for inquiry, reflection, and growth. May it continue to thrive for future generations. And finally, she would like to give a heartfelt thanks to Elena and Ruth, who stood beside her from the early days of LEAP, played an instrumental role in restructuring the MSc programme, and now, most fittingly, join her in co-editing this book.

Elena Panagiotopoulou warmly thanks all those who have inspired and supported her professional journey. Heartfelt thanks go to Katerina Fotopoulou—long-time collaborator, supervisor, mentor and friend. To collaborators and dear friends from Katlab, who were present in many meaningful ways from the early days. She is also grateful to her supervisors and tutors, as well as fellow trainees during her psychotherapy training at Tavistock Relationships, for the shared emotional journey and their friendship. A special note of appreciation goes to the staff and students of the MSc in Early Child Development and Clinical Applications for being a constant source of energy and inspiration for this book, with special thanks to the Deputy Director, Mariana Pereira, for her invaluable support and boundless passion. Also, her thanks to the Postgraduate Studies Leadership Team at Anna Freud for their continued support and confidence in her. Of course, thanks go to the co-editors of this book, Alejandra and Ruth, for their dedication, insight, and collaboration in bringing this work to life—and especially Alejandra, for inspiring creativity, and for her trust and opportunities over the years. Finally, Elena dedicates the book to Daphne and Lea, born just days before this book began, and their parents—a reminder of how every beginning holds wonder.

Ruth Roberts has been incredibly fortunate to work with several supportive academics throughout her academic career. She would like to thank Dr Kaye Kerr who supported her undergraduate Honors at University of Winnipeg in Canada, as well as Professor Kristin Laurens and Professor Helen Fisher who supported her Masters and early career research at the Institute of Psychiatry, Psychology and Neuroscience at Kings College London. She would especially like to thank Professor Essi Viding, who supported her PhD and early career research at the Psychology and Language Department at University College London, for showing her how to optimally navigate parenthood while maintaining academic rigour. And finally, she would like to give a warm thanks to Alejandra and Elena, for the forging of their mutual ideas and interests into LEAP and being so inspiring and supportive in their shared academic pursuits.

Jointly, we would like to acknowledge the various academics, clinicians, and researchers who have inspired us not only through their work, but also through their ability to balance that work with family and personal life—an important working model for all of us.

And finally, to our families, who in their different ways keep us always in touch with the joys, challenges, and realities of family life.

Main introduction

Alejandra Perez, Elena Panagiotopoulou, and Ruth Roberts

There is abundant interest in infancy and early parenthood coming from various fields of research and clinical practice: unsurprising given the importance of these life stages for child development. An understanding of infants' experiences, behaviour, relationship-forming, and general development, as well as of parents' own complex experiences, cannot be adequately gained within the confines of a single discipline. The need for an interdisciplinary approach is especially acute when studying early parenthood and infancy, where the intertwined effects of biology, cultural environment, unconscious experiences, and the parent-infant relationship are now widely accepted to be very significant. Each perspective contributes another small piece to a large and highly complex jigsaw puzzle. Of course, there is now more cross-fertilisation between different areas of study, with old divisions between clinicians and researchers, and between different theoretical and clinical approaches, not being as stark as they once were. There are increasing numbers of 'clinically-informed' researchers and 'research-informed' clinicians. Psychoanalytic ideas are applied more widely across various settings, while current research in neuroscience and developmental psychology informs many early-years clinical and education settings.

The importance of infancy and early parenthood for later development

Infancy is the period of early childhood that spans from birth to around 12–24 months (typically the first year of life but sometimes extended to two years). It is a period of rapid development and a critical window for shaping physical, cognitive, emotional, and social foundations influencing future learning, behaviour, and well-being. While key brain structures and networks are present at birth, rapid and significant brain development happens in the first two years of life (e.g. Gilmore et al., 2018). Early experience plays a key role in shaping and optimising postnatal brain development, especially the emergence of higher-order functions (see Ilyka et al., 2021). Caregiver-infant interactions have been found to be associated with children's structural, functional, and connectivity measures, and such associations are long-term and can be observed even decades later (Ilyka et al., 2021). Positive

DOI: 10.4324/9781003530473-1

environmental factors, such as responsive caregiving and stimulating activities, can significantly enhance a child's cognitive and socio-emotional development, for instance fostering secure attachment and promoting emotional resilience (e.g. Bowlby, 1982). Conversely, negative early experiences, including neglect, trauma, or exposure to chronic stress, profoundly affect brain development and increase vulnerability to emotional and cognitive difficulties (e.g. Gunnar & Quevedo, 2007; McCrory et al., 2010), for example contributing to anxiety and difficulties in forming healthy relationships later in life (Bowlby, 1982). Together, biological and environmental factors work in tandem, creating a dynamic framework that moulds a child's emotional, cognitive, and physical health. This makes the early years, and particularly infancy, a critical window of opportunity but also vulnerability, hence stressing the importance of prevention and early intervention that promotes optimal growth and development.

Infancy and early parenthood are deeply intertwined, as an infant's development is profoundly shaped by the environment provided by the parent(s)/caregiver(s). Importantly, the child-caregiver relationship is bi-directional, meaning that parenting and child characteristics influence one another (e.g. Maccoby, 1992). While caregivers shape the child's environment, a child's temperament, behaviour, and emotional cues also impact caregiving responses (e.g. Lengua & Kovacs, 2005). In other words, a child's behaviour (e.g., being overly challenging) can influence how a parent responds (e.g., becoming more controlling), which, in turn, can affect the child's behaviour, creating a back-and-forth influence between the two.

Apart from child characteristics, parental experiences also play a crucial role in shaping their caregiving. Parents' internal world, for instance, experiences carried from their own childhoods, profoundly influence their parenting behaviours (e.g. Burke et al., 2021), even if these emotional experiences are "unremembered" (Fraiberg et al., 1975). While nurtured parents tend to provide consistent and responsive care, those who experienced trauma or insecure attachments that remain unprocessed may unintentionally and unknowingly pass these patterns on to their children. This intergenerational transmission of attachment and trauma emphasises the need for parental support to break cycles of dysfunction that perpetuate distress across generations and promote healthy development and relationships.

Last but not least, while the parent's role is crucial during the early years of a child's life, it is important to recognise that their influence begins even before birth, as the prenatal stage lays the biological and psychological foundation for future growth. During this period, the foetus is highly sensitive to maternal influences, with the parent's physical and emotional well-being directly impacting the child's health and development (e.g. see Mandl et al., 2024). Additionally, this stage is transformative for parents, as they prepare for caregiving, influencing their emotional readiness and future parenting behaviours. Supporting parental well-being during pregnancy is, therefore, essential for fostering a healthy start for both child and caregiver.

The origins of this book

The idea for this book originated in the thinking involved in restructuring the MSc Early Child Development and Clinical Applications at University College London, run in conjunction with the Anna Freud. This restructuring ultimately included two main changes: the addition of a clinical placement for students in an early-years setting; and the expansion of the syllabus through the introduction of current neurobiological and developmental research, diverse cultural viewpoints, and a range of approaches to parent-infant clinical and educational work, all alongside key psychoanalytic ideas. The clinical placement provides students with real-life work experience, while also helping to crystallise the value of psychoanalytic concepts for them: these concepts are not rigidly defined 'facts' that the clinician just has to know, rather, they help the clinician to think through the complexity of what they are seeing. Clinical placements also expose students to multidisciplinary teams and help them understand both the value and the challenges that these bring. Moreover, presenting a diversity of perspectives to students early in their career can serve to illustrate, albeit in overview, the far-reaching implications of pursuing any one approach. It also aims to create a platform for meaningful dialogue and exchange of ideas, whereby academic knowledge might be translated into practice and research, generating new ways of working.

Creating a dialogue: the challenges

A meaningful dialogue must start from the premise that one has an interest to understand the other's perspective. While we have observed more and more of such openness among academics and clinicians working on infant development and early parenthood experiences, there are still obstacles in the way of a fuller integration of the different approaches. One of the challenges of multidisciplinary (and attempted interdisciplinary) work is the sometimes-alienating effect of each discipline's technical language, or jargon, which is often inaccessible to those outside that discipline. First, each perspective or methodology must be sufficiently understood – and so must be explained in accessible language – in order for it to 'converse' with others. This, of course, comes with the risk that the complexity and nuance of an idea or term might be missed or misunderstood through over-simplification. However, by not attempting to communicate ideas beyond the borders of a particular field, there is equally a risk that that field becomes isolated, and that opportunities for valuable new applications are missed.

This book aims to juxtapose a range of viewpoints on early parenthood and infancy from authors working within different clinical and research perspectives. The themes of the discussion chapters in this book have emerged out of this juxtaposition. It is our hope that, through this diversity of insights, the reader can reach a broader understanding of two highly complex and intertwined life stages, as well as identify areas for their own further reflection and exploration.

Psychoanalytic perspectives

An important body of theory in the study of early parenthood and infancy is psychoanalysis. This discipline's contributions involve both theories of the mind and psychological development, and clinical work with adults, parents, infants, and children. A psychoanalytic perspective focuses on subjective individual experience, which is formed out of a mixture of conscious and unconscious thoughts, feelings, and wishes—those remembered and unremembered, mentally represented and unrepresented   as well as early relationships and experiences. Psychoanalysis examines the specific meanings of these mental and relational experiences for each individual, and its theories have derived predominantly from in-depth, long-term clinical work with patients (i.e. psychoanalytic case studies). A psychoanalyst's understanding of a particular patient emerges from a combination of their own past clinical experience and knowledge; reflection upon what transpired in a session or sequence of sessions; self-reflection (including the analyst's subjective and counter-transferential feelings); free-floating attention; and the attribution of retrospective meaning (Kohon, 2019). While there exist core concepts in psychoanalysis (e.g. the System Unconscious, transference, counter-transference, and unconscious phantasy), there is no single systematic, integrated, comprehensive psychoanalytic theory, but rather multiple 'psychoanalytic theories'. Psychoanalysis is a body of thought that is in continuous development as concepts are refined and expanded and, thus, is in a state of constant tension. Sandler (1983) emphasised the 'elasticity' of psychoanalytic concepts, arguing that their meaning is context-dependent. However, as both Sandler (1983) and Kohon (2019) explain, this is central to the nature of psychoanalysis: it is a body of theoretical formulations of varying degrees of abstraction, focused on a formidably complex subject—human psychic reality.

There is a considerable challenge in developing a dialogue between psychoanalysis and other disciplines, which lies in language. As outlined above, psychoanalytic concepts are elastic and context-dependent, and most cannot be understood without considering the wider psychoanalytic theory of the mind (the metapsychology). Kohon (2005) gives the example of Freud's theory of the Oedipus Complex, which, he explains, would be incoherent if not understood in the context of a theory of the unconscious and psychoanalytic ideas about sexuality. An additional difficulty has arisen from the use of everyday language to convey ideas that belong to a specifically psychoanalytic theory of the mind (for example, sexuality, projection, containment, holding, and so on). However, the rich possibilities of engaging psychoanalysis in conversation with other fields makes it worth attempting to bridge these linguistic and conceptual gaps.

The unique value of a psychoanalytic approach to understanding human experience lies in its rigorous observation of the way in which each individual ascribes their own particular meanings to events, to themselves and others, and to the world. Psychoanalysts are also interested in how unconscious dynamics influence these ascriptions of meaning (Blass & Carmeli, 2007). Starting with Freud's case studies, we can see that he wanted not only to describe particular phenomena, but also to infer the different underlying mechanisms, motivations, and drivers of action in each circumstance. In general, the purpose of such in-depth clinical exploration is not to produce universal theories, but rather to understand the complex mechanisms of an individual's behaviours and beliefs, development of personality, formation of relationships, and general well-being. Some of the knowledge or hypotheses derived from case studies may prove relevant to other cases or situations; however, this is not assumed in psychoanalysis (Kohon, 2019).

Psychoanalysis was the first branch of psychology to explore babies' psychic experiences, and to emphasise their importance in the formation of the mind and in general development. Although its origins are in clinical work with adult patients, psychoanalysis developed and expanded to encompass work with parents, parents and infants (parent-infant psychotherapy), and children. Of particular relevance for this book are psychoanalytic-therapeutic work with parents, and parent-infant psychotherapy, as well as psychoanalysis with expectant parents and those in the early stages of parenthood. The earliest pioneers of psychoanalytic research on infants were Anna Freud, Donald Winnicott, and Melanie Klein, all of whom were observing and working with parents, infants, and young children in the 1940s. While Sigmund Freud attached considerable importance to infancy in his theories of the mind, most of his formulations relied on reconstructions from adult analytic patients and their retrospective views of their childhoods. Anna Freud, however, by paying close analytic attention to children themselves and documenting her observations, formed a deeper understanding of the changes and defences that arise at each stage of development. Her 'double approach' integrated direct observations and reconstructions, and led her to conceive the idea, among others, that the innate urge for new experiences and relationships can be as strong as the drive to repeat past experiences (i.e. transference) (Midgley, 2013). Winnicott, working as a paediatrician and psychoanalyst, saw parallels between the analyst-patient and mother-infant relationships (Winnicott, 1965). His view of the relational environment as necessary for the development of the self stems from his understanding of this earliest relationship between mother and baby. Both Anna Freud and Winnicott brought to their psychoanalytic thinking their knowledge from, and interest in, allied professions—education and paediatrics respectively—thereby opening new possible sources of contributions to psychoanalytic theory beyond the analytic consulting room. Klein was also innovative, not only in being one of the first to work psychoanalytically with children, but also in working with children with severe psychological disturbances and psychoses. She focused on children's play as a communication of their unconscious and, thus, expanded psychoanalytic work beyond the realm of verbal communication (that is, free association) (Perez, 2023).

Parent-infant psychotherapy (PIP, or as it is sometimes referred to in this book, psychoanalytic parent-infant psychotherapy, or PPIP) was developed to support the early relationship between parents and infants. This type of therapy has its basis in psychoanalysis, where consideration of parents' unconscious conflicts and the developing internal world of the infant informs the work. However, PIP is also greatly influenced by research into infants' socio-emotional development, by neuroscience, and by investigations into the psychological and biological changes that occur in new parents. Two important aims of PIP work are to break the pathological, intergenerational repetition of trauma between parents and baby, and to support infants' development (Steele & Baradon, 2004). PIP also allows opportunities to explore and work on the particular triangular relationships and dynamics in the family (Perez, 2018). Joyce (2005) and Perez (2018) have emphasised that, while there is a pull toward the repetition of trauma, motherhood can also be a period of psychic change, in which women are more open to revisiting and working through unconscious conflicts as they live the new experience of being a mother. The PIP therapist works at various levels: that of the parents' reawakened unconscious conflicts, of their defences, and of the transference dynamics, as well as of the emerging relationship with the infant (Perez, 2018).

Psychoanalysis has enlarged our understanding of parenthood and infancy by exploring the unconscious phantasies that are revived when people become parents; the unconscious intergenerational repetition of trauma and abuse; and the integral part played by very early, pre-verbal, and bodily experiences in the formation of the mind and unconscious phantasies, and in overall development. All of these, of course, have powerful long-term implications for future relationships and general well-being.

Developmental psychology perspectives

Another important perspective is that offered by developmental psychology, which scientifically studies how physical, cognitive, emotional, and social capacities emerge, change, and develop across the lifespan. This perspective is crucial to understanding how both infants and parents learn, mature, and adapt to their circumstances. This approach recognises the interplay of biological, psychological, and environmental factors that all influence development.

The study of infantile physical development focuses on the growth and development of the brain and body, and the accompanying attainment of motor skills, reflexes, and coordination, which help the infant to slowly gain independence. Cognitive development refers to infants' capacity to learn and think, and how this is fostered through sensory experiences and interactions with others. Emotional development encompasses the infant's growing recognition and expression of emotions, and their engagement in social interactions. Social development includes the formation of attachments with caregivers, as well as the infant's evolving social skills (e.g. smiling, making eye contact, imitating facial expressions, etc), which they use to engage with others and explore the world around them. Developmental psychology encompasses and studies all of the above forms of development. It also considers how both the infant's innate characteristics, such as genetics and temperament, and environmental factors, such as quality of parenting and cultural context, interact and influence development.

Regarding the experience of parents, research into physical changes and developing capacities during pregnancy and early parenthood, and the psychological aspects of these transition periods, has attracted more interest in the field of developmental psychology in recent years. Initially, the focus on pregnancy and early parenthood was only in relation to the impact those had on the developing child. However, there is an increasing recognition of pregnancy and parenthood as developmental stages in their own right, with all of their accompanying changes and developing capacities (Osofsky, 1982).

Theories in developmental psychology derive from research studies that adopt a variety of methods, encompassing behavioural observation, controlled experiments, interviews, surveys, correlational studies, and archival research. Findings from many such studies have enabled developmental psychologists to understand the underlying mechanisms of human behaviour, relationship development, and mental health, and have, thus, greatly contributed to parenting and early-years practices.

A core framework within developmental psychology is that of attachment theory, where some argue has been the most influential framework in social and behavioural sciences (Thompson et al., 2022). This is because the large body of attachment research has helped understand infants' innate need to form emotional bonds with other people and how these shape children's emotional, social, cognitive, and behavioural development. Within its range of methodologies, attachment research has included longitudinal twin studies looking at the relation of genetics and environment in infants' attachment and across the lifespan (e.g. Fearon et al., 2006). In addition, attachment research has considered how the parents' prenatal attachment representations play a role in their future relationships with their child (Fonagy et al., 1991) and in the child's development (Perez et al., 2025). Finally, attachment theory and research have had a significant impact on improving policy and care settings (Cassidy et al., 2013).

Neuroscience perspectives

Neuroscience is another perspective that offers critical insights into infancy and early parenthood. It is an interdisciplinary field, integrating biology, psychology, medicine, and cognitive science, to study the nervous system, with a primary focus on how the brain develops, processes information, and adapts to experiences. Neuroscience includes branches like molecular, cellular, cognitive, behavioural, affective, social, developmental, computational, and clinical neuroscience, each focusing on different aspects of the study of the nervous system.

Brain development begins soon after conception with rapid brain growth occurring throughout infancy. Brain volume is about 35% of adult volume 2–3 weeks after birth, doubling in size in the first year of life and reaching approximately 80% of adult weight by the age of two. One the main contributions of neuroscience to understanding infancy is that it is a critical period of neuroplasticity, where the brain rapidly forms and refines neural connections in response to early experiences. For example, secure attachment promotes the development of brain regions specialised in emotional regulation, stress response, and social functioning, enhancing infants' resilience and ability to adapt to changing environments, whereas neglect, deprivation, or chronic stress have been found to lead to developmental vulnerabilities, affecting brain structure and function (e.g. Gunnar & Quevedo, 2007; Schore, 2001). Importantly, neuroscience has not only provided insights into the infant brain but also the parental brain, which undergoes significant rewiring during pregnancy and the transition to parenthood. Such neurobiological changes, discussed in more detail in various chapters of this book, facilitate the development of effective caregiving, while also increasing parents' susceptibility to mental health difficulties (c.g. Barba-Müller et al., 2019).

Advances in neuroscience methods have allowed researchers to study not only adult but also infant brain structure and activity in real time. Functional Magnetic Resonance Imaging (fMRI) and Electroencephalography (EEG) are commonly employed to study the brain during specific tasks. fMRI measures blood oxygenation levels and is best for studying brain structures and networks, such as for face processing or emotion regulation. EEG measures electrical activity from neurons and is best for studying real-time neural activity, such as responses to speech sounds. While fMRI poses some challenges by requiring infants to stay still and is commonly conducted during sleep, EEG is more tolerant of movement and can be more easily used during awake states. Neuroimaging measures are often combined with behavioural data, for example obtained through observations or standardised assessments, thus allowing researchers to correlate real-world behaviours with brain activity. Longitudinal studies are particularly helpful in studying development over time, offering insights into how infant brain development may impact later physical, cognitive, emotional, and social outcomes. Last but not least, certain neuroscience methods, such as dual EEG and fNIRS (Functional Near-Infrared Spectroscopy) hyperscanning, have allowed researchers to study infants and parents together, providing insights into dyadic brain activity, bonding, and co-regulation.

Socio-cultural perspectives

Considering socio-cultural perspectives is important in creating a well-rounded picture of early parenthood and infancy, acknowledging the profound influence of cultural norms, societal structures, and community practices on parenting and infant development. Universally, parents across cultures aim to nurture and protect their infant and help the infant meet physical, social, and emotional milestones, however there is considerable variation in what this looks like and how this is achieved (Bornstein, 2013). Culture shapes ideas about how people should think, feel and behave in order to be members of the group (Bornstein, 2013). As such, cultural values shape parenting behaviours, such as feeding practices, sleeping arrangements, and childcare, as well as parental expectations and what behaviours should be encouraged or discouraged in infants and children (Bornstein, 2013). Ideas and advice about parenting are often passed on through the generations and via those in the community. Parenting practices and expectations all have an impact on parents' experiences and parental mental health, as well as infants' well-being and development. Cultural variations encourage us to consider our assumptions about what is normative in parenting practice, the parent-infant relationship, and infant development.

Socio-cultural perspectives also highlight the importance of societal factors, such as healthcare accessibility, parental leave policies, and division of parental labour, as well as community support systems and access to mental health support, all of which can significantly affect parenting experiences and infant outcomes. Environments rich in stimulation, emotional support, and social connection foster better cognitive, emotional, and physical health (Rakesh et al., 2024). Conversely, children exposed to poverty or discrimination face higher risks for developmental delays and mental health challenges (Wright et al., 2013). Socio-cultural perspectives also provide insight into societal norms and attitudes about the ways families are created, including assisted reproduction, and potential barriers to family building. Although much of the existing research on early childhood development has traditionally focused on the nuclear family structure, we now see a great diversity in family structures and configurations, including single parents, extended families, same-sex parents, and non-biological parents and caregivers (Golombok, 2015). It is important that all who work with parents and infants consider these influences to ensure that interventions, parenting programmes, and public policies are culturally sensitive and effective in addressing diverse family needs.

Learning about socio-cultural experiences of infancy and early parenthood often requires researchers to move away from standardised assessments, which may not be optimised to capture the diversity of parental beliefs, values, and experiences. Researchers may use interviews to gather in-depth explorations of cultural narratives or conduct case studies to capture unique individual perspectives. Examples of this can be found in the case study presented by Jones and Thackary in Chapter 10, which explores the experiences of an expectant transgender parent, Chapter 23 by Kanazawa, who used discussion groups to explore research participants' expectations following a parenting readiness programme, and Chapter 16, which brings together qualitative research by Silverio and Dasgupta to examine the socio-cultural context of birth. Researchers may also use parent-infant observation to examine interactions between parents and infants, which can help identify patterns and variations in parent-infant relationships and behaviours, influenced by the surrounding context. Two examples of this are Chapter 29 by Abedi and Chapter 36 by Schraer, both of which draw on clinical observations of parents and infants from different cultural backgrounds. Although beyond the scope of this book, ethnographic studies offer researchers the opportunity to immerse themselves in communities to better understand cultural norms and practices. These qualitative and observational methods enable a deep exploration of specific contexts, yielding rich insights into how cultural norms, societal structures, and individual experiences shape parenting practices and infant development.

How we selected and invited guest authors

This book brings together a diverse collection of guest authors from a range of backgrounds and disciplines, each offering expertise on topics related to conception, pregnancy, birth, transitioning to parenthood, early infancy, and the early parent-child relationship.

To assemble this collection, we extended invitations to those we had previously engaged with in professional or academic capacities. We also conducted a search for additional academics, clinicians, and researchers, who are actively engaged in innovative work in early child development. It was not possible to be fully comprehensive and representative of all views in one book, but we did select authors who could present novel ideas and offer insight into the experiences of underrepresented and under-researched populations. While not all readers may agree with every perspective presented in this book, we believe that fostering an inclusive dialogue is essential for advancing our understanding of the early years.

The resulting collection of authors reflects a deliberate effort to incorporate a range of viewpoints and bring together theoretical insights, research, and practical applications. This diversity of perspectives enables a nuanced examination of the many factors that influence the experiences of parents and infants, encouraging critical reflection and highlighting the complexity of early infant development and parenthood.

Overview of the book

The book's structure follows the chronology of becoming a parent, moving through 1) conception; 2) pregnancy and the prenatal stage; 3) birth; 4) transition to parenthood; 5) infancy (up to one year); and 6) the early parent-infant relationship. Each section comprises chapters from psychoanalytic, neuroscientific, and developmental psychology research, alongside socio-cultural perspectives, allowing the reader the choice between reading the book thematically or according to a particular perspective. However, some chapters include more than one perspective, demonstrating how cross-fertilisation in this subject area is already very much a reality. There are also some chapters that do not subscribe to any of the four main perspectives, but rather introduce other views that shine a helpful light on the topics and perspectives at hand. Each section ends with a discussion chapter written by the editors, in which they describe the themes that have emerged from their readings of the preceding chapters. These discussions were developed in a similar way, albeit not formally, to qualitative thematic analysis (Braun & Clarke, 2012), where themes have been identified from the material.

Reading the book by perspective

A psychoanalytic perspective is offered in the chapters by Perez in every section of the book, serving to explain key psychoanalytic ideas about conception, pregnancy, parenthood, infancy, and the parent-infant relationship. These key psychoanalytic concepts are exemplified in Perez' chapters through clinical material from individual psychoanalytic work with expectant and new parents, as well as parent-infant work with families. Further chapters presenting psychoanalytic perspectives are those by Fine (Chapter 3) on conception; Goulder (Chapter 13) on birth; Salomonsson (Chapter 18) and Thompson (Chapter 19) on the transition to parenthood; de Rementeria (Chapter 32) and Ogbuagu (Chapter 35) on the parent-infant relationship. All of these chapters offer clinical vignettes from varied psychoanalytic work in different settings, such as postnatal classes, a Child Health Centre in Stockholm (Sweden), parent-infant psychotherapy, and even infant observation. Finally, some chapters draw on psychoanalytic theories to help elucidate findings from bodily-self studies (Chapter 22 by Panagiotopoulou), cycles of marginalisation in minority groups (Chapter 29 by Abedi), and cultural practices in birth and child-rearing (Chapter 36 by Schraer).

A developmental perspective on infancy can be found: in Part V on infancy in the chapters by Perez (Chapter 25), Oliveira and Mesquita (Chapter 26), Swanson and Erickson (Chapter 27), and Bremner and Southgate (Chapter 28); in Section VI on the parent-infant relationship in the chapters by Perez (Chapter 31) and Roberts (Chapter 34), which also offer developmental perspectives of attachment and mentalisation respectively. These chapters mainly refer to recent research in the field. A developmental perspective on conception, pregnancy, and parenthood is alluded to in the chapters by Perez (Chapters 1, 7, 12 and 20), Panagiotopoulou and Preston (Chapter 9), Salomonsson (Chapter 18), Thompson (Chapter 19), and Rutherford (Chapter 21). These chapters refer to a combination of developmental studies and clinical work.

Neuroscience perspectives, including neurobiological, can be found in the chapters by Barba-Müller (Chapter 8) on pregnancy, Dahan (Chapter 14) on birth, Rutherford (Chapter 21) on the transition to parenthood, Oliveira and Mesquita (Chapter 26), Swanson and Erickson (Chapter 27), and Bremner and Southgate (Chapter 28) on infancy, and, finally, Lucas and Vrticka (Chapter 33) on parent-infant attachment. The bodily-self chapters by Panagiotopoulou and Preston (Chapter 9), Veale, Munns and Preston (Chapter 15), and Panagiotopoulou (Chapter 22) also touch on brain changes during pregnancy, birth, and the postnatal period, respectively.

Socio-cultural perspectives can be found: in Part I on conception in the chapters by Grace (Chapter 2), Fine (Chapter 3), Daniels and Meadows (Chapter 4), and Jadva (Chapter 5); in Part II on pregnancy and the prenatal stage in the chapter by Jones and Thackery (Chapter 10) and touched upon by Panagiotopoulou and Preston (Chapter 9); in Section III on birth in chapters by Perez (Chapter 12), Goulder (Chapter 13), Dahan (Chapter 14), Veale, Munns and Preston (Chapter 15), and Silverio and Dasgupta (Chapter 16); in Part IV on transition to parenthood in the chapter by Kanazawa (Chapter 23); in Part V on infancy in the chapters by Oliveira and Mesquita (Chapter 26) and Abedi (Chapter 29); and in Part VI on the parent-infant relationship in chapters by Ogbuagu (Chapter 35) and Schraer (Chapter 36), and touched upon by de Rementeria (Chapter 32) and Roberts (Chapter 34).

Reading the book thematically

Regarding the major themes of the book, Part I: 'Conception' covers topics including the conscious and unconscious experiences of people conceiving or trying to conceive, both naturally and through assisted reproduction; sources of information and cultural influences in current fertility and reproductive health education; donor conception and information-sharing with donor-conceived children; and the use of surrogacy to build a family.

Part II: 'Pregnancy and the prenatal stage' covers physical and psychological changes in pregnant parents from a psychoanalytic and neurobiological lens; bodily self during pregnancy; and a socio-cultural perspective on the experience of pregnancy of a transgender man.

Part III: 'Birth' covers the significant changes that occur during birth and navigating new relationships after birth; traumatic birth experience; psycho-neurobiological processes during birth; bodily self during birth; and social-cultural perspectives regarding the 'triple burden' faced by perinatal women, experiences of violence during birth, and the time-bind of motherhood.

Part IV: 'Transition to parenthood' covers psychological and neurobiological changes and challenges in the transition to parenthood; psychoanalytic thinking about the parental couple and the experience of making space for a third; bodily self after birth; and a socio-cultural perspective on low births in Japan and a parenthood readiness education intervention.

Part V: 'Infancy' covers psychoanalytic and attachment perspectives on the infant's inner world; the biological basis of attachment; the role of individual factors in infant development; development of bodily and conceptual self-awareness in infancy; and a socio-cultural perspective on psychological therapies for Muslim families and faith identity.

Part VI: 'The early parent-infant relationship' covers affect regulation in infants and parents; navigation of separations; psychoeducation for parents; parental mentalisation; and how therapeutic intervention can help support and improve parent-infant relationships.

Considerations

Inclusive language

We recognise that some of the terminology in the book is gender-focused (e.g. 'mother' as opposed to 'parent') or gives legal and/or biological connotations (e.g. 'parent' as opposed to 'caregiver'). While it is our intention to be inclusive, these terms are at times required due to the nature of the research (e.g. research with biological parents on brain structure and function changes related to pregnancy and childbirth) or clinical observations (e.g. psychological changes in pregnant women and mothers in Winnicott's concept of 'primary maternal preoccupation'). At times, it can be assumed that the findings and observations might be applicable to other groups of people. However, there is still a lack of research and clinical observations to state this and there is a need to explore this further. We recognise that this is a limitation of this book.

Clinical material and confidentiality

Some of the chapters in this book include clinical and/or research interview vignettes. The authors of these chapters have changed potentially personally identifying information that relates directly or indirectly to individuals in order to disguise and safeguard the confidentiality, privacy, and data protection rights of those concerned. In some cases, authors have asked the people involved for additional permission to publish.

References

Barba-Müller, E., Craddock, S., Carmona, S., & Hoekzema, E. (2019). Brain plasticity in pregnancy and the postpartum period: Links to maternal caregiving and mental health. *Archives of Women's Mental Health, 22*(2), 289–299.

Blass, R. B., & Carmeli, Z. (2007). The case against neuropsychoanalysis: On fallacies underlying psychoanalysis' latest scientific trend and its negative impact on psychoanalytic discourse. *The International Journal of Psychoanalysis, 88,* 19–40.

Bornstein M. H. (2013). Parenting and child mental health: A cross-cultural perspective. *World Psychiatry: Official Journal of the World Psychiatric Association (WPA), 12*(3), 258–265.

Bowlby, J. (1982). *Attachment and loss: Vol. 1. Attachment* (2nd ed.). New York: Basic Books.

Braun, V., & Clarke, V. (2012). Thematic analysis. In H. Cooper, P. M. Camic, D. L. Long, A. T. Panter, D. Rindskopf, & K. J. Sher (Eds.), *APA handbook of research methods in psychology, Vol. 2. Research designs: Quantitative, qualitative, neuropsychological, and biological* (pp. 57–71). American Psychological Association.

Burke, J., Fitzhenry, M., Houghton, S., & Fortune, D. G. (2021). Breaking the cycle of intergenerational trauma: Evaluating the impact of parental adverse childhood experiences on parenting group outcomes using a mixed-methods approach. *Children and Youth Services Review, 130,* Article 106223.

Cassidy, J., Jones, J. D., & Shaver, P. R. (2013). Contributions of attachment theory and research: A framework for future research, translation, and policy. *Developmental Psychopathology, 25*(4 Pt 2), 1415–1434.

Fearon, R. M. P., Van IJzendoorn, M. H., Fonagy, P., Bakermans-Kranenburg, M. J., Schuengel, C., & Bokhorst, C. L. (2006). In search of shared and nonshared environmental factors in security of attachment: A behavior-genetic study of the association between sensitivity and attachment security. *Developmental Psychology, 42*(6), 1026–1040.

Fonagy, P., Steele, H., & Steele, M. (1991). Maternal representations of attachment during pregnancy predict the organization of infant-mother attachment at one year of age. *Child Development, 62* (5), 891–905.

Fraiberg, S., Adelson, E., & Shapiro, V. (1975). Ghosts in the nursery: A psychoanalytic approach to the problems of impaired infant-mother relationships. *Journal of the American Academy of Child Psychiatry, 14*(3), 387–421.

Gilmore, J., Knickmeyer, R., & Gao, W. (2018). Imaging structural and functional brain development in early childhood. *Nature Reviews Neuroscience, 19,* 123–137.

Golombok, S. (2015). *Modern families: Parents and children in new family forms.* Cambridge: Cambridge University Press.

Gunnar, M., & Quevedo, K. (2007). The neurobiology of stress and development. *Annual Review of Psychology, 58*, 145–173.

Ilyka, D., Johnson, M. H., & Lloyd-Fox, S. (2021). Infant social interactions and brain development: A systematic review. *Neuroscience & Biobehavioral Reviews, 130*, 448–469.

Joyce, A. (2005). The parent-infant relationship and parent-infant mental health. In T. Baradon, C. Broughton, I. Gibbs, J. James, & J. Woodhead (Eds.), *The practice of psychoanalytic parent-infant psychotherapy* (pp. 5–24). London: Routledge.

Kohon, G. (2005). The Oedipus complex. In S. Budd & R. Rusbridger (Eds.), *Introducing Psychoanalysis*. London: Routledge.

Kohon, G. (2019). *Concerning the nature of psychoanalysis: The persistence of a paradoxical discourse*. London: Routledge.

Lengua, L. J., & Kovacs, E. A. (2005). Bidirectional associations between temperament and parenting and the prediction of adjustment problems in middle childhood. *Journal of Applied Developmental Psychology, 26*(1), 21–38.

Maccoby, E. E. (1992). The role of parents in the socialization of children: An historical overview. *Developmental Psychology, 28*(6), 1006–1016.

Mandl, S., Alexopoulos, J., Doering, S., Wildner, B., Seidl, R., & Bartha-Doering, L. (2024). The effect of prenatal maternal distress on offspring brain development: A systematic review. *Early Human Development, 192*, 106009.

McCrory, E., De Brito, S. A., & Viding, E. (2010). Research review: The neurobiology and genetics of maltreatment and adversity. *Journal of Child Psychology and Psychiatry, 51*(10), 1079–1095.

Midgley, N. (2013). *Reading Anna Freud*. London: Routledge.

Osofsky, H. J. (1982). Developmental aspects of expectant and new parenthood. In H. J. Prill, M. Stauber, & P. G. Pechatschek (Eds.), *Advances in psychosomatic obstetrics and gynecology*. Berlin, Heidelberg: Springer.

Perez, A. (2018). From pathological merger to a reflective, triangular space: Parent-infant psychotherapy with a mother with Borderline Personality Disorder, *Journal of Infant, Child, and Adolescent Psychotherapy, 17*(1), 15–27.

Perez, A. (2023). Infant research-rooted therapies in the UK. In B. Hyppertz (Ed.), *Underlying assumptions in psychoanalytic schools: A comparative perspective*. London: Routledge.

Perez, A., Steele, M., Fonagy, P., Fearon, P., Segal, F., & Steele, H. (2025). Predictions of adolescents' responses to the Youth Self-Report from parental attachment interviews collected during pregnancy: A 17-year longitudinal study. *Attach Human Development, 16*, 1–15.

Rakesh, D., McLaughlin, K. A., Sheridan, M., Humphreys, K. L., & Rosen, M. L. (2024). Environmental contributions to cognitive development: The role of cognitive stimulation. *Developmental Review, 73*, 101135.

Sandler, J. (1983). Reflections on some relations between psychoanalytic concepts and psychoanalytic practice. *The International Journal of Psychoanalysis, 64*, 35–45.

Schore, A. N. (2001). The effects of early relational trauma on right brain development, affect regulation, and infant mental health. *Infant Mental Health Journal, 22*(1–2), 201–269.

Steele, M., & Baradon, T. (2004). Clinical use of the adult attachment interview in parent-infant psychotherapy. *Infant Mental Health Journal, 25*(4), 284–299.

Thompson, R. A., Simpson, J. A., & Berlin, L. J. (2022). Taking perspective on attachment theory and research: Nine fundamental questions. *Attachment & Human Development, 24*(5), 543–560.

Winnicott, D. W. (1965). The theory of the parent-infant relationship. *International Psycho-Analytical Library, 64*, 37–55.

Wright, M. O., Masten, A. S., & Narayan, A. J. (2013). Resilience processes in development: Four waves of research on positive adaptation in the context of adversity. In S. Goldstein & R. Brooks (Eds.), *Handbook of resilience in children*. Boston, MA: Springer.

Part I

Conception

Chapter 1

Psychoanalytic perspectives on conception

Alejandra Perez

Psychoanalysis has contributed to our understanding of the conscious and uncon-scious experiences of people trying to conceive a baby, whether successfully or unsuccessfully (and whether naturally or with assisted technology), and those of people where pregnancy was unplanned. Alongside shedding light on these psych-ical experiences around pregnancy and new parenthood, psychoanalysis has also been interested in the other definition of the term 'conception'; that is, the forming of a thought or an idea. Conceiving a thought is a developmental process of the mind, starting with a sensory input, which arises internally from our body or exter-nally from our environment—in either case this input will require some form of processing in the mind. From there we form a representation of the input, and finally develop a narrative around it that helps us to make sense of ourselves and the world around us. However, this process is also greatly influenced by our early childhood experiences, our internalised relationships with our primary figures, our perception of these, as well as our current relationships and our socio-cultural context.

Conceiving a baby involves both the biological and the mental kind of concep-tion. The person who is planning or trying to conceive might begin to imagine their future baby and themselves as a parent, which will give rise to various feelings and begin to foster expectations in connection with these mental representations. It is important to note that the term 'representations' has been used differently in different fields. While it is beyond the scope of this chapter to explain all these definitions, it is important to highlight one key difference. In developmental and cognitive psychology, the concept of representation is understood broadly as an internalisation of the external world, developed progressively by the particular environment that the person is in, their own actions, and the consequences of these actions. Psychoanalysis, on the other hand, has focused on understanding the unconscious elements that influence the internalisation of the external world. Unconscious elements include thoughts, fantasies, and feelings that are felt to be unbearable (and so are repressed from consciousness), or sensory and raw experi-ences that have never formed into a representation nor reached consciousness (see Chapter 25 for an overview on the development of the baby's inner representa-tions). Thus, an imagined baby will emerge from a mixture of conscious thoughts, feelings, and wishes, as well as remembered and unremembered experiences of

DOI: 10.4324/9781003530473-3

early relationships, represented and unrepresented bodily experiences, unconscious phantasies, thoughts, and conflicts. In psychoanalysis, the English spelling of 'phantasy' (with a 'ph') is to distinguish the unconscious elements and processes from the more colloquial use of 'fantasy', which refers to conscious imaginings or daydreams. Importantly, the 'imagined baby'—or the internal representation of the unborn baby—can play an important role in the future relationship with the real baby once it is born, as well as playing a part in the expectant parent's experience of conception and pregnancy.

On being able to conceive

In many instances conception happens naturally, without much conscious effort. Conception can be fulfilling, generating a sense of purpose and meaning—as something that we can do; something that defines who we are. However, when conception is difficult or does not happen (when it is hoped for), it can confront a person with their limitations and powerlessness in a process that is not entirely within their control. Most of the clinical literature focuses on people who are not able to conceive, and the psychological impact that this can have on them, or else it considers the emotional difficulties of conceiving through assisted reproduction. However, it is important to note that some people who plan and are able to conceive naturally can also be subject to intense feelings of powerlessness, inadequacy, fear, and stress. At times, the rapidity and newness of the biological process of conception can feel beyond one's conscious control. At other times, it is the upcoming changes, and the uncertainty of parenthood and an as-yet unknown baby that can feel overwhelming. Equally, there are instances where conception awakens unconscious conflicting feelings of excitement and fear; a fear of the force of change, and of things coming together to create something new.

The space to allow creation

Conceiving either a baby or an idea is a creative act, and creation is very much part of life and being human. For a baby to be conceived, there must be at least two elements (sperm and ovum) and a space (a uterus, or laboratory for assisted reproduction) to enable conception. Similarly, a mental conception of the unborn baby implies the coming together of two elements: a stimulus and a representation of it; one's internal thoughts and feelings, and the external situation of planning and trying to conceive with another (be it a partner, friend, or donor). It also requires a mental space in which these elements can come together and allow a new thought or representation to emerge. This may sound straightforward, but the necessary elements and space may each bring complications. The external situation includes the person's early childhood, their current relationships and sources of support, their socio-cultural situation, and so on. The internal aspect or 'inner reality' includes the ways in which these external experiences have been internalised in our minds to create an individual subjective experience—which is partly conscious and partly unconscious—alongside more innate drives and make-up, unconscious phantasies, and bodily experiences (represented and unrepresented). The mental space to conceive a baby will be influenced by both of these situations, internal and external. Several psychoanalysts have written on the process of creativity, but Winnicott's (1956) theory on transitional phenomena is of particular relevance here. He emphasised the importance for human development of an intermediate space between inner reality (our subjective experience) and the external world, as it allows a bridging between the two. If there is no intermediate space in which to process, regulate, and understand ourselves and the world, external situations and inner reality can be experienced as traumatic. For expectant parents, the conception of the imagined baby requires some form of transitional space, through which inner reality—filled with hopes, fears, expectations, and unconscious fantasies—can be reconciled with the external reality of the growing baby, and the changes being introduced by new parenthood.

Clinical vignette: A planned pregnancy that feels 'too soon' and 'unexpected'

Bianca and Charlie had been together for a couple of years and felt ready to start a family. Bianca got pregnant on their first try. They both felt happy, but also shocked and anxious. For Bianca, she felt panicked about the change in her life that would occur when the baby was born. She had imagined that it would take time to get pregnant—much-needed time to feel ready to become a mother. Previously, when thinking about juggling her career and raising a baby, this had felt manageable to her, but, as soon as she actually became pregnant, she began to experience doubt. Conception, for both Charlie and Bianca, seemed to come about too soon. Charlie described feeling stressed about the responsibility of a baby, who he imagined would be demanding, create financial stress, and claim all of Bianca's attention. What's more, for both of them, getting pregnant felt unexpected and out of their control, as if something had happened to them instead of them having actively conceived. After a month in parent-infant psychotherapy, Bianca suddenly remembered getting her first menstrual period. She was one of the first in her group of friends to get her period, and she was celebrated with excitement and admiration by her friends and her mother. However, she also remembered the fear and confusion that she felt about the changes in her body: it felt so intense, violent, strange; so suddenly upon her. She felt that her body was changing too quickly, and she was fearful of what else lay ahead. She felt conflicted about the joy and excitement that her friends and mother expressed about her starting to menstruate. She described wanting to withdraw into herself. It is as if the intense bodily change was psychically too overwhelming to bear; as if she lacked a 'transitional space' (Winnicott, 1956) either within her own mind or in those around her. Both at that earlier time of first menstruation, and now in early pregnancy, such a transitional space was needed to enable her to psychically hold the changes taking place until they felt more her own, at which time she could claim her body once again.

Conflicts about creation: Tension, loss, and feeling excluded

People can experience very positive feelings about conceiving: for example, a general sense of being productive and creative; hopes for the future; the reality of a longed-for baby and becoming a parent; or a satisfying, rewarding feeling of being able to conceive. However, some people may also experience, consciously and/or unconsciously, conflicted feelings about conceiving. Conception (and pregnancy, birth, the first few months of breastfeeding, and feeding and holding a baby) is an intensely physical experience. Psychoanalytic work has tried to explore and understand the different levels of our experience, starting from the physical, somatic level (sensorial input via our bodies) and leading to the more organised narrative of our conscious thoughts and feelings. Many of these early physical and bodily experiences remain within us, and may be reawakened in the process of conception. On a very simple level, things coming together for creation also implies that all elements are changed. Inevitably, what once was is now transformed—and often might be experienced as lost. For example, an expectant parent may feel that their previous life, sense of self, and relationships are irreversibly changed or gone. Most people will experience mixed feelings (at least unconsciously), including uncertainty around not yet knowing what has been created. These feelings of loss, uncertainty, and fear of the unknown can make an expectant parent feel deeply conflicted, since they also long to have a baby and become a parent.

Freud was interested in the various experiences of internal conflict, which were central to his understanding of the human mind. He postulated the existence of two opposing drives within us (1920). While psychoanalytic views on Freud's theories of the drives vary (see Laplanche, 2004), some of his descriptions of the life and death drives are certainly of relevance for understanding the psychic tensions in people going through conception. Freud described the 'life drive' as an inherent drive to create life and ideas, to grow and transform, to bind bodily energy, and to move forward in development. On the other hand, the 'death drive' aims to reduce or remove stimulation, tension, and/or change, at times by 'unbinding', in order to restore an earlier psychic state. Conception necessarily follows the life drive, and a person can feel confronted by this rush to grow and change, which can cause the unbalancing of a formerly quiet, tensionless state.

Moving on from the biological/mind frontier, Freud was also interested in children's understanding of their parents' sexual life, and of their own origins, as well as their ideas about conception. He described the conflict between love and hate experienced by children when becoming aware of the sexual and exclusive relationship between their parents. This new awareness can lead a child to feel a mixture of emotions—excitement, exclusion, and confusion, as well as anxiety about the imagined violent parental sexual intercourse. In Freud's view, the child's first thoughts about conception are conflicted, with intense opposing feelings of love and hate (these are elaborated on in his work on the Oedipus complex and the primal scene: Freud, 1918; Freud, 1940).

Clinical vignette: Fear of being excluded

Tom had felt confident in his relationship with Ana. Together they had faced various challenges in their lives (family losses, changes in work, etc.), which had made them feel stronger and more connected to one another. Tom was convinced that he wanted to stay with Ana for the rest of his life, and to build a family with her. When Ana became pregnant, his initial feelings were of pride and happiness: they were forming a baby together and beginning the next stage of their lives. However, one evening, while struggling to get to sleep, Tom had an intrusive thought that the baby was not his. He suddenly feared that Ana had slept with another man, and that this was in fact that other man's baby. He felt quite shaken by the intensity of the thought and the jealousy, anger, and fear that it aroused in him. In the morning, he tried to reassure himself that this baby was his, but he felt quite disturbed by his thoughts. In therapy he described how excluded he felt from the process of conceiving. He knew rationally that a part of him, his sperm, had created the embryo now in Ana's body, but he could not help feeling that it was someone else's, or perhaps—as he now began to feel—solely Ana's. He began to feel excluded from the pregnancy, from the excitement Ana felt about the changes in her body, and the images from the scans. He started to resent the pregnancy, to spend more time at work, and to withdraw, as he also felt ashamed of these feelings. In therapy, he began to understand that a part of his wish to have a family with Ana was to feel a secure bond with her. He had always feared that he would lose her, either by her dying or by her becoming interested in someone else. He remembered a close friend at school who had suddenly become the popular one with girls, and how he had felt left behind. He also remembered how close his parents had been. As an only child he had felt loved and cared for, yet also that his parents really enjoyed going out together without him; that they felt an excitement about each other that they did not feel about him. Ana had changed that for him: he felt special, important, the 'exciting one'. Now, Ana's excitement about the pregnancy and their unborn baby felt to Tom as though he were being excluded, and so, in turn, he had started to exclude himself. Slowly, as he voiced some of his fears and feelings, he felt better able to become more involved in the pregnancy, and to imagine his future as a father.

Reawakening of the past

Conceiving or planning to conceive a child can take us back to our own beginnings—how was I conceived? Was it a joyful conception? Was I wanted? Did my mother enjoy being pregnant with me? Conceiving a child means that, consciously or unconsciously, we are in touch with thoughts, feelings, fantasies, and bodily experiences of this coming-together and creating. Our own different experiences and internalisations of conception (narratives formed consciously or unconsciously), our fears and fantasies, can reawaken at this time. Raphael-Leff (1993) describes how conception is the beginning of what she calls 'an inside story' for each expectant parent, which is built from their psychic reality, illusions, and internal representations of primary figures.

Clinical vignette: Giving up to avoid the pain of failure

Alicia wanted to get pregnant and create a family. She felt that she had a good relationship with her partner, and that it was a good time in her life to have a baby. After two unsuccessful attempts, she became convinced that she was infertile. She was reluctant to have a fertility check-up or to continue trying. At a second therapy consultation meeting, she described how she felt that her mother had not enjoyed being with her when she was a child, that she had really wanted a son, and how she had seemed to "*give up*" on Alicia when she did not get good marks in her first years at school. Alicia remembered how painful it was to try to get good marks in order to gain her mother's love, and how each low mark confirmed for her that she was not worthy of that love. She seemed to have internalised this defeatist view of herself: that there was no point in trying since she was, as she felt, an unwanted, wrong child. Failing to get pregnant on her first few tries reawakened this painful feeling of being unwanted, and the hopelessness that she had felt as a child. Alicia described feeling as though this hoped-for baby did not want her; that she was not fit to be a mother. She had unconsciously defended against this feeling of being unwanted by giving up on trying to conceive. Despite her success at work and the confidence this gave her, and despite the connection and trust that she felt with her partner, the failed pregnancy attempts reawakened this early experience that she had forgotten about. It took time for Alicia to separate her childhood experiences with her mother from her own sense of self, as she confronted her feelings of powerlessness in trying to conceive. She slowly began to see herself as having something worthwhile; that is, a wish to conceive and to have a baby, which was not contingent on feeling wanted or unwanted by others.

References

Freud, S. (1918) From the history of an infantile neurosis. In J. Strachey (Ed. & Trans.), The Standard Edition of the Complete Psychological Works of Sigmund Freud, 17:1–124. London: Vintage, The Hogarth Press.

Freud, S. (1920) Beyond the pleasure principle. In J. Strachey (Ed. & Trans.), The Standard Edition of the Complete Psychological Works of Sigmund Freud, 18:1–64. London: Vintage, The Hogarth Press.

Freud, S. (1940) An outline of psycho-analysis. In J. Strachey (Ed. & Trans.), The Standard Edition of the Complete Psychological Works of Sigmund Freud, 21:27–84. London: Vintage, The Hogarth Press.

Laplanche, J. (2004). The so-called 'death drive': A sexual drive. *British Journal of Psychotherapy*, 20(4):455–471.

Raphael-Leff, J. (1993). *Pregnancy: The inside story*. London: Sheldon Press.

Winnicott, D. W. (1956) [1975] Chapter XVIII. Transitional objects and transitional phenomena. Through paediatrics to psycho-analysis (International Psycho-Analytical Library (No. 100, pp. 229–242). London: Hogarth Press & Institute of Psycho-Analysis.

Chapter 2

Fertility and reproductive health education for family building

Bola Grace

Global perspective

Global health policies and various stakeholder groups have emphasised the importance of improving women's health and enhancing knowledge of contraception,
both as part of pregnancy prevention and as pregnancy planning. However, in terms
of general fertility awareness, there is a higher body of literature regarding the prevention of pregnancy versus planning for pregnancy. A relatively large number of
research studies have been conducted globally to assess education levels regarding
contraception for pregnancy prevention; however, fewer studies have focused on
achieving pregnancy.

In sexual and reproductive health education, the emphasis has traditionally been
on preventing pregnancy rather than planning for it. This imbalance in focus on
pregnancy prevention versus attainment is likely the result of many years of cam-
paign efforts aimed at reducing abortion rates, as well as unplanned and unwanted
pregnancies (Sikaluzwe et al., 2018). Since unwanted pregnancies, particularly in
adolescence, remain a significant factor in negative outcomes for mother and child,
perpetuating cycles of poverty and poor health, public health initiatives over several decades have rightly prioritised campaigns to improve availability and access
to contraception (Altshuler et al., 2015).

These global campaigns are justified; evidence indicates that between a third
and a half of all pregnancies worldwide are unintended, with approximately 80%
of women affected not using modern contraception. Literature evidence shows
that unintended pregnancy is one of the most serious health issues, especially in
low and middle-income settings (Aragaw et al., 2023; Pillai et al., 2023). These
serious issues highlight the ongoing importance of contraception from a global
perspective.

Family planning: A historical perspective

The origins of family planning can be traced to the decline in birth rates from the late
nineteenth century, which occurred unevenly across social classes and was associated with the demographic transition and the role of individual rational action. In

DOI: 10.4324/9781003530473-4

the pre- and early-twentieth century, artificial methods of contraception were still stigmatised, being linked to non-marital sex and perceived immorality. Historians attribute much of the decline in birth rates during this period to the of natural methods (Szreter, 1996). By the early twentieth century, various factors—including concerns about population fitness, the perceived 'over-breeding' of lower classes, eugenics, feminism, and broader cultural changes—influenced attitudes towards family size.

The transition of contraception from being morally unacceptable to state-sanctioned occurred during the 1920s and 1930s. Activists employed diverse arguments, yet a shared approach was to dissociate contraception from sex and link it to broader social benefits, such as improving women's health, increasing population fitness, and alleviating poverty (Hawkes, 1996). As discussions of sexuality were tied to procreation within marriage, promoting the 'respectable' or non-sexual aspects of contraception became a key strategy. The National Birth Control Association, established in the 1920s, changed its name to the Family Planning Association in 1939. Hawkes and Weeks (Weeks, 1989) both regard this as significant, linking contraception to the rise of social planning and state intervention at the time. Hawkes further argues that the concepts of 'family planning' and 'planned families' enabled the state to address concerns regarding non-marital sexuality and reproduction.

Have we left family out of family planning?

While the term 'family planning' encompasses achieving one's desired number of children and spacing pregnancies, it is more commonly associated with limiting family size. In general usage, it has become synonymous with contraception, birth control, and the prevention of unintended pregnancies. According to the Oxford English Dictionary, family planning is defined as "the practice of controlling the number of children one has and the intervals between their births, particularly by means of contraception or voluntary sterilisation". This prevailing emphasis on preventing unintended pregnancies reveals a gap in the literature that warrants further exploration. While the prevention of unintended pregnancies remains critical, relatively little attention has been paid to the global decline in fertility rates, which in many high-income countries are now below replacement level. Some explanations for this reduction include delayed childbearing and involuntary childlessness.

Although the term 'family planning' is firmly established in both general literature and scientific discourse in the context of pregnancy prevention, our literature review highlighted the absence of a widely recognised equivalent term for achieving pregnancy. The term 'proception' (Te Velde et al., 2012) has been proposed to describe behaviours aimed at achieving conception; however, it has not gained widespread usage. Similarly, 'family building' appears in the literature, yet no clear definition is provided, and its origins within fertility awareness remain unclear. Misunderstandings surrounding the concept of family planning in the context of achieving pregnancies may lead to disparities in public health messaging on reproductive health. While continued advocacy for contraception remains crucial within fertility awareness campaigns, there is a need to achieve greater balance in messaging.

Addressing issues faced by individuals trying to conceive requires improved fertility-related terminology and more inclusive public health approaches. In their work, Grace et al. (2022), define family building as: "the construction or formation of a family, which can include steps or actions taken by an individual towards having children. In contrast to family planning, the intent focuses on pregnancy planning and childbearing rather than pregnancy prevention. However, it can also include actions taken to space the number of children one has."

The importance of fertility and reproductive health education

Childbearing at advanced maternal and paternal ages has markedly increased in many high-income countries over the past two decades. In response, educators, healthcare professionals, charities, reproductive health groups, and government policymakers have made a concerted effort to improve fertility education. Since earning potential typically increases with age, delaying parenthood can be viewed as a rational economic decision, with economic considerations such as studying, employment, and career progression frequently cited as key reasons for postponing childbearing (Leung et al., 2016). However, economic motivations are not the only factors; collectively, they remain among the most significant (Brand & Davis, 2011; Mills et al., 2011). Changing social norms regarding the ideal age for parenthood, improved access to education, the availability of contraception, and advances in assisted reproductive technologies are also contributing factors.

Evidence has shown that delayed childbearing is not always a conscious choice but is influenced by a complex interplay of financial and emotional stability, relationship status, health, and fertility considerations (Koert et al., 2021). Nonetheless, a lack of awareness regarding the impact of advancing maternal age on fertility and increased risks associated with delayed childbearing often contributes to reduced likelihood of conception (Harper et al., 2017).

The demographic shift towards delayed family building has become an increasing public health and clinical concern due to higher risks of adverse maternal and foetal outcomes. While most women who try to conceive before the age of 35 are likely to succeed naturally, the risk of infertility and poor outcomes increases significantly for those who face difficulty conceiving beyond this age. Therefore, improving fertility knowledge remains an essential component of public health strategies aimed at preventing involuntary childlessness and supporting individuals in achieving their family-building goals (Harper et al., 2021; Cheshire et al., 2024).

An understanding of reproductive cycles and fertility is important not only for pregnancy prevention but also for pregnancy planning. Education should enable both men and women to appreciate how their fertility declines with age due to a combination of genetic factors. These further emphasize the importance of fertility awareness, which is defined as

> The understanding of reproduction, fecundity, fecundability, and related individual risk factors (e.g. advanced age, sexual health factors such as sexually transmitted infections, and life style factors such as smoking, obesity) and non-individual risk factors (e.g. environmental and work place factors); including the awareness of societal and cultural factors affecting options to meet reproductive family planning, as well as family building needs.
>
> (Zegers-Hochschild et al., 2017)

The rapid advancement of assisted reproductive technologies highlights the focus on potential solutions rather than addressing the root cause: insufficient fertility awareness and education. Improving fertility knowledge and awareness across reproductive age groups has significant potential to reduce the impact of infertility caused by modifiable factors, underscoring the importance of robust fertility education (Martins et al., 2023). Furthermore, fertility education can enhance reproductive autonomy, improve body literacy, and enable individuals to make informed health decisions beyond their childbearing intentions.

Sources of fertility and reproductive health information

Improving fertility and reproductive education requires a thorough understanding of the sources from which individuals obtain reproductive health and fertility information. Online sources are frequently cited as popular avenues for accessing fertility information across reproductive age groups (Grace et al., 2023a). Factors driving this preference include ease of access, perceived anonymity, and the speed with which information can be obtained. A critical element in addressing fertility education is evaluating whether these sources meet people's needs and whether the information provided is accurate and reliable. Such evaluations are essential for implementing effective strategies to disseminate reproductive health knowledge. Understanding how individuals access reproductive health information also presents opportunities for improving communication and outreach.

The significance of accessing reliable health-related information has become even more apparent since the COVID-19 pandemic, during which an 'infodemic' contributed to widespread confusion and health-related harm (WHO, 2021). The term 'infodemic', a blend of 'information' and 'epidemic', refers to the overabundance of information—both accurate and inaccurate—in digital and physical spaces, leading to confusion, risk-taking behaviour, and adverse health outcomes (Zarocostas, 2020). An infodemic can also result in mistrust of health authorities, undermine public health responses, and contribute to increased mortality. Several pervasive myths and rumours regarding the impact of COVID-19 vaccines on reproductive health and fertility further highlight the need for trusted and reliable sources of information (Grace et al., 2023a; Harper et al., 2021).

Research has consistently shown that the internet has long been one of the most popular sources for seeking (in)fertility information. People use the internet to feel better informed, to address emotional, social, and psychological needs, and to aid decision-making processes. While online educational materials available via websites and social media platforms can empower individuals and improve patient care (Harper et al., 2017), there are associated risks, including the potential for misinformation, misunderstanding of data, and unmet informational needs.

Considering broader population groups

While discussions on fertility and reproductive health continues to focus on women, it remains critical to consider the needs of broader population groups and key stakeholders.

Engaging men

Literature evidence (Grace et al., 2019) supports the perception that fertility is a "woman's issue", highlighting the negative impact of stereotypical male and female roles in reproductive health. A review of evidence (Hammarberg et al., 2017) has shown that men's fertility awareness is low. Additionally, from a public health perspective, men have traditionally been disengaged from fertility and reproductive health discussions and unaware of the impact of paternal health on the child. Despite growing evidence (Fleming et al., 2018) on the significance of paternal health on the health of the child, one of the main reasons for the poor inclusion of men in fertility and reproductive health discussions and research is the overarching interest in reproductive outcomes in terms of offspring. Evidence shows that various stakeholders, including at a societal level, have succumbed to traditionally held beliefs regarding male involvement and interest in fertility and reproductive health. However, more recent evidence is highlighting that men do want to be involved and engaged on the topic (Grace et al., 2019). There needs to be a change in societal attitudes towards men's reproductive health if men are to play a more informed role in fertility and reproductive health, in order to improve health equity for both men and women.

Educating healthcare professionals

Although healthcare professionals are often cited as the most trusted sources of fertility and reproductive health information, evidence shows that they can have low knowledge of fertility-related topics themselves (Garcia, et al., 2017; Grace et al., 2023b), with substantial gaps in understanding as well as misconceptions on fertility and infertility treatment. In their study, Grace et al. (2023b) showed that healthcare professionals did not feel confident educating patients and were often unsure of where the responsibilities for fertility education lie. It is therefore important to ensure that healthcare professionals themselves are educated and trained on this subject, in order to ensure that patients in their care are provided with accurate and reliable information regarding fertility and reproductive health.

Planting the seed young

Evidence highlights significant gaps in the education of young people regarding reproductive health (Biswakarma et al., 2024; Delbaere, 2024). As comprehensive reproductive health and sex education plays a crucial role in promoting overall health and well-being, it remains important to provide boys and girls with age-appropriate education to enhance fertility awareness, normalise discussions about reproductive health, and challenge taboos surrounding the subject. Such education can help reduce misinformation and encourage positive attitudes towards sex and reproductive health.

Language matters

Finally, while the improvement of fertility and reproductive health education is not intrinsically controversial, knowing how to effectively communicate these topics effectively can be challenging. From a public health perspective, there are several risks and unintended consequences, such as increasing anxiety, perceived shaming, guilt, unnecessary alarming, fear-mongering, and unintended pronatalist messaging. If not executed correctly, fertility education campaigns can have a negative effect, become counter-productive, or even result in backlash. In their recommendation article, Mertes et al. (2023) provide a framework for getting the language right. These include being mindful of reproductive autonomy; avoiding blame; offering a positive focus; considering the needs of both men and women; and ensuring that messages are tailored to relevant audience.

References

Altshuler, A. L., Gaffield, M. E., & Kiarie, J. N. (2015). The WHO's medical eligibility criteria for contraceptive use: 20 years of global guidance. *Current Opinion in Obstetrics and Gynecology*, *27*(6), 451–459. https://doi.org/10.1097/GCO.0000000000000212

Aragaw, F. M., Amare, T., Teklu, R. E., Tegegne, B. A., & Alem, A. Z. (2023). Magnitude of unintended pregnancy and its determinants among childbearing age women in low and middle-income countries: Evidence from 61 low and middle-income countries. *Frontiers in Reproductive Health*, *17*(5), 1113926. https://doi.org/10.3389/frph.2023.1113926

Biswakarma, R., Maslowski, K., Reiss, M. J., & Harper, J. C. (2024). Parenthood intentions of 16–18-year-olds in England: A survey of school students. *Human Fertility*, *27*(1). https://doi.org/10.1080/14647273.2024.2310639

Brand, J. E., & Davis, D. (2011). The impact of college education on fertility: Evidence for heterogeneous effects. *Demography*, *48*(3), 863–887. https://doi.org/10.1007/s13524-011-0034-3

Cheshire, J., Chu, J., Boivin, J., Dugdale, G., Harper, J., & Balen, A. (2024). The Fertility Education Initiative: responding to the need for enhanced fertility and reproductive health awareness amongst young people in the United Kingdom. *Human Fertility*, *27*(1). https://doi.org/10.1080/14647273.2024.2417940

Delbaere, I., De Vos, M., Somers, S., Condorelli, M., Pening, D., Bogaerts, A., Vandepitte, H., Stoop, D., Harper, J., & Mertes, H. (2024). "Do I want children later in life?": Reproductive intentions of 1700 adolescents. *European Journal of Contraception and Reproductive Health Care*, *29*(3), 85–92. https://doi.org/10.1080/13625187.2024.2335651

Fleming, T. P., Watkins, A. J., Velazquez, M. A., Mathers, J. C., Prentice, A. M., & Stephenson, J. (2018). Origins of lifetime health around the time of conception: Causes and consequences. *The Lancet*, *391*(10), 555–557. https://doi.org/10.1016/S0140-6736(18)30312-X

García, D., Vassena, R., Prat, A., & Vernaeve, V. (2017). Poor knowledge of age-related fertility decline and assisted reproduction among healthcare professionals. *Reproductive BioMedicine Online*, *34*(1), 32–37. https://doi.org/10.1016/j.rbmo.2016.09.013

Grace, B., Shawe, J., Johnson, S., & Stephenson, J. (2019). You did not turn up... I did not realise I was invited...: Understanding male attitudes towards engagement in fertility and reproductive health discussions. *Human Reproduction Open*, *1*(3), 1–7.

Grace, B., Shawe, J., Barrett, G., Usman, N. O., & Stephenson, J. (2022). What does family building mean? A qualitative exploration and a new definition: A UK-based study. *Reproductive Health*, *19*, 203. https://doi.org/10.1186/s12978-022-01511-w

Grace, B., Shawe, J., & Stephenson, J. (2023a). A mixed methods study investigating sources of fertility and reproductive health information in the UK. *Sexual & Reproductive Healthcare*, *36*, 100826. https://doi.org/10.1016/j.srhc.2023.100826

Grace, B., Shawe, J., & Stephenson, J. (2023b). Exploring fertility knowledge amongst healthcare professional and lay population groups in the UK: A mixed methods study. *Human Fertility*, *26*(2), 302–311. https://doi.org/10.1080/14647273.2022.2153349

Hammarberg, K., Collins, V., Holden, C., Young, K., & McLachlan, R. (2017). Men's knowledge, attitudes, and behaviours relating to fertility. *Human Reproduction Update*, *23*(4), 458–480.

Harper, J., Boivin, J., O'Neill, H. C., Brian, K., Dhingra, J., Dugdale, G., Edwards, G., Emmerson, L., Grace, B., Hadley, A., Hamzic, L., Heathcote, J., Hepburn, J., Hoggart, L., Kisby, F., Mann, S., Norcross, S., Regan, L., Seenan, S., Stephenson, J., Walker, H., & Balen, A. (2017). The need to improve fertility awareness. *Reproductive Biomedicine and Society Online*. *Apr 8*(4), 18–20. doi: 10.1016/j.rbms.2017.03.002. PMID: 29774262; PMCID: PMC5952813.

Harper, J. C., Hammarberg, K., Simopoulou, M., Koert, E., Pedro, J., Massin, N., Fincham, A., & Balen, A. (2021). The International Fertility Education Initiative: Research and action to improve fertility awareness. *Human Reproduction Open*. https://doi.org/10.1093/hropen/hoab031

Hawkes, G. (1996). *Sociology of sex and sexuality*. McGraw-Hill Education.

Leung, M. Y. M., Groes, F., & Santaeulalia-Llopis, R. (2016). The relationship between age at first birth and mother's lifetime earnings: Evidence from Danish data. *PLoS ONE*, *11*(1), e0146989. https://doi.org/10.1371/journal.pone.0146989

Martins, M. V., Koert, E., Sylvest, R., Maeda, E., Moura-Ramos, M., Hammarberg, K., Harper, J., & Collaboration o. b. o. E. s. I. R. H. E. (2023). Fertility education: Recommendations for developing and implementing tools to improve fertility literacy. *Human Reproduction*, *39*(2), 293–302. https://doi.org/10.1093/humrep/dead253

Mertes, H., Harper, J., Boivin, J., Ekstrand Ragnar, M., Grace, B., Moura-Ramos, M., Rautakallio-Hokkanen, S., Simopoulou, M., Hammarberg, K., & on behalf of the

International Reproductive Health Education Collaboration (IRHEC). (2023). Stimulating fertility awareness: the importance of getting the language right. *Human Reproduction Open, 2023*(2), hoad009. https://doi.org/10.1093/hropen/hoad009

Pillai, V. K., & Nagoshi, J. L. (2023). Unmet family planning need globally: A clarion call for sharpening current research frameworks. *Open Access Journal of Contraception, 20*(14), 139–147. https://doi.org/10.2147/OAJC.S378042

Sikaluzwe, M., Phiri, M., Lemba, M., Shasha, L., & Muhanga, M. (2018). Trends in prevalence and factors associated with unintended pregnancies in Zambia (2001–2018). *BMC Pregnancy and Childbirth, 24*, 148. https://doi.org/10.1186/s12884-024-06311-7

Szreter, S. (1996). *Fertility, class, and gender in Britain, 1860–1940.* Cambridge Studies in Population, Economy and Society in Past Time, 41. Cambridge University Press.

Te Velde, E., Habbema, D., Leridon, H., & Eijkemans, M. (2012). The effect of postponement of first motherhood on permanent involuntary childlessness and total fertility rate in six European countries since the 1970s. *Human Reproduction, 27*, 1179–1183.

Weeks, J. (1989). *Sex, politics, and society: The regulation of sexuality since 1800.* Longman.

World Health Organization. (2021). Infodemic. Available from: www.who.int/health-topics/infodemic#tab=tab_1

Zarocostas, J. (2020). How to fight an infodemic. *The Lancet, 395*(10225), 676. https://doi.org/10.1016/S0140-6736(20)30461-X

Zegers-Hochschild, F., Adamson, G. D., Dyer, S., Racowsky, C., de Mouzon, J., Sokol, R., Rienzi, L., Sunde, A., Schmidt, L., Cooke, I. D., Simpson, J. L., & van der Poel, S. (2017). The international glossary on infertility and fertility care. *Human Reproduction, 32*, 1786–1801.

Chapter 3

Psychoanalytic perspectives on assisted donor conception

Katherine Fine

Assisted conception

The decision by couples or individuals to create a family through assisted conception often follows the discovery that they cannot have a baby in the conventional way. Over the last 50 years, significant advances have been made in reproductive medicine, marked by the milestone birth of Louise Brown, the first human to have been born after conception by in vitro fertilisation in 1978.

There are significant emotional and psychological consequences to using each of the new reproductive techniques to conceive a family. These radical fertility treatment developments (how else would one describe them) continue within the context of enormous social change and geopolitical challenges.

The use of donated eggs, sperm, and embryos has increased considerably. Today we encounter a greater variety of family forms in our clinical practice than ever before. This affects both how we think about what constitutes a family, as well as how we create one.

The psychoanalytic perspective on early parenthood and infancy

An adult's wish to have a family inevitably reawakens early anxieties and developmental struggles. Early parenthood resonates with powerful conscious and unconscious memories of the infant and child in mourning.

The growing infant is faced with the painful task of having to relinquish his first love, his mother, or the one who gives birth and to allow for the presence of a powerful and sexually potent other / father (in phantasy). Ehrensaft (2015) attests to the hurdles that need to be overcome. Over time the infant/child becomes increasingly able to mourn the loss of his exclusive relationship with his mother, aware that she is part of a (reproductive) parental couple, with their own exclusive relationship.

All being well and by working through complicated and painful developmental hurdles along the way, the growing child is increasingly able to bear feelings of

DOI: 10.4324/9781003530473-5

frustration and loss. The maturing young person continues this journey, endeavouring to take ownership of his or her body and his or her mind.

Becoming an adult and considering having a baby of their own, the seed of the potential of forming his/her own sexual couple relationship is sown. The wish or lack of desire to conceive a family depends very much on early history, relationships, and personal scenarios. Raphael-Leff (2014)

What does it mean to conceive?

The notion of conception is rich with symbolic representation, embedded in deeply emotional experiences. Where psychological conflicts involve fertility, this reaches into the deepest layers of the individual psyche. Apfel and Keylor (2002)

For women, this could mean a wish to be pregnant, rather than to be a mother. Maybe to recapture or to repair a sense of a lost or damaged internal babyhood and, for her impregnated, lactating body to be witnessed. Zoja (1998) suggests pregnancy may represent a woman's attempt to initiate a birth of self, by re-affirming her own fertility. Or, as Raphael-Leff (2007) suggests, to actualise unconscious phantasies in reality.

A woman who is confident in her capacity to have a healthy baby can trust in her sexual identity and femininity that she too can be a mother, like her own mother. If she fails to get pregnant, however, she may believe in phantasy that her reproductive organs are either permanently immature, or destroyed beyond repair; thus reinforcing feelings of omnipotence or helplessness. Pines (1993)

For men, powerful conscious and unconscious phantasies may also reawaken early anxieties and developmental struggles. The notion of an embryo and a foetus lodged inside the woman's womb can leave men feeling alienated, with no tangible connection to the physical reality of a pregnancy. For men, proven fertility can feel like an affirmation of their sense of manhood and potency when symbolic and concrete thinking converge. Schofield (2015)

Typically, in fertility clinics, attention is focused on the female partner for historical and medical reasons. Yet, figures suggest that male-factor infertility accounts for 30% of all cases: Miles, Keitel, Jackson, Harris and Licciardi (2009). Men who are infertile show high levels of distress and guilt about their infertility and the affect it has on their loved ones. Schofield (2015)

In the process of painfully reworking what is referred to by Raphael-Leff (2007) as a sense of a person's own "generative identity", the self can be subjected to profound disappointment, inadequacy, or shame. Feeling as if their life is empty and has no meaning, it seems shattered by the loss of the ideal partner, conception, birth, family, or children.

The potential of working through this internal experience may well be akin to creating a baby of the mind. Creative capacities may be re-found, akin to when childhood feelings of helplessness and rage are mastered; procreation identified in symbolic terms as an essentially healing task towards integration in the depressive position. Klein (1957)

Note: Psychoanalytic theory and practice concerns itself with *fantasy*, not just at the conscious level but also at a deeper unconscious level. This is normally referred to as *phantasy*.

Conceiving a family using donated gametes

The decision to build a family through the use of donated eggs, sperm, or embryos may result from a variety of circumstances: infertility in one or both partners of a heterosexual couple; the absence of a partner for a single person; or of a partner of the opposite sex in same sex relationships. Lingiardi, V., & Carone, N. (2019)

There are significant issues encountered by people when conceiving a family using donated gametes; that is a sexually reproducing organism, especially an ovum or sperm. In assisting conception, recipients may imagine that they are simply acquiring a factor of reproduction. Donor Conception can indeed offer a marvellous solution, but it is not just about procreation, making a baby, or creating a donor conceived child.

Navigating:

> … the resurfacing of early primal scenes and oedipal dramas … connected to psychological strategies and defences, particularly denial, to ward off anxieties generated by introducing an outside party into the most intimate arena of family life—conception of a child.
>
> (Fine (2015), p.15)

Is to take account of "*introducing an outside party*": starting with the medical investigative intervention. In raising a family with donor conceived children, the imagined donor is ever present. It may mean family life becomes suffused with imaginings, daydreams, and questions. In fiction it is often told:

> When she was old enough to go with her {*single*} mother to the market she looked at the faces of the men who sold vegetables and wondered if one of them was her father.
>
> (Faulks, 2022)

How does the fact of the donor shape a sense of family?

The HFEA reports on 'fertility trends' that 2% of all babies born in the UK were conceived through in vitro fertilization (IVF) and women over the age of 45 are using donor eggs more often than their own eggs, for the first time. (2018)

Linda and Susie

Here is a brief excerpt from a discussion I had with Linda and Susie, half-siblings conceived through the same anonymous sperm donor, but to different mothers, in different families, with additional half-siblings as yet untraced. They were fifteen

years old when I met them. Linda and Susie were born a few weeks apart, but did not know of each other until they were ten years old. Fine (2015)
They seemed at ease with the (non-identifiable) donor not being a part of their lives.

> They were receptive to the notion of him, but more in the sense of general curiosity. They both imagined the donor was probably married and had children of his own, although neither seemed to consider that if he had any, the donor's own children would be their half siblings. In their discussion with me they seemed to be reflecting on the nature of his "gift" and what his motivation might have meant in terms of exploring his 'fit', in their family.
>
> You'd have to decide how much you would make them part of your life, would you have Christmas dinner together? Also, he has his own life, he's probably married and has kids of his own.

Linda would not think of calling her donor 'dad' or anything like that. When she was little she used to think about the donor as the ideal dad sort of figure, whereas now she doesn't really want to know who he is because:

> ... chances are he is not going to be that ideal figure that I have in my mind and I have a happy life and I have a half-sister that I really love ... I don't have the need to meet him, I don't feel that my life is any less for not having him in it.

While there may be a temptation for recipients to think that, in using a donated sperm, egg, or embryo, this is simply a one-off fertility treatment, actually they are receiving the genetic history and psychological legacy of (the donor's) family. The donor becomes part of the family, in phantasy and in reality, for life. Hence: *Donor Conception for Life* (Fine, 2015).

The psychoanalytic perspective on early parenthood and infancy of donor-assisted conception

The choices available in creating the longed-for family in donor conception can far exceed expectations of choice in a more conventional conception.

> Involving a donor(s) as an external party to procreation raises many complex psychological, social and relational issues. This challenges our fundamental preconceptions about "who is family" and "how babies are made."
>
> (Fine, 2015, p.4)

Prospectively, crossing family boundaries and 'norms' facilitates sometime extreme options; for example, by becoming a new parent at over 60 years of age. The potential of using reproductive techniques to conceive presents a position of such omnipotence, it may risk becoming a defence against intense feelings of ambivalence, shame, and loss. This raises complex moral, practical, and psychological issues. Imagine if by 2040 it is possible to produce embryos from the skin cells of people of any age or gender. Golombok (2020)

In a new generation of 'Preparation for (donor conception) parenthood' workshops, Fine and Mitchell (2015) outline how a couple's infertility can produce the same sense of bereavement as in a death, yet, there is no body, just a void, with no embryos, simply an empty space into which a child cannot, or will not, come. This is a 'non-event' loss, a point of transition that needs to be processed before thinking of the alternative. Within a partnership, mourning is likely to happen at different times for each person.

Spontaneous lovemaking may be replaced by what Montuschi (2015 in Fine and Mitchell, 2015) calls "baby making" sex. Failure to conceive can leave an intense feeling of frustrated desire. She suggests it deprives the couple of "an unthinking conception", the joy of conceiving through lovemaking.

Infertile women who, with egg or embryo donation, still carry the pregnancy in their bodies face a different kind of loss. Conception taken out of the bedroom can leave single women and single men feeling bereft, compounding as it does a sense of being unable, thus far, to maintain a successfully generative partnership. Same sex couples may feel a sense of loss at their inability to give their partner the one small, but vital, missing gamete. Lingiardi, V., & Carone, N. (2019)

The end of the genetic line can mean the loss of a personal and cultural heritage of the 'mini me', so called by many. Failing to give a genetically related grandchild to their parents has been described by some as a death of hopes and dreams. Taking the decision to pursue assisted reproduction may involve an agonising series of decisions. At its most excruciating, it is not uncommon for seven or eight failed IVF attempts to have been endured. Group workshops, couple, or individual therapy may be invaluable in working through and deciding on a way forward. Fine (2015)

Family Marionn

A couple who met in their early 40s wanted a family.

> Mr Marionn had previously had a vasectomy; their first son was conceived by DI [donor insemination]. The baby tragically died at 18 months old. Their second son Elliot, was born of double donation, a donor sperm from one family and a donor egg from another family, carried in utero by Mrs Marionn.
>
> Elliot was nine years old when the family presented for help; he was angry and depressed. His parents had once mentioned that he was donor conceived, but it had never been discussed since. The couple were helped to face the pain and loss of having had to use donor gametes, compounded by the grief at the death of their first child. ...
>
> In family therapy it became clear that Elliot felt he could not live up to his dead brother. Through therapy he realised he was a son who was loved for being himself and his parents' gratitude was for being able to have him, their precious boy.

In conclusion, the work of mourning the loss of the longed-for and imagined baby/child/family continues, life-long. Each stage of family life has its own characteristic anxieties to be addressed and the developmental tasks ahead involve all members of the family. Establishing a sense of belonging to their family may also mean integrating the knowledge of half-siblings and the donor's own family.

In generating a family reverie, however, the task of mourning the loss of a 'natural' conception offers the possibility, if not the promise, of re-defining the very nature of modern family life. The family boundaries are redrawn, donor inclusive, where fears are suitably addressed, for example by discussing the facts openly with family and friends, so the potential for a more ordinary and satisfactory outcome is possible. Feelings can hopefully be experienced in a much more satisfying way than was thought imaginable at the outset.

References

Apfel, R. J., & Keylor, R. G. (2002). Psychoanalysis and infertility. Myths and realities. *International Journal of Psychoanalysis*, 83(Pt 1):85–104. doi: 10.1516/0020757021601702

Ehrensaft, D. (2015). Ch. 6. When baby makes three or four or more: Attachment, individuation and identity in assisted conception families. In K. Fine (Ed.) *Donor Conception for Life*. London: Karnac.

Faulks, S. (2022). *Snow Country*. London: Vintage.

Fine, K. (Ed.) (2015). *Donor Conception for Life: Psychoanalytic Reflections on New Ways of Conceiving the Family*. London: Routledge.

Golombok, S. (2020). *We Are Family: What Really Matters for Parents and Children*. London: Scribe UK.

HFEA gov.UK (2018) *UK Statistics for IVF and DI Treatment, Storage, and Donation*. London: HFEA (non departmental public body sponsored by the Dept of Health and Social Care), Government Office in London.

Klein, M. (1957). *Envy and Gratitude*. London: Tavistock

Lingiardi, V., & Carone, N. (2019). Challenging Oedipus in changing families: Gender identifications and access to origins in same-sex parent families created through third-party reproduction. *The International Journal of Psychoanalysis*, 100(2):229–246. doi: 10.1080/00207578.2019.1589381

Miles, L. M., Keitel, M., Jackson, M., Harris, A., & Licciardi, F. (2009). Predictors of distress in women being treated for infertility. *Journal of Reproductive and Infant Psychology*, 27(3):238–257.

Pattis Zoja, E. (1998). *Abortion: Loss and Renewal in the Search for Identity*. London: Routledge.

Pines, D. (1993). *A Woman's Unconscious Use of Her Body. A Psychoanalytic Perspective*. London: Virago Press.

Raphael-Leff, J. (2007). Femininity and its unconscious 'Shadows': Gender and generative identity in the age of biotechnology. *British Journal of Psychotherapy*, 23:497–515.

Raphael-Leff, J. (2014). *Dark Side of the Womb: Pregnancy, Parenting and Persecutory Anxieties*. London: Karnac.

Schofield, A. (2015). Ch 5. It takes a second to be a father...... But a lifetime to be a Daddy. In K. Fine (Ed.) *Donor Conception for Life*. London: Routledge.

Chapter 4

Psychosocial aspects of donor conception and seeking identity of donors

Ken Daniels and Letitia Meadows

Introduction

The practice of donor conception where the gametes of a third party, who is usually unknown, are used has undergone major changes since its inception and those changes reflect how the socio-cultural context of the practice is impacting on parents and their offspring.

Parents who used donor insemination (DI), the earliest of the donor conception (DC) methods, were originally encouraged to see this as a medical treatment and a means of overcoming the male partner's infertility so they could have a baby. The successful birth of a child, however, raised issues for the parents, the most significant being decision-making about what information, if any, would be shared with the child. This 'family issue', with its heavy reliance on psychology and sociology, meant that DI could no longer simply be seen as a solely medical intervention. This led to the recognition of DI as being about treating infertility and building a family (Daniels, 2004). The focus on the family has been the subject of much debate and conflict between the different professions (Daniels & Thorn, 2001) particularly on issues such as secrecy and information sharing with offspring and the related issue of the anonymity of the donors. In recent years, as those conceived as a result of DI, and more generally DC, have become adults they have begun to demand information about 'their donor', including the possibility of meeting him/her. There has also been an expressed desire by donor conceived persons (DCPs) to be able to know and potentially meet their half-siblings as they are frequently seen as 'family'. It is for this reason that this chapter has a focus on not only the psychosocial aspects of donor conception but also includes the emerging voices of those who resulted from DI and how those voices have the potential to impact on the perspective of early parenthood and infancy.

Parenthood following donor conception

Most people expect to conceive and become parents (if they wish to) without having to involve doctors in the process. The discovery of infertility is invariably challenging not only to the infertile partner but also to the couple because it is they who

DOI: 10.4324/9781003530473-6

wish to have a child. Socio-cultural perspectives such as shame and stigma overlay personal views such as failure, inadequacy, and loss. When donor conception is suggested as an alternative pathway to family creation it is presented into this cauldron of intense feelings and views. This solution to the 'problem' is dependent on how the 'problem' is viewed. It was once suggested that a child is not the cure for infertility (Harper & Aitken, 1981) recognising that there are many issues associated with infertility that are likely to impact on the way in which parenthood and relationships with the infant are seen and acted on.

It needs to be noted that the relatively recent advent of what is commonly referred to as social infertility, where a partner/s decide not to engage in sexual intercourse as the means of conceiving, does not or is unlikely to raise the above issues or at least not in the same ways.

The possible use of DC raises significant issues concerning how "family" is viewed. Blood ties or genetic connection have traditionally been seen as fundamental to family formation and continuing the "family line"(van den Akker, 2006), an example being the way in which physical likeness is highlighted in social encounters, especially when a baby is very young. He/she is expected to look like one or both parents (Isaksson etal., 2019). Those considering the use of DC are forced to confront the fact that this will be different for them. How they understand and manage this difference is likely to impact on their view of parenthood and relationship with a child. In the case of DI, the male partner is likely confronted with issues associated with the traditional view of masculinity, and what it may mean for another man's semen to "replace" his and how he will relate to the resultant child. For the female partner, what might it mean for her to have the semen of an unknown person inserted into her body and carry the resultant child? The couple's ability to discuss these issues and arrive at an appropriate level of understanding and agreement seem fundamental to shared parenthood.

An early study by the first author and colleagues (Daniels et al., 1996; Gillett et al., 1996) explored the degree of congruence between partners in 50 couples regarding having had a child as a result of DI. For both males and females, their feelings about DI before, during, and after treatment did not correlate with their perceived view of their partner's feelings. Of particular note were the views about the donor, which did not correlate well. However, all but one of the couples agreed that the DI child had brought them closer together. The authors stated that the findings suggest for many couples acceptance in to the DI programme was less than ideal and only improved with having treatment and then conceiving. They further stated that the data highlights the need for psychosocial assistance to be made available to couples prior to the commencement of treatment. That assistance, we suggest, will have as a main focus the transitioning of thinking concerning the basis of family formation.

Between 1999 and 2006, the first author and Dr Petra Thorn conducted several weekend parent preparation workshops for couples who were considering using DI. The workshops had a group work format and a psychoeducational focus (Thorn and Daniels, 2003). Research was undertaken (Daniels et al., 2007: Thorn & Daniels,

2006) with those who participated (n=60) between 1999 and 2001. Two important findings were that: 1) the levels of confidence in using DI increased for most couples as a result of participating in the workshops, and this positively impacted on their intention to share information about DI with future children and 2), there was a pattern of convergence in the majority of the couples who had not previously held the same views, regarding sharing the family history with any resultant child. The design of the workshops was modified and used in the UK with their research supporting that from the German workshops (Crawshaw & Montuschi, 2014).

Infertility is a significant challenge for most couples and the decision to use donated gametes adds another level of potential challenges. The results of the study in Germany show that would-be parents reported their levels of confidence regarding the use of DI increased as a result of the workshops and this had a flow-on effect in relation to their openness regarding their family history sharing. The previous pattern of maintaining, or trying to, maintain secrecy was no longer felt to be in the best interests of their parenting roles.

The adult donor conceived person

The voices of donor conceived persons (DCPs) have become prominent over the past two decades(Daniels, 2020; Hertz et al., 2013; Schrijvers et al., 2019; Turner & Coyle, 2000).The rights and needs of DCPs to information about their origins and identity have gained traction and international visibility. In 2019 an international group of DCPs prepared their International Principles for Donor Conception and Surrogacy (the Principles), including the right to identity and to preserve connections between offspring and their biological, social, and gestational 'family'. These principles and the group received a standing ovation by the United Nations for the 30th Convention on the Rights of the Child (UN Presentation Committee, 2019).

Growing numbers of DCPs are arguing that they have a right to information about 'their' donor and many want the opportunity to meet them (Hertz et al., 2013). For offspring, there is a connection—a blood tie—that raises questions about how the family is thought of. Of note is that many DCPs who are angry are frequently those who have discovered the nature of their conception by accident. Direct-to-consumer (DTC) DNA testing, ancestry websites, and online chat groups have contributed to increased access to information (Newton, 2022). This, alongside more formal practices of identity-release sperm donation (when the DCP may access information at a certain age) and open-identity donation (when the donor's identity is known to recipients), have reconfigured the socio-cultural dimensions that have traditionally dominated DC, in particular, the secrecy regarding the use of donor gametes to build a family.

Increasingly, parents desire to move away from secrecy because of its negative impact on their relationship with their children (Turner & Coyle, 2000; Nordqvist 2014). Moreover, a study about parents' decision to share information with their offspring identified that maintaining secrecy entailed significant pressures (Daniels et al., 2011). Parents may hold complex beliefs that inform their decision to share information, however, some of these include the right of the child to know about the family-building history and a desire for openness and honest family relationships (Isaksson et al., 2016). Parents' decision-making and confidence to share their family-building story may be enhanced by appreciating the complementary interface with the adult DCP voice and desire for openness.

For many DCPs there is a desire for early, clear and trustworthy information about their origins, including information about the donor, their medical history, and the presence of any half-siblings (UN Presentation Committee, 2019). Indeed, early disclosure about the nature of family building is recommended and appears to afford the most positive outcome for all parties (Daniels, 2004). Conversely, there is evidence that unexpected and late disclosure may evoke distress and erode trust in family members (Turner & Coyle, 2000). In the absence of information about their origins, some DCPs had suspected something was hidden from them and wished they had been told earlier (Daniels, 2020). Schrijvers et al. (2019) found that adult DCPs sought open and early communication about the nature of their conception and to talk about their thoughts and feelings about being donor conceived.

With the move towards openness, there is a growing need to address the place of the donor as this concerns the family-building story and where the donor fits as part of the family system (Grace & Daniels, 2007). In Hertz et al. (2013) research with DCPs, most participants sought contact with the donor and over half sought to be known by them. This did not necessarily mean they wished to develop a relationship with the donor. Rather, DCPs may seek the donor for clues about their own identity, health, and ancestry (Hertz et al., 2013). Interestingly, while parents had held early decision-making power about using donor gametes to build a family and initiated any process of information sharing, DCPs in Hertz et al. (2013) study assumed control over the later process of searching for and linking with the donor. This inevitably extends upon (and challenges) the immediate natal family because offspring relocate 'their' donor's position in the family system via their consideration of the donor's biological *and* the social contribution to their identity.

In a study by Daniels (2020), the interest of DCPs in half-siblings surpassed their interest in the donor. Many DCPs may value the opportunity to connect with peers who have insight into their experience (Schrijvers et al., 2019). Hertz (2022) found that connecting with half-siblings provided a resource for offspring to explore their identity and genetic origins and afforded a sense of belonging for offspring and membership, albeit varied, to a collective of donor siblings.

Currently, there is debate concerning what psychosocial support should be available to parents seeking to build their family using donor gametes and their offspring, including who is appropriately skilled and qualified to provide this, who should resource this, and when this support should/can be available to service users (Crawshaw et al., 2022). These tensions sit alongside a diversifying client profile and changing needs. While some recipient parents and donors are seeking support in navigating openness (Daniels, 2015; Schrijvers et al., 2019), DCPs and donors may seek assistance to navigate linking and complex intersecting family systems. The management of associated boundaries is an emerging issue that requires attention.

For parents who are focused on overcoming their infertility, it is a challenging time to consider the enduring importance of family building for the DCP. Yet, the goal of successful conception for recipient parents using donor gametes is merely the beginning of an evolving family experience across the life course that intersects with the rights and needs of DCPs, the presence of donors and their families, and donor conceived half-siblings and their families (IICO, 2024). There may be multiple and intersecting relationships to navigate and an uncertain path ahead. The psychosocial needs of those on the receipt of treatment including recipient parents, DCPs and donors remain both neglected and of vital importance.

Conclusions

This chapter has, as its central focus, the meanings and understandings that are attached to family and in particular the contribution that sperm and eggs make to these understandings. For most heterosexual couples this is not an issue as the meanings of gametes are intertwined with the meanings associated with family. The dominant socio-cultural thinking is that family is based on the genetic contributions of the parents. When this is not the case and 'donated' gametes are utilised to form the family this is likely to impact on the couple's relationship and further impact on the relationship with the resultant child. Research and innovative practice cited suggest that parents benefit from being able to consider, along with others, the issues surrounding how they will understand and manage this form of family creation and building. Fast forwarding to those persons whose family-building history included DC and who are now adults, their voices are reinforcing the view that their parents needed to be transparent and honest about their decision-making as this has impacted on them in significant ways. The understanding of family for them is frequently different from their parents. For them the family constellation involves the donor and half-siblings as well as the wider family network. The issue of access to information about these persons along with the possibility of meeting them has become a matter of considerable debate and advocacy among adult DCPs. The nature of the relationships and particularly boundary management, between all the various parties, is an increasingly important practice issue.

References

Crawshaw, M., & Montuschi, O. (2014). It 'did what it said on the tin'– Participant's views of the content and process of donor conception parenthood preparation workshops. *Human Fertility*, *17*(1), 11–20. https://doi.org/10.3109/14647273.2014.881562

Crawshaw, M., Pericleous-Smith, A., & Dark, S. (2022). Counselling challenges associated with donor conception and surrogacy treatments–time for debate. *Human Fertility*, *25*(5), 806–812. https://doi.org/10.1080/14647273.2021.1950850

Daniels, K. (2004). *Building a Family with the Assistance of Donor Insemination*. Dunmore.

Daniels, K. (2015). Understanding and managing relationships in donor assisted families. In K. Fine (Ed.), *Donor Conception for Life* (pp. 181–208). Karnac. https://doi.org/10.4324/9780429473920-8

Daniels, K. (2020). The perspective of adult donor conceived persons. In K. Beier, C. Brügge, P. Thorn, & C. Wiesemann (Eds.), *AssistierteReproduktionmitHilfeDritter: Medizin-Ethik-Psychologie-Recht* (pp. 443–459). Springer Berlin Heidelberg. https://doi.org/10.1007/978-3-662-60298-0_29

Daniels, K. R., Gillett, W. R., & Herbison, G. P. (1996). Successful donor insemination and its impact on recipients. *Journal of Psychosomatic Obstetrics & Gynecology, 17*(3), 129–134. https://doi.org/10.3109/01674829609025673

Daniels, K. R., Grace, V. M., & Gillett, W. R. (2011). Factors associated with parents' decisions to tell their adult offspring about the offspring's donor conception. *Human Reproduction, 26*(10), 2783–2790. https://doi.org/10.1093/humrep/der247

Daniels, K.R., & Thorn, P. (2001). Sharing information with donor insemination offspring: A child-conception versus a family-building approach. *Human Reproduction, 16*(9), 1792–1796. https://doi.org/10.1093/humrep/16.9.1792

Daniels, K., Thorn, P., & Westerbrooke, R. (2007). Confidence in the use of donor insemination: An evaluation of the impact of participating in a group preparation programme. *Human Fertility, 10*(1), 13–20. https://doi.org/10.1080/14647270600973035

Gillett, W. R., Daniels, K. R., & Herbison, G. P. (1996). Feelings of couples who have had a child by donor insemination: The degree of congruence. *Journal of Psychosomatic Obstetrics & Gynecology, 17*(3), 135–142. https://doi.org/10.3109/01674829609025674

Grace, V. M., & Daniels, K. R. (2007). The (ir)relevance of genetics: Engendering parallel worlds of procreation and reproduction. *Sociology of Health & Illness, 29*(5), 692–710. https://doi.org/10.1111/j.1467-9566.2007.01010.x

Harper, P., & Aitken, J. (1981). Child is not the cure for infertility: Workshop on Infertility: A report of proceedings of a national workshop held in September, 1981 / jointly sponsored by the Institute of Family Studies and the Citizens' Welfare Service of Victoria Australian Government 1981. Accessed 12/12/24. Available from: http://trove.nla.gov.au/work/25848469?selectedversion=NBD2203650

Hertz, R. (2022). Sociological accounts of donor siblings' experiences: Their importance for self-identity and new kinship relations. *International Journal of Environmental Research and Public Health, 19*(4), 2002. https://doi.org/10.3390/ijerph19042002

Hertz, R., Nelson, M. K., & Kramer, W. (2013). Donor conceived offspring conceive of the donor: The relevance of age, awareness, and family form. *Social Science & Medicine, 86*, 52–65. https://doi.org/10.1016/j.socscimed.2013.03.001

International Infertility Counselling Organisation (IICO) (2024). IICO Statement about Psychosocial Counselling and Professional Support related to involuntary childlessness, including Implications over the life course, September 2024. Accessed 12/12/2024. Available from: www.IICO-Statement-about-Psychosocial-Counselling-and-Professional-Support-related-to-involuntary-childlessness-and-its-life-course-implications-September-2024.pdf

Isaksson, S., Skoog-Svanberg, A., Sydsjö, G., Linell, L., & Lampic, C. (2016). It takes two to tango: Information-sharing with offspring among heterosexual parents following identity-release sperm donation. *Human Reproduction, 31*(1), 125–132. https://doi.org/10.1093/humrep/dev293

Isaksson, S., Sydsjö, G., Svanberg, A.S. & Lampic, C. (2019). Managing absence and presence of child–parent resemblance: A challenge for heterosexual couples following sperm donation. *Reproductive Biomedicine & Society online, 8*, 38–46. https://doi.org/10.1016/j.rbms.2019.07.001

Newton, G. (2022). Doing reflexivity in research on donor conception: Examining moments of bonding and becoming. In R. M. Shaw (Ed.), *Reproductive citizenship: Technologies, rights and relationships* (pp. 279–301). Springer Nature Singapore. https://doi.org/10.1007/978-981-16-9451-6_12

Nordqvist, P. (2014). The drive for openness in donor conception: Disclosure and the trouble with real life. *International Journal of Law, Policy and the Family, 28*(3), 321–338. https://doi.org/10.1093/lawfam/ebu010

Schrijvers, A., Bos, H., van Rooij, F., Gerrits, T., van der Veen, F., Mochtar, M., & Visser, M. (2019). Being a donor-child: Wishes for parental support, peer support and counseling. *Journal of Psychosomatic Obstetrics & Gynecology, 40*(1), 29–37. https://doi.org/10.1080/0167482X.2017.1396313

Thorn, P., & Daniels, K. R. (2003). A group-work approach in family building by donor insemination: Empowering the marginalized. *Human Fertility, 6*(1), 46–50. https://doi.org/10.1080/1464770312331368993

Thorn, P., & Daniels, K. R. (2006). Vorbereitung auf die FamilienbildungmitdonogenerInsemination-die BedeutungedukativerGruppenseminare. *Journal für Reproduktionsmedizin und Endokrinologie. Journal of Reproductive Medicine and Endocrinology, 3*(1), 49–53.

Turner, A. J., & Coyle, A. (2000). What does it mean to be a donor offspring? The identity experiences of adults conceived by donor insemination and the implications for counselling and therapy. *Human Reproduction, 15*(9), 2041–2051. https://doi.org/10.1093/humrep/15.9.2041

UN Presentation Committee 2019. (2019). *International Principles for Donor Conception and Surrogacy (the Principles).* November 19, 2019, United Nations 30th Anniversary of the Convention on the Rights of the Child Palais des Nations, Geneva, Accessed 12/12/24. Available from: The Geneva Principles – Donor Conceived UK.

Van den Akker, O. (2006). A review of family donor constructs: Current research and future directions. *Human Reproduction Update, 12*(2), 91–101. https://doi.org/10.1093/humupd/dmi038

Chapter 5

The social and psychological aspects of forming a family through surrogacy

Vasanti Jadva

Surrogacy remains a highly controversial method of family building. Despite the continued debates and controversies surrounding surrogacy, the practice has become a more familiar method of assisted reproduction amongst the general population, partly resulting from high profile celebrities openly sharing their use of surrogacy to have a child. Within the UK, surrogacy laws came into place in 1985 in the form of the Surrogacy Arrangements Act following public outrage over British surrogate, Kim Cotton, being paid to gestate a pregnancy for a couple from the USA (Brahams, 1987). Despite the restrictive surrogacy laws that were hastily brought in, surrogacy births have continued to grow in the UK, and subsequent legislative changes have made it easier for gay couples and single men to have a child in this way. International surrogacy or cross-border surrogacy, where intended parents travel overseas for surrogacy, is a growing phenomenon, yet the exact prevalence remains unknown. Data from the USA showed that between 2010 and 2014 over 10,000 infants were born through surrogacy with 18% being to non-US residents (Perkins et al., 2018). Within the UK, the number of applications for a parental order, which transfers legal parenthood from the surrogate to the parents of a surrogacy-born child, rose from 121 in 2011 to 435 in 2021. Data from 2020–2021 showed that 145 parental orders were granted for surrogacy arrangements taking place in England, with 76 for the USA, 44 for Ukraine and 39 for other countries (Horsey et al., 2022). Not everyone who uses surrogacy applies for a parental order and thus these numbers are likely to be an underestimate (Jadva et al., 2021).

Surrogacy can vary based on several factors, including whose gametes are used for treatment. Within the literature the terms gestational and traditional surrogacy identify whether the surrogate's egg is used for the pregnancy. In gestational surrogacy (also referred to as host or full surrogacy), the intended parents' gametes, or donor gametes, are used for conception, and the surrogate achieves a pregnancy using *in vitro* fertilisation (IVF). With traditional surrogacy (sometimes referred to as straight or partial surrogacy), the surrogate uses her egg for the pregnancy, and she is, therefore, genetically and gestationally related to the resultant child. In the UK, one of the intended parents must be the genetic parent of the child to obtain a parental order. During surrogacy arrangements in the UK, it is common

DOI: 10.4324/9781003530473-7

for close relationships to be formed between intended parents and their surrogate as they generally maintain direct contact with each other throughout gestation (MacCallum et al., 2003; Jadva et al., 2019). Close relationships have also been reported by UK couples whose surrogate lives overseas, particularly amongst those with American surrogates (Jadva et al., 2021). However, this contrasts sharply with intended parents whose surrogate lives in low- or middle-income countries such as India or Thailand, where language and cultural differences make direct contact more difficult (Ziv & Freund-Eschar, 2015; Riggs et al., 2015; Lamba et al., 2018; Jadva et al., 2019). Furthermore, intended parents may deliberately choose destinations where they do not need to form a direct relationship with the surrogate (Jadva et al., 2021). Overseas destinations for surrogacy differ in policy and practice, which could have implications for families and the child as he/she grows up. Given the different ways in which surrogacy is practiced, it is more useful to view it as an umbrella term (Jadva., 2020). Such a definition better reflects the diversity of factors that may influence the psychological health of the people involved.

Several concerns have been raised about the outcomes for surrogates, i.e. the woman who gestates the pregnancy for someone else. While in the past it was more common to call surrogates, surrogate mothers, the term 'mother' is no longer used with surrogates in the UK context (Jadva et al., 2020). Terminology, therefore, changes over time and differs globally. For example, 'surrogate mother' is used within India and 'gestational carrier' is commonly used in the USA. One of the main psychological concerns for surrogates is whether she will experience psychological problems as a result of gestating a pregnancy for someone else. A study of 95 surrogates in the USA found low rates of postnatal depression in surrogates two weeks after the pregnancy (Parkinson et al., 1999). A UK study of 34 surrogates, interviewed a year after the birth of the surrogacy child, found that two reported some difficulties with handing over the child at the time of the interview, with 32% recalling having experienced some difficulties in the weeks following the birth. Thus, although the initial weeks may be difficult, this lessened over time (Jadva et al., 2003). These difficult experiences were often explained in relation to their hormonal levels or feeling sad that the surrogacy arrangement had ended. When 20 of these surrogates were interviewed 10 years later, they did not show any longer-term psychological problems, with many showing high levels of self-esteem (Jadva et al., 2015). A qualitative study of surrogates 20 years after they had carried a surrogacy pregnancy found that many recognised the emotional effort of maintaining relationships with the families they had helped. Surrogates were reported to have positive experiences of surrogacy, which they had integrated into their sense of identity (Shaw et al., 2024). The impact of surrogacy on the surrogate's own children has also been a cause for concern. A UK study of 34 surrogates' children aged 12–25 years found them to show good levels of psychological well-being and reported close family relationships, with many feeling proud of their mothers (Jadva & Imrie, 2014). However, a US study of 13 children aged 7–17 years found that a third of the children reported negative feelings about their mother's involvement in surrogacy. More research is needed to understand these different findings. A prospective study following the surrogate's family and assessing the psychological health of the children during the pregnancy, and in the years that follow, would enable a better evaluation of the impact of surrogacy on the surrogate's own family.

A number of recent cross-sectional studies have been conducted examining family functioning and child outcomes within families headed by gay couples who have had a child through surrogacy (Golombok et al., 2018; Carone et al., 2018; D'Amore et al, 2024). In a European study of two-parent families with a young infant living in the UK, the Netherlands, or France, gay-father families formed through surrogacy were found to show no differences to a comparison group of lesbian-mother families formed through sperm donation and heterosexual parent families formed through IVF, in relation to parenting stress, depression, anxiety, or relationship satisfaction. Similarly, a study of two-parent gay-father families with children aged 4–9 years were found to be similar to lesbian-mother families on measures of quality of parenting and parent-child interaction (Golombok et al., 2018). However, parents who perceived higher levels of stigma reported their children to have higher levels of externalising problems (Golombok et al., 2018). While the perceived stigma may not have been due to the method of conception itself, several studies have shown an association between stigmatisation of gay and lesbian parent families and externalising problems in children (Bos & Gartrell, 2010; Bos & van Balen, 2008) and parental mental health (Goldberg and Smith., 2011). Given the negative perceptions of surrogacy practices prevalent in many countries, as well as in digital spaces (See Horsey & Mahmoud, 2025), it is possible that parents may feel stigmatised about their use of surrogacy, which may lead to negative consequences for family functioning and child outcomes.

Recent studies have begun to examine the psychological outcomes for families headed by single men who have a child through surrogacy. An Italian study of gay and heterosexual single fathers with a 3–10-year-old child born using surrogacy found few differences in parenting, parent-child relationships, and child outcomes when compared to two-parent gay-father families and heterosexual parent families. The only difference that was found suggested greater parenting stress among the single-father groups compared to the other two groups (Carone et al., 2020). This may be due to single fathers parenting as a lone parent, where they take on a greater parental load compared to two-parent arrangements. Indeed, in a study comparing single fathers to single mothers with a child born using donor conception, no differences were found in relation to parent mental health or parenting stress (Jones et al., 2022). In an observational study of parent-child play of single gay and single heterosexual fathers of 3–10-year-old children, an indirect relationship was found between higher frequency of microaggressions experienced by fathers and lower sensitivity towards their child (Carone et al., 2021), showing the negative impact that stigma can have on parent-child relationships.

The only in-depth longitudinal psychological study of children born through surrogacy has been a 20-year follow-up study in the UK of 42 families formed through surrogacy. The study also included families formed through egg donation, sperm donation, and unassisted conception (Golombok et al., 2004, 2006a, 2006b, 2011, 2013, 2017, 2023). The families were seen over seven time points from when the child was aged 1 to age 20 years. Despite the concerns that had been raised about the potentially negative consequences of surrogacy for family relationships and children's psychological well-being, the findings showed more positive parenting among surrogacy families. For example, when the children were aged 14, the mothers in the surrogacy families showed less negative parenting and reported greater acceptance of their children and fewer problems in family relationships, compared to mothers who had children born through gamete donation. Furthermore, no differences were found between the surrogacy-born children and their counterparts in terms of self-esteem or psychological adjustment (Golombok et al., 2017). Most of the adolescents reported feeling positive or unconcerned about their surrogacy birth, and some of those not in contact with their surrogate were curious about her and wanted to know, for example, her reasons for becoming a surrogate (Zadeh et al., 2018). At age 20, young adults continued to feel unconcerned about the method of their conception, with 2 of the 15 young adults born through surrogacy reporting that it made them feel special or unique (Jadva et al., 2023).

To summarise, there are a growing number of studies showing that the outcomes for families formed through surrogacy are similar to families formed through other forms of reproductive donation and to families that have not used assisted reproduction to have their child. Studies of gay couples and single men using surrogacy have similarly found good outcomes, and children are well adjusted. Given the negative societal attitudes towards surrogacy that remains and indeed may even have increased in recent years, the impact of stigma on family functioning and child outcomes remains a cause for concern. Despite the growth of cross-border surrogacy arrangements, research evaluating the impact of international surrogacy for children is limited. Children born to international surrogates may not know their surrogate or egg donor. It is not known, for example, how the child may feel about having a surrogate from a disadvantaged background, who is from a different culture and who they may never meet. Or about having a surrogate who was paid a vast amount of money for carrying and giving birth to them. Research focusing on children's perspectives about their birth following more recent forms of surrogacy, including international surrogacy, remains limited. Understanding how the myriad ways in which surrogacy is now practiced can affect the psychological outcomes of those involved will be an important area of future research.

References

Bos, H., & Gartrell, N. (2010). Adolescents of the USA National Longitudinal Lesbian Family Study: Can family characteristics counteract the negative effects of stigmatization? *Family Process*, *49*(4), 559–572. https://doi.org/10.1111/j.1545-5300.2010.01340.x

Bos, H. M., & van Balen, F. (2008). Children in planned lesbian families: Stigmatisation, psychological adjustment and protective factors. *Culture, Health & Sexuality*, *10*(3), 221–236. https://doi.org/10.1080/13691050701601702

Brahams, D. (1987). The hasty British ban on commercial surrogacy. *The Hastings Center Report, 17*(1), 16–19.

Carone, N., Baiocco, R., Lingiardi, V., & Barone, L. (2020). Gay and heterosexual single father families created by surrogacy: Father–child relationships, parenting quality, and children's psychological adjustment. *Sexuality Research & Social Policy: A Journal of the NSRC, 17*(4), 711–728. https://doi.org/10.1007/s13178-019-00428-7

Carone, N., Baiocco, R., Manzi, D., Antoniucci, C., Caricato, V., Pagliarulo, E., & Lingiardi, V. (2018). Surrogacy families headed by gay men: Relationships with surrogates and egg donors, fathers' decisions over disclosure and children's views on their surrogacy origins. *Human Reproduction, 33*(2), 248–257. https://doi.org/10.1093/humrep/dex362

Carone, N., Lingiardi, V., Baiocco, R., & Barone, L. (2021). Sensitivity and rough-and-tumble play in gay and heterosexual single-father families through surrogacy: The role of microaggressions and fathers' rumination. *Psychology of Men & Masculinities, 22*(3), 476–487. https://doi.org/10.1037/men0000267

D'Amore, S., Green, R. J., Mouton, B., & Carone, N. (2024). European gay fathers via surrogacy: Parenting, social support, anti-gay microaggressions, and child behavior problems. *Family Process, 63*(2), 1001–1024. https://doi.org/10.1111/famp.12950

Golombok, S., MacCallum, F., Murray, C., Lycett, E., & Jadva, V. (2006a). Surrogacy families: Parental functioning, parent-child relationships and children's psychological development at age 2. *Journal of Child Psychology and Psychiatry, and Allied Disciplines, 47*(2), 213–222. https://doi.org/10.1111/j.1469-7610.2005.01453.x

Golombok, S., Murray, C., Jadva, V., Lycett, E., MacCallum, F., & Rust, J. (2006b). Non-genetic and non-gestational parenthood: Consequences for parent-child relationships and the psychological well-being of mothers, fathers and children at age 3. *Human Reproduction, 21*(7), 1918–1924. https://doi.org/10.1093/humrep/del039

Golombok, S., Blake, L., Casey, P., Roman, G., & Jadva, V. (2013). Children born through reproductive donation: A longitudinal study of psychological adjustment. *Journal of Child Psychology and Psychiatry, and Allied Disciplines, 54*(6), 653–660. https://doi.org/10.1111/jcpp.12015

Golombok, S., Blake, L., Slutsky, J., Raffanello, E., Roman, G. D., & Ehrhardt, A. (2018). Parenting and the adjustment of children born to Gay Fathers through aurrogacy. *Child Development, 89*(4), 1223–1233. https://doi.org/10.1111/cdev.12728

Golombok, S., Ilioi, E., Blake, L., Roman, G., & Jadva, V. (2017). A longitudinal study of families formed through reproductive donation: Parent-adolescent relationships and adolescent adjustment at age 14. *Developmental Psychology, 53*(10), 1966–1977. https://doi.org/10.1037/dev0000372

Golombok, S., Jones, C., Hall, P., Foley, S., Imrie, S., & Jadva, V. (2023). A longitudinal study of families formed through third-party assisted reproduction: Mother-child relationships and child adjustment from infancy to adulthood. *Developmental Psychology, 59*(6), 1059–1073. https://doi.org/10.1037/dev0001526

Golombok, S., Murray, C., Jadva, V., MacCallum, F., & Lycett, E. (2004). Families created through surrogacy arrangements: Parent-child relationships in the 1st year of life. *Developmental Psychology, 40*(3), 400–411. https://doi.org/10.1037/0012-1649.40.3.400

Golombok, S., Readings, J., Blake, L., Casey, P., Marks, A., & Jadva, V. (2011). Families created through surrogacy: Mother-child relationships and children's psychological adjustment at age 7. *Developmental Psychology, 47*(6), 1579–1588. https://doi.org/10.1037/a0025292

Goldberg, A. E., & Smith, J. Z. (2011). Stigma, social context, and mental health: Lesbian and gay couples across the transition to adoptive parenthood. *Journal of Counseling Psychology, 58*(1), 139–150. https://doi.org/10.1037/a0021684

Horsey, K., Gibson, G., Lamanna, G., Priddle, H., Linara-Demakakou, E., Nair, S., Arian-Schad, M., Thackare, H., Rimington, M., Macklon, N., & Ahuja, K. (2022). First clinical report of 179 surrogacy cases in the UK: Implications for policy and practice. *Reproductive Biomedicine Online, 45*(4), 831–838. https://doi.org/10.1016/j.rbmo.2022.05.027

Horsey, K., & Mahmoud, Z. (2025). *It's time to call out surrogacy misinformation.* 3rd Feb 2025. Bionews 1275. www.progress.org.uk/its-time-to-call-out-surrogacy-misinformat ion/. Accessed Feb 2025.

Jadva, V. (2020). Postdelivery adjustment of gestational carriers, intended parents, and their children. *Fertility and Sterility, 113*(5), 903–907. https://doi.org/10.1016/j.fertnst ert.2020.03.010

Jadva, V., Gamble, N., Prosser, H., & Imrie, S. (2019). Parents' relationship with their surrogate in cross-border and domestic surrogacy arrangements: Comparisons by sexual orientation and location. *Fertility and Sterility, 111*(3), 562–570. https://doi.org/10.1016/j.fer tnstert.2018.11.029

Jadva, V., & Imrie, S. (2014). Children of surrogate mothers: Psychological well-being, family relationships and experiences of surrogacy. *Human Reproduction, 29*(1), 90–96. https://doi.org/10.1093/humrep/det410

Jadva, V., Imrie, S., & Golombok, S. (2015). Surrogate mothers 10 years on: A longitudinal study of psychological well-being and relationships with the parents and child. *Human Reproduction, 30*(2), 373–379. https://doi.org/10.1093/humrep/deu339

Jadva, V., Jones, C., Hall, P., Imrie, S., & Golombok, S. (2023). 'I know it's not normal but it's normal to me, and that's all that matters': Experiences of young adults conceived through egg donation, sperm donation, and surrogacy. *Human Reproduction, 38*(5), 908–916. https://doi.org/10.1093/humrep/dead048

Jadva, V., Murray, C., Lycett, E., MacCallum, F., & Golombok, S. (2003). Surrogacy: The experiences of surrogate mothers. *Human Reproduction, 18*(10), 2196–2204. https://doi. org/10.1093/humrep/deg397

Jadva, V., Prosser, H., & Gamble, N. (2021). Cross-border and domestic surrogacy in the UK context: An exploration of practical and legal decision-making. *Human Fertility, 24*(2), 93–104. https://doi.org/10.1080/14647273.2018.1540801

Jones, C., Zadeh, S., Jadva, V., & Golombok, S. (2022). Solo fathers and mothers: An exploration of well-being, social support and social approval. *International Journal of Environmental Research and Public Health, 19*(15), 9236. https://doi.org/10.3390/ijerph1 9159236

Lamba, N., Jadva, V., Kadam, K., & Golombok, S. (2018, April). The psychological well-being and prenatal bonding of gestational surrogates. *Human Reproduction, 33*(4), 646–653, https://doi.org/10.1093/humrep/dey048

MacCallum, F., Lycett, E., Murray, C., Jadva, V., & Golombok, S. (2003). Surrogacy: The experience of commissioning couples. *Human Reproduction, 18*(6), 1334–1342. https:// doi.org/10.1093/humrep/deg253

Parkinson, J., Tran, C., Tan, T., Nelson, J., Batzofin, J., & Serafini, P. (1999). Perinatal outcome after in-vitro fertilization-surrogacy. *Human Reproduction, 14*(3), 671–676. https:// doi.org/10.1093/humrep/14.3.671

Perkins, K. M., Boulet, S. L., Jamieson, D. J., Kissin, D. M., & National Assisted Reproductive Technology Surveillance System (NASS) Group (2016). Trends and outcomes of gestational surrogacy in the United States. *Fertility and Sterility, 106*(2), 435–442.e2. https://doi.org/10.1016/j.fertnstert.2016.03.050

Riggs, D. W., Due, C., & Power, J. (2015). Gay men's experiences of surrogacy clinics in India. *The Journal of Family Planning and Reproductive Health Care, 41*(1), 48–53. https://doi.org/10.1136/jfprhc-2013-100671

Shaw, K., Imrie, S., Hall, P., & Jadva, V. (2024). 'It's all settled on the right page' surrogates' feelings and reflections of surrogacy two decades on. *Human Reproduction, 39*(12), 2734–2742. https://doi.org/10.1093/humrep/deae216

Zadeh, S., Ilioi, E. C., Jadva, V., & Golombok, S. (2018). The perspectives of adolescents conceived using surrogacy, egg or sperm donation. *Human Reproduction, 33*(6), 1099–1106. https://doi.org/10.1093/humrep/dey088

Ziv, I., & Freund-Eschar, Y. (2015). The pregnancy experience of Gay couples expecting a child through overseas surrogacy. *The Family Journal, 23*(2), 158–166. https://doi.org/10.1177/1066480714565107

Chapter 6

Conception

A discussion

Alejandra Perez and Ruth Roberts

The chapters in this section explore several topics related to conception through a range of perspectives. In Chapter 1, Perez offers a psychoanalytic perspective on conception and uses psychoanalytic theories and illustrative clinical vignettes to explore the conscious and unconscious experiences that occur when people are trying to conceive. In Chapter 2, Grace draws on empirical evidence to highlight the importance of education in bringing awareness about the impact of advancing age on fertility and enabling informed health decisions about family building. In Chapter 3, Fine uses psychoanalytic theories and clinical examples to discuss challenges faced by those considering donor conception. In Chapter 4, Daniels and Meadows examine psychosocial considerations of donor conception, drawing on empirical evidence to discuss challenges faced by parents and donor conceived children. Finally, in Chapter 5, Jadva presents empirical evidence to explain the complexity and challenges faced by those using surrogacy to build their family.

The rapidly changing landscape of conception

The increasing age of conception

In her chapter, Grace discusses how, in high-income countries, childbearing at older ages has increased over the past two decades. This is commonly due to economic factors, such as education and employment opportunities, but changes in social norms about the ideal age for conception, increased access to contraception, and advances in reproductive technology have also contributed to increasing parental age. However, advanced maternal age is associated with decreased fertility and increased risks in pregnancy (Harper et al., 2021). Grace highlights a growing need for education to provide clear, destigmatising information, tailored to specific audiences, which explains fertility decline and associated risk factors. Increased awareness is essential to prevent involuntary childlessness and allow people to make informed decisions about family building.

DOI: 10.4324/9781003530473-8

Rules and regulations for assisted reproduction

Reproductive technologies have provided methods to build a family when natural conception is not possible, however, rules and regulations around assisted reproduction are variable. Jadva reports that, although it has become more visible through stories of celebrity use of surrogacy in the media, it remains controversial. Laws and regulations vary widely across the world, with it being illegal in some countries, and other countries having no laws regarding surrogacy. This has raised concerns about negative and unregulated surrogacy practice in some countries. Despite this, there has been a rise in the use of international surrogacy given difficulties with finding a surrogate in the home country, regulations about how surrogates can be paid, and how the surrogacy journey is managed, and laws around parental rights and responsibilities. For example, in the UK, legal parentage is given to the surrogate at birth and one of the intended parents must be genetically related to the child to receive parental status. There are large differences in how much surrogates can be paid, which creates concerns about the potential exploitation of women from disadvantaged backgrounds.

Daniels and Meadows explain the changes in how children born of donor conception access information about their origins. Changes to donor conception practice increasingly allow for donor conceived persons (DCPs) to access information either right from the point of conception or when the DCP reaches a certain age. This is a positive shift away from secrecy that was previously common in donor conception. DCPs are also able to more easily access information through home DNA testing kits, ancestry websites, and through online internet groups. However, Daniels and Meadows highlight the limited guidance and support in accessing information and potential difficulties managing boundaries and complexities of potentially large family systems arising from donor conception.

The space and time needed to conceive and build a family

While biological conception (the physical act of the sperm fertilising an egg) may be a matter of hours or days, the mental assimilation of the thoughts, feelings, conscious imaginings, and unconscious phantasies that emerge during conception, and preparing to build a family, require more time. The chapter by Grace highlights the limited focus on family planning in research literature, in global health policies, and in health education campaigns.

In their respective chapters, Perez and Fine explore the various unconscious phantasies and intense feelings that arise in many expectant parents who are trying or have conceived either naturally or through assisted reproduction. Moreover, both authors consider how such challenges during the conception stage may impact the expectant parents' sense of their forming family and their roles within it. These chapters point to the importance of psychoanalytic therapy in exploring expectant parents' experiences, fantasies, and conflicts, thereby helping them as they prepare to form a family. Awareness of the psychological impact of conception is important for expectant parents, as many are surprised by the intensity of the experience of pregnancy, and by the rapid, major changes it ushers in. Further knowledge and education about the difficulties that expectant parents might face are important. Some early longitudinal studies of families who conceived through assisted reproduction suggest that the extra time that these expectant parents have (compared to unassisted reproduction) might help them on their journey through parenthood. These studies showed good outcomes in terms of parenting, parent-child relationships, and child development. Some authors (see Golombok et al., 2023) postulate that, while on the one hand these families face challenges with regards to conceiving, and working through their feelings about assisted reproduction, on the other hand, they have more time to think about the work of building their family.

The chapters by Fine, Daniels and Meadows, and Jadva, however, note that, as assisted reproduction is now much more common and effective, this can result in an accelerated conception process for many people. This of course brings advantages, but also disadvantages. Fine explains that expectant parents must take time to first mourn their sense of loss around being unable to conceive naturally, then work to understand their feelings about the imagined (if unknown) or known donor (and we assume this also applies to feelings about the surrogate), and about their future baby, and how all these feelings correspond to their idea of building a family.

This section of the book also draws attention to the importance of parents being open with their children about their conception through donated gametes or embryos, and/or through surrogacy—the beneficial effect of such openness is now well established by longitudinal studies (see Daniels, 2004). However, these chapters highlight how, for such families, exploring their future child's possible thoughts and feelings about their conception is a task necessarily brought forward to the very beginning of the reproductive process. In such a situation, the expectant parents need support and guidance from the earliest stage of conception, in how to think about the assisted conception and then how to navigate building a family.

Advantages and challenges of having extensive information and choices about conception

Advances in assisted reproductive methods have helped many people who otherwise would be unable to have a baby. Access to information online has also helped many to prepare for pregnancy, or has otherwise supported their conception journey. Online information and communities have particularly helped those who do not have access to psychological support or up-to-date, reliable information about conception, pregnancy, and parenthood, and those who are afraid of, or resistant to, in-person consultations with health professionals. There is now more information about and awareness of the physical, emotional, and relationship changes that occur during pregnancy, and certain health and age-related issues that can lead to infertility. There are also more options regarding fertility treatments, which are more accessible by a wider population.

These advances are invaluable. However, they have also brought new challenges. Having more choice, in this instance, has not always made it easier for people trying to conceive to know what is right for them. In terms of the greater variety of fertility treatments, for some people this has meant having more options to try after initial unsuccessful attempts. This can bring hope to people wanting to be parents, nurturing their wish to persevere. However, this greater choice can, for others, prolong and increase the stress created by continuing with treatments, with the many physical, emotional, relational, and financial difficulties that they entail—and all of this without any certainty that conception will result. Sometimes making the decision to stop, and to mourn the idea of a life with children, is difficult when there are more, possibly effective treatments available.

A person's experience of conception is so personal and individual, and yet conception, then pregnancy and parenthood, exist within a much wider socio-cultural realm. Expectant parents are exposed to many different views, sources of information, and expectations in their social, work, and family circles, and so need support in understanding their own experience.

In her chapter, Grace describes how highly valued online information is by many expectant parents, given the ease of access, the perceived privacy of online research, and the speed with which such information can be obtained. However, she also points to its pitfalls, citing a paper by Zarocostas (2020), who refers to the plethora of both accurate and inaccurate information as an 'infodemic' ('information' combined with 'epidemic'). This deluge of information too often leads people into confusion, risk-taking behaviour, and adverse health outcomes.

Socio-cultural perspectives on conception

Need for knowledge

Daniels and Meadows emphasise the donor conceived child's need and right to know about their conception and birth, as well as the identity of their donor and any half-siblings they have. The authors note how parents using donor conception have increasingly moved away from secrecy surrounding their child's conception and parentage. Their previous studies have shown that secrecy around their child's donor conception have caused parents significant stress and had a negative impact on their relationship with their child, with unexpected and late disclosures causing distress and mistrust. There is now more understanding of the needs of DCPs, which is a desire to have clear and accurate information about their origins, including information about their donor, medical history, and potential half-siblings. This information allows DCPs to explore their identity and genetic origins, and may provide a sense of belonging within a group of donor siblings. Fine also notes how a sense of belonging may also come from being able to integrate the awareness of the donor and any half-siblings within the family unit.

Jadva also highlights the importance of need for knowledge regarding surrogacy. Longitudinal research into domestic surrogacy has found more positive parenting, greater acceptance of their children, and fewer family relationship problems than families who used donor conception, with young people born to surrogacy feeling positive or unconcerned about their conception (Golombok et al., 2023). Less research has examined the impact of international surrogacy. Jadva raised important questions about how children born to international surrogates might feel about not being able to meet their surrogate, having a surrogate from a different culture, who may not speak the same language. Jadva considers how a child produced by such a surrogate pregnancy might feel about the financial, social, and other power imbalances between their parents and the surrogate. Families who use surrogates in countries that have been found to have negative surrogacy practices may be less inclined to be open about their path to conception.

Beyond a physical and biological process

Daniels and Meadows also highlight how perceptions around donor conception have shifted from being a purely medical process, designed to solve the problem of infertility, to consider the complex needs of the family. Both Daniels and Meadows and Fine discuss issues about family genetics in donor conceived families. Having a genetic connection and continuation of the family blood line has been considered by some as essential for family functioning. Fine notes how some people feel inadequate when faced with not being able to carry on the genetic line and must mourn the loss of personal and cultural heritage. Daniels and Meadows also note that many people focus on who the baby looks like, searching for whether the baby looks like one or both parents, and parents of DCPs must navigate this difference right from when the baby is born. In addition to genetics, as discussed above, the successful conception of a pregnancy through donor conception marks the start of a continually changing family dynamic that involves the rights and needs of the child, the acknowledgement and possible presence of the donor, half-siblings and their families, and navigation of family boundaries.

Revisiting the concept of being a parent and forming a family

Ideas about parenthood and forming a family have evolved over time, influenced by changes in society and culture. Bornstein (2013) noted that parenting is not done in isolation; it is shaped by the socio-cultural context in which it takes place. Each culture has deeply held and accepted ideas about how a parent should feel, think, and act. We now recognise the importance of early parenthood and the parent-infant relationship for children's development. This was made possible, in part, by Freud's theories on development as far back as the early 1900s (Freud, 1900; Freud, 1905). No doubt changes throughout history have influenced how parenting was and is constructed. Given the many and various histories across different countries and epochs, there exist myriad constructions of parenting and family-formation.

As people begin to think about, plan, and try to form a family, it is worth revisiting the origin of the word 'parent'. It comes from the Latin *parēns,* the noun form of the verb *'parere'*, meaning to bring forth, develop, or educate. Houghughi and Long (2005, p.5) defined parenting as the "purposive activities aimed at ensuring the survival and development of children". As the focus for many people during the conception stage is on being able or not being able to get pregnant, it is perhaps important to emphasise that the developmental journey taken by parents and children is lifelong, no matter their family configuration, conception history, or socio-cultural background.

References

Bornstein, M.H. (2013). Parenting and child mental health: a cross-cultural perspective. *World Psychiatry.* 12(3):258–65. doi: 10.1002/wps.20071

Daniels, K. (2004). *Building a family with the assistance of Donor insemination.* Auckland: Dunmore.

Freud, S. (1900). The interpretation of dreams. In J. Strachey (Ed. & Trans.), The Standard Edition of the Complete Psychological Works of Sigmund Freud, 4:ix–627. London: Vintage, The Hogarth Press.

Freud, S. (1905). Three essays on the theory of sexuality. In J. Strachey (Ed. & Trans.), The Standard Edition of the Complete Psychological Works of Sigmund Freud, 7:123–246. London: Vintage, The Hogarth Press.

Golombok, S., Jones, C., Hall, P., Foley, S., Imrie, S. & Jadva, V. (2023). A longitudinal study of families formed through third-party assisted reproduction: Mother-child relationships and child adjustment from infancy to adulthood. *Dev Psychol.* 59(6):1059–73. doi: 10.1037/dev0001526

Harper, J.C., Hammarberg, K., Simopoulou, M., Koert, E., Pedro, J., Massin, N., Fincham, A. & Balen, A. (2021). The International Fertility Education Initiative: Research and action to improve fertility awareness. *Human Reproduction Open.* 4:hoab031. doi: 10.1093/hropen/hoab031

Houghughi, M.S. & Long, N. (eds.) (2004). *Handbook of parenting: Theory and research for practice.* London: Sage.

Zarocostas, J. (2020, February 29). How to fight an infodemic. *The Lancet.* 395(10225):676. Available from: www.thelancet.com/article/S014067362030461X/fulltext

Part II

Pregnancy and the prenatal stage

Chapter 7

Physical and psychological changes

A psychoanalytic perspective

Alejandra Perez

Pregnancy is a period defined by great physical and psychological demands and changes. It marks the beginning of a developmental watershed, and, like childbirth and parenthood, is a major turning point in one's life. While pregnancy involves intense emotional and mental upheaval, it is also a period of psychological opportunity. Many expectant parents begin to revisit and work through internal conflicts, reshaping identifications and perceptions of self and others through the integration of these new experiences. This is not to say that all women (or men) must become parents in order to achieve psychological development, rather that pregnancy, birth, and parenthood are unique experiences that can lead to a particular type of psychic growth.

People may have a wide range of experiences during pregnancy, and these sets of experiences can in turn differ considerably from person to person. A person's early childhood, early relationships (and how these were internalised), current relationships, and physical state will all play important parts in their experience.

As well as involving much change in itself, pregnancy unfolds on the cusp of further change. On one hand, pregnancy entails the achievement of conception and the palpable, rapid physical changes of the pregnant body; future parenthood can seem imminent and intensely real. On the other hand, this period brings deep uncertainty—about the survival and well-being of the foetus, the anticipation of birth, and what the baby and parenthood will be like. Some expectant parents find the uncertainty and waiting stressful, and this not knowing about the future becomes filled with fears and unconscious phantasies.

Physical changes during pregnancy

The bodily changes during pregnancy are significant and these occur in a relatively short time. These changes are the body's normal response to needing to accommodate and nurture a growing foetus (Chandra and Paray, 2024). They comprise physical (external characteristics), physiological (internal processes and functions), and biochemical (hormonal) changes, which begin after conception and affect every organ system in the body: the respiratory, musculoskeletal, reproductive, endocrine, cardiovascular, neurological, gastrointestinal, and immunological systems, as well as changes to the breasts and skin (Lockitch, 1997). While these changes are

DOI: 10.4324/9781003530473-10

part of normal pregnancy, they may be experienced as symptoms of medical disease (Soma-Pillay et al., 2016). Any bodily experience generates a psychological demand to be represented and given meaning. However, because these particular physical changes so closely resemble illness, pregnancy poses an additional challenge to the pregnant person: they must try to form a representation of a healthy life growing inside them, while having the experience of being unwell.

For the non-pregnant expectant parent, their partner's bodily changes may make them feel frightened, powerless, and excluded. Raphael-Leff (1993) described how partners have the additional challenge of finding their place within the mother-baby dyad, and of maintaining contact with the growing baby despite not undergoing these major bodily changes themselves. Indeed, their place might not feel as easily or clearly established as the pregnant expectant parent.

The inter-connection between body and mind in psychoanalysis

Throughout his work, Freud emphasised the intertwining of the body and the psyche from the very start of life, where mental representations and unconscious phantasies emerge to make sense of bodily sensations, and to regulate tensions and energy from internal and external stimuli (1923). Importantly, he distinguished the physical body (or soma) from the libidinal body. The former is the biological organisation and can manifest in illness and pain, while the latter includes the drives, unconscious phantasies, and mental representations of the body (such as the place where sexuality, aggression, and narcissism take place). A drive, as Freud conceives it, "is a measure of the demand made upon the mind for work in consequence of its connection with the body" (Freud, 1915, p.122). The psychic figuration or construction of our libidinal, represented bodies is a complicated process, especially at times of great physical and somatic stress such as illness or pregnancy.

The pregnant body's demands on the mind

It follows that the demands placed on the psyche of the pregnant woman are considerable, given the bodily changes she is undergoing, and the need for her to begin to represent the still-forming, growing, unknown baby. Winnicott (1956) described the importance of the primary caregiver's capacity to imaginatively elaborate the somatic parts, feelings, and functions of both the pregnant body and the future baby.

The speed and number of bodily changes that take place during pregnancy are unlike any other in the course of a woman's life, except those occurring during infancy and, in some instances, in the process of dying. These rapid changes require a psychic quickness and flexibility from expectant mothers, in order that they can give these changes meaning and make them bearable. From conception through pregnancy and into the first few months of their babies' lives, some mothers struggle, in various ways, to mentally integrate these different somatic experiences—their own and those of their foetus or baby (Perez, in press).

Symbiosis and separation

Pregnancy has also been described as an important phase in a woman's lifelong process of separation and individuation from her own mother—a woman stops being only a daughter and begins to become a mother to another (Pines, 1982). Alongside this separation and attendant revision of identity, the pregnant woman must also physically and mentally come together with the growing baby inside her. In this sense, pregnancy is a symbiosis, where mother and baby live together and share the mother's body, with the baby depending on the mother. Raphael-Leff (1993, p.8) calls pregnancy a 'strange union' because, "when so much of life is dedicated to maintaining our integrity as distinct beings, this bodily tandem is an uncanny fact".

Winnicott (1956) described the importance of the mother entering a state where she withdraws from the world and orients herself to the infant, a state he termed 'primary maternal preoccupation'. This involves a complex capacity of closeness and separation: the mother needs to identify completely, almost symbiotically, with her growing baby's experience of complete dependence, and at the same time understand the separateness of the baby's individual needs. The pregnant woman is therefore in constant flux, moving between experiences of symbiosis and individuation. Many people struggle to manage the back-and-forth between these two states.

Imagining baby

During pregnancy, expectant parents very often begin to imagine their unborn baby, attributing to them a personality and picturing their future relationship (Perez et al., 2025). Some of this imagining is conscious and reflects the hopes and wishes the expectant parent has for their child. Imagining or forming a representation of the unborn baby during pregnancy has been considered important for the future parent-child relationship, as studies have found these to be predictive of future mother-infant relationships (e.g. Benoit et al., 1997). However, a more recent longitudinal study (conducted by the editors of this book) found that mothers described many changes in their representations and feelings towards their baby within the first year. Interestingly, mothers who, during pregnancy, had the clearest mental representation of their baby (which included the baby's personality, and positive feelings towards the baby), experienced a significant shift toward feeling disconnected from the baby at birth, then ended the first year post-birth with a strong connection to the baby but also a fear of separation. In contrast, mothers who had a less clear mental representation of their unborn baby during pregnancy, yet who felt curiosity and positive feelings toward the baby, underwent a more gradual, steady transition into getting to know and love their child. These findings indicate the difficulty that some parents face when their imagining of the baby is too far removed from their actual experience with the real baby once born.

Psychoanalytic clinical work with expectant parents has contributed to our understanding of the various unconscious elements involved in the imagining of the unborn baby. For a start, the rapid physical changes in the pregnant body and the need to psychically represent these, alongside the vacuum created by not knowing what the baby and parenthood will be like, create a tense psychical space. For many expectant parents, their minds are quickly filled up with remembered and unremembered (unconscious) early experiences and phantasies.

At first these unconscious phantasies are closely linked to early bodily experiences, and while they gradually grow in sophistication, they continue throughout life (see Chapter 25 for an overview of unconscious phantasies and the inner world).

Some analysts argue that a person's early experiences form an integral part of pregnancy. For example, Kulish (2011) postulates that becoming pregnant may carry an unconscious wish for continuity of the self between the past as a daughter or son, their present as a pregnant woman or expectant partner, and their future as a parent.

Coping with pregnancy: Projection, identification, and an in-between state

The experiences of expectant mothers' bodily changes and their growing, unborn baby are varied and ever-changing in the first months. Some expectant mothers seem to take in these changes and delight that their bodies can accommodate a new being, feeling a sense of purpose and self-gratification. Others oscillate between these moments of adaptation and pleasure, and moments of fear or disturbance at the unfamiliar bodily changes. For example, Alba, in her third trimester, was halfway through expressing her joy at having decorated the nursery for her future baby, when she stopped and, in a panicked voice, described the physical sensation of pressure of the baby inside her, pushing against her chest: *"What if I can't breathe? What if this baby crushes my lungs?"* For that brief moment, the growing baby was the object of all her projected fears, and her feelings of uncertainty and danger, becoming a crushing force that threatened her survival.

Both the baby and pregnancy itself may become associated with early unconscious phantasies. For example, pregnancy may fulfil a person's early childhood wish to be like their mother, to identify with a creative mother, and to feel that one holds something important within oneself (Deutsch, 1933). Pregnancy can also feel full of conflict for some expectant parents, if it represents an unconscious wish for triumph over one's own parents (Deutsch, 1945), or fear of transgression (Leuzinger-Bohleber, 2001; Pines, 1990) by becoming a parent.

While many expectant mothers might experience such moments of fear during pregnancy as a normal process of accommodating physically and psychically an 'unknown other' within them, other pregnant women can become much more psychically destabilised. For example, by the reawakening of early traumatic experiences or unconscious anxieties, leading to a process of splitting. In this process, they project all of their hatred and disturbance onto the baby, who is now experienced as a threat, and either avoided or met with hostile and murderous feelings (Schumacher, 2008). Other expectant mothers come to identify with a rejected and deficient body, and become detached and depressed, or anxious and overbearing, with all of the badness projected onto the external world. For other women who have experienced early trauma, the ongoing process of separation and the need to recognise the baby as separate awaken early feelings of complete dependence and fear of annihilation. These, in turn, are defended against with a delusion of merger with their baby (Perez, 2018). Sometimes the expectant mother cannot bear to think about or imagine the baby: Spinelli (2010) describes cases where denial of pregnancy becomes lethal, with expectant mothers projecting destructive internal forces onto the baby, and then going on to kill their newborn.

However, in other cases, mothers' not-thinking about their baby can, by contrast, act as an unconscious mechanism to protect the growing unborn baby. A useful example can be found in several women who had suffered prolonged physical pain and/or illness and panic during a first pregnancy or post-partum period, and who went on to have a second pregnancy while in psychoanalysis (Perez, in press). Each of these mothers navigated her second pregnancy through a complex process of what I have called 'creative disavowal' of her unborn baby. I have described this as the creation of an in-between mental state capable of protecting the baby from the violent bodily experiences, primitive anxieties, and hatred that these mothers felt. The analytic work in each case involved containing the mother's intense hostile and primitive unconscious phantasies, and giving meaning to her somatic experiences, while also creating space for the psychological or imagined baby to be born and held. Piccini (2021), Horney (1926), and Kristeva (2014) write about the pleasure and passion that pregnant women can experience alongside the physical and psychical violence of carrying and birthing a child. It is a capacity to connect to this pleasure and passion that is needed and, at times, this can only be achieved through such creative disavowal.

Clinical vignette: A twisted, stuck pain

Tara had had a traumatic experience breastfeeding her firstborn twins. She had developed infectious mastitis several times and been left feeling panicked, stuck, and with no one to help her. Tara first came to see me many years after that experience, when her twins were adolescents, and she was about to marry a new partner. A few years after that, she became pregnant and initially felt hopeful, imagining a loving baby. However, when she felt her breasts growing and becoming more sensitive and tender, this triggered the bodily memory of her first breastfeeding experience, along with the panic and claustrophobia that she had felt. Our sessions became filled with this reawakened pain and panic. She stopped talking and thinking about her unborn baby. In one session, while describing her mastitis, she said, *"It's something inside, that grows, and then can become hardened … it becomes solid … so quick … and once it's hard and twists, there's no way … it was just so fast … so painful …"* I spoke to her about her longing for a loving baby and her fear of this pain turning bad inside her. There was a moment of confusion, and she asked, *"What baby?"* Then, after a pause, she said, *"Oh, this baby. I had forgotten. Yes."* Similar moments continued to happen as she spoke of her body and the pain that she had endured in that first pregnancy. I understood that forgetting about her baby was a way of keeping a distance between the growing baby and the pain and panic that she felt. After a few weeks, she began to talk about new passions in relation to work and friends. She became livelier and more hopeful. When her baby was born, Tara immersed herself in the baby's life. She told me that the first feed had been difficult, adding, *"But yes, we knew this"*, as though her baby and her fear of breastfeeding him had always been in her mind, but kept safely separate. Imagining, and thinking and speaking about, her unborn baby felt too dangerous: I think that she felt, quite concretely, that this baby would be at risk of being destroyed if kept side by side with the physical and psychic hostility that she was experiencing. Now she began to speak more about her thoughts and feelings about her baby, perhaps because she now knew that she and her baby had survived (Perez, in press).

References

Benoit, D., Parker, K.C.H., & Zeanah, C.H. (1997). Mothers' representations of their infants assessed prenatally: Stability and association with infants' attachment classifications. *Journal of Child Psychology and Psychiatry*, 38(3):307–11.

Chandra, M., & Paray, A.A. (2024). Natural physiological changes during pregnancy. *Yale Journal of Biology and Medicine*, 97(1):85–92.

Deutsch, H. (1933). Motherhood and sexuality. *Psychoanalytic Quarterly*, 2:476–48.

Deutsch, H. (1945). *The psychology of women, Vol. 2: Motherhood.* New York: Grune & Stratton.

Freud, S. (1915). Instincts and their vicissitudes. In J. Strachey (Ed. & Trans.), The Standard Edition of the Complete Psychological Works of Sigmund Freud, 14:109–140. London: Vintage, The Hogarth Press.

Freud, S. (1923). The ego and the id. In J. Strachey (Ed. & Trans.), The Standard Edition of the Complete Psychological Works of Sigmund Freud, 19:1–66). London: Vintage, The Hogarth Press.

Horney, K. (1926). The flight from womanhood: The masculinity-complex in women, as viewed by men and by women. *The International Journal of Psychoanalysis*, 7:324–339.

Kristeva, J. (2014). Reliance, or maternal eroticism. *Journal of the American Psychoanalytic Association*, 62(1):69–85.

Kulish, N. (2011). On childlessness. *Psychoanalytic Inquiry*, 31:350–365.

Leuzinger-Bohleber, M. (2001). The 'Medea fantasy': An unconscious determinant of psychogenic sterility. *The International Journal of Psychoanalysis*, 82(2):323–345.

Lockitch, G. (1997). Clinical biochemistry of pregnancy. *Critical Reviews in Clinical Laboratory Sciences*, 34(1):67–139.

Perez, A. (2018). From pathological merger to a reflective, triangular space: Parent-infant psychotherapy with a mother with borderline personality disorder. *Journal of Infant, Child, and Adolescent Psychotherapy*, 17(1):15–27.

Perez, A. (in press). 'What baby?': creative disavowal during second pregnancy – A protective, parallel world. *International Journal of Psychoanalysis.* http://dx.doi.org/10.1080/00207578.2025.2483299

Perez, A., Panagiotopoulou, E., Vourda, M.C., Pereira, M. McCrory, E., & Roberts, R. (2025) Trajectories of change in mothers' parenting confidence and relationship with baby: A 15-month qualitative longitudinal study. *BMC Pregnancy and Childbirth.* 2025 Jul 3; 25(1):709. https://doi.org/10.1186/s12884-025-07683-0.

Piccini, O. (2021). The mother's body, the role of pleasure in the mother-infant relationship, and the traumatic risk. *International Forum of Psychoanalysis,* 30:129–138.

Pines, D. (1982). The relevance of early psychic development to pregnancy and abortion. *The International Journal of Psychoanalysis,* 63:311–319.

Pines, D. (1990). Pregnancy, miscarriage and abortion. A psychoanalytic perspective. *The International Journal of Psychoanalysis,* 71:301–307.

Raphael-Leff, J. (1993). *Pregnancy: The inside story.* London: Sheldon Press.

Schumacher, B. (2008). "I can't live without my child": Motherhood as a "solution" to early trauma. *British Journal of Psychotherapy,* 24:317–327.

Soma-Pillay, P., Nelson-Piercy, C., Tolppanen, H., & Mebazaa, A. (2016). Physiological changes in pregnancy. *Cardiovascular Journal of Africa,* 27(2):89–94.

Spinelli, M. (2010). Denial of pregnancy: A psychodynamic paradigm. *Journal of the American Academy of Psychoanalysis and Dynamic Psychiatry,* 38(1):117–131.

Winnicott, D.W. (1956) [1975]. Chapter XXIV. Primary maternal preoccupation. *Through paediatrics to psycho-analysis (International Psycho-Analytical Library* (No. 100, pp. 300–305). London: Hogarth Press & Institute of Psycho-Analysis.

Chapter 8

Neurobiological perspectives on pregnancy

Erika Barba-Müller

John Bowlby once said, "It is fortunate for their survival that babies are so designed by Nature that they beguile and enslave mothers" (1958, p.369). While babies are undeniably captivating, nature not only endows them with charm but also prepares the mother's brain to fulfil this evolutionary role, adapting during pregnancy to nurture and raise her child.

Gestation is a common yet extraordinary process, in which the female body undergoes numerous adaptations in a precise, coordinated, and dynamic manner as pregnancy progresses. Most organs adjust to support the growing foetus, some through subtle changes, others through dramatic adaptations. Recent neuroimaging studies reveal unique plastic transformations in the brain, deepening our understanding of the remarkable neurobiological foundations of motherhood.

Pioneering research on maternal brain changes

The first mention of pregnancy-related brain changes appeared in 2002 when Oatridge and colleagues observed structural alterations in the maternal brain. However, methodological limitations led to the study being largely overlooked.

In 2008, we undertook a longitudinal study at the Autonomous University of Barcelona to investigate these changes in greater depth. Magnetic resonance imaging was employed to scan couples planning to become parents, capturing images both before pregnancy and after childbirth. A control group of non-parent couples was also included. The initial findings were presented in my doctoral thesis (Barba-Müller, 2015) and subsequently published in *Nature Neuroscience*, incorporating a third time-point measurement conducted on the mothers two years postpartum (Hoekzema et al., 2017). This study provided the first evidence that pregnancy induces specific morphological changes in the human brain.

Whereas the brains of fathers and non-parent couples showed no significant changes, striking neural transformations were observed in mothers. Notably, every mother in our study exhibited a consistent reduction in grey matter volume, symmetrically distributed across both hemispheres. These changes occurred regardless of conception method, delivery type, or feeding practices.

DOI: 10.4324/9781003530473-11

At the two-year postpartum mark, most grey matter reductions remained observable. To further investigate this persistence, we conducted follow-up scans six years after childbirth and confirmed that the brain changes endured (Martínez-García et al., 2021). Interestingly, cross-sectional studies suggest that these modifications may persist for decades, indicating a long-lasting transformation (de Lange et al., 2020; Orchard et al., 2020).

Hormones as potential contributing factors

During pregnancy, the endocrine system undergoes a monumental adjustment. Yet even modest changes in sex steroid hormone levels—smaller than those observed in pregnancy—are known to influence human brain structure and function (Comasco et al., 2014; Comasco & Sundström-Poromaa, 2015).

Moreover, animal studies suggest that hormones are the primary driver of pregnancy-related neural changes. In fact, brain modifications can be induced in virgin female rats through hormonal treatments that mimic pregnancy (Kinsley et al., 2006).

Hoekzema and colleagues (2022), at Amsterdam University, conducted a second pre-post pregnancy study incorporating several enhancements, including the addition of hormonal measurements throughout pregnancy. The results closely mirrored those of the Barcelona research. Additionally, they revealed a strong correlation between neurostructural changes and third-trimester oestradiol levels, suggesting that this sex steroid hormone may play a key role in inducing this neuroplastic adaptation.

Which brain regions are modified?

In both the Barcelona and Amsterdam samples (Barba-Müller, 2015; Hoekzema et al., 2017, 2022), grey matter volume reductions were primarily observed in the anterior and posterior cortical midline, as well as specific bilateral sections of the lateral prefrontal and temporal cortex. These areas significantly overlap with brain regions activated during Theory of Mind tasks in fMRI paradigms; tasks designed to assess the ability to infer others' thoughts, feelings, and intentions.

Additionally, pregnancy-related structural brain changes were associated with fMRI responsiveness to own-baby cues, as well as with measures of maternal-foetal bonding, nesting behaviour, and predicted indicators of postpartum mother-infant attachment.

Taken together, these findings suggest that pregnancy-induced brain remodelling supports the maternal transition, facilitating key processes essential for newborn care.

The significance of Theory of Mind in caregiving

Theory of Mind (ToM) is crucial for interpersonal understanding, and in the context of infant care, it becomes essential for survival. Newborns are entirely dependent on caregivers to meet their basic needs, and a mother with good ToM skills may be better equipped to interpret her baby's signals and respond appropriately. This accurate responsiveness is critical not only for the baby's immediate well-being but also for long-term psychological health, as it lays the foundation for secure attachment, emotional development, and bonding (Fonagy, 1996).

Of course, the ability to accurately infer a newborn's needs is not exclusive to biological mothers. Adoptive mothers, fathers, and other caregivers can also interpret and respond to a baby's cues. However, pregnancy appears to enhance these functions. Interestingly, this enhancement extends beyond understanding a baby's needs to general social processing, such as recognising novel faces and rapidly detecting potential threats (Anderson & Rutherford, 2011; Pearson et al., 2009). This suggests that pregnant women develop heightened sensitivity in processing social information; a logical adaptation given that in human societies, both support and threats typically come from others.

The role of the Default Mode Network in identity shifts

The brain areas reshaped by pregnancy not only overlap with regions involved in ToM tasks but also significantly coincide with the Default Mode Network (DMN). This is unsurprising, as the DMN plays a key role in ToM and social inferences while also being central to self-referential processing.

The DMN is typically suppressed during externally focused tasks or goal-directed behaviours. Conversely, it is activated during resting states and internally oriented processes such as daydreaming, self-reflection, and referencing information to oneself—including inferring others' mental states or performing ToM tasks. It integrates and makes sense of external events in the context of prior internal information, constructing a coherent internal narrative or sense of self (Menon, 2023; Yeshurun et al., 2021).

Pregnancy reshapes the DMN both structurally and functionally. In pregnant women, functional connectivity within the DMN is increased, suggesting that the transition to motherhood enhances the network's temporal coherence (Hoekzema et al., 2022). These modifications may represent the neural correlates of the profound, life-altering experience of motherhood; a transformation that extends beyond behaviour to include shifts in identity.

In this context, notable clinical research has explored the inner dynamics accompanying the transition into motherhood. These studies focus on phenomena such as the reorganisation of identifications, mourning processes, and the earliest symbiotic relationship between mother and child, among other psychological processes. This transformation is so profound that some authors have described it as a pseudo-transient pathological state (Brazelton & Cramer, 1991), a process akin to a developmental stage (Benedek, 1959), or a special psychological condition characterised by "heightened sensitivity" or "normal devotion" (Winnicott, 1958/2018).

Maternal motivation and the mesolimbic reward circuit

Maternal care is the most prominent and widespread example of altruism in the animal kingdom and may represent the foundational form of prosocial behaviour from which all others evolved (Panksepp, 1998). Studies across various animal species have investigated the emergence of strong maternal motivational drives and identified the mesolimbic reward circuit as a key player in promoting altruistic maternal responsiveness toward offspring.

To determine whether pregnancy in humans is associated with subcortical changes, particularly within the mesolimbic reward circuit, we measured a core structure within this system: the ventral striatum, a region crucial for processing reward, motivation, and emotional responses (Hoekzema et al., 2020). The findings revealed that pregnancy alters the anatomy of the ventral striatum. Moreover, this structural change predicted functional responses to offspring cues postpartum, suggesting that pregnancy primes the maternal reward circuit to respond more robustly to infant cues, thereby increasing the newborn's motivational salience.

Grey matter volume reduction: a signature of a neural refinement

It may seem paradoxical that becoming a mother—a period marked by the acquisition of substantial new knowledge—coincides with a decrease, rather than an increase, in grey matter volume. Typically, such reductions are associated with neurodegenerative processes. However, a similar phenomenon occurs during adolescence, a developmental stage characterised, among other things, by the emergence of executive functions mediated by the prefrontal cortex. Interestingly, adolescence is also marked by a decrease in grey matter, a process attributed to synaptic pruning, as shown in a postmortem study (Petanjek et al., 2011). Consequently, in adolescence, grey matter reduction is widely interpreted as a sign of the brain's refinement and optimisation of neural circuits.

Apparent parallels between pregnancy and adolescence have prompted us to analyse the morphometric characteristics of cortical alterations in these two hormonally driven transitional stages (Carmona et al., 2019). We compared brain scans obtained before and after pregnancy with longitudinal data from female adolescents over two years of pubertal development. The results revealed that both first-time mothers and adolescent girls exhibited a similar monthly rate of volumetric reductions and a comparable anatomical alteration profile. These findings provide preliminary evidence that pregnancy, like adolescence, represents a sensitive period during which hormonal priming induces an enhanced state of neuroplasticity, potentially serving an adaptive role in responding to forthcoming environmental demands.

In my view, pregnancy and adolescence share five key similarities: 1) elevated sex steroid hormone levels, 2) reductions in grey matter volume, 3) identity shifts, 4) some cognitive specialisations, and 5) an increased psychological vulnerability.

Mental health vulnerabilities during pregnancy and postpartum

Periods of significant hormonal changes—such as puberty, pregnancy, and menopause/andropause—are marked by heightened vulnerability in terms of mental health and emotional balance.

Regarding pregnancy, postpartum depression and anxiety have gained increasing recognition, and they affect an estimated 10% to 20% of first-time mothers. However, less attention has been given to the fact that both disorders can also emerge during pregnancy, with an estimated prevalence of 15.6% (Fisher et al., 2012). Notably, a review suggests that antenatal depression rates may exceed those observed in the first year postpartum (Underwood et al., 2016) and that postpartum depression and anxiety often stem from symptoms initially present during pregnancy (Heron et al., 2004).

While an in-depth discussion of peripartum mental disorders is beyond the scope of this chapter, a comprehensive review is available in Barba-Müller et al. (2018). For those interested in cognitive aspects, see Orchard (2023) and Callaghan and Pawluski (2024).

Here, I want to emphasise that while pregnancy-related brain plasticity is adaptive and serves an evolutionary purpose—the continuation of the human species—it is not without risks. Just as pregnancy carries physical risks, such as an increased likelihood of diabetes, preeclampsia, and other complications, its psychological impact must not be overlooked. Just as women's physical health during pregnancy and childbirth is prioritised through routine obstetric care and skilled birth attendance—practices that have saved countless lives—there is an equally important opportunity to focus on psychological prevention and intervention during this critical period.

Pregnancy and the postpartum period are times of heightened mental vulnerability, predisposing mothers to peripartum mental disorders. The associated suffering has profound consequences for the mother, her partner, and her child. Moreover, the baby is particularly sensitive to the mother's emotional state, making the perinatal period a crucial window for identifying and supporting women at risk. Addressing maternal mental health during this time not only supports the mother but also has a preventive effect on the baby's well-being, achieving two objectives with one effort. Conversely, if mood disorders persist, they can have far-reaching consequences for the child.

Insights from MRI scanning during pregnancy

A recent study examined 110 first-time pregnant women during late pregnancy and postpartum. The findings reveal significant reductions in cortical volume and thickness before childbirth, which partially recovered in the early postpartum period (Patermina-Die et al., 2024).

Using a single-case longitudinal design, Pritschet et al. (2024) conducted 26 brain scans of one individual, capturing neuroanatomical changes from preconception through pregnancy and up to two years postpartum. The findings illustrate a dynamic landscape of brain changes throughout the maternal transition, characterised by a gradual, unfolding curve.

These studies highlight a distinct pattern of cortical reductions during pregnancy, reaching their lowest point around childbirth and gradually reversing as the postpartum period progresses, though they do not fully return to pre-pregnancy levels.

Conclusion

The integration of interdisciplinary knowledge is essential for advancing a comprehensive understanding of the human brain and mind. In this chapter, we have explored how recent in-vivo neuroscientific research confirms what experience and clinical observation have long suggested: pregnancy is a life-altering event. It is not merely an experience a woman undergoes; it is a transformation that reshapes her at a fundamental level.

Pregnancy represents a period of unparalleled neuroplasticity in adult life, during which a woman's brain undergoes profound changes to meet the unique challenges of gestation and caregiving; a process that sustains humanity and lays the foundation for social relationships. This transformation coincides with that of the baby, whose brain is shaped by early experiences. Thus, during this stage, two significant windows of neuroplasticity align: that of the mother and that of the baby.

From a mental health perspective, this period represents a crucial target for enhancing care and providing treatment when needed, making it a promising strategy for mental health prevention.

References

Anderson, M.V., & Rutherford, M.D. (2011). Recognition of novel faces after single exposure is enhanced during pregnancy. *Evolutionary Psychology, 9*(1), 47–60.

Barba-Müller, E. (2015). *Morphologic brain changes induced by pregnancy. A longitudinal magnetic resonance imaging study* [Ph.D. Thesis, Universitat Autònoma de Barcelona]. www.tdx.cat/handle/10803/319448

Barba-Müller, E., Craddock, S., Carmona, S., & Hoekzema, E. (2018). *Brain plasticity in pregnancy and the postpartum period: Links to maternal caregiving and mental health.* Archives of Women's Mental Health.

Benedek, T. (1959). Parenthood as a developmental phase. *Journal of the American Psychoanalytic Association, 7*, 389–417.

Bowlby, J. (1958). The nature of the child's tie to his mother. *International Journal of Psycho-Analysis, 39*(5), Article 5.

Brazelton, T.B., & Cramer, B.G. (1991). *The earliest relationship: Parents, infants, and the drama of early attachment.* Da Capo Press.

Callaghan, B.L., & Pawluski, J.L. (2024). *Cognition and motherhood: A key to understanding perinatal mental health?* Archives of Women's Mental Health.

Carmona, S., Martínez-García, M., Paternina-Die, M., Barba-Müller, E., Wierenga, L.M., Alemán-Gómez, Y., ... & Hoekzema, E. (2019) Pregnancy and adolescence entail similar neuroanatomical adaptations: A comparative analysis of cerebral morphometric changes. *Human Brain Mapping, 40*(7), 2143–2152.

Comasco, E., Frokjaer, V.G., & Sundström-Poromaa, I. (2014). Functional and molecular neuroimaging of menopause and hormone replacement therapy. *Frontiers in Neuroscience, 8*, 388.

Comasco, E., & Sundström-Poromaa, I. (2015). Neuroimaging the menstrual cycle and premenstrual dysphoric disorder. *Current Psychiatry Reports, 17*(10), 77.

de Lange, A.G., Barth, C., Kaufmann, T., Anatürk, M., Suri, S., Ebmeier, K.P., & Westlye, L.T. (2020). The maternal brain: Region-specific patterns of brain aging are traceable decades after childbirth. *Human Brain Mapping, 41*(16), 4718–4729.

Fisher, J., Mello, M.C., Patel, V., Rahman, A., Tran, T., Holton, S., & Holmes, W. (2012). Prevalence and determinants of common perinatal mental disorders in women in low- and lower-middle-income countries: A systematic review. *Bulletin of the World Health Organization, 90*, 139–149.

Fonagy, P. (1996). The significance of the development of metacognitive control over mental representations in parenting and infant development. *Journal of Clinical Psychoanalysis, 5*, 67–86.

Heron, J., O'Connor, T.G., Evans, J., *et al.* (2004). The course of anxiety and depression through pregnancy and the postpartum in a community sample. *Journal of Affective Disorders, 80*(1).

Hoekzema, E., Barba-Müller, E., Pozzobon, C., *et al.* (2017). Pregnancy leads to long-lasting changes in human brain structure. *Nature Neuroscience,* 20(2).

Hoekzema, E., Tamnes, C.K., Berns, P., Barba-Müller, E., *et al.* (2020). Becoming a mother entails anatomical changes in the ventral striatum of the human brain that facilitate its responsiveness to offspring cues. *Psychoneuroendocrinology, 112*, 104507.

Hoekzema, E., van Steenbergen, H., Straathof, M., *et al.* (2022). Mapping the effects of pregnancy on resting state brain activity, white matter microstructure, neural metabolite concentrations and grey matter architecture. *Nature Communications, 13*(1), 6931.

Kinsley, C.H., Trainer, R., Stafisso-Sandoz, G., *et al.* (2006). Motherhood and the hormones of pregnancy modify concentrations of hippocampal neuronal dendritic spines. *Hormones and Behavior, 49*(2), 131–142.

Martínez-García, M., Paternina-Die, M., Barba-Müller, E., *et al.* (2021). Do pregnancy-induced brain changes reverse? The brain of a mother six tears after parturition. *Brain Sciences, 11*(2), 168.

Menon, V. (2023). 20 years of the default mode network: A review and synthesis. *Neuron, 111*(16), 2469–2487.

Oatridge, A., Holdcroft, A., Saeed, N., *et al.* (2002). Change in brain size during and after pregnancy: Study in healthy women and women with preeclampsia. *American Journal of Neuroradiology, 23*(1), 19–26.

Orchard, E.R., Rutherford, H.J.V., Holmes, A.J., & Jamadar, S.D. (2023). Matrescence: Lifetime impact of motherhood on cognition and the brain. *Trends in Cognitive Sciences, 27*(3), 302–316.

Orchard, E.R., Ward, P.G.D., Sforazzini, *et al.* (2020). Relationship between parenthood and cortical thickness in late adulthood. *PloS One, 15*(7).

Panksepp, J. (1998). *Affective neuroscience: The foundations of human and animal emotions.* Oxford University Press.

Paternina-Die, M., Martínez-García, M., Martín de Blas, D., *et al.* (2024). Women's neuroplasticity during gestation, childbirth and postpartum. *Nature Neuroscience, 27*(2), 319–327.

Pearson, R.M., Lightman, S.L., & Evans, J. (2009). Emotional sensitivity for motherhood: Late pregnancy is associated with enhanced accuracy to encode emotional faces. *Hormones and Behavior, 56*(5), 557–563.

Petanjek, Z., Judaš, M., Šimic, G., *et al.* (2011). Extraordinary neoteny of synaptic spines in the human prefrontal cortex. *PNAS, 108*(32), 13281–13286.

Pritschet, L., Taylor, C.M., Cossio, D., *et al.* (2024). Neuroanatomical changes observed over the course of a human pregnancy. *Nature Neuroscience, 27*, 2253–2260.

Underwood, L., Waldie, K., D'Souza, S., Peterson, E.R., & Morton, S. (2016). A review of longitudinal studies on antenatal and postnatal depression. *Archives of Women's Mental Health, 19*(5), 711–720.

Winnicott, D. W. (2018). Primary maternal preoccupation. In *Through paediatrics to psychoanalysis: Collected papers* (pp. 300–305). Routledge. (Original work published 1958).

Yeshurun, Y., Nguyen, M., & Hasson, U. (2021). The default mode network: Where the idiosyncratic self meets the shared social world. *Nature Reviews. Neuroscience, 22*(3), 181–192.

Chapter 9

The bodily self during pregnancy

Elena Panagiotopoulou and Catherine E.J. Preston

Pregnancy is a period of heightened embodiment during which women become acutely aware of their physical bodies. Pregnant bodies undergo rapid and substantial transformations, both externally (i.e. size, shape, and weight) and internally (i.e. bodily sensations), as they grow and transform into vessels for another life. These physiological changes are accompanied by external shifts in social responses and expectations, often placing additional pressure on women. Together, these adjustments and adaptations profoundly impact women's lived, felt sense of their bodies: from how they perceive and feel about their changing body (body image) to their sense of ownership and control (body ownership and agency) and awareness of signals coming from within their body (bodily awareness). The prepartum experience of the body can, in turn, deeply influence women's identity and well-being and, ultimately, their relationship with baby and child's development.

Body image

Pregnant women are required to balance social expectations about body ideals and ideals of being a good mother (Kirk & Preston, 2019). Experiencing rapid bodily changes during pregnancy is quite complex and cannot be thought about outside of the cultural, social, and political discourses that frame our lives and exert pressure on us (Lemma, 2015). These changes are often in conflict with, and push women further away from, transnational socio-cultural ideals of the female body, such as the unrealistic aspiration to a thin ideal (e.g. Duncombe et al., 2008). Managing own and others' expectations, also imposed through social media platforms like Instagram, can have negative consequences, with an increased appearance comparison and pressure to "bounce back" (e.g. Arellano et al., 2025). These pressures can lead to body image disturbances, that is negative perceptions, feelings, beliefs, and attitudes towards one's body (Cash et al., 2004) with important repercussions on both mother's and newborn's health (Spinoni et al., 2023). Negative experiences of the prepartum body are linked to maternal depression (e.g. Silveira et al., 2015), impaired maternal-foetal and mother-infant attachment (e.g. Fuller-Tyszkiewicz et al., 2013), lower breastfeeding intentions and breastfeeding rates (e.g. Morley-Hewitt & Owen, 2020), as well as more unhealthy behaviours, such as smoking

DOI: 10.4324/9781003530473-12

during pregnancy (Duncombe et al., 2008) and skipping meals, self-induced vomiting, and laxative use as extreme weight control conducts (e.g. Clark & Odgen, 1999). In contrast, body image satisfaction during pregnancy has been found to be associated with better mother-infant relationship quality, lower depression and anxiety, and higher levels of interoception, e.g. body listening and body trusting (Kirk & Preston, 2019).

Interestingly, research examining body image during pregnancy has yielded conflicting findings, indicating wide variation in women's responses, from distress to liberation (e.g. Meireles et al., 2015). Some studies report improvement of prepartum body satisfaction, with recognition of the functionality of the pregnant body being a protective factor for negotiating bodily changes (e.g. Watson et al., 2016). For some women, the pregnant body becomes symbolic of life, fertility, and femininity, hence, protecting pregnant women from the pressures of achieving an ideal body shape or size. In a recent qualitative study conducted by the editors of this book, we found that pregnant women prioritised the desire to be healthy and have a healthy baby over their appearance (Arellano et al., 2025). This is in line with evidence that the brain during pregnancy adjusts to focus more on bodily sensations related to foetal well-being, while placing less emphasis on sensations linked to physical appearance (Dahan, 2021). However, many studies report worsening of prepartum body satisfaction (Crossland et al., 2023). The lack of consensus over how pregnant women experience their changing bodies reflects the complexity and heterogeneity of women's experiences, as well as methodological limitations. These include but are not limited to: lack of standardised validated measures designed specifically for the pregnant population, and suboptimal sample sizes and lack of independent samples for the development and validation of pregnancy body satisfaction scales (Kirk & Preston, 2019); retrospective reports of pre-pregnancy body satisfaction, which can be biased (e.g. Munns et al., 2024), as well as limited use of qualitative methods to better understand the range and nuances of women's body image experiences during pregnancy (e.g. Watson et al., 2016).

Body ownership, agency, and control

The experience of pregnancy creates a unique duality—the woman's sense of self may shift as she integrates the experience of nurturing a new life within her own body. This can profoundly influence a woman's sense of ownership, the feeling that the body belongs to herself, as well as agency, the experience of initiating and controlling an action. The feeling of losing control of the pregnant body has been noted in the literature (Hodgkinson et al., 2014), with studies reporting that pregnant women: perceive their bodies as undertaking pregnancy-related changes of their own accord (Schmied and Lupton, 2001); consider their bodies as strangers to them (Clark et al., 2009); and feel a loss of ownership of their bodies (Arellano et al., 2025). This sense of sharing the body with the foetus results in conflicting attitudes: a comforting feeling of co-existing harmoniously with baby, alongside a feeling of being invaded by the baby (Schmied & Lupton, 2001).

Another way in which women experience a lack of control over their bodies is through the dissolution of social boundaries. Pregnancy often brings a woman's body into public focus, sometimes leading to unsolicited comments, attention or touch by family, friends or even strangers (Johnson et al., 2004). This public scrutiny, for instance comments about belly size, can lead to feelings of insecurity about the baby's development (Arellano et al., 2025), but also insecurity about their own appearance and feelings of exposure or objectification.

Last but not least, the healthcare system's role in monitoring pregnancy often places women's bodies under medical scrutiny. Routine examinations and medical interventions may contribute to feelings of reduced agency, as pregnant women may feel like their bodies are being controlled by the medical authority rather than by themselves (e.g. Kırlı & Kaya, 2025).

Bodily awareness

During the prepartum period, women undergo changes in how they internally perceive their bodies, turning their attention towards signals coming from within their body, such as the baby's kicking (Clark et al., 2009). Such perceptual experiences that are unique to this period can strengthen the connection between the mother and baby and, ultimately, enhance a sense of purpose and meaning in the transformation of the body, helping women adapt positively to these changes (Clark et al., 2009). More generally, interoceptive signals coming from the inside of the body can not only provide us with information about physical states, e.g., hunger, but also emotional states, such as heart rate (Craig, 2002). Interoceptive awareness is linked to body image experiences in pregnant women (Kirk & Preston, 2019), with prepartum body image satisfaction being associated with higher levels of interoception, e.g., body listening and body trusting. Listening to and trusting the body is also important for coping with the complex experience of blurry self-other boundaries between mother and foetus (Schmied & Lupus, 2001), whereas interoception can also mitigate negative effects of body appearance dissatisfaction on maternal bonding (Stafford et al., 2024).

Recent evidence points to the important role of touch, which is now recognised as a cross-modal sensory system as it is both an exteroceptive (coming from outside the body) and interoceptive signal (generating sensations within the body). Self-touch of the bump offers opportunities for connecting and communicating with the baby, whereas having the partner touch the bump helps feel that the experience can be shared with them, further contributing to a positive prepartum body experience (Arellano et al., 2025).

Neural changes

Physical changes to the body during pregnancy are accompanied by widespread changes in the brain (e.g. Paternina-Die et al., 2024). However, the reasons for these neural changes remain largely unknown. Postnatal brain changes are thought to support caregiving behaviours (e.g. Kim et al., 2016), and, given that an absence or obsession on infant care can be a marker of perinatal psychopathology, these brain changes may also relate to the increased risk of mental health issues after birth (Kim et al., 2016). Importantly, preparation for caregiving begins well before birth. A mother's emotional bond with her baby develops throughout pregnancy and influences both prenatal behaviours (e.g., quitting smoking for the baby's health, Jussila et al., 2020) and postnatal mother-infant relationships (Trombetta et al., 2021). Because the baby is physically located within the mother's body during pregnancy, information from her own body may play a key role in prenatal bonding, which is supported by behavioural studies (e.g. Kirk & Preston, 2019). At the same time, however, the bodily experience (both in terms of feelings about external appearance and interpretation of interoceptive signals) is closely linked to psychological well-being (e.g. Kirk & Preston, 2019), which is also at higher risk prenatally (O'Hara & Wisner, 2014).

Predictive theories of neural processing suggest that our experiences, including those of our bodily states, are based on predictions rather than real-time sensory information. When there is a mismatch between predicted and actual body states, the brain can either update its predictions to align with current bodily information or adjust the body state to match the prediction (Paulus & Stein, 2006). A failure to resolve these discrepancies can contribute to thoughts and behaviours associated with mental health issues (e.g. Paulus & Stein, 2006). During pregnancy, the body undergoes major changes, which may increase prediction errors in the brain. For instance, hormonally driven changes in blood vessels increase blood volume by up to 50%, leading to stronger and faster heartbeats (Meah et al., 2016). Outside of pregnancy, rapid heartbeats often signal anxiety (Paulus & Stein, 2006), so previously learned predictions about heart rate and emotions may no longer be accurate, increasing prediction errors. To deal with this, the brain may start disregarding unreliable bodily signals. However, because bodily information remains crucial for informing about and bonding with the foetus, the brain has to carefully balance how it uses these signals. Navigating this balance in the context of continuous bodily change during pregnancy may help explain the increased risk of mental health challenges and the aforementioned experiences of reduced body ownership and control commonly reported during this period.

Interplay of different aspects of bodily self

It is apparent that different aspects of the bodily self—the lived, felt sense of the body—are interlinked, influencing one another. How a person perceives and feels about their changing body appearance is deeply influenced by their sense of agency and control, and their perception of the body from within. Positive experiences in one of these areas often enhance the others, while challenges in one aspect can lead to negative impacts on the other two. These changes may be underpinned by neural changes throughout gestation, which rebalance the weighting of bodily information away from informing about emotional state in favour of foetal well-being.

These fundamental changes enable the brain to deal with a dramatically changing bodily state while preparing for parenthood, but also may represent vulnerability to psychological well-being. Understanding this interplay and the underlying neural mechanisms can help provide better support for pregnant individuals as they navigate these shifts.

References

Arellano, A., Roberts, R., Perez, A., & Panagiotopoulou, E. (2025). *External and internal influences on prepartum body image: A qualitative study.* Research Square.

Cash T. F. (2004). Body image: Past, present, and future. *Body Image, 1*(1), 1–5.

Clark, A., Skouteris, H., Wertheim, E. H., Paxton, S. J., & Milgrom, J. (2009). The relationship between depression and body dissatisfaction across pregnancy and the postpartum: A prospective study. *Journal of Health Psychology, 14*(1), 27–35.

Clark, M., & Ogden, J. (1999). The impact of pregnancy on eating behaviour and aspects of weight concern. *International Journal of Obesity and Related Metabolic Disorders: Journal of the International Association for the Study of Obesity, 23*(1), 18–24.

Craig A. D. (2002). How do you feel? Interoception: The sense of the physiological condition of the body. *Nature Reviews: Neuroscience, 3*(8), 655–666.

Crossland, A. E., Munns, L., Kirk, E., & Preston, C. E. J. (2023). Comparing body image dissatisfaction between pregnant women and non-pregnant women: A systematic review and meta-analysis. *BMC Pregnancy and Childbirth, 23*(1), 709.

Dahan, O. (2021). The birthing brain: A lacuna in neuroscience. *Brain and Cognition, 150*(105722), 105722.

Duncombe, D., Wertheim, E. H., Skouteris, H., Paxton, S. J., & Kelly, L. (2008). How well do women adapt to changes in their body size and shape across the course of pregnancy?. *Journal of Health Psychology, 13*(4), 503–515.

Fuller-Tyszkiewicz, M., Skouteris, H., Watson, B. E., & Hill, B. (2013). Body dissatisfaction during pregnancy: A systematic review of cross-sectional and prospective correlates. *Journal of Health Psychology, 18*(11), 1411–1421.

Hodgkinson, E. L., Smith, D. M., & Wittkowski, A. (2014). Women's experiences of their pregnancy and postpartum body image: A systematic review and meta-synthesis. *BMC Pregnancy and Childbirth, 14*, 330.

Johnson, S., Burrows, A., & Williamson, I. (2004). 'Does my bump look big in this?' The meaning of bodily changes for first-time mothers-to-be. *Journal of Health Psychology, 9*(3), 361–374.

Jussila, H., Pelto, J., Korja, R., Ekholm, E., Pajulo, M., Karlsson, L., & Karlsson, H. (2020). The association of maternal-fetal attachment with smoking and smoking cessation during pregnancy in The FinnBrain Birth Cohort Study. *BMC Pregnancy and Childbirth, 20*(1), 741.

Kim, P., Strathearn, L., & Swain, J. E. (2016). The maternal brain and its plasticity in humans. *Hormones and Behavior, 77*, 113–123.

Kirk, E., & Preston, C. (2019). Development and validation of the Body Understanding Measure for Pregnancy Scale (BUMPS) and its role in antenatal attachment. *Psychological Assessment, 31*(9), 1092–1106.

Kırlı, G., & Kaya, Ş. D. (2025). Medicalization of female life stages: A qualitative research. *BMC Health Services Research, 25*, 322.

Lemma, A. (2015). *The body in psychoanalysis: Contemporary developments*. Routledge.

Meah, V. L., Cockcroft, J. R., Backx, K., Shave, R., & Stöhr, E. J. (2016). Cardiac output and related haemodynamics during pregnancy: A series of meta-analyses. *Heart, 102*(7), 518–526.

Meireles, J. F., Neves, C. M., de Carvalho, P. H., & Ferreira, M. E. (2015). Body dissatisfaction among pregnant women: An integrative review of the literature. *Ciencia & saude coletiva, 20*(7), 2091–2103.

Morley-Hewitt, A. G., & Owen, A. L. (2020). A systematic review examining the association between female body image and the intention, initiation and duration of post-partum infant feeding methods (breastfeeding vs bottle-feeding). *Journal of Health Psychology, 25*(2), 207–226.

Munns, L. B., Crossland, A. E., McPherson, M., Panagiotopoulou, E., & Preston, C. E. J. (2024). Developing a new measure of retrospective body dissatisfaction: Links to postnatal bonding and psychological well-being. *Journal of Reproductive and Infant Psychology, Aug 6*, 1–16. doi: 10.1080/02646838.2024.2386077.

O'Hara, M. W., & Wisner, K. L. (2014). Perinatal mental illness: Definition, description and aetiology. *Best Practice & Research. Clinical Obstetrics & Gynaecology, 28*(1), 3–12.

Paternina-Die, M., Martínez-García, M., Martín de Blas, D., Noguero, I., Servin-Barthet, C., Pretus, C., Soler, A., López-Montoya, G., Desco, M., & Carmona, S. (2024). Women's neuroplasticity during gestation, childbirth and postpartum. *Nature Neuroscience, 27*(2), 319–327.

Paulus, M. P., & Stein, M. B. (2006). An insular view of anxiety. *Biological Psychiatry, 60*(4), 383–387.

Schmied, V., & Lupton, D. (2001). The externality of the inside: Body images of pregnancy. *Nursing Inquiry, 8*(1), 32–40.

Silveira, M. L., Ertel, K. A., Dole, N., & Chasan-Taber, L. (2015). The role of body image in prenatal and postpartum depression: A critical review of the literature. *Archives of Women's Mental Health, 18*(3), 409–421.

Spinoni, M., Singh Solorzano, C., & Grano, C. (2023). A prospective study on body image disturbances during pregnancy and postpartum: The role of cognitive reappraisal. *Frontiers in Psychology, 14*, 1200819.

Stafford, L., Munns, L., Crossland, A. E., Kirk, E., & Preston, C. E. J. (2024). Bonding with bump: Interoceptive sensibility moderates the relationship between pregnancy body satisfaction and antenatal attachment. *Midwifery, 131*, 103940.

Trombetta, T., Giordano, M., Santoniccolo, F., Vismara, L., Della Vedova, A. M., & Rollè, L. (2021). Pre-natal attachment and parent-to-infant attachment: A systematic review. *Frontiers in Psychology, 12*, 620942.

Watson, B., Broadbent, J., Skouteris, H., & Fuller-Tyszkiewicz, M. (2016). A qualitative exploration of body image experiences of women progressing through pregnancy. *Women and Birth: Journal of the Australian College of Midwives, 29*(1), 72–79.

Chapter 10

Qualitative study of a transgender father in his third trimester

Dominic Jones and Lisa Thackeray

There is growing scholarly interest in the lives and rights of people who do not conform to prevailing expectations of gender. Non-conformity in how people perform, express, or embody social norms, conventionally associated with sex differences, encompasses a multitude of minority identities, including transgender (Aguirre-Sánchez-Beato, 2018). Being transgender (or trans) generally connotes having a gender identity—an inner sense of gender—that differs from sex assigned at birth. Although not all, many trans people make social, legal, or medical transitions to affirm and embody their gender identity. In this chapter on expectant parenthood, we share the experience of George, a transgender man assigned female at birth, during his third trimester of pregnancy.

Speculation on the 2021 Census (ONS, 2024) suggests 0.3% of the adult population of England and Wales—144,000 people—may identify as trans or non-binary (Biggs, 2024). The proportion of transgender adults who have children is similarly speculative, with estimates in the USA broadly between a quarter and a half (Dierckx *et al.*, 2015; Stotzer *et al.*, 2014). This is less than the general population. However, it is evident that many transgender people are parents, want to become parents, and plan for parenthood (Moseson *et al.*, 2021). Many may have formed families before they identified as trans or transitioned. And for those who have already legally or medically transitioned, there are multiple pathways to family formation. Options include adoption, fostering, and step-parenthood, as well as biological and technologically assisted reproduction. Although medical transitioning (i.e., hormone therapy and surgery) can have consequences for fertility, it is possible for many transgender men, with child-bearing reproductive systems, to conceive, carry, and give birth themselves (Light *et al.*, 2014).

Recent explorative research with trans men have identified tensions between the body as a place to enact and embody a masculine gender identity, and as a place to bear children. This can complicate decisions around parenthood (Tasker & Gato, 2020). Riggs (*et al.*, 2023) conducted focus groups with nulliparous trans men regarding their views of pregnancy. Many reported cultural barriers to reproductive autonomy. Planning a family would entail the "unpacking" of cultural norms felt to be odds with their identities, such as pronatalism regarding their sex assigned at birth, and the constraints of conventional fatherhood. Trans men who have given

DOI: 10.4324/9781003530473-13

birth and nurse their infants have also reported challenges related to the changing size and function of breast tissue (MacDonald *et al.*, 2016). This has been captured by Charter (*et al.* 2023) as a difficulty "inhabiting the pregnant body". Their surveys and interviews with trans parents reveal additional, concrete challenges, such as pausing testosterone therapy and negative experiences with healthcare professionals. Pregnancy, however, was seen by many as a functional sacrifice, necessary to achieve the life goal of forming a family. New meanings of fatherhood were often constructed to make the transition to parenthood possible.

Qualitative study

Our participant, pseudonymised as George, had medically transitioned and lived as a trans man for nearly a decade before conceiving and carrying a gestational pregnancy to term. While in his third trimester, he took part in semi-structured interviews with us, as part of a longitudinal project, the LEAP Study.[1] In order to analyse George's account of expectant parenthood, with attention to the construction of meaning, we utilised the technique of Interpretative Phenomenological Analysis (Smith, Flowers & Larkin, 2022). This involves a double hermeneutic of interpreting how another person has interpreted an episode of their life. We examined how George made sense of his own reactions, feelings, and expectations, as well as perceived challenges and sources of support, during his pregnancy. This involved iterative reading, coding, and the distillation of themes identified in the analysis of interviews. Below, we explore three Personal Experiential Themes that emerged from George's account of pregnancy.

Formation of a new role and identity

George identified as a father. When asked what fatherhood meant to him, he described it as an open question. He referred to language conventions and anatomy, and despite these, saw himself as only marginally different from the conventional idea of manhood. He was a father, in his view, simply because he was a man. Contrastingly, he spoke at length about the functions of parenthood; the *doing* of fatherhood, involving nurturing, protecting, and provisioning for the child. In his understanding of these labours of love and sacrifice, we observe commonly held, contemporary ideals of the parental couple, with a less gendered division of labour. Where George felt trepidation about these tasks, he was reassured by his and his partner's shared moral standpoints. They could not go far wrong, so long as they helped their child grow to be themselves, and not feel moulded, pressured, or a disappointment.

With a positive pregnancy test, George immediately assumed this parental identity and role. However, the preceding period of trying to conceive was challenging. One reason for this was stopping hormone therapy.

> It just felt like a lifetime because it had been over a year since I'd stopped testosterone. So, coming off hormones- my hormones readjusting, all of that, was

quite a, uh, rocky road, not the most enjoyable transition experience. So, I think it was just really exciting to finally have what we had been working towards all that time.

This discontinuity with his previous bodily experience, eight and a half years of hormone therapy, appeared manageable for George because other long-standing goals were finally coming together. His sense of himself as a man, and as somebody planning and desiring a family with his partner, remained a guiding thread down this metaphorical "rocky road" of the transition to parenthood.

Surroundings of the pregnancy

Against the backdrop of this manageable albeit intense period, were "additional layers of stress" originating in the outside world. Antenatal healthcare appointments were slow and disrupted by (mal)administration. For example, George's birth certificate recognises his identity as a man. This led healthcare staff to cancel appointments, as they could not readily process a man booking medical appointments for *his* pregnancy; to procure an appointment, he and his partner had to file a formal complaint. The theme of intrusion of the outside world was also evident when George reflected on his hopes for his future child.

> I hope [my baby] doesn't experience any difficulty from other people externally because they don't come from a typical kind of family. I hope that they don't feel short-changed by that. I guess, I hope that it doesn't upset them or bother them that they were birthed by a man, that they were birthed by their dad. I just want them to, you know, be able to flourish and not have barriers or hardship.

Stepping back from the outside world and focusing on a private space enabled George to soothe the tumult and anxiety of pregnancy. This is a familiar element of expectant parenthood; George regulated his immediate, private surroundings, and described it as "nesting". He found ways of attending to his social and home environment: provisioning toys, activities, and food for the coming baby, and preferring to spend time inside, "keeping cosy". He and his partner enlisted the help of their mothers, as experts, and in the early stages they informed few other people about the pregnancy. This safe and insular space was foundational. However, after initial troubles with healthcare staff, continuity of care with a midwife became another important source of support.

Growth of the baby and body

Much of George's account of pregnancy was physical, including fatigue, nausea, and other medical symptoms. The idea of the foetus had to be gradually built up through medical scans and sonography; early images appeared "blob" and "frog-like". When George shared how the representation of the baby in utero slowly unfolded, his sentences were fragmented, perhaps reflecting both excitement and anxiety as he attempted to describe a significant, complex, and nuanced experience. Excitement, as recognisable parts of the baby came into view: hands, feet, an ear, and so on. But, also anxiety, with an urgent need to see more of the baby, and to have reassurance of its viability and health. George described "voids" and painful stretches of time during which he was left waiting for these signs. The experience of the body's changes (swelling, light bleeding, nausea, and fatigue), he said, were impossible to prepare for and felt far out of one's control.

But, in one significant way, George's body did not change. Reflecting on having had a double mastectomy, George expressed a nuanced sense of concern.

I feel sad that I won't be able to breastfeed [my baby] because you know, it gets rammed down your throat, like 'breast is best' and so- you know, although I don't regret having top-surgery because it's been five years of a much more comfortable and happy life having done it, and I don't think I would trade that for being able to breastfeed now, but even still, like, it makes me sad that I can't do that, and you know, wondering about like, ohh, but will there be long term implications of that, or like, you know, will I pick the wrong formula?

George did not regret this aspect of his transition, as it had helped him live a happier life as in individual. However, he shared his sadness and wondered about complications for the future nourishment and growth of his baby. This was particularly felt against the normative pressure ("breast is best") to nurse infants. George experienced concern about his ability to fulfil his baby's needs, find the appropriate alternatives, and what implications there could be.

Discussion

Ultimately, birthing and rearing a much-wanted baby was central to George's experience of pregnancy. Beyond this, his focus was on managing anxieties and providing optimal conditions to raise the child, with parental moral values mattering most. Regarding fatherhood, there was a focus on parental function rather than identity, and perhaps only a secondary significance of labels and language. This theme has been discussed elsewhere, as trans and non-binary parents have indicated a shift away from static identities (of "mothers" and "fathers") towards a "doing" of parenthood (Bower-Brown, 2022). The lifegoals of George, to form a family as a parental couple, provided a strong foundation from which to embark upon the tumultuous "road" of pregnancy.

In our interview, it did not appear that George struggled to "inhabit the pregnant body" with regards to his identity as a transgender man. Coming off testosterone in order to conceive required him to dwell in uncertainty and was a difficult period. But, having made the adjustment, and then conceiving, George could state plainly that he was a man, he was going to birth, and that this would make him a father. Unlike the participants of MacDonald's (et al., 2016) study, George would not be in a position to nurse his infant after birth because of his mastectomy. However, the idea of nursing did not appear to disturb him, and he instead shared a sense of sadness and concern about formula feeding. George noted that this was not a regret and could not be traded for the comfort and happiness of his transition, but it was a part of parenthood he was anticipating ways to navigate. Where he raised other challenges of pregnancy, these closely corresponded with the materiality of pregnancy itself: the physical shifts, trimester by trimester, which are simply part of gestating a foetus.

In the clinical context, transgender people have identified a tendency of healthcare professionals to reduce their needs to gender alone, as if, for example, the common cold was instead a "trans cold" (Women and Equalities Committee, 2015). We have explored an account of "trans parenthood" and noted elements of the experience related to trans identity and medical transitioning. However, it is important to emphasise that, in George's transition to parenthood, when obstacles and concerns related to being transgender did arise, they mostly did so from sources external to his private life; for example in healthcare settings, in concerns about the acceptance of non-traditional family forms, and the pressure of 'breast being the best'. Where this stress arose, it existed alongside George's main preoccupations, which were the tribulations, as well as excitements and joyous anticipations, of starting a family.

Note

1 www.annafreud.org/research/current-research-projects/longitudinal-experiences-and-adjustments-in-parenthood-study-leaps/

References

Aguirre-Sánchez-Beato, S. (2018). Trans terminology and definitions in research on transphobia: A conceptual review. *Quaderns De Psicologia, 20*(3), 295–305.

Biggs, M. (2024). Gender identity in the 2021 census of England and Wales: How a flawed question created spurious data. *Sociology, 58*(6), 1305–1323.

Bower-Brown, S. (2022). Beyond Mum and Dad: Gendered assumptions about parenting and the experiences of trans and/or non-binary parents in the UK. *LGBTQ+ Family: An Interdisciplinary Journal, 18*(3), 223–240.

Charter, R., Ussher, J. M., Perz, J., & Robinson, K. H. (2023). Transgender men and pregnancy. In D. W. Riggs, J. M. Ussher, K. H. Robinson, & S. Rosenberg (Eds.), *Trans Reproductive and Sexual Health: Justice, Embodiment and Agency* (pp. 62–80). Abingdon, Oxon: Routledge.

Dierckx, M., Motmans, J., Mortelmans, D., & T'sjoen, G. (2015). Families in transition: A literature review. *International Review of Psychiatry, 28*(1), 36–43.

Light, A. D., Obedin-Maliver, J., Sevelius, J. M., & Kerns, J. L. (2014). Transgender men who experienced pregnancy after female-to-male gender transitioning. *Obstetrics & Gynecology, 124*(6), 1120–1127.

MacDonald, T., Noel-Weiss, J., West, D., Walks, M., Biener, M., Kibbe, A., & Myler, E. (2016). Transmasculine individual's experiences with lactation, chestfeeding, and gender identity: A qualitative study. *BMC Pregnancy and Childbirth, 16*(106). https://doi.org/10.1186/s12884-016-0907-y

Moseson, H., Fix, L., Hastings, J., Stoeffler, A., Lunn, M. R., Flentje, A., Lubensky, M. E., Capriotti, M. R., Ragosta, S., Forsberg, H., & Obedin-Maliver, J. (2021). Pregnancy intentions and outcomes among transgender, nonbinary, and gender-expansive people assigned female or intersex at birth in the United States: Results from a national, quantitative survey. *International Journal of Transgender Health, 22*(1–2), 30–41.

Office for National Statistics (ONS). (2024). Sexual orientation and gender identity quality information for Census 2021. *ONS website, methodology*. Updated 12 September 2024.

Riggs, D., Pfeffer, C., White, F. R., Hines, S., & Pearce, R. (2023). Young men, trans/masculine and non-binary people's views about pregnancy. In D. W. Riggs, J. M. Ussher, K. H. Robinson, & S. Rosenberg (Eds.), *Trans Reproductive and Sexual Health: Justice, Embodiment and Agency* (pp. 156–174). Abingdon, Oxon: Routledge.

Smith, J., Flowers, P., & Larkin, M. (2022). *Interpretative Phenomenological Analysis* (2nd ed.). London: Sage.

Stotzer, R., Herman, J., & Hasenbush, A. (2014). Transgender parenting: A review of existing research. *The Williams Institute*. Retrieved on 23 January 2023 from https://williamsinstitute.law.ucla.edu/publications/transgender-parenting/.

Tasker, F., & Gato, J. (2020). Gender identity and future thinking about parenthood: A qualitative analysis of focus group data with transgender and non-binary people in the United Kingdom. *Frontiers in Psychology, 11*(865). https://doi.org/10.3389/fpsyg.2020.00865

Women and Equalities Committee. (2015). Oral evidence: Transgender Equality Inquiry. 8 September 2015. HC 390.

Chapter 11

Pregnancy and the prenatal stage

A discussion

Alejandra Perez and Elena Panagiotopoulou

The chapters of this section explore physical and psychological changes that occur during pregnancy, focusing on a range of perspectives. In Chapter 7, Perez discusses prepartum bodily changes and their psychological impact through a psychoanalytic lens. She presents clinical work and refers to empirical research to emphasise how these changes require expectant mothers to navigate a constant shift between symbiosis and separation, with their experience influenced by early childhood experiences, current relationships, and physical state. Unconscious processes like projection, identification, and creative disavowal often emerge as defences against early anxieties and feelings of loss. In Chapter 8, Barba-Müller, explores neurobiological empirical research, particularly longitudinal neuroimaging studies, on prepartum changes, highlighting how pregnancy-induced brain plasticity supports maternal transition and newborn care, while increasing susceptibility to mental health issues. In Chapter 9, Panagiotopoulou and Preston, drawing on empirical quantitative and qualitative data, focus on the experience of the body, exploring how prepartum bodily changes affect body image, ownership, and awareness, and linking these changes to neural mechanisms and psychological vulnerability. In Chapter 10, Jones and Thackeray offer a socio-cultural perspective on pregnancy through a case study of a transgender father in his third trimester. Using Interpretative Phenomenological Analysis (IPA), they explore themes like identity formation, the ambiguous growth of the baby, and managing stress, emphasising that pregnancy should not be confined to traditional gender roles.

Medical interventions and social contact: The experience of intrusion on the pregnant body

During pregnancy, expectant parents must not only navigate their thoughts and feelings about their changing bodies, but they must also face external pressures. From routine medical interventions to societal expectations and public scrutiny, the pregnant body becomes a site of regulation and debate, something that some expectant parents find intrusive.

In their chapter, Panagiotopoulou and Preston explain that pregnant women must navigate not only their own expectations but also those imposed by others

DOI: 10.4324/9781003530473-14

regarding their body's appearance, such as an aspiration for a thin ideal, often rein-forced through social media platforms like Instagram. These external pressures can negatively impact body image and, in turn, mental health. Unsolicited comments, attention, and physical touch from family, friends, and even strangers can foster insecurity about a pregnant individual's appearance and contribute to feelings of exposure or objectification (Arellano et al., 2025; Johnson et al., 2004). Importantly, Panagiotopoulou and Preston suggest that this public scrutiny of the pregnant body also leads to a loss of autonomy and control over their body. Yet this experience is not exclusive to women. Social expectations and cultural norms related to one's sex assigned at birth create unique barriers to reproductive autonomy for transgender individuals (Riggs et al., 2023), affecting their capacity to make decisions about parenthood.

Another form of intrusion can be experienced in healthcare settings. Panagiotopoulou and Preston explain that, while medical oversight is essential for ensuring maternal and foetal health, regular check-ups and interventions can some-times subject women's bodies to medical scrutiny and override personal autonomy. Pregnant individuals may feel that medical professionals have more control over their bodies than they do themselves. Negative interactions with healthcare profes-sionals are also described by the transgender father in Jones and Thackeray's case study in Chapter 10, with staff cancelling appointments and seeking clarification as they could not readily understand why a man was booking medical appointments for his pregnancy.

On the whole, this experience of intrusion seems multifactorial, stemming from both an internal loss of control and an external shift in others' responses to the pregnant body. While not universal—since some expectant parents find support and reassurance in medical interventions and social contact—others can feel pres-sured, with this negatively shaping both their pregnancy experience and percep-tion of themselves. This challenge can affect all pregnant individuals, including transgender people, who face additional social and cultural barriers. For these rea-sons, some expectant parents withdraw to feel protected from external contact. As Jones and Thackeray highlight, the intersection of medicine and social influ-ence brings forward crucial questions about bodily autonomy, consent, and the balance between care and control. Raising public awareness of the profound impact of social pressures on pregnant people's experiences and their ability to adjust to pregnancy-related bodily changes is, therefore, crucial.

Reconciling the changing pregnant body with one's internal world

In addition to the challenges that pregnant people experience in connection with the outside world, many also have to navigate their changing body in relation to their internal world, a world that may be largely unconscious, and from which fears, anx-ieties, and wishes may emerge or reawaken. The chapter by Perez draws attention to how some of the rapid bodily changes during pregnancy resemble illness, and so expectant parents are faced with the challenge of forming a mental representation of themselves and their baby as healthy, while having the experience of being unwell. Panagiotopoulou and Preston's chapter offers a neuroscientific perspective, as the authors describe the demands that these rapid bodily changes place on a pregnant person's neural processing. Instead of the brain naturally adjusting when one's bodily experiences differ from those that had been expected, the sheer quantity of major bodily changes occurring concurrently leads to a high rate of prediction error. Moreover, the pregnant person's brain has the difficult task of disentangling bodily information crucial for the growing foetus' survival from more unreliable signals (such as the natural increase in rapid heartbeats during pregnancy). The chapter by Jones and Thackeray, describes the additional challenge for George, as a transgender man having to stop testosterone therapy for the duration of pregnancy.

The chapter by Barba-Müller explains how internally-focused thought processes—daydreaming, self-reflection, mind-wandering, autobiographical memory, mental exploration of future situations, self-reflection, and remembering the past—become more dominant through the reshaping of a set of brain regions known as the Default Mode Network (DMN). Perez brings clinical material to exemplify how some of these forms of internally-oriented thinking are intensely present in expectant parents. All these chapters demonstrate how bodily changes during pregnancy become psychically demanding. In particular, Perez explores how remembered and unremembered (unconscious) early experiences and conscious imaginings and unconscious phantasies play an important part in how pregnant bodily changes are experienced. While some expectant mothers can celebrate the changes in their bodies, which allow them to accommodate a new human being, others may experience fear or disturbance. Panagiotopoulou and Preston point to conflicting findings in the research examining body image in pregnant women and go on to highlight the methodological limitations of these studies. An additional factor in these conflicting findings may also relate to unconscious phantasies surrounding the pregnant body. Perez describes how the experience of having a body inside one's body can bring back positive early experiences of symbiosis and togetherness for a pregnant woman, yet might also arouse claustrophobic anxieties, or awaken fears of being invaded from within.

The beginning of a new developmental stage and a changing identity

The changes that occur during pregnancy are quite extensive and not limited to the body. Expectant parents go through emotional, psychological, social, and relationship transformations, some of which are temporary, circumscribed by the duration of the pregnancy, while others constitute lifelong changes. Together with conception, pregnancy forms the beginning of a new stage in life: parenthood. Pregnancy is an opportunity to work through internal relationships and conflicts, to revisit one's own identity and sense of self and others, and then to assimilate the changes of this new stage in life.

The chapter by Perez describes how pregnancy, for some women, may become associated with early unconscious wishes to identify with a creative mother and, thus, to feel that they have something valuable inside them (Deutsch, 1933). Pregnancy may also be associated with a wish to maintain a sense of continuity of the self, acting as a link between one's past as a daughter or son, to one's present as a pregnant woman or expectant partner, and future as a parent (Kullish, 2011). Early experiences, and how these were internalised, can also have a great impact on the expectant parents' development of their identity as parents, as in the clinical cases of Tom and Alicia described by Perez in Chapter 1. At a brain level, Barba-Müller explains how the reshaping of the brain region DMN during pregnancy also enables the development of a new identity by activating states of self-reflection, and by integrating experiences of external events within the context of prior internal information. The bodily experience is also relevant: as Panagiotopoulou and Preston state in their chapter, experiences in the body can affect both a woman's identity and her future relationship with her child. In their chapter, Thackeray and Jones cite a focus group study of pregnant transgender men (Riggs et al., 2023), where the men reported that cultural norms were at odds with their identity as fathers. A similar viewpoint was described by George who explained that his own life experience and not cultural norms helped develop his identity as a father and form his beliefs and intentions around happiness and raising his future child.

In psychoanalytic literature, pregnancy has also been described as an important point in a woman's lifelong process of separation and individuation from her own mother, in the sense that a woman stops being only a daughter and now becomes a mother herself (Pines, 1982). This transition period is also paradoxical in the sense that a woman may be separating from own mother, yet also, at times, is psychically growing closer to her through identifying with her, and by sharing a body symbiotically with a foetus. This makes for an emotionally very intense period for the pregnant woman.

The physical and mental adjustments involved in preparing for the baby

The significant physical and emotional changes that occur during pregnancy are thought to help prepare the pregnant woman for motherhood. Barba-Müller's (2015) groundbreaking research demonstrated that pregnancy leads to long-lasting structural changes in the female human brain, specifically in regions of the brain enlisted to perform theory of mind tasks (such as the cognitive ability to infer the thoughts, feelings, and intentions of others). Pregnancy brain changes have also been associated with the mother's responsiveness to her own and her baby's cues, with bonding and nesting behaviour, and with predicted post-partum mother-infant attachment. In their chapter, Panagiotopoulou and Preston present research into how pregnant women prioritise their body's functionality and their baby's health over their own appearance.

Winnicott's (1956) concept of 'primary maternal preoccupation' explains the expectant mother's mental state at a more unconscious level. He explained the highly developed capacity of the pregnant woman to identify almost symbiotically with her growing baby's needs. However, we are increasingly aware of just how diverse people's experiences of pregnancy are. The chapter by Perez presents clinical work with several women who endured panic triggered by prolonged physical pain and/or illness during a first pregnancy, and who, during their second pregnancy, cut off from consciously thinking about their unborn baby. Perez describes this as an unconscious defence mechanism—what she terms 'creative disavowal'—aimed at forming an in-between mental state capable of protecting the baby from the violent, painful bodily experiences and the resulting primitive anxieties and hatred that these expectant mothers felt. Freud (1936) had a developmental view of defence mechanisms, in which the use of a given mechanism could be age-appropriate at a certain stage of development, but of concern at another. As pregnancy is the beginning of a new stage of development, associated with heightened emotions and intense bodily changes (including brain changes), as well as various socio-economic implications for the pregnant person, it should be expected that some expectant parents will return to different or earlier defence mechanisms. While these chapters describe the various changes precipitated by pregnancy, they also indicate the wide range of experiences that pregnant people can have.

Pregnancy as a period of mental health vulnerability

While awareness of postpartum depression and anxiety has been increasing, less emphasis is placed on psychological struggles during pregnancy. Drawing from different perspectives, all chapters explore why pregnancy is a time of heightened mental health vulnerability, shaped by a mix of psychological, hormonal, neurological, and socio-cultural factors.

Perez explains that pregnancy brings deep uncertainties about the foetus' survival, the process of birth, and the realities of parenthood. Some expectant parents find these uncertainties stressful, where early and unconscious anxieties come to fill this void. In line with this, the participant of Jones and Thackeray's case study, George, described how difficult he found to endure the uncertainty during pregnancy, breaking out as catastrophic anxiety. Reflecting on psychoanalytic clinical work, Perez notes that while many expectant mothers process these fears and anxieties as part of a normal process of accommodating an 'unknown other' within them, others become more psychically destabilised. In these more concerning cases, the pregnant women cope, some by projecting destructive internal forces onto the baby and avoiding it or meeting it with hostility (Schumacher, 2008), while others by projecting the badness to the external world, and becoming detached and depressed, or anxious and overbearing.

Stressors originating in the outside world are also identified in this section. Panagiotopoulou and Preston discuss how societal ideals and expectations—such as pressure to compare appearance—can lead to negative experiences of the prepartum body, which are linked to maternal depression (e.g., Silveira et al., 2015). Negative interactions with healthcare professionals can contribute to feelings of isolation during pregnancy, which Jones and Thackeray identify as a significant risk factor for postnatal depression.

From a neurobiological perspective, while the neurobiological changes during pregnancy facilitate the maternal transition and support the development of key processes essential for caring for the newborn, Barba-Müller explains that the significant hormonal changes imply a heightened vulnerability in terms of mental health and emotional balance. Moreover, Panagiotopoulou and Preston describe how predictive theories of neural processing can explain increased vulnerabilities to mental well-being, due to failure to resolve discrepancies between expected and actual body states, thus leading to thoughts and behaviours linked to mental health issues (Paulus & Stein, 2006).

The mental health challenges discussed in this section can have profound effects not only on mothers and fathers but also on their children. With babies highly sensitive to their parents' emotions, the perinatal period becomes a crucial window for identifying and supporting at-risk expectant parents.

References

Arellano, A., Roberts, R., Perez, A., & Panagiotopoulou, E. (2025). *External and internal influences on prepartum body image: A qualitative study*. [Preprint]. Research Square.

Barba-Müller, E. (2015). *Morphologic brain changes induced by pregnancy. A longitudinal magnetic resonance imaging study* [Ph.D. Thesis]. Universitat Autònoma de Barcelona.

Deutsch, H. (1933). Motherhood and sexuality. *Psychoanalytic Quarterly, 2*, 476–48.

Freud, A. (1936) [1992]. *The ego and the mechanisms of defence*. London: Routledge.

Johnson, S., Burrows, A., & Williamson, I. (2004). 'Does my bump look big in this?' The meaning of bodily changes for first-time mothers-to-be. *Journal of Health Psychology, 9*(3), 361–374.

Kulish, N. (2011). On childlessness. *Psychoanalytic Inquiry, 31*, 350–365.

Paulus, M. P., & Stein, M. B. (2006). An insular view of anxiety. *Biological Psychiatry, 60*(4), 383–387.

Pines, D. (1982). The relevance of early psychic development to pregnancy and abortion. *The International Journal of Psychoanalysis, 63*, 311–319.

Riggs, D., Pfeffer, C., White, F. R., Hines, S., & Pearce, R. (2023). Men, trans/masculine and non-binary people's views about pregnancy. In Riggs, D., Ussher, J.M., Robinson, K.H. & Rosenberg, S. (Eds.), *Trans reproductive and sexual health: Justice, embodiment and agency* (pp. 156–174). Abingdon, Oxon: Routledge.

Schumacher, B. (2008). "I can't live without my child": Motherhood as a "solution" to early trauma. *British Journal of Psychotherapy, 24*, 317–327.

Silveira, M. L., Ertel, K. A., Dole, N., & Chasan-Taber, L. (2015). The role of body image in prenatal and postpartum depression: A critical review of the literature. *Archives of Women's Mental Health, 18*(3), 409–421.

Winnicott, D. W. (1956) [1975]. Chapter XXIV. Primary maternal preoccupation. *Through Paediatrics to Psycho-Analysis (International Psycho-Analytical Library* (No. 100, pp. 300–305). London: Hogarth Press & Institute of Psycho-Analysis.

Part III

Birth

Chapter 12

Hopes, fears, and change during birth

Alejandra Perez

Birth marks the beginning of a baby's life in the world outside its mother's body; it is the definitive physical separation of the baby from the mother. Psychoanalytically, separating from and uniting with our mother/primary caregiver (and our unconscious internal object or caregiver) are thought of as a continual, ongoing process that forms part of the development of our minds and personalities. For the baby, the mother/caregiver is essential to their physical, mental, and emotional life, and to the fulfilment of their various needs. However, the separation from mother/caregiver stimulates the baby's development of a memory or mnemic image of her, as a way of coping with her absence. This mnemic image, or memory, enables the baby to wait for her return, and it also generates feelings of desire. The baby's internal world slowly grows to include not only basic needs being met or unmet, but also feelings towards the other, imagination, the beginnings of symbolisation, and unconscious phantasies (for further discussion on the internal world see Chapter 25). For many parents, the opposite direction of force comes into play, where the birth of their baby begins the getting to know their baby, separate and distinct from the fantasies (conscious and unconscious) and expectations of their imagined baby.

Experiences of birth vary widely, but labour always entails risk. Most birth complications (such as perinatal tears, a labour that does not progress, an abnormal heartbeat in the baby, perinatal asphyxia, or excessive bleeding in the mother) are treatable with medical interventions, but can be fatal without them. For example, 95% of maternal deaths occur in low- and lower-middle-income countries, indicating the impact of the inequality of access to high-quality healthcare (WHO, 2020). Neonatal mortality, meanwhile, accounts for 53.1% of deaths of children under five years old in low- and middle-income countries, demonstrating just how vulnerable newborn babies are (Li et al., 2021). It is not surprising, then, that childbirth can stir up difficult emotions for some expectant parents, including a fear of the mother and/or baby dying or being harmed, a sense of lack of control, and anxieties surrounding the need for—versus the availability of—external help during labour.

After birth, the baby continues to grow and develop, now greatly supported by continual interactions with parents and others. For the parents, birth entails an

DOI: 10.4324/9781003530473-16

intensification of the care that they must provide to ensure their baby's survival. Parents are therefore faced with their infant's fragility and complete dependence on them. They must also become acquainted with their baby's individual needs and preverbal forms of communication. Importantly, after birth parents are constantly confronted with their 'real' baby, which inevitably will differ in many ways from the 'imagined' baby in their minds.

My own interest in working clinically with parents and babies, as well as in conducting research in this area, began with my psychoanalytic work with people who became parents in the course of their analysis. Each of these individuals had their own unique experience of pregnancy and childbirth, coloured by many different factors, yet for most of them it was an intensely emotional and, at times, turbulent period. However, many of their difficulties—which were rooted in deep, unconscious conflicts or preverbal experiences that had provoked rigid defences— became more amenable to exploration, and their defences grew more flexible, as they became parents. In psychoanalysis, the view is that unconscious phantasies and experiences with the 'real' other are always at play. I think that the ongoing encounter with the 'real' baby, interacting with the parents' powerful, pervasive unconscious phantasies and past experiences, is what helped them to move toward psychic change.

Birth: Separation and continuity of being

In terms of the baby's experience of being born, psychoanalysis was the first field to speculate on babies' subjective experiences. Moreover, it asserted the importance of these experiences in the child's socio-emotional development, as well as the importance of the baby's experience of birth in the development of the mind. Freud (1926) posited a continuity from intrauterine life to post-birth, yet that birth also constituted an "impressive caesura" and so the first experience of anxiety. Bion (1977) focused on the continuity and connection between prenatal and postnatal life (birth being the first of many caesuras; demarcations of inner and outer reality; past, present, and future; life and death). The baby, when born, might find the outside world overwhelming and too complex to make sense of. This may give the baby a feeling akin to death and annihilation, until some relief can be found in the processing of these raw and intense experiences through the help of another (parent/caregiver) (see Chapter 31 for a further description of this process of regulation). Similarly, Winnicott (1949) believed that the caregiver environment was essential in helping the baby with the (over)stimulating experience of now being in the external world. Winnicott's focus, however, was not so much on babies making sense of the world, but on them being able to have continuity of being. Without an adequate caregiver environment, the baby's focus is skewed greatly toward adapting and surviving, which is disruptive to the baby's development of self (and thus results in the creation of a false self). In this sense, birth also marks this particular process, where the parent can allow or hinder this development and continuity of being.

For the mother, birth is also an important caesura at a physical, emotional, and mental level, and can be experienced as traumatic (see Chapter 13 for further discussion on traumatic births). Similarly to the baby's experience, the ongoing separations and coming-together of parents and baby form an essential part in the development of parental life. Many times, a parent's difficulty in being able to embrace the separations and continuities of parenthood are rooted in early experiences and/or unconscious phantasies about separation from their own primary or internal caregiver. Several psychoanalysts have noted the conflicting feelings that women may experience during childbirth: fears about their bodies being violently ruptured, broken, and destroyed by the baby's arrival, as well as tenderness when confronted with an entirely dependent infant (Kristeva, 2014).

Birth stories: Expectations, hopes, and fears

The intense physical experience of birth, like pregnancy, creates a similarly intense psychological demand to integrate these various experiences (Kristeva, 2014; Pines, 1990; Balsam and Harris, 2012). Some parents' conflicting feelings about birth—this combined separation from and meeting with their baby—can be seen in some of their expectations, conscious and unconscious phantasies, hopes, and fears. The stories that a parent has heard of their own birth (their 'birth story') can symbolise their inter-psychic experiences and conflicts (Dobrich, 2022). These can also, at times, reflect their unconscious fears about their baby's birth and the future. Birth stories often reflect a struggle with life under the threat of death.

In terms of more conscious expectations, a previous qualitative longitudinal study of ten first-time mothers, followed from the third trimester of pregnancy to the end of their babies' first year of life (Perez et al., 2025), found that most mothers had many strong expectations about pregnancy and childbirth, and that they were disappointed by their actual experiences. Overall, in this low-risk sample, most mothers' parenting confidence improved with time, as did their relationship with their baby. However, two mothers who had felt very confident during pregnancy lost all their confidence after going through a difficult birth. The findings from this study indicated the complexity of the emotional recovery for mothers who experience a traumatic or difficult birth, and showed that this recovery involves two different elements: recovery from the frightening experience of birth, and grief and mourning for former expectations about birth and becoming a parent. Most mothers in this study anticipated and prepared for difficulties, and those who found the experience easier were those who did not plan too rigidly for upcoming problems and took them more 'in their stride', thus recognising the uncertainty of birth, the ever-changing nature of parenthood, and the individuality of their baby. Similarly, a study by Borelli and colleagues (2018) looked at expectant mothers' coping strategies for childbirth, and found that they highlighted the importance of being flexible regarding birth plans and in anticipation of unforeseen events, since birth entails so much uncertainty.

Change: The arrival of a third

The birth of a baby is not only a separation of mother-foetus, it also marks the arrival of a third person into the parents' lives, and the formation of a new family configuration. Freud's (1897) formulation of the Oedipus complex introduced the conflicting thoughts and feelings that can arise from the awareness of a third, as well as the developmental importance of such conflict. It is beyond the scope of this chapter to explain and discuss the context and psychoanalytic concepts of sexuality, the dynamic unconscious, the system unconscious that are necessary to understand Freud's theory. Instead, I will limit myself to describing their relevance to understanding some parents' experiences when having a baby. One simple aspect of birth is that it changes a dyad into a triad. There are various family configurations, and the terms 'dyad', 'triad', and 'third' should not be understood as indicating solely the number of people involved, but rather the type of relationship that exists. A dyad, in this sense, can describe parents in a couple; co-parents; a single parent and their 'adult' world (either externally, as friends, family, and colleagues, or internally in the mind, i.e. the relationship one has with work, or our self-image in the world); or, the dyadic relationship a parent has with their 'imagined' baby, and so on. The value of the dyad is that it allows an immersion; that is, a particular intensity of feeling that can develop and be properly felt and understood, as it is experienced in what is felt to be a safe place, kept separate from more distant 'others'. Meanwhile, the value of triadic relationships is that they enable a separation from this intense dyad, allowing one to see the complexities and wider context of where each individual—and the dyad—sits. The triad thus supports the development of a more reflective capacity. Again, a 'third' should not only be understood as one particular person, but as another type of relationship through which one becomes aware of 'an-other' having a place adjoining or added to the dyad. This can be: the baby joining the parental couple dyad; the father joining the mother-baby dyad (and vice-versa, and including co-parents, same-sex parents, etc.); the 'real' baby joining the parent and 'imagined' baby dyad, and so on. Most of us move through and fluctuate between various dyadic and triadic relationships, both externally with others and internally in our minds, throughout the course of our lives.

Freud (1897) posited the developmental importance for the child of becoming aware of the relationship between the parents. Britton (1989) explains that, when the infant becomes aware of even the possibility of the mother's relationship with another, the infant realises that this relationship excludes him or her. However, this awareness also allows the baby to experience him- or herself as an observer, and as being observed, fostering self-reflection and creating a new psychic space, which Britton terms 'triangular space', or a third position.

In a similar way, the arrival of the baby can also permit the birth of a third position in the parents' minds. On one hand, the baby begins to form an individual dyadic relationship with each parent (in the case of a two-parent family), with the third 'other' taking the observer position. On the other hand, the parent is also now aware of the real baby, which invites reflection and consideration from the known dyad of parent and their imagined baby. These experiences of a third are developmentally important for the parent, but can also bring up or reawaken intense feelings of exclusion, fear, and anger (and subsequent guilt). The recognition and acceptance of the baby's individuality and difference—as a third—can also leave parents feeling the loss of an idealised, imagined baby; an idea and ideal that will need to be mourned. Becoming aware of these conflicting feelings can allow for a more complex picture of their baby and of parenthood, and, in this way, can allow a movement towards psychic flexibility and change.

Clinical vignette: Meeting baby

John and Sophie were in their third trimester, expecting their firstborn son, when they came to parent-infant psychotherapy. They felt anxious following an ultrasound scan to check the baby's growth. Despite the doctors' reassurances that the baby was developing normally, they remained preoccupied about the birth and their baby's survival. Sophie had heard many stories from friends about possible birth complications, and she spent many sleepless nights terrified by the prospect of labour. She had frightening dreams of their baby dying at birth, which John found so disturbing and unbearable to hear that he asked her to stop telling him about them. In the sessions, they both talked about feeling that their fears were irrational, yet they could not stop worrying. John then spoke about his birth story, as had been told to him by his mother when he was a young adolescent, and which he had not spoken about since. John was one of two identical twins. His twin brother died at birth, and John was told that, while his parents had been very sad about losing his brother, they were very happy to see John so strong and happy. John never talked about his birth again, as he felt conflicted when thinking about it. His birth felt like a profound split, where his life, strength, and happiness came at the expense of the tragic death and loss of his twin brother. He had begun to imagine his unborn baby as he had imagined his brother—small, fragile, and dead. He had also begun to fear that Sophie was not strong enough for labour, and she shared similar fears—they both felt that their baby's birth was surrounded by death. Despite their fears and a long labour, the arrival of their baby was without complications. John then described his surprise at holding his baby for the first time: his baby looked, felt, moved, and sounded different from how he had imagined him. This moment crystallised how fixed his mental image of a weak, dead baby had been. John was now struck by a new fear, born of the feeling that this baby was a stranger to him. However, John experienced this fear as a much more manageable one, and he felt able now to get to know his son.

References

Balsam, R.H., & Harris, A. (2012). Maternal embodiment: A conversation between Rosemary Balsam and Adrienne Harris. *Studies in Gender & Sexuality*, 13:33–52.

Bion, W. R. (1977). *Two papers: The grid and caesura*. London: Karnac.

Borelli, S.E., Walsh, D., & Spiby, H. (2018). First-time mothers' expectations of the unknown territory of childbirth: Uncertainties, coping strategies and 'going with the flow'. *Midwifery*, 63:39–45.

Britton, R. (1989). The missing link: Parental sexuality in the Oedipus complex. In R. Britton, M. Feldman, & E. O'Shaughnessy (Eds.), *The Oedipus complex today: Clinical implications* (pp. 83–101). London, England: Karnac.

Dobrich, J. (2022). The creative use of birth stories in psychoanalytic treatments. *Psychoanalytic Social Work*, 29:109–122.

Freud, S. (1897). Letter 71: Extracts from the Fliess papers. In J. Strachey (Ed. & Trans.), The Standard Edition of the Complete Psychological Works of Sigmund Freud, 1:263–266). London: Vintage, The Hogarth Press.

Freud, S. (1926). Inhibitions, symptoms and anxiety. In J. Strachey (Ed. & Trans.), The Standard Edition of the Complete Psychological Works of Sigmund Freud, 20:75–176. London: Vintage, The Hogarth Press.

Kristeva, J. (2014). Reliance, or maternal eroticism. *Journal of the American Psychoanalytic Association*, 62(1):69–85.

Li, Z., Karlsson, O., Kim, R. & Subramanian, S.V. (2021). Distribution of under-5 deaths in the neonatal, postneonatal, and childhood periods: A multicountry analysis in 64 low- and middle-income countries. *International Journal for Equity in Health*, 20:109.

Perez, A., Panagiotopoulou, E., Vourda, M.C., Pereira, M., McCrory, E. & Roberts, R. (2025, July). Trajectories of change in mothers' parenting confidence and relationship with baby: A 15-month qualitative longitudinal study. *BMC Pregnancy Childbirth*. 25(1):709. https://doi.org/10.1186/s12884-025-07683-0.

Pines, D. (1990). Pregnancy, miscarriage and abortion. A psychoanalytic perspective. *The International Journal of Psychoanalysis*, 71:301–307.

Winnicott, D. W. (1975) [1975]. Chapter XIV. Birth memories, birth trauma, and anxiety. *Through Paediatrics to Psycho-Analysis (International Psycho-Analytical Library)* No. 100, pp. 174–193. London: Hogarth Press & Institute of Psycho-Analysis.

World Health Organization (WHO) (2020). Available at: www.who.int/news-room/fact-she ets/detail/maternal-mortality

Chapter 13

Traumatic births

Claudia Goulder

Introduction

Where does a difficult birth end and trauma begin? Thinking of my own births, I see how nuanced and subjective the experience is: the delivery that appeared more complicated, involving a brightly lit operating theatre, higher statistical risk, and a raft of medics on standby (it was twins), felt less traumatic than the first, an objectively more straightforward affair.

If we look at the research, around a third of women report experiencing psychological trauma during birth (Alcorn et al., 2010; Soet et al., 2003). This has often been associated with medical intervention and has been defined as a perception of 'actual or threatened injury or death to the mother or her baby' (Beck, 2010). However, the same author argues that the perception of trauma is in the 'eye of the beholder' (Beck, 2004) and must be defined by the woman experiencing it.

Qualitative studies exploring 'traumatic births' identify interactions with care providers as a more important factor than medical intervention or type of birth. A perceived lack of control and involvement in decision-making, for instance, can be crucial to the experience of trauma versus something more ordinary, more digestible. Women will often describe feeling disconnected, helpless, and isolated during a birth that comes to be regarded as traumatic.

While not all traumatic birth experiences result in post-traumatic stress disorder (PTSD, the diagnostic label for a chronic, ongoing mental condition linked to trauma), research indicates that negative care provider interactions are a significant risk factor (James, 2015). Yet, while more policies and procedures are implemented and there is an increasing number of bodies set up to look at failing services (Maternity Matters, 2007; NICE, 2010), there is a rising rate of medical interventions (e.g., induced labour and c-sections) and falling rate of 'spontaneous' births in this country). Maternity services and staff within them can be found to defend rather than think about the work they do (Obholzer and Roberts, 1994) and need to be encouraged and supported to do so, so that the containers can be contained.

DOI: 10.4324/9781003530473-17

Working with pre- and postnatal couples in the community

The charity Pregnant In West London was founded amid a scarcity of affordable birth-preparation education, offering free antenatal classes for expectant mothers and fathers in the community. Those who attend are socially and culturally diverse with a high proportion originally from countries outside of the UK. With English as a second language and less familiarity with the overall 'system', there is often more scope for frightening experiences of powerlessness and overwhelm during childbirth.

Midwives in the local area encourage women and their partners to attend in the second or third trimester. Classes cover subjects including labour, birth nutrition, mental health, first aid, pain relief, and coming home with baby. Their aim is to empower young women and their partners through education about the birthing process and beyond, giving them ownership and confidence to make informed choices and to ask questions they may not otherwise have thought to.

My role has been to lead sessions on mental health, encouraging emotional preparation for the birth and postpartum period. Among its challenges has been to know how to best prepare people for something that is, ultimately, not possible to fully prepare for. I try to educate but also make space for couples to voice their concerns, hopes, phantasies, fears, and explore their inner worlds together, in the hopes they can continue to do this beyond the groups. An important element is to help people come to terms with the possibility of things not going to plan.

In this chapter, I will draw more on my work with the postnatal classes, termed 'birth reflections'. These have been running intermittently for four years. They are for new mums, dads, and babies to come together and think about their recent experience; the move from pregnancy to parenthood, the birth itself, and the recovery period, which is also a period of adjustment to a new sort of life—life with a baby outside the womb.

Aspects of trauma in birth

In my previous job in an NHS hospital, it was broadly assumed that a traumatic delivery was one where there was a medical emergency: an emergency c-section, haemorrhaging during the pre- or post-partum period, or significant tear, for instance. The baby could have been physically damaged during the delivery or the survival of either mother or child become uncertain. In these cases, a 'birth debrief' might have been offered by a member of the midwifery team, an opportunity to go through the ordeal with someone else, to make sense of what happened, awful as it may have been, and perhaps (hopefully) make space in the mind for the new baby. Unfortunately, this service, once open to anyone no matter how the birth was 'on paper', has been significantly cut.

Referrals of women to the perinatal mental health service, where I worked as a psychotherapist, were usually when things had become chronic and there was a serious risk for baby and parent. Women who were referred with symptoms of postnatal depression, psychosis, anxiety, insomnia, PTSD, intrusive thoughts, and others, often ended up speaking of births that were not necessarily obviously traumatic, but had left an indelible mark on them, contributing to the deterioration of their mental health. Experience, even the dramatic one of giving birth, is something we would hope can be digested over time, eventually woven into the tapestry of one's life. Trauma, however, can leave a vacuum where the ordinary working through of events is possible. Just as a physical trauma might leave a body part isolated, temporarily or not, from the overall system because of an actual severing, a psychological trauma can see the mental system, whose function is usually to cope with and manage experiences (big and small), become overwhelmed. Many I have worked with felt their trauma as a failure in care, hospital staff seeming overly controlling or adding to panic instead of allaying it, overzealous monitoring, rigid reactions to things not being 'straightforward'. This often chimed with a pre-existing early experience, for instance, of being a 'difficult' or 'nuisance' baby in an environment where there was no space or time for this; a wound from an earlier time was effectively reopened.

The child psychotherapist and former midwife Louise McNally O'Higgins (2011) writes how the "emotional drivers for (some) midwives may include the wish to control distress and eliminate suffering, influenced in turn by their need to remain in control and in charge. This group struggles with uncertainty and tries to be logical and detached". This is far more likely when midwives themselves are not given enough support or are put under too much pressure, within a dysfunctional or defensively driven system. These things can replicate earlier experiences, putting a poor experience of lack of care into a whole different category.

Many women who attend the community group are pleased to be able to speak about their experience—good or bad. They may not have recognised the part their birth played on subsequent difficulties, such as feeding issues, or lack of capacity to take pleasure in things, and are usually interested in how their own pasts and perceptions of things could link with the experience. Making this connection is often a first step to feeling more real, more alive—to their baby, their partner, and to themselves. One woman, in her late 20s, came amid difficulties bonding with her baby. She said she did not have a "terrible" delivery—"the medical staff did what they had to do to get her (baby) out safely" (a 'category 2 caesarean section' was performed after what is known as a 'failure to progress' in labour, causing concern for the health of mother and baby) —but it was as if the whole thing happened 'to' her. She felt unsafe, there were decisions made she did not feel a part of, an attempt to insert a cannula into a vein she had told them was no good, but they did anyway, then talk by hospital staff of using a general anaesthetic versus regional, as if she were not there. She spoke out, emboldened (she said) by what she had been told in the antenatal classes, saying she would like to be awake if she could in surgery, to be a part of the birth of her baby. This is, thankfully, what happened. Yet still a troubling sense of disempowerment and detachment had been left in both parents. She says she was unable to feel much when she was handed her baby. "I just didn't know what was going on. I couldn't feel any of it was mine." When she had difficulty feeding while still in hospital she was given a bottle of formula, which — while helping alleviate guilt and panic in the short term—she wondered added to the sense of failure in the longer term.

Another new mother described being tormented by a thought that had lodged in her mind. It centred upon the foetal scalp electrode (sometimes called a clip) they attached to her baby's scalp through her vagina, during a prolonged labour, which could then pick up the heartbeat. She felt every time the baby cried out or woke from sleep in distress in subsequent weeks, he was remembering the pain of this 'clip' piercing his skin. We can see this as a remnant of a trauma. The insertion of the device had been one thing on top of many that had felt overwhelming and alarming, after many hours in labour, with a midwife who gave the impression of impatience and dissatisfaction with the job.

During labour, a woman is in her most primitive state and needs strong emotional containment to feel safe enough to ride the contractions and keep pushing. She might need reminding, for instance, that it is an alive baby that she is going to meet shortly. Midwives find themselves doing this because otherwise the process can very quickly become something detached and isolated—a horrific experience of pain, which can feel closer to deadliness than to bringing new life into the world. The real separate baby can be forgotten and the mother, particularly when under pressure or in a state of panic, can feel as if she has been told to push something out that is already either dead or best kept inside. This can add to the sense of trauma, because she is in effect torn in two. At this point in labour the fear will either be recognised and responded to by a midwife, who might (in more favourable circumstances) work to look after the mother more closely, tapping in to what she is capable of and what she is doing this for (e.g., She is strong, creative, with good things inside her and in store. If she continues to push, she will not die or cause death, she is doing what she is supposed to even if it feels painful and frightening right now), or left to increase. This is a pivotal moment, often recounted by mothers and fathers, where things can turn a corner or descend. If fear escalates it has a paralysing effect on the body. As seen in nature when an animal feels threatened or disturbed, the stress hormone catecholamine shuts down labour. Similarly, when a labouring woman does not feel safe or protected or when the progress of her normal labour is altered, catecholamine levels rise and labour slows down or stops (Lothian, 2004). The need for further medical intervention, either an epidural, or assistance in delivery with forceps or ventouse, or surgical intervention (c-section), then increases.

Truth as antidote to trauma

In psychoanalytic terms there is always a conflict between seeking truth and guarding against it: we have two motivational categories, one determined by desire for pleasure and avoidance of pain, one determined by the emergence of truth and desire for emotional growth. My belief is all can be helped to have these truths recognised, and they serve as an antidote to the defensive traumatised mind—nourishment for parents as milk is to the child. Such 'truths' can be:

1   The baby has been created by mother and father, but is crucially a part of mother. There is a real difference in their experiences from conception and this must be recognised by both. The baby comes between them. They are separated by it, partly because their experience and relationship to it is different from the start. Can each member of a couple remain interested in what the other is going through?
2   There is, we can imagine, a part of the mother that feels it is wrong to push her baby out. Some women feel this more consciously than others and can continue to feel guilty for ejecting their baby, for a long time after. This must be acknowledged. Guilt and shame, dread and persecution do not belong solely to the traumatised. These are important facets of all individuals, requiring attention just like love and creativity.
3   Birth is an earth-shattering separation—separation of mother from baby. Baby from mother. As with all developmental steps these lines are painful, difficult, and stimulating of powerful defensive mechanisms—holding on at all costs, for instance. The baby also represents separation of the couple as they know themselves to be, a dyad.

There is often attention on the see-saw of love and hate that exists in feelings towards the baby and one another. By making these ideas more accessible in people's minds, and between couples, it seems they are freer to access these paradoxes internally and to reach some of these ideas and feel able to share them with one another.

I will give one final example of how the interplay of past and present, internal and external reality, profoundly influences the perception of a birth and level of trauma associated. A woman in her early thirties described her birth experience as a "car crash"; the birth centre she and her partner had expected to be under the care of had been full the night she went into spontaneous labour, and she had been sent to a different ward where the emphasis was not on natural, unassisted delivery and midwife-led care. It was a busy ward with no option for water birth. The midwife they had was perceived as cold and detached. The 36-hour labour ended in an epidural (injection of medication in the back that numbs spinal nerves and blocks pain signals to the brain), ventouse (assisted) delivery, and significant tear. She and the baby had survived, but to her and the father it felt like a disaster. The mother could not sleep at night, even though the baby slept well in proceeding weeks. Over time it emerged that her chaotic childhood meant she had frequently been left, literally holding baby siblings and caring for others, as a child, and at night, when her parents would be unavailable, she remembered feeling very scared. She associated to this in the group and realised that panicked feeling had returned the instant the birth centre had not answered the doorbell and they had been sent to the unfamiliar labour ward. Letting go into sleep seemed to be associated with a 'letting go' into something terrifying. Talking of this, many in the group nodded along, as it seemed that, although her experience was extreme, they could identify with this idea.

There seems to be great power in offering a space to new parents to face this together. Whatever the true experience of birth, it is my strong belief it deserves our fullest attention and we can help people process their own stories through giving them a chance to speak but also listen to others.

References

Alcorn KL, O'Donovan A, Patrick JC, Creedy D, Devilly GJ. (2010). A prospective longitudinal study of the prevalence of post-traumatic stress disorder resulting from childbirth events. *Psychol Med*, 40:1849–59.

Beck CT. (2004). Birth trauma: In the eye of the beholder. *Nurs Res*, 53(1):28–35.

Beck CT, Watson S. (2010). Subsequent childbirth after a previous traumatic birth. *Nurs Res*, 59(4):241–9.

James S. (2015). Women's experiences of symptoms of post traumatic stress disorder (PTSD) after traumatic childbirth: a review and critical appraisal. *Arch Womens Ment Health*, 18:761–71.

Lothian J. (2004). Do not disturb: The importance of privacy in labour. *Perinat Educ*, 13(3): 4–6.

Maternity Matters (2007). Choice, access and continuity of care in a safe service. Available at: https://dera.ioe.ac.uk/id/eprint/9429/7/dh_074199_Redacted.pdf

McNally O'Higgins L. (2011). A psychoanalytic perspective on hospital midwifery and birth. *J Infant Observation*, 14(2): 129–144.

NICE (2010) National Institute for Health and Clinical Excellence. Pregnancy and complex social factors: A model for service provision for pregnant women with complex social factors. *NICE Clinical Guidelines*, No. 110

Obholzer A, Roberts VZ. (1994). *The unconscious at work: Individual and organisational stress in the human services*. Hove: Routledge.

Soet JE, Brack GA, Dilorio C. (2003). Prevalence and predictors of women's experiences of psychological trauma during childbirth. *Birth*, 30(1):36–46.

Pregnant In West London: www.onewestminster.org.uk/directory/20888; https://westlondondoulas.com/

Chapter 14

Birthing consciousness

Psycho-neurobiology of childbirth

Orli Dahan

Introduction: The science of birth

The birthing process is a complex interplay of physiological, psychological, and neurological factors (Olza et al., 2020). Yet there is a significant gap in our understanding of the psycho-neurobiological aspects of physiological childbirth. From a psychological perspective, numerous studies have examined childbirth as a traumatic event or the psychopathological consequences of birth on postpartum maternal well-being (e.g., Shorey et al., 2023); far fewer have explored the experience of childbirth as a positive, life-altering event (Dahan, 2023a; Olza et al., 2018). Even more concerning, few neuroscientific studies have been conducted to determine the brain areas that function during physiological childbirth, and the data we do have about maternal brain functioning during and after pregnancy explain the vast neurofunctional and neuroanatomical changes only in terms of preparing for motherhood, not even mentioning childbirth (Dahan, 2021).

The functional magnetic resonance imaging (fMRI) studies conducted recently to examine pain levels in women with epidurals stand out as exceptions to the lack of research concerning the maternal brain during different types of births (Wang et al., 2023). However, although labour pain is central to many women's childbirth narratives, the overemphasis on this aspect and its management through epidurals obscures the complexity of the birthing experience. To reduce neurobiological research about childbirth to epidural neurological effects is to diminish the rich and varied experiences of countless women.

This chapter aims to address this gap in current research by examining the relationship between the type of childbirth and its psychological and neurobiological mechanisms, particularly the phenomenon of hypofrontality. Based on research I have conducted from various perspectives on "birthing consciousness"— a unique state of consciousness of retreat experienced by women during physiological childbirth—I will explore a few hypotheses about the psycho-neurobiological mechanisms underlying physiological births versus medicalised births.

DOI: 10.4324/9781003530473-18

A tentative taxonomy of births

The categorisation of types of childbirth is often dependent on the lens through which childbirth is viewed. Various classifications exist, some more common and accepted than others, yet none fully capture the complexity of the birth experience. For instance, from a medical perspective, childbirth is often dichotomised into vaginal births versus caesarean sections, focusing solely on where the foetus emerges (e.g., Negrini et al., 2021). Clearly, this classification overlooks the subjective experiences of the birthing woman. A finer-grained classification might categorise births into five physiological types: natural birth, vaginal birth with epidural, instrumental birth, unplanned caesarean, and planned caesarean (Dekel et al., 2019).

Childbirth also can be categorised from a psychological perspective as either traumatic or empowering (Dahan, 2023a), which can be applied to the finer-grained classification, because empirical research suggests a correlation between traumatic birth experiences and instrumental or emergency caesarean births (Dekel et al., 2019). Social and interpersonal perspectives also can inform classifications, ranging from private and intimate freebirth, where there is no professional medical assistance, to highly medicalised births with little privacy (Feeley & Thomson, 2016).

Here I use a simple categorisation of physiological birth, characterised by minimal medical intervention, versus medicalised birth, involving more medical intervention. This is a physiological categorisation that also captures the psychological experience of birthing, including the link between more medicalised births and poorer postpartum mental health (Dekel et al., 2019). It should be noted, though, that while this simple categorisation provides a useful framework for the current discussion, a more comprehensive taxonomy is necessary when attempting to fully capture the diverse range of birthing experiences and inform evidence-based practices.

What can we say about the psycho-neurobiology of physiological birth?

The phenomenon of birthing consciousness

On the psychological level, many women have described experiencing physiological birth as being "in the zone" or "on another planet". Those for whom this has happened have also experienced less affective pain: as labour intensified, they modified their pain experience by focusing and retreating to a private world (Dahan, 2020). Based on many qualitative studies that have described these transcendent experiences that many women have experienced during physiological birth (Olza et al., 2018), it is plausible to conclude that women in labour may enter a distinct altered state of consciousness (ASC). An ASC is a unique psychophysiological experience characterised as a temporary state of deviation in perceptions, feelings, and cognition capacities that significantly hinders the ability to function as one's usual self (Dahan, 2020).

I have termed the experience of an ASC during physiological birth "birthing consciousness" (Dahan, 2020). Birthing consciousness is a profound physiological and psychological experience characterised by altered perception—a heightened awareness of bodily sensations and a diminished sense of time and space; emotional transformation—experiencing intense emotions, ranging from euphoria to profound peace, often accompanied by a sense of the transcendent; and cognitive shifts—a focus on the present moment and a reduced capacity for self-reflection and analytical thought. These factors help the birthing woman to handle the intense labour pain, which, although typically perceived as negative, can be associated with positive feelings in many women (Dahan 2020, 2023a).

Birthing consciousness is a peak experience that usually leads to feelings of empowerment, increased self-confidence, and enhanced coping abilities (Dahan, 2020, 2023a, 2023b). It also may have physiological benefits, such as reduced pain perception and shorter labour duration (Hishikawa et al., 2019). Odent and I (Dahan & Odent, 2023) have theorised that birthing consciousness may even trigger the foetus' ejection reflex, accelerating the crucial second stage of labour. While these hypotheses require further empirical investigation, the potential benefits of birthing consciousness on both the physiological and psychological aspects of childbirth are significant.

A hypothesis concerning the neurobiological mechanism of birthing consciousness: Transient hypofrontality

Although no neurobiological research has been conducted to date to determine the brain mechanism during physiological birth, the similarity of the phenomenological and cognitive features of birthing consciousness and transient hypofrontality suggests a strong affinity between the two states (Dahan, 2020, 2021). Hypofrontality refers to a decrease in activity in the prefrontal cortex, a brain region associated with higher-order cognitive functions such as planning, decision-making, and self-awareness. Transient hypofrontality has been linked to various ASCs, including meditation, hypnosis, psychedelic experiences, and highly intensive physiological effort such as running a marathon (Dietrich & Al-Shawaf, 2018).

I have posited that birthing consciousness exemplifies an adaptive ASC that harnesses the neurophysiological mechanisms of transient hypofrontality, something that likely conferred significant evolutionary advantages for women during childbirth when natural birth was the only option for reproductive success, before the advances of modern obstetrics (Dahan, 2020, 2021). There are several potential benefits of transient hypofrontality during birth. It may contribute to pain management by modulating pain perception and enhancing coping mechanisms (Dahan, 2020). It also may influence the body's biochemistry by reducing stress and anxiety, thereby promoting optimal hormonal levels like oxytocin and beta-endorphins, which promote the physiological birthing process (Romano & Lothian, 2008). Ultimately, this ASC may allow women to more fully engage with the physiological processes of birth.

Analysing data from existing studies on neuroanatomical and neurofunctional changes in the maternal brain before and after birth supports the hypothesis that transient hypofrontality during birth may be an adaptive trait promoting physiological birth (Dahan, 2021). One finding that bolsters the hypothesis is that of opposing grey matter volume changes before and after birth. While first-time mothers were found to experience a significant reduction in grey matter volume throughout pregnancy (Hoekzema et al., 2020), there was found to be an increase in grey matter volume in the postpartum period (Luders et al., 2020). These alterations, particularly concentrated in the cerebral cortex, may be linked to the brain's preparation for childbirth and the occurrence of transient hypofrontality (Dahan, 2021).

Other findings involve changes in prefrontal cortical function. Pregnant women were found to exhibit altered decoding of psycho-biological alarm signals, with significant differences between early and late pregnancy. For instance, activation across the prefrontal cortex in response to fearful faces was found to be higher in the second trimester than in the third (Roos et al., 2011). Women in late pregnancy were also found to display diminished and delayed processing of angry facial expressions (Raz, 2014). Further, while women in the first trimester were found to respond neurally to anxiety chemosignals (in the case cited, anxiety sweat), albeit with atypical spatial distribution, women in the third trimester in the study showed no detectable neural response to anxiety sweat (Lübke et al., 2017). These findings suggest that pregnancy induces significant changes in brain function, particularly in the prefrontal cortex, which may have implications for behaviour and emotion regulation of women during birth. The brain may promote a beneficial state of partial dissociation, reducing stress and anxiety as the due date nears. This could facilitate the onset of labour and increase the likelihood of the birthing woman entering a state of birthing consciousness (Dahan, 2021).

In addition, a new study by Paternina-Die et al. (2024) suggests that different modes of birth influence the trajectory of brain changes during the postpartum period. It was found that women who give birth physiologically may experience a slower return to baseline levels in certain brain networks, such as the default mode and frontoparietal networks, compared to those who undergo caesarean birth (Paternina-Die et al., 2024). This could indicate that the mode of birth plays a significant role in shaping brain mechanisms, perhaps providing indirect support for the transient hypofrontality hypothesis: the pregnant woman's brain prepares for a physiological birth by preparing her to engage the transient hypofrontality mechanism during birth (McCormack & Thomason, 2024).

The mental experience during birthing consciousness: Flow

An alternative approach to indirectly explore birthing consciousness and to attempt to validate its associated hypotheses as to the brain mechanism of transient hypofrontality is to use the measure of "flow". The mental state of flow, characterised by intense focus and intrinsic motivation, has been linked to a transient hypofrontality brain mechanism, particularly during demanding physical activities (Stoll

& Pithan, 2016). While other theories exist, the hypofrontality model remains the most widely supported explanation for the neural basis of flow (Clark, 2023). The assessment of flow through self-report questionnaires provides a non-invasive method for investigating this state, even concerning complex events like childbirth.

A recent online study that my colleagues and I undertook (Dahan et al., 2024) of 766 women with birth experiences investigated the relationship between the mode of birth and the mental state of flow during childbirth. By utilising the FSS self-report questionnaire (Jackson & Marsh, 1996), we found that women who experienced physiological birth reported higher levels of flow compared to those who underwent vaginal birth with medical interventions or caesarean birth. This research represents the first empirical validation of the link between the birthing experience and the flow state, providing further support for the hypothesis of the existence of the psycho-neurobiological mechanism during physiological birth of birthing consciousness (Dahan et al., 2024).

What can we say about the psycho-neurobiology of medicalised birth?

Given the lack of research on the brain state during childbirth (medicalised or physiological), I propose to discuss the question of psychological and brain mechanisms during medicalised childbirth by inference. In other words, what can we say about the psychological experience during medicalised childbirth and how the brain might be affected by what happens in a medicalised birth?

Medical interventions, such as labour induction and epidurals, can disrupt the natural progression of labour (Romano & Lothian, 2008) and potentially interfere with the development of birthing consciousness (Dahan & Odent, 2023). Although many interventions can be lifesaving, medical interventions usually start a cascade of further interventions that alter hormonal levels, increase stress, interrupt normal labour, and significantly increase the risk of unplanned cesarian sections (Romano & Lothian, 2008).

Here, a note about the birth environment is crucial. Across the spectrum of human experience, individuals exhibit a keen awareness of their immediate environment. This intuitive recognition of the environment's impact on one's emotional state is equally pertinent to the childbirth experience (Goldkuhl et al., 2023). Thus, it is understandable why the conditions typically found in a standard hospital birthing room set up to allow for medical interventions would make it nearly impossible to enter into or sustain the meditative state of flow, which involves a certain degree of healthy dissociation (Dahan, 2020). These conditions include bright fluorescent lights, strangers, loud noises, strong odours (Dahan, 2023b), frequent vaginal examinations (Shabot, 2021), and restrictions on food, drink, and movement (Romano & Lothian, 2008). Childbirth is an intimate process that demands intimate conditions (Newton, 1987), and the birth environment of most medicalised births is the opposite of intimate (Dahan & Odent, 2023; Newton, 1987). It hardly seems plausible that a meditative state could be achieved under such circumstances even when not undergoing childbirth, let alone while experiencing labour pains. Further, currently in most Western hospitals there is no continuous professional one-on-one support for birthing mothers, which, if provided, could decrease the rate and need of various medical interventions (Bohren et al., 2017).

I assume that these factors affect the neurological and psychological mechanisms and thus the process of birth (Dahan, 2023b). Various medical interventions could impair birthing consciousness, interfere with the maintenance of flow, and disrupt the state of transient hypofrontality, and a public situation such as a standard hospital birthing room could hyperactivate the prefrontal cortex (Dahan & Odent, 2023). Future empirical studies should test these assumptions (Dahan, 2023b).

Conclusion

This chapter is rich in hypotheses—rather than evidence—about the psycho-neurobiology of childbirth. This reflects the significant gap in our understanding of the birthing brain and highlights the urgent need for more research in this area. I believe that better understanding the psycho-neurobiological mechanisms underlying birthing consciousness and hypofrontality could have significant implications for childbirth practices. By promoting environments that support these psychophysical mechanisms, we may be able to substantially enhance the birthing experience and optimise maternal outcomes.

References

Bohren, M. A., Hofmeyr, G. J., Sakala, C., Fukuzawa, R. K., & Cuthbert, A. (2017). Continuous support for women during childbirth. *Cochrane Pregnancy and Childbirth Group*, July 6. https://doi.org/10.1002/14651858.CD003766.pub6

Clark, F. E. (2023). In the zone: Towards a comparative study of flow state in primates. *Animal Behavior and Cognition, 10*(1), 62–88. https://doi.org/10.26451/abc.10.01.04.2023

Dahan, O. (2020). Birthing consciousness as a case of adaptive altered state of consciousness associated with transient hypofrontality. *Perspectives on Psychological Science, 15*(3), 794–808. https://doi.org/10.1177/1745691620901546

Dahan, O. (2021). The birthing brain: A lacuna in neuroscience. *Brain and Cognition, 150*, 105722. https://doi.org/10.1016/j.bandc.2021.105722

Dahan, O. (2023a). Birthing as an experience of awe: Birthing consciousness and its long-term positive effects. *Journal of Theoretical and Philosophical Psychology, 43*(1), 16–30. https://doi.org/10.1037/teo0000214

Dahan, O. (2023b). Navigating intensive altered states of consciousness: How can the set and setting key parameters promote the science of human birth? *Frontiers in Psychiatry, 14*, 1–14. https://doi.org/10.3389/fpsyt.2023.1072047

Dahan, O., & Odent, M. (2023). Not just mechanical birthing bodies: Birthing consciousness and birth reflexes. *Journal of Perinatal Education, 32*(3), 1–12. https://doi.org/10.1891/JPE-2022-0007

Dahan, O., Zibenberg, A., & Goldberg, A. (2024). Birthing consciousness and the flow experience during physiological childbirth. *Midwifery, 138*, 104151. https://doi.org/10.1016/j.midw.2024.104151

Dekel, S., Ein-Dor, T., Berman, Z., Barsoumian, I. S., Agarwal, S., & Pitman, R. K. (2019). Delivery mode is associated with maternal mental health following childbirth. *Archives of Women's Mental Health, 22*, 817–824. https://doi.org/10.1007/s00737-019-00968-2

Dietrich, A., & Al-Shawaf, L. (2018). The transient hypofrontality theory of altered states of consciousness. *Journal of Consciousness Studies, 25*(11–12), 226–247.

Feeley, C., & Thomson, G. (2016). Why do some women choose to freebirth in the UK? An interpretative phenomenological study. *BMC Pregnancy and Childbirth, 16*, 1–12. https://doi.org/10.1186/s12884-016-0847-6

Goldkuhl, L., Gyllensten, H., Begley, C., Nilsson, C., Wijk, H., Lindahl, G., Uvnas-Moberg, K. & Berg, M. (2023). Impact of birthing room design on maternal childbirth experience: Results from the Room4Birth randomized trial. *HERD: Health Environments Research & Design Journal, 16*(1), 200–218. https://doi.org/10.1177/19375867221124232

Hishikawa, K., Kusaka, T., Fukuda, T., Kohata, Y., & Inoue, H. (2019). Anxiety or nervousness disturbs the progress of birth based on human behavioral evolutionary biology. *The Journal of Perinatal Education, 28*(4), 218–223. https://doi.org/10.1891/1058-1243.28.4.218

Hoekzema, E., Tamnes, C. K., Berns, P., Barba-Müller, E., Pozzobon, C., Picado, M., Lucco, F., Martinez-Garcia, M., Desco, M., Ballesteros, A., Crone, E. A., Vilarroya, O., & Carmona, S. (2020). Becoming a mother entails anatomical changes in the ventral striatum of the human brain that facilitate its responsiveness to offspring cues. *Psychoneuroendocrinology, 112*, 104507. https://doi.org/10.1016/j.psyneuen.2019.104507

Jackson, S. A., & Marsh, H. W. (1996). Development and validation of a scale to measure optimal experience: The Flow State Scale. *Journal of Sport and Exercise Psychology, 18*(1), 17–35. https://doi.org/10.1123/jsep.18.1.17

Lübke, K. T., Busch, A., Hoenen, M., Schaal, B., & Pause, B. M. (2017). Pregnancy reduces the perception of anxiety. *Scientific Reports, 7*(1), 9213. https://doi.org/10.1038/s41598-017-07985-0

Luders, E., Kurth, F., Gingnell, M., Engman, J., Yong, E. L., Poromaa, I. S., & Gaser, C. (2020). From baby brain to mommy brain: Widespread gray matter gain after giving birth. *Cortex, 126*, 334–342. https://doi.org/10.1016/j.cortex.2019.12.029

McCormack, C., & Thomason, M. (2024). Pregnancy restructures the brain to prepare for childbirth and parenthood. *Nature, 636*, 583–584. https://doi.org/10.1038/d41586-024-03942-w

Negrini, R., da Silva Ferreira, R. D., & Guimarães, D. Z. (2021). Value-based care in obstetrics: Comparison between vaginal birth and caesarean section. *BMC Pregnancy and Childbirth, 21*(1), 333. https://doi.org/10.1186/s12884-021-03798-2

Newton, N. (1987). The fetus ejection reflex revisited. *Birth, 14*(2), 106–108. https://doi.org/10.1111/j.1523-536X.1987.tb01464.x

Olza, I., Leahy-Warren, P., Benyamini, Y., Kazmierczak, M., Karlsdottir, S. I., Spyridou, A., Crespo-Mirasol, E., Takacs, L., Hall, P. J., Murphy, M., Jonsdottir, S. S., Downe, S., & Nieuwenhuijze, M. J. (2018). Women's psychological experiences of physiological childbirth: A meta-synthesis. *BMJ Open, 8*(10), e020347. http://orcid.org/0000-0002-9614-9496

Olza, I., Uvnas-Moberg, K., Ekström-Bergström, A., Leahy-Warren, P., Karlsdottir, S. I., Nieuwenhuijze, M., Villarmea, S., Hadjigeorgiou, E., Kazmierczak, M., Spyridou, A., & Buckley, S. (2020). Birth as a neuro-psycho-social event: An integrative model of maternal experiences and their relation to neurohormonal events during childbirth. *PLoS One, 15*(7), e0230992. https://doi.org/10.1371/journal.pone.0230992

Paternina-Die, M., Martínez-García, M., Martín de Blas, D., Noguero, I., Servin-Barthet, C., Pretus, C., Soler, A., Lopez-Montoya, G., Desco, M., & Carmona, S. (2024). Women's neuroplasticity during gestation, childbirth and postpartum. *Nature Neuroscience, 27*(2), 319–327. https://doi.org/10.1038/s41593-023-01513-2

Raz, S. (2014). Behavioral and neural correlates of cognitive–affective function during late pregnancy: An event-related potentials study. *Behavioural Brain Research, 267*, 17–25. https://doi.org/10.1016/j.bbr.2014.03.021

Romano, A. M., & Lothian, J. A. (2008). Promoting, protecting, and supporting normal birth: A look at the evidence. *Journal of Obstetric, Gynecologic & Neonatal Nursing, 37*(1), 94–105. https://doi.org/10.1111/j.1552-6909.2007.00210.x

Roos, A., Robertson, F., Lochner, C., Vythilingum, B., & Stein, D. J. (2011). Altered prefrontal cortical function during processing of fear-relevant stimuli in pregnancy. *Behavioural Brain Research, 222*(1), 200–205. https://doi.org/10.1016/j.bbr.2011.03.055

Shabot, S. C. (2021). Why 'normal' feels so bad: Violence and vaginal examinations during labour–a (feminist) phenomenology. *Feminist Theory, 22*(3), 443–463. https://doi.org/10.1177/14647001209207

Shorey, S., Downe, S., Chua, J. Y. X., Byrne, S. O., Fobelets, M., & Lalor, J. G. (2023). Effectiveness of psychological interventions to improve the mental well-being of parents who have experienced traumatic childbirth: A systematic review and meta-analysis. *Trauma, Violence, & Abuse, 24*(3), 1238–1253. https://doi.org/10.1177/1524838021 1060808

Stoll, O., & Pithan, J. M. (2016). Running and flow: Does controlled running lead to flow-states? Testing the Transient Hypofontality Theory. In L. Harmat, F. Ørsted Andersen, F. Ullén, J. Wright, & G. Sadlo (Eds.), *Flow experience* (pp. 65–75). Springer. https://doi.org/10.1007/978-3-319-28634-1_5

Wang, J. J., Yang, F. P. G., Tsai, C. C., & Chao, A. S. (2023). The neural basis of pain during labor. *American Journal of Obstetrics and Gynecology, 228*(5), S1241–S1245. https://doi.org/10.1016/j.ajog.2023.02.012

Chapter 15

The bodily self during birth

Sarah E. Veale, Lydia B. Munns, and Catherine E.J. Preston

Birth is a profoundly physical experience as the baby emerges from the mother's body, marking the transition from a single, unified body to two distinct beings. Birth is thought of as an existential moment that is a key meaningful life event (Prinds et al., 2014). This process involves not only a physical separation of mother and baby, but also carries profound transformation of both the maternal body and the maternal brain (Paternina-Die et al., 2024).

This dual transformation is deeply rooted in the physical and emotional connection between mother and baby, with the bodily self—the lived, felt sense of the body—being central to shaping the birthing experience (Meyer et al., 2022). During pregnancy and beyond, the brain undergoes significant neuroplasticity thought to shape the transition to motherhood (Paternina-Die et al., 2024). Postpartum changes in grey matter, particularly in Theory-of-Mind regions, are detectable even decades later, highlighting the permanence of these changes (Orchard et al., 2021).

Medicalisation and obstetric violence

Historically, pregnancy and birth were regarded as physiological events that occurred naturally, without intervention. However, with advancements in medicine, maternity has become increasingly medicalised, framing pregnant women and their babies as patients in need of treatment (Shaw, 2013). In Western societies, the female body is objectified and valued predominantly for appearance. During pregnancy, however, the body's role in developing a baby takes on primary importance and can liberate women from social pressures of how their body should look (Hodgkinson et al., 2014). The extent to which this shift from appearance to functionality is felt varies among individuals (Crossland et al., 2023), but it arguably peaks during birth, when the connection to the body as a functional, life-giving entity is critical (Prinds et al., 2014). However, Shabot (2017) argues that over-medicalised childbirth can objectify the maternal body, instead of focusing on appearance, reducing the body to an instrument to be controlled by medical authorities. While advances in obstetric medicine has saved countless lives, unnecessary interventions mean that, instead of experiencing birth as a moment of profound connection and meaning, the maternal body is reduced to an object, merely performing

DOI: 10.4324/9781003530473-19

the function of giving birth and thus alienating women from their own embodied experiences. This aligns with the notion that obstetric violence reflects broader patriarchal dynamics, where women's bodies are treated as passive objects, alienated and prone to shame (Shabot & Korem, 2018). Such practices fundamentally undermine the bodily self, severing the relational and social connections that are crucial during childbirth (Meyer et al., 2022).

The negative consequences of medicalisation of pregnancy and birth can be substantial and long lasting for both mother and baby. Birth interventions pose a significant risk factor for negative experiences and are associated with adverse health outcomes for the child in both the short and long term compared to unassisted, spontaneous vaginal births (Peters et al., 2018). Negative birth experiences can also increase the risk of maternal mental health issues (Chen et al., 2022; Simpson & Catling, 2016), negatively impact breastfeeding practices (Mojab, 2008), and disrupt the maternal-infant bond—critical for the child's emotional and social development (Smorti et al., 2020). Mode of delivery also influences feelings of embodiment during birth, with vaginal births, especially those without pain relief, reported as providing an intense embodied experience, whereas caesarean sections are more likely to be associated with feelings of bodily disconnection, and even a sense of disconnection from the infant (Lupton & Schmied, 2013).

Historical narratives of birth

The cultural and historical context of childbirth has profoundly shaped how women experience their bodies during birth. For centuries, myths and narratives have framed the female body as chaotic, flawed, and in need of external control. These ideas disconnected women from their bodily self during birth, perpetuating a legacy of disempowerment.

Religious and philosophical traditions often portrayed childbirth as a form of punishment or chaos. The Biblical story of Eve's punishment with labour pain established a cultural association between childbirth and divine retribution. Philosophers like Plato reinforced this perspective, viewing bodies, particularly women's bodies, as 'vulgar' and 'disorderly', in contrast to the rational soul (Wolfarth, 2024, p.82). This framing diminished women's agency, casting their bodies as unruly and in need of management.

In the eighteenth and nineteenth centuries, as scientific advancements began to dominate maternity care, the pregnant body became a focus of medical scrutiny. Yet, even during this period, professional bodies failed to claim authority of care over the pregnant body (Oakley, 1984). This mystery gave rise to conflicting views within the medical literature. On one hand, Chavasse (1878, p.172) asserted that "nature is perfectly competent to bring, without the assistance of man, a child into the world". On the other hand, practitioners like Dr John Grigg (1789) criticised women for rejecting professional medical oversight, accusing them of clinging to "ancient, erroneous opinions and customs" (p.144).

Midwives and birth attendants, meanwhile, have long been central to childbirth, intervening through practices rooted in embodied knowledge, such as administering herbs or stimulating the uterus via breast stimulation, orgasm, or semen (Oakley, 1984, p.194). However, as obstetrics became institutionalised, these practices were replaced by medical interventions like inductions, which emerged as obstetrics sought to free itself from superstition and religion (Oakley, 1984). This shift sidelined women's embodied knowledge and cemented the dominance of male-led medical authority over childbirth.

Body trust and maternal agency

At the heart of reclaiming the bodily sense of self is the concept of body trust. Childbirth has been described as the "fulfilment of bodily purpose" (Prinds et al., 2014), a moment where the body's capabilities align with the lived experience of the birthing mother. This alignment fosters a sense of connection to the self and the baby, affirming the relational and embodied nature of birth. Body trust is thought to be an important construct both during and outside the perinatal period (Crossland et al., 2022) and is associated with prenatal bonding (Stafford et al., 2024) as well as breastfeeding intentions (Munns & Preston, 2025), behaviours (Munns et al., 2025), and experience (Flacking et al., 2021). Trusting and listening to bodily signals is also intuitively central to labour and birth to follow signals from the body throughout delivery, such as knowing when to push (Cheyney, 2011). The use of unnecessary birth interventions may mask or prevent such signals from the body, thus compromising body trust. Given the profound nature of birth as an existential experience, undermining body trust during birth and the wider perinatal period may have negative long-lasting consequences (Munns et al., 2025). This is concerning given that a recent qualitative study found that up to 60% of women felt a sense of failure regarding their birth experience (Schneider, 2018).

The birthing brain

Perinatal neural changes may also influence birth experiences. Many of the neural adaptations observed during pregnancy and postnatally are linked to preparing for parenthood and caregiving behaviours (Kim et al., 2016). However, some distinct neural changes occurring during pregnancy are thought to specifically occur to prepare the body for birth (Dahan, 2021). For instance, pregnancy is marked by widespread decreases in grey matter volume (Paternina-Die et al., 2024; Pritschet et al., 2024), while postnatal changes (associated with caregiving) typically involve increases in grey matter (Kim et al., 2016). This may therefore implicate the point of birth as a key moment underlying perinatal neural plasticity. Physiological changes also occur in pregnancy, both internally and externally, as the body accommodates the growing baby. Internal bodily sensations (interoception) such as pain and hunger, which changes profoundly throughout gestation, are thought to play a role in emotional well-being (Paulus & Stein, 2010). Given that pregnancy brings heightened physiological changes, sensations like increased heart rate, which is commonly associated with fear and anxiety outside of pregnancy, may be experienced even in neutral emotional states. According to predictive theories of the brain, this shift could mean that certain bodily signals are ignored because they are no longer reliable (Seth, 2013). However, as discussed above, successful labour requires heightened bodily awareness. Thus, it is plausible that the brain adapts during pregnancy to prioritise foetal and birth-related bodily sensations while deprioritising others, such as those tied to body appearance or non-essential cognitive and emotional processes (Dahan, 2021).

These shifts in how the brain processes bodily cues could explain the altered states of consciousness and heightened embodiment reported during unassisted vaginal birth (Lupton & Schmied, 2013). Interventions like caesarean sections, which prevent vaginal birth, are associated with different neural signatures postnatally (Swain et al., 2011), suggesting that these embodied states apparent during birth might play an important role in transitioning from pregnancy to motherhood.

Honouring the bodily self in birth

The bodily sense of self during birth is shaped by a complex interplay of cultural, historical, and individual factors. For centuries, patriarchal and medicalised narratives have disconnected women from their bodies, casting childbirth as chaotic and in need of external control. Yet, alternative perspectives emphasise the potential for birth to be an empowering and embodied experience when prioritising body trust.

By dismantling the legacy of objectification and medicalisation along with reclaiming childbirth as a relational, embodied event, women can reassert agency over their experiences even when interventions are needed. This reimagining requires an increased understanding of how maternal body and brain prepare for birth, as well as maternity care practices that honour the lived experiences of labouring women, creating environments that support body trust and celebrate the transformative potential of birth.

References

Chavasse, P. H. (1878). *Advice to a wife on the management of her own health and on the treatment of some of the complaints incidental to pregnancy, labour, and suckling, with an introductory chapter especially addressed to a young wife.* The American News Company.

Chen, Y., Ismail, F., Xiong, Z., Li, M., Chen, I., Wen, S. W., & Xie, R.-H. (2022). Association between perceived birth trauma and postpartum depression: A prospective cohort study in China. *International Journal of Gynaecology and Obstetrics: The Official Organ of the International Federation of Gynaecology and Obstetrics, 157*(3), 598–603.

Cheyney, M. (2011). Reinscribing the birthing body: Homebirth as ritual performance. *Medical Anthropology Quarterly, 25*(4), 519–542.

Crossland, A. E., Munns, L., Kirk, E., & Preston, C. E. J. (2023). Comparing body image dissatisfaction between pregnant women and non-pregnant women: A systematic review and meta-analysis. *BMC Pregnancy and Childbirth, 23*(1), 709.

Crossland, A., Kirk, E., & Preston, C. (2022). Interoceptive sensibility and body satisfaction in pregnant and non-pregnant women with and without children. *Scientific Reports, 12*(1), 16138.

Dahan, O. (2021). The birthing brain: A lacuna in neuroscience. *Brain and Cognition, 150*(105722), 105722.

Flacking, R., Tandberg, B. S., Niela-Vilén, H., Jónsdóttir, R. B., Jonas, W., Ewald, U., & Thomson, G. (2021). Positive breastfeeding experiences and facilitators in mothers of preterm and low birthweight infants: A meta-ethnographic review. *International Breastfeeding Journal, 16*(1), 88.

Grigg, J. (1789). *Advice to the female sex in general, particularly those in a state of pregnancy and lying-in: The complaints incident to their respective situations are specified and treatment recommended ... To which is added ... some directions relative to the management of children in the first part of life.* S. Hazard.

Hodgkinson, E. L., Smith, D. M., & Wittkowski, A. (2014). Women's experiences of their pregnancy and postpartum body image: a systematic review and meta-synthesis. *BMC Pregnancy and Childbirth, 14*, 330.

Kim, P., Strathearn, L., & Swain, J. E. (2016). The maternal brain and its plasticity in humans. *Hormones and Behavior, 77*, 113–123.

Lupton, D., & Schmied, V. (2013). Splitting bodies/selves: women's concepts of embodiment at the moment of birth: Women's concepts of embodiment at the moment of birth. *Sociology of Health & Illness, 35*(6), 828–841.

Meyer, S., Cignacco, E., Monteverde, S., Trachsel, M., Raio, L., & Oelhafen, S. (2022). 'We felt like part of a production system': A qualitative study on women's experiences of mistreatment during childbirth in Switzerland. *PLOS ONE, 17*(2), e0264119.

Mojab, C. G. (2008). The impact of traumatic childbirth on health through the undermining of breastfeeding. In Banyard, V. L., Edwards, V. J., & Kendall-Tackett, K. (eds.), *Trauma and physical health* (pp. 79–104). Routledge. www.taylorfrancis.com/books/edit/10.4324/9780203885017/trauma-physical-health-victoria-banyard-valerie-edwards-kathleen-kendall-tackett?refId=a9eebf57-8c17-40e4-b07b-42da6fedd0f4&context=ubx

Munns, L. B., & Preston, C. (2025). The role of bodily experiences during pregnancy on mother and infant outcomes. *Journal of Neuropsychology, 19*, 131–151.

Munns, L. B., Noonan M. A. P., Romano, D. L., & Preston, C. E. J. (2025). Interoceptive and exteroceptive pregnant bodily experiences and postnatal well-being: A network analysis. British Journal of Health Psychology, 30(3), e70002.

Oakley, A. (1984). The captured womb: A history of the medical care of pregnant women. Oxford: Blackwell.

Orchard, E. R., Ward, P. G. D., Chopra, S., Storey, E., Egan, G. F., & Jamadar, S. D. (2021). Neuroprotective effects of motherhood on brain function in late life: A resting-state fMRI study. *Cerebral Cortex (New York, N.Y.: 1991), 31*(2), 1270–1283.

Paternina-Die, M., Martínez-García, M., Martín de Blas, D., Noguero, I., Servin-Barthet, C., Pretus, C., Soler, A., López-Montoya, G., Desco, M., & Carmona, S. (2024). Women's neuroplasticity during gestation, childbirth and postpartum. *Nature Neuroscience, 27*(2), 319–327.

Paulus, M. P., & Stein, M. B. (2010). Interoception in anxiety and depression. *Brain Structure & Function, 214*(5–6), 451–463.

Peters, L. L., Thornton, C., de Jonge, A., Khashan, A., Tracy, M., Downe, S., Feijen-de Jong, E. I., & Dahlen, H. G. (2018). The effect of medical and operative birth interventions on child health outcomes in the first 28 days and up to 5 years of age: A linked data population-based cohort study. *Birth*, *45*(4), 347–357.

Prinds, C., Hvidt, N. C., Mogensen, O., & Buus, N. (2014). Making existential meaning in transition to motherhood–A scoping review. *Midwifery*, *30*(6), 733–741.

Pritschet, L., Taylor, C. M., Cossio, D., Faskowitz, J., Santander, T., Handwerker, D. A., Grotzinger, H., Layher, E., Chrastil, E. R., & Jacobs, E. G. (2024). Neuroanatomical changes observed over the course of a human pregnancy. *Nature Neuroscience*, *27*(11), 2253–2260.

Schneider, D. A. (2018). Birthing failures: Childbirth as a female fault line. *Journal of Perinatal Education*, *27*(1), 20–31.

Seth, A. K. (2013). Interoceptive inference, emotion, and the embodied self. *Trends in Cognitive Sciences*, *17*(11), 565–573.

Shabot, S. C., (2017). Constructing subjectivity through labour pain: A Beauvoirian analysis. *European Journal of Women S Studies*, *24*(2), 128–142.

Shabot, S. C., & Korem, K. (2018). Domesticating bodies: The role of shame in obstetric violence. *Hypatia*, *33*(3), 384–401.

Shaw, J. C. A. (2013). The medicalization of birth and midwifery as resistance. *Health Care for Women International*, *34*(6), 522–536.

Simpson, M., & Catling, C. (2016). Understanding psychological traumatic birth experiences: A literature review. *Women and Birth: Journal of the Australian College of Midwives*, *29*(3), 203–207.

Smorti, M., Ponti, L., Ghinassi, S., & Rapisardi, G. (2020). The mother-child attachment bond before and after birth: The role of maternal perception of traumatic childbirth. *Early Human Development*, *142*(104956), 104956.

Stafford, L., Munns, L., Crossland, A. E., Kirk, E., & Preston, C. E. J. (2024). Bonding with bump: Interoceptive sensibility moderates the relationship between pregnancy body satisfaction and antenatal attachment. *Midwifery*, *131*, 103940.

Swain, J. E., Kim, P., & Ho, S. S. (2011). Neuroendocrinology of parental response to baby-cry. *Journal of Neuroendocrinology*, *23*(11), 1036–1041.

Wolfarth, J. (2024). *Milk*. Weidenfeld & Nicolson.

Chapter 16

The socio-cultural context of birth

Sergio A. Silverio and Tisha Dasgupta

The 'triple burden' faced by perinatal women

Women embarking on their journey to new motherhood—for a first or subsequent child—may be overwhelmed by many factors relating to decisions about healthcare[1]. As cultural norms change, it is important to re-theorise about women's identity work, as well as their cognitive, emotional, psychological, and physical labour associated with conception, pregnancy, birth, and the postpartum period. This work, in the context of increasingly pressurised healthcare systems and those facing acute or chronic health system shocks, has previously been conceptualised as a 'triple burden' faced by perinatal women (Silverio et al., 2024).

The first burden perinatal women face is that of increased anxiety related to the uncertainty associated with being pregnant or postpartum in these situations. These fears can be generated from the threat of infection, or fears of welfare within the struggling healthcare system, which lacks resources and staffing (i.e. the social shock of 'Brexit' causing high-levels of foreign-born healthcare professional staff attrition; Iacobucci, 2016). Women are therefore concerned not only about their own health, but also the health of their unborn or newly born babies, with greater levels of anxiety stemming from poorer levels of understanding about the health system shocks. With respect to women who suffer a pregnancy loss, a stillbirth, or neonatal death, this confusion is further compounded by the lack of continuity in information shared between each section of the healthcare system (i.e. gynaecology, maternity, primary care, etc.), which they have to navigate to seek answers (Silverio, Easter, et al., 2021; Silverio, George-Carey et al., 2024).

Second, perinatal women face the burden of access *to* and engagement *with* healthcare services. This can present in two ways—first, where there is physical restriction to services, whereby service provision has been reduced, relocated afar, or closed altogether (Jardine et al., 2021; Silverio et al., 2021); or second, where for whatever reason women choose to not engage with services or do not feel they are eligible candidates (Dixon-Woods et al., 2006) for the healthcare system with which they are provided and expected to utilise.

Finally, the third burden perinatal women are faced with is that of health decision-making. This can cover a multitude of different actions: prenatal screening or

DOI: 10.4324/9781003530473-20

testing (Green et al., 2004); having an early elective abortion (Lokubal et al., 2022) or a termination of pregnancy due to foetal abnormality (Lafarge et al., 2014); where to give birth (Greenfield et al., 2021); whether or not to vaccinate during pregnancy (Dasgupta et al., 2024) and/or vaccinate their newborn (Skirrow et al., 2024); whether or not to breastfeed (Roberts et al., 2023); and—in the cases where a baby is ill or expected to die—decisions around paediatric palliative and end-of-life care (Malcolm & Knighting, 2022); postmortem examination (Lewis et al., 2019); and to the decision to have any further ("penumbra") children (Reid, 2007; p.181).

Cultural, structural, and direct violence faced by women

Pregnant women utilise healthcare services, not because they are unwell, but in order to bring a second life into the world. While many women leave their health-care setting healthy, and with a healthy baby, obstetric violence pervades (Castañeda et al., 2022) and there remain concerns about the levels of racial discrimination that exist within healthcare systems (Silverio et al., 2022; Silverio, Varman et al., 2023), and which may be causing such disparity in maternal mortality in the post-partum period, among minority ethnic women (Awe et al., 2022; Birthrights, 2022; Esan et al., 2022; Gohir, 2022). Although it is important to acknowledge improvements in reduction of racialised violence in obstetric and maternal health settings, we must also be cognisant of new and emergent issues that may arise. Recently, modern understanding of racial discrimination in maternity care has been conceptualised as embodying different levels of violence to which women may be subjected (Silverio, Varman et al., 2023).

The first, and perhaps most profound, is conceivably the most insidious form of violence, would be that of 'cultural violence' whereby divisions occur on the basis of ethnic identity, race, and/or religio-cultural practices, and minority ethnic persons are constructed as 'other', who in turn may embody an ingrained fear and/or expectation of encountering racialised discrimination. This type of violence may not be overtly presented or outwardly witnessed, but is internalised by women of minoritised and marginalised groups, and can lead to further disparities in their maternity outcomes (Saluja & Bryant, 2021).

The second level of violence encountered would be that of 'structural violence' whereby social injustice becomes ingrained within a system, service, or is natural-ised as part of the workplace culture within a healthcare setting. This renders the system difficult for minoritised people to access and navigate as they face systemic unconscious bias. Although not completely explicit, this workplace culture can be highly destructive and may present itself differently between staff themselves (where in-group/out-group roles develop and socio-economic or identity statuses become more important; Silverio et al., 2022), and between staff and the minori-tised patients they look after (where more traditional notions of racism based on skin colour or cultural background are weaponised; Silverio, Varman, et al., 2023).

If the prior two levels of violence are being enacted in a healthcare setting, the third becomes inevitable: 'direct violence'. With this type of violence, we witness actions which cause real and direct threat to a woman's life or diminishes her right to access and engage with safe and equitable healthcare, via means of direct physical, mental, and/or psycho-emotional harm caused to women from minoritised and marginalised groups. Here, healthcare practitioners' loss of all notion of cultural humility or cultural competency (Greene-Moton & Minkler, 2020) can—in the worst of circumstances—result in unnecessary and inexcusable loss of life.

The time-bind of motherhood

Women—particularly mothers—are crucial to the health and well-being of their families, their children, and societies more broadly. The toll they pay for being this central hub to so many spokes is often heavy, and, over time, scholars have conceptualised mothering as comprising certain shifts, rendering mothers in a 'time-bind' (Hochschild & Machung, 1989). It is vital to understand the health of a population as fluid; and one can better comprehend societal health by studying those who themselves are often responsible for the maintenance of the health of those around them: women—more specifically, mothers. Women have experienced a change in the way they organise their lives—with new 'shifts' emerging through necessity and need, not want or knowing. Therefore, in relation to their social and familial identities, there has been an extension of such 'shifts', accounting for the new roles that women have assumed in times of social and health crises (Silverio, 2025).

The 'First Shift' is from paid employment whereby women leave their mothering duties and seek gainful employment to ensure they can provide—either in part or fully—for the financial maintenance of the home. This shift, while removing mothers from their familial role, provides them with a social role, through which they can attract status and a sense of purpose away from motherhood.

The 'Second Shift' is said to resemble providing care to any children as well as to a spouse or partner. This shift re-inserts the mother into her familial role, making her the central hub to the many spoked members of the family. Although this may be a desired role by many women, it can also lead to judgements of women being made through only their (re)productive potential (Silverio, 2021), and, where ruptures in the familial unit occur, can lead to the worse outcomes, such as maternal anxiety, attachment issues, ambivalence, abandonment, or infanticide (Silverio, Wilkinson, et al., 2021).

The 'Third Shift' is conceptualised as managing the family's social responsibilities, which can range from home-schooling to socialising their children, while also establishing and maintaining relationships with friends and relatives, and even neighbours and colleagues. Again, this positions mothers in a wider social role, which can be both fatiguing, and can prioritise the identity of mother over woman, something that has previously been conceptualised as the 'paradox of loss' (Nicolson, 2001).

And, finally, it is easy to conceptualise a 'Fourth Shift', whereby healthcare-giving responsibilities to those within their familial nucleus (or wider social circle) have become a core part of the maternal identity (Silverio, 2025). With this new way of performing motherhood, women are often othered by systems and structures (Agarwal, 2022), and expected to account for new socio-cultural shifts, picking up the slack in the system; offering themselves as a resource, where formalised care structures are not otherwise available or are being restricted due to socio-cultural changes in provision.

Summary: Intersectional factors and the socio-cultural context of birth

Whilst usually a time of anticipatory joy, the perinatal period can be replete with concerns about health (Pilkington & Bedford-Dyer, 2021) and the new identity of motherhood. This is especially true when—as we recently faced—country-wide or global health system shocks change the way in which perinatal care—both physical (Silverio et al., 2021; Silverio et al., 2023) and mental (Bridle et al., 2022; Pilav et al., 2022)—is delivered. If we overlay onto the burdens discussed above, through an intersectional lens, the picture becomes more complex. For example, women belonging to minority ethnic groups (Silverio, Varman, et al., 2023); or those who do not speak the language of the country in which they are seeking care (Bridle et al., 2021; Rayment-Jones et al., 2021); those with chronic illness (Ralston et al., 2021); and those who belong to a sexual minority group (Mamrath et al., 2024), among other marginalised groups, are at a heightened risk of experiencing more numerous complexities when navigating maternity care. Birth and the perinatal period overall is experienced vastly differently by women who belong to one or more of these minoritised and marginalised groups, each unique to their own socio-cultural context. It is important, as we think to the future, that we focus on building ethical and resilient maternal, perinatal mental health, child, and family healthcare systems (Jackson et al., 2024; Redhead et al., 2025) in which women can trust, with which they want to engage, and which provides the safest possible high-quality care for all, regardless of creed, race, or socio-cultural identity.

Note

1 We use the words 'woman' and 'women' to represent all pregnant and birthing people, recognising that whilst the majority of people who become pregnant and give birth identify as women; there is a proportion of non-binary, trans-masculine, and gender dysphoric people who also become pregnant and will give birth.

References

Agarwal, P. (2022). *(M)otherhood: On the choices of being a woman.* Canongate.
Awe, T., Abe, C., Peter, M., Agboola, J., Adebayo, S., & Anderson, T. (2022). *The Black maternity experiences survey: A nationwide study of Black women's experiences of maternity services in the United Kingdom.* FiveXMore.

Birthrights. (2022). *Systemic racism, not broken bodies. An inquiry into racial injustice and human rights in UK maternity care: Executive summary*. Birthrights.

Bridle, L., Bassett, S., & Silverio, S. A. (2021). "We couldn't talk to her": A qualitative exploration of the experiences of UK midwives when navigating women's care without language. *International Journal of Human Rights in Healthcare, 14*(4), 359–373. https://doi.org/10.1108/IJHRH-10-2020-0089

Bridle, L., Walton, L., van der Vord, T., Adebayo, O., Hall, S., Finlayson, E., Easter, A., & Silverio, S. A. (2022). Supporting perinatal mental health and wellbeing during COVID-19. *International Journal of Environmental Research and Public Health, 19*(3), 1777. https://doi.org/10.3390/ijerph19031777

Castañeda, A. N., Hill, N., & Johnson Searcy, J. (2022). Introduction (pp. 13–24). In A. N. Castañeda, N. Hill, & J. Johnson Searcy (Eds.), *Obstetric violence: Realities and resistance from around the world*. Demeter Press.

Dasgupta, T., Boulding, H., Easter, A., Sutedja, T., Khalil, A., Mistry, H. D., Horgan, G., Van Citters, A. D., Nelson, E. C., von Dadelszen, P., Duncan, E. L., The Resilient Study Group, Silverio, S. A., & Magee, L. A. (2024). Post-pandemic maternity care planning for vaccination: A qualitative study of the experiences of women, partners, health care professionals, and policymakers in the United Kingdom. *Vaccines, 12*(9), 1042. https://doi.org/10.3390/vaccines12091042

Dixon-Woods, M., Cavers, D., Agarwal, S., Annandale, E., Arthur, A., Harvey, J., Hsu, R., Katbamna, S., Olsen, R., Smith, L., Riley, R., & Sutton, A. J. (2006). Conducting a critical interpretive synthesis of the literature on access to healthcare by vulnerable groups. *BMC Medical Research Methodology, 6*(35), 1–13. https://doi.org/10.1186/1471-2288-6-35

Esan, O. B., Adjel, N. K., Saberlan, S., Stephens, E., Adeyemi, K., Thomas, R., Johnson, P., & Smith, L. (2022). *Summary report: Mapping existing policy interventions to tackle ethnic health inequalities in maternal and neonatal health in England: A systematic scoping review with stakeholder engagement*. NHS Race & Health Observatory.

Gohir, S. (2022). *Invisible: Maternity experiences of Muslim women from racialised minority communities*. Muslim Women's Network UK.

Green, J. M., Hewison, J., Bekker, H. L., Bryant, L., Richardson, S., Jones, D., Thompson, A., Halliday, J., & Noble, S. (2004). Psychosocial aspects of genetic screening of pregnant women and newborns: A systematic review. *Health Technology Assessment, 8*(33), iii–125. https://doi.org/10.3310/hta8330

Greene-Moton, E., & Minkler, M. (2020). Cultural competence or cultural humility? Moving beyond the debate. *Health Promotion Practice, 21*(1), 142–145. https://doi.org/10.1177/1524839919884912

Greenfield, M., Payne-Gifford, S., & McKenzie, G. (2021). Between a rock and a hard place: Considering "freebirth" during Covid-19. *Frontiers in Global Women's Health, 2*(603744), 1–11. https://doi.org/10.3389/fgwh.2021.603744

Hochschild, A. R., & Machung, A. (1989). *The second shift: Working parents and the revolution at home*. Viking Penguin.

Iacobucci, G. (2016). Brexit could worsen NHS staff shortages, doctors warn. *BMJ, 353*, i3604. https://doi.org/10.1136/bmj.i3604

Jackson, L., Greenfield, M., Payne, E., Redhead, C., Harris, J., Davie, P., Easter, A., Roberts, D., Silverio, S. A., & Magee, L. A. (2024). A consensus statement on perinatal mental health during the COVID-19 pandemic and recommendations for post-pandemic recovery and re-build. *Frontiers in Global Women's Health*, *5*(1347388), 1–8. https://doi.org/10.3389/fgwh.2024.1347388

Jardine, J., Relph, S., Magee, L. A., Mistry, H. D., Khalil, A., von Dadelszen, P., Easter, A., Harris, J., & Knight, M. (2021). Maternity services in the UK during the coronavirus disease 2019 pandemic: A national survey of modifications to standard care. *BJOG: An International Journal of Obstetrics & Gynaecology*, *128*(5), 880–889. https://doi.org/10.1111/1471-0528.16547

Lafarge, C., Mitchell, K., & Fox, P. (2014). Termination of pregnancy for fetal abnormality: A meta-ethnography of women's experiences. *Reproductive Health Matters*, *22*(44), 191–201. https://doi.org/10.1016/S0968-8080(14)44799-2

Lewis, C., Riddington, M., Hill, M., Mahoney, J., Smith, T., Johnson, E., Thompson, P., Riley, D., & Anderson, K. (2019). "The communication and support from the health professional is incredibly important": A qualitative study exploring the processes and practices that support parental decision-making about postmortem examination. *Prenatal Diagnosis*, *39*(13), 1242–1253. https://doi.org/10.1002/pd.5575

Lokubal, P., Corcuera, I., Balil, J. M., Martinez, L., Rodriguez, F., Alvarez, P., Gonzalez, R., Fernandez, A., & Sanchez, J. (2022). Abortion decision-making process trajectories and determinants in low-and middle-income countries: A mixed-methods systematic review and meta-analysis. *eClinicalMedicine*, *54*(101694), 1–25. https://doi.org/10.1016/j.eclinm.2022.101694

Malcolm, C., & Knighting, K. (2022). A realist evaluation of a home-based end-of-life care service for children and families: What works, for whom, how, in what circumstances and why? *BMC Palliative Care*, *21*(31), 1–17. https://doi.org/10.1186/s12904-022-00921-8

Mamrath, S., Greenfield, M., Fernandez Turienzo, C., Fallon, V., & Silverio, S. A. (2024). Experiences of postpartum anxiety during the COVID-19 pandemic: A mixed methods study and demographic analysis. *PLoS One*, *19*(3), 1–22. https://doi.org/10.1371/journal.pone.0297454

Nicolson, P. (2001). *Postnatal depression: Facing the paradox of loss, happiness and motherhood*. John Wiley.

Pilav, S., Easter, A., Silverio, S. A., De Backer, K., Sundaresh, S., Roberts, S., & Howard, L. (2022). Experiences of perinatal mental health care among minority ethnic women during the COVID-19 pandemic in London: A qualitative study. *International Journal of Environmental Research and Public Health*, *19*(4), 1–15. https://doi.org/10.3390/ijerph19041975

Pilkington, P. D., & Bedford-Dyer, I. (2021). Mothers' worries during pregnancy: A content analysis of Reddit posts. *Journal of Perinatal Education*, *30*(2), 98–107. https://doi.org/10.1891/J-PE-D-20-00018

Ralston, E. R., Smith, P., Chilcot, J., Silverio, S. A., & Bramham, K. (2021). Perceptions of risk in pregnancy with chronic disease: A systematic review and thematic synthesis. *PLoS One*, *16*(7), 1–15. https://doi.org/10.1371/journal.pone.0254956

Rayment-Jones, H., Harris, J., Harden, A., Silverio, S. A., Fernandez Turienzo, C., & Sandall, J. (2021). Project20: Interpreter services for pregnant women with social risk factors in England: What works, for whom, in what circumstances, and how? *International Journal for Equity in Health*, *20*(233), 1–11. https://doi.org/10.1186/s12939-021-01570-8

Redhead, C. A. B., Silverio, S. A., Payne, E., Greenfield, M., Barnett, S. M., Chiumento, A., Holder, B., Skirrow, H., Torres, O., Power, C., Weiss, S. M., Magee, L. A., Downe, S., Frith, L., & Cameron, C. (2025). A consensus statement on child and family health during the COVID-19 pandemic and recommendations for post-pandemic recovery and re-build. *Frontiers in Child and Adolescent Psychiatry, 4*(1520291), 1–8. https://doi.org/10.3389/frcha.2025.1520291

Reid, M. (2007). The loss of a baby and the birth of the next infant: The mother's experience. *Journal of Child Psychotherapy, 33*(2), 181–201. https://doi.org/10.1080/007541 70701431339

Roberts, D., Jackson, L., Davie, P., Zhao, C., Harrold, J. A., Fallon, V., & Silverio, S. A. (2023). Exploring the reasons why mothers do not breastfeed, to inform and enable better support. *Frontiers in Global Women's Health, 4*(1148719), 1–7. https://doi.org/10.3389/fgwh.2023.1148719

Saluja, B., & Bryant, Z. (2021). How implicit bias contributes to racial disparities in maternal morbidity and mortality in the United States. *Journal of Women's Health, 30*(2), 270–273. https://doi.org/10.1089/jwh.2020.8874

Silverio, S. A. (2021). Women's mental health a public health priority: A call for action. *Journal of Public Mental Health, 20*(1), 60–68. https://doi.org/10.1108/JPMH-04-2020-0023

Silverio, S. A. (2025). A hidden crisis: Women's mental health after the pandemic. *The Psychologist, 38*(1/2), 54–57.

Silverio, S. A., De Backer, K., Brown, J. M., Dasgupta, T., Easter, A., George-Carey, R., Memtsa, M., Storey, C., Khalil, A., Horgan, G., Mistry, H. D., Nelson, E. C., von Dadelszen, P., Duncan, E. L., & Magee, L. A. (2023). Reflective, pragmatic, and reactive decision-making by maternity service providers during the SARS-CoV-2 pandemic health system shock: A qualitative, grounded theory analysis. *BMC Pregnancy and Childbirth, 23*(368), 1–15. https://doi.org/10.1186/s12884-023-05641-2

Silverio, S. A., De Backer, K., Dasgupta, T., Easter, A., Khalil, A., George-Carey, R., Memtsa, M., & Magee, L. A. (2022). On race and ethnicity during a global pandemic: An 'imperfect mosaic' of maternal and child health services in ethnically-diverse South London, United Kingdom. *eClinicalMedicine, 48*(101433), 1–10. https://doi.org/10.1016/j.eclinm.2022.101433

Silverio, S. A., De Backer, K., Easter, A., von Dadelszen, P., Magee, L. A., & Sandall, J. (2021). Women's experiences of maternity service reconfiguration during the COVID-19 pandemic: A qualitative investigation. *Midwifery, 102*(103116), 1–9. https://doi.org/10.1016/j.midw.2021.103116

Silverio, S. A., Easter, A., Storey, C., Khalil, A., Mistry, H. D., & George-Carey, R. (2021). Preliminary findings on the experiences of care for parents who suffered perinatal bereavement during the COVID-19 pandemic. *BMC Pregnancy and Childbirth, 21*(840), 1–13. https://doi.org/10.1186/s12884-021-04292-5

Silverio, S. A., George-Carey, R., Memtsa, M., Khalil, A., Storey, C., & Magee, L. A. (2024). Preliminary findings on the experiences of care for women who suffered early pregnancy losses during the COVID-19 pandemic: A qualitative study. *BMC Pregnancy and Childbirth, 24*(522), 1–16. https://doi.org/10.1186/s12884-024-06721-7

Silverio, S. A., Harris, E. J., Jackson, L., Payne, E., Roberts, D., & Davie, P. (2024). Freedom for some, but not for Mum: The reproductive injustice associated with pandemic 'Freedom Day' for perinatal women in the United Kingdom. *Frontiers in Public Health, 12*(1389702), 1–14. https://doi.org/10.3389/fpubh.2024.1389702

Silverio, S. A., Varman, N., Barry, Z., Khazaezadeh, N., Rajasingam, D., Magee, L. A., & Matthew, J. (2023). Inside the 'imperfect mosaic': Minority ethnic women's qualitative experiences of race and ethnicity during pregnancy, childbirth, and maternity care in the United Kingdom. *BMC Public Health*, *23*(2555), 1–11. https://doi.org/10.1186/s12889-023-17505-7

Silverio, S. A., Wilkinson, C., Fallon, V., Brown, J. M., Easter, A., Storey, C., Magee, L. A., Mistry, H. D., Von Dadelszen, P., & Stephenson, J. (2021). When a mother's love is not enough: A cross-cultural critical review of anxiety, attachment, maternal ambivalence, abandonment, and infanticide. In C.-H. Mayer & E. Vanderheiden (Eds.), *International handbook of love: Transcultural and transdisciplinary perspectives* (pp. 291–315). Springer.

Skirrow, H., Lewis, C., Haque, H., Alaeze-Ibeh, A., Sahota, D., & Dixon, S. (2024). 'Why did nobody ask us?': A mixed-methods co-produced study in the United Kingdom exploring why some children are unvaccinated or vaccinated late. *Vaccine*, *42*(22), 1–13. https://doi.org/10.1016/j.vaccine.2024.126172

Chapter 17

Birth

A discussion

Alejandra Perez and Ruth Roberts

The chapters in this section use a range of perspectives to examine several topics related to internal and external factors influencing parents' experiences and types of childbirth. In Chapter 12, Perez uses psychoanalytic theories and an illustrative clinical vignette to explain the profound changes that occur during birth for the parent and the baby, and the navigation of the separation involved in birth and the building of new family relationships. In Chapter 13, Goulder draws on her expertise running postnatal classes and qualitative and empirical literature to describe the experience and impact of trauma during childbirth. She highlights the importance of support following a traumatic birth. In Chapter 14, Dahan draws on empirical evidence to consider the psycho-neurobiological processes that occur during birth, exploring the concepts of birthing consciousness, transient hypofrontality and flow, and how these differ during medicalised versus unmedicalised births. In Chapter 15, Veale, Munns, and Preston use empirical research, as well as historical and cultural perspectives, to examine the bodily self during childbirth, exploring medicalisation of the body and bodily trust. Finally, in Chapter 16 Silverio and Dasgupta examine the socio-cultural context of birth, drawing on empirical evidence to explore the challenges faced by women in accessing appropriate healthcare, navigating new roles following birth, and the additional complexities faced by women of minoritised and marginalised groups.

Different ways of thinking about birth

Medical classifications

In Chapter 14, Dahan describes how, despite there existing various classifications on type of childbirth, none fully capture the complexity of the birth experience. She explains how medical classifications focus on the physiological experiences of birth, and we noted how medical classifications usually focused on the level of intervention involved. Vaginal birth can be completely unassisted with no pain relief or intervention (often called natural birth). Vaginal birth can also involve some level of intervention including induction (involving physical or pharmaceutical procedures), pain relief (e.g., Entonox, commonly known as gas and air), and

DOI: 10.4324/9781003530473-21

physical or pharmaceutical assistance for delivery of the placenta. Vaginal birth may also include increased levels of intervention, including use of epidural (e.g., pain relief administered into the space around the spinal nerves) or instrumental assistance during delivery (e.g., via a physical intervention such as forceps or ventouse). Childbirth may also happen non-vaginally, via caesarean section. This can be planned (e.g., when the pregnancy is high risk or parental preference) or unplanned (e.g., emergencies, or when vaginal birth is not progressing). We note how these classifications are often focused on the risks and benefits to mother and baby (University Hospitals Dorset NHS Foundation Trust, n.d.).

Subjective classifications

Dahan highlights that medical classifications do not consider the subjective experiences of the birthing woman, which can be classed as either subjectively empowering or traumatic. The subjective experience of trauma is incredibly important; all authors in this section consider potential sources of traumatic experience during childbirth and the various ways they impact on the mother and baby. Goulder also highlights that experience of trauma during childbirth must be defined by the mother.

Perez notes how parents' experiences of birth vary widely. Labour always entails some risk to the birthing parent and the baby, involves the physical separation between them, and intensification of the care that the parent must provide to ensure their baby's survival. Perez explains that these facts can be experienced differently depending on the meaning (conscious and unconscious) these have for the parents, as well as the emotions and past experiences that can become reawakened during this process. Goulder and Veale, Munns, and Preston note how medicalised births often seek to take control over the birthing experience, particularly via use of intervention, and this can contribute to women's experience of trauma during childbirth.

Social and contextual classifications

While out of scope of this section, Dahan also notes the growing recognition of experiences of different groups of people, which can be helpful to consider when thinking about classification of births. This includes births involving transgender individuals and births with parents with special needs. There are also births that involve difficult or unexpected experiences, including stillbirths, and we also add emergency births to this group. In all of these cases, experiences may not be represented in the chapters in this book and further consideration may be needed to ensure an optimal birthing experience.

Additionally, Dahan discussed how the place of birth, for example home birth versus birth in a hospital, will also have an impact on the birth experience. Dahan notes how a more comprehensive taxonomy is needed to fully capture the diverse range of birthing experiences and inform evidence-based practices.

External and internal factors influencing the birthing experience

There is a growing interest among clinicians and researchers in this field in trying to understand the differences between individual birthing experiences. This increased engagement with the subject of childbirth is likely a result of more women reporting their experience of it as traumatic, and is probably also influenced by recent studies indicating that the experience of childbirth can have a significant impact on the mother's postpartum psychological state (Bell & Andersson, 2016) and the early mother-infant relationship (Re-Murray & Fisher, 2001). The existing research has looked at a wide range of external and internal factors. The external factors include: poor medical care or lack of access to medical care, increasing health risks to the birthing parent and baby; medical interventions themselves (by stopping the natural physiological preparation for birth and/or by contributing to the birthing parent's sense of lack of control); poor or insufficient social and/or emotional support; poor or insufficient information about the process of birth; and childbirth complications (such as stillbirth, life-threatening haemorrhages, etc.). Internal factors that have been considered are: the birthing parent's mental state during the birth (see, for example, Dahan's description of 'flow'—others yet to be considered include psychotic and depressive states); unconscious subjective experiences of separating from the baby; and fear of dying. The birthing experience is a highly complex phenomenon, given the range and interplay of individual factors and external circumstances, and thus it varies significantly from person to person.

The authors in this section and the previous one (on pregnancy) put forward different arguments for and against the use of medical interventions during pregnancy and childbirth. On one hand, it is clear that medical interventions can make the difference in reducing infant and maternal mortality and birth complication rates. On the other hand, as Dahan explains, the natural neurobiological changes that occur during childbirth help the birthing parent to cope with intense labour pains, and medical interventions in this sense have a negative effect by interrupting this natural process. In their chapter, Veale, Munns, and Preston underline the importance of the bodily self, arguing that medicalised births disconnect women from their bodies and from feelings of trust in their bodies. Medical interventions, then, are described as either life-saving or physically and psychologically detrimental. These are strikingly opposing views, which raise important aspects that should be considered. Expectant mothers also differ in the ways in which they perceive birth (both consciously and unconsciously) and the process of physical separation from their baby; specifically whether and how much these processes awaken unconscious conflicts, intense feelings of loss, fear of death, or a sense of annihilation.

Meanwhile, in her chapter, Perez provides a clinical example of an expectant father, John, who felt painfully confronted by fear for his baby's survival. For John, gaining an understanding of the origins of this fear enabled him to begin getting to know his baby. In this sense, childbirth—for both the birthing and the non-birthing parent—is an important stage in the process of integrating past experiences and becoming open to new ones. In a similar vein, Goulder, in her chapter, emphasises the need for psychoeducation and other opportunities for expectant and new parents to talk about their experiences, giving them the chance to work through intense and difficult feelings.

Mental states during birth

The intense physical experience of giving birth also has a psychological parallel. In her chapter, Dahan focuses on the neurobiological process of hypofrontality in childbirth, and proposes that the birthing mother enters a mental state that she has termed 'birthing consciousness'. This state is defined by a heightened awareness of bodily sensations, an altered perception of time and space, intense shifts of emotion—ranging from euphoria to profound peace—and a reduced capacity for self-reflection and analytical thought.

As far back as 1956, Winnicott postulated a particular mental state—'primary maternal preoccupation'—in women in their last trimester of pregnancy and post-partum. Recent research has demonstrated the neurobiological changes that occur during these periods, resulting in changes in mental states. For example, Dahan, in her chapter, delineates these neurobiological, giving rise to a 'birthing consciousness', which helps the birthing mother to regulate pain, and to reduce stress and anxiety. Informed by her psychoanalytic work, Perez describes the different unconscious mechanisms that are mobilised to help the mother navigate her intense fear, anxiety, and physical pain, and so to protect the new baby. Both chapters by Dahan and Veale, Munns, and Preston appeal for more support for birthing mothers, to help them connect to their bodies and to the natural process enabling them to give birth. Following Winnicott's line of thinking, Perez explores the different ways in which the physical experiences of pregnancy and childbirth are represented psychically, and sheds light on how clinical work can help expectant and new parents to integrate and make sense of their experiences. The great importance of psychoanalytic work during this period is in helping parents to create a space in their minds where they can get to know and bond with their new baby. This is a greater challenge for parents who have suffered a traumatic birth.

Traumatic births

The different authors in this section illuminate important contributions to the topic of what makes a birth traumatic. The challenge of addressing this subject is that the experience of childbirth is a highly complex and individual experience, influenced by multiple external and internal factors. In addition, while the term 'traumatic birth' is used frequently in clinical and maternal health literature, its meaning is defined somewhat differently. In her chapter, Goulder sets the scene by bringing Beck's (2004) definition of "a perception of 'actual or threatened injury or death to the mother or her baby'". The strength of this definition is that it encompasses both external and internal factors. Some authors have focused on the various ways in which medical interventions can negatively impact the woman's bodily trust, diminishing her sense of agency and control, and causing her to feel violently intruded upon. Meanwhile, other authors point to the real physical danger of childbirth for the birthing mother and the baby, so that medical intervention can sometimes make the difference between life and death, or else avoid serious complications. Still other authors have focused on the internal unconscious anxieties and conflicts that are reawakened by the prospect of giving birth. Significantly, all of these authors allude to the ways in which birth can be experienced not only as a frightening, painful, or traumatic experience (of separation, loss, death, passivity, and so on) but also as a progression to a new stage of life, where diverse physical and mental changes are required to make space for a new member of the family.

Socio-cultural aspects of childbirth

The importance of accessible, high-quality care

Access to and quality of care during and in preparation for childbirth is essential. However, the chapters in this section describe the various limitations and challenges within maternity services and the resulting impact for birthing parents. In her chapter, Perez noted how inequality of access to high-quality healthcare in low- and middle-income countries contributed to high levels of infant and maternal mortality. Goulder remarked on the importance of accessible and affordable birth preparation education, particularly for parents who are from diverse social and cultural backgrounds. Parents who do not speak the language or who are not familiar with the healthcare system may feel powerless or overwhelmed during childbirth.

Goulder also notes reductions in important services supporting parents following childbirth, such as debriefing services for parents who have experienced a traumatic birth. She highlights how midwives may seek to be logical and detached when faced with pressures and uncertainty in their role and they may not receive adequate support, particularly when healthcare systems take a defensive approach. Support for midwives and those caring for birthing mothers is important as they are the frontline in providing support and guidance during labour. Dahan noted that in Western hospitals there is rarely continuous, individualised support for birthing mothers.

Silverio and Dasgupta describe a triple burden on expectant women resulting from a struggling healthcare system. The first is related to anxiety and uncertainty about themselves and/or their baby being at risk due to the lower quality of services. The second relates to access to and engagement with services, which may be difficult when there is poor communication and services are hard to access or when women do not feel like they are eligible for the service for a range of reasons and then choose not to engage. Additionally, women may feel overwhelmed by the number of health-related decisions they need to make during the course of pregnancy, birth, and the postnatal period.

Silverio and Dasgupta also describe how women from marginalised and minoritised backgrounds face discrimination within maternity services, which may be experienced as violence. They explain two forms of violence: cultural and structural. 'Cultural violence' involves the construction of minority ethnic individuals as 'other', which can lead to an ingrained fear or expectation of racial discrimination. This form of violence is often subtle and internalised, rather than overtly expressed or witnessed. 'Structural violence' involves systemic barriers for minoritised individuals, making it difficult for them to access and navigate services due to unconscious bias, but can also manifest in workplace culture and between staff. When cultural and structural violence are present, 'direct violence' often becomes inevitable, with women from minoritised and marginalised groups experiencing physical and/or emotional harm.

Increases in medicalised childbirth

Several authors note an increase in the medicalisation of maternity services. Veale, Munns, and Preston described how historically, women's bodies were viewed as flawed, vulgar, and disorderly, with childbirth being seen as a form of punishment. They highlight that, in the eighteenth and nineteenth centuries, the pregnant body became a focus of medical scrutiny, however pregnancy and childbirth continued to be mysterious, and women were criticised for rejecting professional oversight. They highlight a loss in practices rooted in women's embodied knowledge giving way to male-led, medical authority over childbirth.

Dahan discussed how increases in medical intervention during childbirth can cause disruption to the usual progression of labour and may interfere with neurobiological processes that are thought to enhance birthing experiences, such as birthing consciousness. Dahan notes that hospitals are not optimised for birthing mothers to enter or sustain the flow associated with birthing consciousness, due to aspects like bright lights and loud noises.

Veale, Munns, and Preston note how in Western society the female body is objectified and valued for its appearance. During pregnancy, the body's role in gestating the baby takes priority and this can reduce societal pressures on bodily expectations. However, the authors also note that increases in medical intervention risks objectifying the female body, not in terms of appearance, but by reducing the body to an object that is performing a function. This reduces women's agency over their experience.

The editors recognise the lack of a medical perspective in this section, which is a limitation of this book. It is important to recognise this as the increase in medicalised births may also be influenced by other, or in addition to other, factors such as increasing age of birthing parents and pre-existing medical conditions (see Blomberg et al., 2014).

Pressures of motherhood

Silverio and Dasgupta note that mothers bear a significant toll in times of social and health crises due to their central role in families, communities, and society. They describe various 'shifts' mothers make in their lives, which are shaped by necessity rather than choice. The first shift involves taking on paid employment, where women provide financially for their families, gaining a social role and sense of purpose separate from motherhood. The second shift involves provision of care within the family, where mothers are the central hub for family life, and women feel responsible for challenges that arise in the family unit. The third shift involves managing social responsibilities and social networks for the family, which can prioritise the identity as a mother over one's individual identity, creating a 'paradox of loss'. The fourth shift involves taking on healthcare responsibilities for family or social circles, often filling gaps left by insufficient formal care systems. These shifts highlight the evolving and multifaceted nature of motherhood, emphasising the heavy social responsibilities mothers carry in addition to the psychological and physical changes discussed before.

References

Beck, C.T. (2004). Birth trauma: in the eye of the beholder. *Nurs Res*, *53*(1):28–35.

Bell, A.F. & Andersson, E. (2016). The birth experience and women's postnatal depression: A systematic review. *Midwifery*, *39:*112–123. doi: 10.1016/j.midw.2016.04.014.

Blomberg, M., Birch Tyrberg, R. & Kjølhede, P. (2014). Impact of maternal age on obstetric and neonatal outcome with emphasis on primiparous adolescents and older women: A Swedish Medical Birth Register Study. *BMJ Open*, *4*:e005840. doi: 10.1136/bmjopen-2014-005840

Re-Murray, H.J. & Fisher, J.R. (2001). Operative intervention in delivery is associated with compromised early mother-infant interaction. *BJOG*, *108*(10):1068.–1075. doi: 10.1111/j.1471-0528.2001.00242.x.

University Hospitals Dorset NHS Foundation Trust. (n.d.). *Types of birth*. Retrieved April 27, 2025, from www.uhd.nhs.uk/services/maternity/services/types-of-birth

Winnicott, D. W. (1956)[1975]. Chapter XXIV. Primary maternal preoccupation. *Through Paediatrics to Psycho-Analysis (International Psycho-Analytical Library* (No.100, pp. 300–306). London: Hogarth Press & Institute of Psycho-Analysis.

Part IV

Transition to parenthood

Chapter 18

Psychological changes and challenges in the transition to parenthood

Björn Salomonsson

A mother-infant dyad

Donna is a 30-year-old woman whom I interviewed with her five-month-old daughter Annie. Donna said:

> I'm no good at this parent-child thing! I don't like pushing the pram. Guess I feel guilty. I know this isn't politically correct. I like to work hard, and now I can't compensate by working harder. Pregnancy was not unplanned, but it went faster than we'd thought. Kind of 'whoops, I guess this was fun'. The entire pregnancy was 'whoops', I never had time to long for a child. I didn't feel well during the latter part of pregnancy. The doctor wanted to put me on sick leave. I told him I don't have time. 'That's just your problem', he said.
>
> Delivery wouldn't start so they did an emergency Caesarean. I woke up after five hours. That 'immediate mother-baby-contact' never appeared. She never liked breastfeeding, just threw herself backwards. I had fantasies of throwing her out of the window. Everybody praises breastfeeding, but there's no scientific evidence that it's better than a bottle! When my husband resumed working, I panicked. Alone with the baby ...

Part of my clinical practice is to do consultant work at a Child Health Centre in Stockholm with young families in various therapeutic settings and with various problems. Some receive an intensive individual or parent-infant psychotherapy with me, where we can explore unconscious conflicts around parenthood and infancy. My perspective also stems from living in an epoch marked by a global trend of having children later in life and of changing gender roles. There is also a sharp rise in the parents' medical and psychological knowledge via internet searches, which can create much anxiety as it is hard to differentiate trustworthy information from exaggerations and misinformation.

At the Centre, I often meet women like Donna (whom I, in contrast, met in a research study). Donna is smart, well-read, has a secure standard of living, a supportive husband, and a treasured job. But motherhood has toppled her calmness, security, and happiness. She switches between acknowledging that her anxiety

DOI: 10.4324/9781003530473-23

about motherhood is incomprehensible—and that it's society's fault. Also, she indicates that burying herself in work tasks is not a sound solution—and yet she cannot accept sick-leave.

Some comments in the interview point to one source of her maternal anxiety; a faltering identification with her mother. When I ask about their relationship, she responds:

> We've a very close and frequent contact … I've an academic education but my parents haven't exactly read Strindberg … My Mum is hasty and doesn't think things through. I asked if she thought anything special when she had me. She looked at me as if I was a Martian: 'Was I supposed to think anything special? I just did what I did'.

This illustrates her identification with a 'non-mothering mother'. Probably, she handled her daughter Donna well, but one can see that Donna was left with few identifications that could support and encourage her as a future mother. As for Donna's contact with her daughter, she says:

> The first 6 weeks I felt absent, due to a wound infection after the Caesarean. Kind of self-centred. I was breastfeeding all the time, but I was tired and fell asleep when I nursed her. The girl refused the breast from 2½ months and onwards. It was a shock being alone with her. Suddenly, I had a child with a strong will. She didn't want to sleep or eat, she was just tired. Then she was too tired to eat. All the time, something didn't work.

Donna's account raises questions about their contact and behaviour. Let us compare with my report of a video recording that was part of a research project, in which this dyad and many others participated (Salomonsson and Sandell, 2011a, b).

> Donna's tempo is fast. Facing Annie's mounting distress, she decides it must be "fart or poo-poo". She names Annie 'Plum-face' and asks, 'Are you a Hawaiian who only knows vowels, ouayah?' The girl wants to be held in mother's arms, but Donna interprets this as appeals to sing or to change the diaper. Donna's garrulous, up-tempo language is evident. This leaves behind a doubt how she might contain the baby's distress. In my countertransference, Annie seemed 'aged' and concerned, and her eyes looked sad.

In my interpretation, Donna projects onto the girl her own anxiety and vexation to depose unlovable and disgusting aspects of herself. This is reflected in her conviction that the girl's fussy panting must be due to fart or poo. I rather believe that Annie signals her emotional distress, which the mother does not capture. This distress is visible in other ways, such as Annie's gaze avoidance and clinging to her mother and then retracting from her. Finally, her mother takes recourse to the ultimate solution. She offers her breast, and the girl grasps it vividly. The impression remains, however, of a dyad in which the child's emotional signals are not introjected by the mother, transformed by her alpha-function, and then returned to the girl in a form that Annie can make use of (Bion, 1962).

My apprehension received confirmation years later, when Donna contacted me about her worries about Annie. She described a chaotic situation at home. Annie had temper tantrums, and family members had to adapt to them. She could not be alone and avoided physical contact. She was afraid of dogs and elevators and grinded her teeth. She was also clever and well-behaved at pre-school. Tearful, her mother recalled that she had always felt a distance between her and Annie: "In the beginning, I had no contact with her". This led to a psychoanalytic child therapy (Salomonsson and Winberg Salomonsson, 2017).

Changes and challenges

Changes and challenges are two neighbouring words. When a change strikes us, we are challenged to ask what it consists of, what feelings arise, if we welcome it or not, and what are its consequences for us and others near to us. The first change that we can study directly is birth. We are ousted from intrauterine life, with its relative passivity and non-volition, to a reality that we must slowly learn to handle ourselves. These changes are at first merely biological, but, very soon, psychological changes and challenges await us as well.

Psychoanalytic theory has always focused on how human cognition and emotion *develop*. This interest was originally a by-product of clinical findings. Analysts discovered that, as their patients struggled with present emotional challenges and talked about them, they often connected them with events in early childhood. Consequently, theory focused on how experiences in childhood and youth were connected with present emotional disorders.

When analysts suggested that children pass through developmental phases, the idea was also that mental disorders were linked with phases when the individual had experienced invincible challenges. As they were towering, unconscious conflicts became fixated that might later derail the individual's mental balance. These phases related both to biological and psychological changes. Classical theory did not describe any phases later than adolescence. Erik Homburger Erikson (1950) changed this in his epigenetic theory of eight developmental stages, covering the entire life cycle. Parenthood occurs in the stages of young and middle adulthood, with their challenges of intimacy versus isolation and generativity versus stagnation, respectively.

Parenthood post Freud

The emotional challenges of parenthood became a topic for mid-century analysts like Winnicott (1960), Benedek (1959), Bibring et al., (1961), and Deutsch (1944). Benedek described parenthood as a developmental phase and argued that the psychodynamic processes of reproduction and parenthood are drive motivations for further development.

Table 18.1 Mother's feelings in pre- and post-natal life

PRENATAL LIFE	POSTNATAL LIFE
In command at work and at home	Not working, bad at home
Goodlooking and desired	Ugly and unattractive
Opinionated about parenting	Puzzled and irresolute as parent
Foetus an abstract and cryptic 'something there'	Baby a concrete and totally present 'someone here'
Kids are uninteresting / cute	Baby is screaming and demanding
Rested and calm	Fagged out and on the alert
Gender equality	Gender inequality
One's parents not central, not needed	Parents central and needed

Benedek did not overlook that, in parenthood, parents also use primary processes that have been operating from infancy. There is, so to speak, a baby in every parent—and the new mother may relive "the pleasure and pains of [her own] infancy" (Benedek, 1959, p.395). This can be an insurmountable challenge. I suggest Donna is a case in point. As a girl, she probably did not get adequate containment from her mother. She became a diligent, successful, and self-contained woman, though with difficulties in understanding a person in a psychological situation very different from her own; a dependent, needy, and helpless baby like Annie.

Every new mother was thus once a child herself who introjected from her mother what it had felt like to be fed, nursed, and cared for. This "long and complicated route" (Mack Brunswick, 1940, p.296) started with the girl being passively fed by the mother, followed by her identifying with the mother's active caretaking and limit-setting. Sometimes, this can yield resentment in the girl and extend into her future pregnancy (H.C. Freud, 2011). She may oscillate between an illusory symbiosis with the mother and an abysmal separation from her. We may observe this when mother and daughter form "a duo chained and addicted to each other" (p.11). This easily leads to unconscious anger towards the baby. To illustrate, Donna asks Annie in the video if she is a Hawaiian who only uses vowels. This can be interpreted as an innocent joke, but, in my impression, it also reveals her helplessness and vexation with the girl. Such feelings also surface in comments during the interview with me.

One surprising discovery of young mothers in research interviews and therapy is that their psychological processes and their babies are actually akin. Both of them need to balance greedy and generous, loving and hateful, progressive and regressive, autonomous and symbiotic impulses. The mother's challenge contains an extra weight in that she must simultaneously be 'the adult in the room' and take care of a helpless baby. When all goes well and she can make peace with her own infantile impulses involved in baby care, it gives her an increased self-esteem (Bibring, 1961), and the baby can form a secure attachment to her. The cases we see at ante- and postnatal clinics, like the one of Donna and Annie, are the ones that did not tread this fortunate pathway.

Before we leave the tribulations of motherhood, let us not forget the father. As Benedek saw it, his emotional attitude "in the family triad is significant from conception on. He responds to the receptive-dependent needs of his wife which are increased by her pregnancy, by her anxieties about parturition and the care of the child". The father's relationship to the child is "directed more by hope than by drive" (400). He soothes, comforts, and plays with the child. Besides this "primary, libidinal gratification, he also experiences a secondary narcissistic gratification in the reassurance of his ego ideal that he is a good father". To summarise, Benedek argued that the father's impact on the child emerged later than that of the mother. Her position may seem old-fashioned, now that there is much focus on fathers' experiences. Yet, her position salutes the psychological consequences of the biological differences between the sexes, a position that I also adhere to—though with the reservation that they are especially important in the baby's first months.

Some two generations after the previously mentioned authors, Jessica Benjamin (1988) integrated Freudian theory, intersubjectivity, feminist theory, and societal changes. She stated that, despite our knowledge of the mother's importance in shaping the child's early attachment and identity, society tends to underestimate her caregiving. This perpetuates a gender polarity of man and woman, of dominator and dominated, all to the detriment for the child as well.

Other contemporary authors include Chodorow (2023), Kristeva (1985), Chasseguet-Smirguel (1976). To describe their work goes beyond the scope of this chapter. In brief, they contributed by de-idealising and de-sanctifying people's views of women and mothers and explored the individuals amid daily chores, hassles, as well as challenged by unconscious intrapsychic and interpersonal conflicts.

Other psychoanalytic contributions include mothers' ambivalence (Parker, 2002, Benoit et al., 1997), rage (Trad, 1991), and sexuality (Laplanche, 1999) in connection with their relation to their baby and partner. An apt metaphor for this focus is "the dark side of the womb" (Raphael-Leff, 2015), referring to the ignorance and debasement of womanhood that may occur both in women and men. When such attitudes—which often are unconscious and sharply contrasting with conscious 'politically correct' values—prevail, the future mother faces a grave challenge.

Parenthood today

The ideas mentioned so far are still relevant to me. However, today's postponement of first-time parenthood has implications that go beyond the ones described by earlier authors. The table summarises these challenges.

The table suggests that the challenges of parenthood revolve around narcissism versus object love, as well as fear of the past, present, and future. In one mother's words, "Before pregnancy, I was fine, in control, fit, and relishing the power of having left my folks and created my own life. Now that I'm a mother, I feel exhausted, unattractive, marginalized, confused and uncertain about mothering my baby."

Today's parents read books and search on the internet. However, this does not help every mother to feel more 'in the saddle'. Old "ghosts in the nursery"

(Fraiberg, 1987) from her past still haunt her. Also, "the medicalization of birth" (Hustvedt, 2022, p.372), which has come to dominate developed cultures, may increase the emotional distance to being a parent. Importantly, such challenges affect both sexes, as seen by the many mothers and fathers who are uncertain of what they can and cannot achieve.

Donna told me she felt like having had only one pregnancy and delivery, referring to the birth of Annie's younger sibling. I cannot find a better way of expressing the torment of a mother who realises that the challenges of parenthood overwhelmed her and that, at the time, there was nobody to talk seriously about it. As it happened in this case, Annie had a later opportunity of receiving child psychotherapy. But the case also illustrates how much more we can do, once we get signals of postnatal suffering in mother and/or baby and have the possibility of suggesting psychotherapy to the mother, the father, or the dyad.

The precondition for this to happen is that the public, health care politicians, and stakeholders, and, last but not least, psychodynamic psychotherapists realise that it is essential to institute qualified support and help to these suffering dyads. The baby's budding personality is brittle and malleable and may influence his or her future development. And due to their parental preoccupation, the parents have easier access to unconscious conflicts. Also, their parental drive (Spitz, 1965) often renders them eager to do their best in trying to avoid transferring (Faimberg, 2005, Salberg and Grand, 2016) to their children whatever negative experience they may have had in their own childhood. These factors indicate the necessity to help these families, because they suffer and because they are often amenable to psychotherapy.

References

Benedek, T. 1959. Parenthood as a developmental phase. A contribution to the libido theory. *Journal of the American Psychoanalytic Association*, 7, 389–417.

Benjamin, J. 1988. *The Bonds of Love: Psychoanalysis, Feminism, and the Problem of Domination*, New York, NY, Pantheon.

Benoit, D., Parker, K. C. & Zeanah, C. H. 1997. Mothers' representations of their infants assessed prenatally: Stability and association with infants' attachment classifications. *Journal of Child Psychology and Psychiatry*, 38, 307–313.

Bibring, G. L., Dwyer, T. F., Huntington, D. S. & Valenstrin, A. F. 1961. A study of the psychological processes in pregnancy and of the earliest mother-child relationship—I. Some propositions and comments. *Psychoanalytic Study of the Child*, 16, 9–24.

Bion, W. R. 1962. *Learning from Experience*, London, Karnac Books.

Chasseguet-Smirgel, J. 1976. Freud and female sexuality: The consideration of some blind spots in the exploration of the "Dark Continent.". *International Journal of Psycho Analysis*, 57, 275–286.

Chodorow, N. J. 2023. *The Reproduction of Mothering: Psychoanalysis and the Sociology of Gender*, Los Angeles, University of California Press.

Deutsch, H. 1944. *The Psychology of Women*, London, Grune and Stratton.

Erikson, E. H. 1950. *Childhood and Society*, New York, W. W. Norton.

Faimberg, H. 2005. *The Telescoping of Generations: Listening to the Narcissistic Links Between Generations*, London, Routledge.

Fraiberg, S. 1987. *Selected writings of Selma Fraiberg*, Columbus (USA), Ohio State University Press.

Freud, H. C. 2011. *Electra vs. Oedipus: The Drama of the Mother-Daughter Relationship*, London, Routledge.

Hustvedt, S. 2022. Umbilical phantoms. *The International Journal of Psychoanalysis*, 103, 368–380.

Kristeva, J. 1985. Stabat Mater. In: ED, T. M. (ed.) *The Kristeva Reader, 160-186.* New York: Columbia University Press.

Laplanche J. 1999. *The unconscious and the id.* London, Rebus Press.

Mack Brunswick, R. 1940. The preoedipal phase of the libido development. *Psychoanalytic Quarterly*, 9, 293–319.

Parker, R. 2002. The production and purposes of maternal ambivalence. In: Hollway, W. & Featherstone, B. (eds.) *Mothering and Ambivalence*, London, Routledge.

Raphael-Leff, J. 2015. *Dark Side of the Womb*, London, Anna Freud Centre.

Salberg, J. & Grand, S. 2016. *Wounds of history: Repair and resilience in the transgenerational transmission of trauma*, Abingdon, Taylor & Francis.

Salomonsson, B. & Sandell, R. 2011a. A randomized controlled trial of mother-infant psychoanalytic treatment. 1. Outcomes on self-report questionnaires and external ratings. *Infant Mental Health Journal*, 32, 207–231.

Salomonsson, B. & Sandell, R. 2011b. A randomized controlled trial of mother-infant psychoanalytic treatment. 2. Predictive and moderating influences of quantitative treatment and patient factors. *Infant Mental Health Journal*, 32, 377–404.

Salomonsson, B. & Winberg Salomonsson, M. 2017. Intimacy thwarted and established: Following a girl from infancy to child psychotherapy. *International Journal of Psychoanalysis*, 98, 861–875.

Spitz, R. 1965. *The First Year of Life*, New York, IUP.

Trad, P. V. 1991. From mothers' milk to mothers' dreams: Maternal destructive separation fantasies. *Contemporary Psychoanalysis*, 27, 34–50.

Winnicott, D. W. 1960. The theory of the parent-infant relationship. *International Journal of Psychoanalysis*, 41, 585–595.

Chapter 19

Psychoanalytic thinking and the parenting couple

Kate Thompson

The creative couple[1]

Couples are drawn together for all manner of conscious and unconscious reasons. A complex web of unconscious projection and introjection create a dynamic between them that encourages development or, its reverse, a kind of psychological statis for both the two individuals and their shared relationship. Mary Morgan describes the challenge to couples of sustaining a "creative couple" state of mind, a place where individual identity and development can thrive, and feelings of separateness and togetherness co-exist in a third space between them.

> Within creative *couple* development, there is a capacity to manage separateness and difference together with intimacy. The other's different thoughts and views can be taken inside the self without too much anxiety that one's own thoughts and views will be lost or annihilated …This capacity supports the individual and the couple in letting go of previous certainties, being able to know and realising that while it may not be immediately apparent, an as-yet-unknown creative outcome to their difficulty might be possible.
>
> (Morgan, 2024)

This couple capacity to develop their own individual thoughts and feelings, while combining them in a new third way, with their relationship in their minds as something at once separate *to* them but made up *of* them, is perhaps the most hopeful foundation for the couple as they contemplate the creation of a child and the lifelong challenge of parenthood. It will ensure they maintain their relationship as a resource to contain the inevitable internal and external pressures that all parents face, alongside the joys.

Case vignette

Mary and Fred were an unmarried couple in their mid-30s. They presented for couple psychotherapy when their daughter, Iris, was 2 years old. The couple reported ricocheting from one flare-up to another, interspersed with periods of

DOI: 10.4324/9781003530473-24

quiet, simmering resentment. Their physical relationship had completely broken down. Their conflict was mostly placed at Fred's door; Mary believed she was reasonable and rational, the grown-up in the relationship.

Mary was the only child of wealthy parents, now both dead. They had her late in life and raised her to stand on her own two feet, worried that she would be left an orphan when they died. Her father suffered from chronic depression, which could be traced back through his family of origin, which was punctuated by suicide and trauma. As a result, her father maintained a distance, interrupted by occasional angry eruptions that were incomprehensible to Mary.

Mary's mother suffered from post-natal depression after she was born and, in the couple therapy, we wondered if this was linked to the previous loss of a full-term baby boy two weeks after his birth, and not long before Mary was conceived. Mary said, when she was young, she couldn't enjoy herself like other children. She would go to classmates' houses and see them running around, shrieking, and jumping on the beds. She thought to herself that they were weird. Only later in life did she realise she was the anomaly.

Perinatal Loss

Marguerite Reid (2007) describes a "penumbra baby ... my work has shown that many babies conceived following a perinatal loss are born in the shadow of the dead baby". Reid goes on to explain how a mother's containment of her infant's distressed feelings is often linked to the infant's fear for survival. She continues:

> Bion (1962) wrote of maternal containment whereby the mother receives and detoxifies painful projections from her baby before returning these detoxified feelings. When there has been perinatal loss, I think it is often difficult for the mother to receive painful projections associated with death. They stir considerable anxiety for her.

Reid believes that this difficulty can inhibit aspects of mother-infant interaction.

Case vignette

Growing up, Mary took refuge in her studies and, in adulthood, became a curator in a well-known museum, specialising in the preserving of antiquities and advising other museums around the world.

Being pregnant and becoming a mother filled Mary with disquiet. There was part of her that was pleased but mostly she dreaded that she would somehow get it wrong. She turned to me in session and said, "*Where was the manual? No-one told me what to do.*"

Fred's parents, like Mary's, never spoke about their emotions although they were a tight unit, with their three children left largely untended to, on the outside of things. Fred's father was a reporter for a local newspaper and his mother a teaching assistant at the school Fred went to. Fred remembered conversations between his parents, about local accidents or disobedient pupils, and feeling alarmed by what he overheard. Fred was also bullied at school, made worse because his mother was part of the teaching staff. He didn't tell anyone about his difficulties and no-one noticed his grades plummeting.

Fred left school with few qualifications. He started drinking, took drugs, and hung out with the wrong crowd. The one thing Fred loved was being in nature. When he met Mary, he was working as a carpenter and renovating an old shepherd's hut in the woods.

Unconscious Couple Fit

We might think of the couple's unconscious fit as Mary being attracted to a man who needed her sensible, 'parental' approach, who was different to her in terms of means, ambition, and lifestyle. Fred's eruptions of passionate feeling and explosions of temper seemed to represent to her a freedom from the confines of a repressed, wealthy, upper-class background. Fred was full of outrageous fun when they first met but, as time went on, suffered from bouts of severe anxiety where he would shout at Mary and be rude to her friends. This anxiety when he believed something was expected of him was interspersed with crippling depression where he found it hard to get out of bed in the morning.

Fred was attracted to Mary's serious steadiness. She seemed to provide the key to a life he aspired to and offered him safety and security, something he had never had. She was interested in him and he loved it that they could talk creatively about ideas.

Over time, however, their initial 'couple fit' changed. Mary's 'reasonable' stance increasingly provided Fred with someone to rebel against while Fred's lack of ambition drove Mary mad. This mutual frustration, located in the other's 'difference', only increased when they fell pregnant.

Each began to hate the difference they located in the other, which represented a split-off part of themselves, despite these variations between them being their initial source of attraction. Their dynamic became stuck in a rigid parent/child coupling with Mary complaining of Fred's lack of responsibility while he scorned her as dull and unnatural.

Couples as parents: Parents as couples

The developmental task of the couple runs parallel to the developmental task of the parents. Both need flexibility of mind and a secure base from which confidence in being good enough makes space for creativity across both spheres. While a potential line of breakage may be present within a couple's dynamic, it can sometimes remain undisturbed before the added pressure of raising a family. Bring a third into the equation, in the form of a child, and a fissure may develop. The necessary, open psychic spaces where development can flourish are not available. Anxiety spawns rigid internal emotional systems and the creative couple relationship will likely be placed under stress.

In Enemies of Promise (1938), Cyril Connolly wrote, "There is no more sombre enemy of good art than the pram in the hall". Alongside the joys and celebration of beginning a family, what happens to a couple's career ambition with the pram in the hall, fast-forwarding them into a new world of domesticity, financial commitment, and responsibility for a wholly dependent child?

Challenges to the parental couple are more acute at specific developmental stages of their child—and within the timeline of their relationship. By specific times in a child's developmental trajectory, I mean times such as birth, weaning, starting nursery, arrival of siblings, the transition to secondary school, the onset of adolescence, moves towards individuation, and launching into the world. Specific times in the couple's timeline can include the birth of children, the course of their sexual life, career successes or disappointments, menopause, financial concerns, caring for an elderly parent, retirement, those kinds of potential vulnerability points in any couple's life together.

Case vignette

Mary found pregnancy difficult and retreated into the familiar world of work, justifying it as "*someone needed to earn the money*". Fred felt increasingly useless and acted out by drinking and falling out with tradesmen he worked with on building sites.

As it was, Mary had a very difficult birth and for a while it looked as if her baby would be born on the bathroom floor at home. The ambulance was late coming, the midwife Mary had organised couldn't get there. Mary felt completely out of control of what was happening to her body, with no idea of what she should do. She described in session that, at one point, her eyes locked on to Fred's and it was clear both were flooded with panic.

Things went from bad to worse for the couple in that Mary struggled to breast-feed despite input from many different professionals. In his response to this difficult situation, Fred kept losing his temper with Mary, just making matters worse. Fred explained to me that the baby wasn't gaining weight and that he was very worried that Mary wasn't able to be a proper mother to Iris. He described a desire to scoop the baby up and to run to his shepherd's hut. In a way, this is largely the dynamic that evolved. No reflection of the love that both had for baby Iris, Fred became her main carer, coupling up with his daughter whom he believed he knew and understood exactly. He excluded Mary, and Iris reacted accordingly, always calling for her father and with little interaction with her mum. A competent/incompetent parenting split arose between the couple and this polarising distance threatened the future of their relationship.

Threats to the secure boundary around the couple, threatening their role as parents

A couple's developmental feat on becoming parents is to adapt their own intimate relationship alongside and within their role as parents. This necessitates mourning the 'couple life' they had previously.

A secure but flexible boundary needs to be maintained around their couple relationship, that can encompass their parenting one but is not subsumed beneath it. Perhaps the most vital influence on outcomes for children, parents need to maintain both roles, connected but separate, and tolerate the fluctuating, temporary dominance of either.

Fisher (1999) describes "children who are hostage to the destructive narcissism of their parents". This encapsulates all manner of pressures that parents can be vulnerable to as they attempt to transition from a couple to a family with a baby. Oedipal tension, such as one half of the couple experiencing feelings of exclusion from the infant/parent dyad or believing him or herself eclipsed by the centrality of the infant in their shared adult life can emerge for even the most devoted new parent. Withstanding these anxieties requires sufficient ego strength, particularly on the part of the non-birthing partner: "in the triangular dynamics of the parental couple's relationship with their new-born, the father's behaviour towards the mother may be a conscious or unconscious attack on the child, who is felt to be a threat to his position alongside his wife" (McCann, 2024).

It is my supposition that Mary and Fred struggled to create open psychic space between them where development can flourish. This third position, separate from their two individual selves, representing the couple they have created, can help keep their relationship secure during this transition to parenthood. Their initial projective couple fit, where Mary was the 'adult parent' and Fred the wayward, depressed adolescent, swapped after Iris was born. Now it was Mary who was depressed while Fred occupied the place of both parents, discovering a new, if narcissistic, meaning to his life. Fisher (1999) describes a longing for the perfect object, which can lead to destructive, defensive relating when contradicted by reality:

> By marriage, I mean to emphasise the passion for and dependence on the intimate other. By narcissism, on the other hand, I do not mean preoccupation with the self, a kind of self-love. Rather, I mean to point to a kind of object relating in which there is an intolerance for the reality, the independent existence of the other, but a longing for another that is perfectly attuned and responsive, and thus not a genuine other at all.
>
> (p.1)

Many couples, as they negotiate their shared relationship, struggle with distance regulation: how close is claustrophobic or engulfing; how separate is abandonment or neglect? The couple's closeness-distance dilemma is further placed under stress with the introduction of a child. On becoming a family, this kind of pressurised claustro-agoraphobic coupling can result in the parents' dynamic becoming split, with one parent teaming up with the child, as a shield from overwhelming couple intimacy or as a foil to a sense of isolation from their partner.

In raising a child, many parents model themselves on their own parents and are attached to their children in reaction to their own experience of being parented,

The bi-directional influence of:

• The parental relationship on the developing creative couple

• The 'couple fit' and its place within the parental relationship

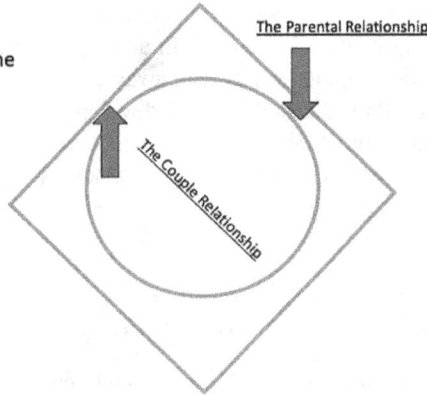

The Parental Relationship

The Couple Relationship

© Thompson, K. 2024

Figure 19.1

whether it be repetition or over-compensation. For example, Mary, who had an angry, unpredictable father, could likely find herself being over-protective of Iris, linked to deep-rooted anxiety she had as a child. Unconsciously, however, the anxiety references Mary's own neglect, which would be confusing for Iris and adversely affect her identity development.

Another common trap for parents is a 'good'/'bad' split between them, perhaps as a reaction to their more ambivalent feelings towards their child. This can arise purely by dint of one being the primary carer while the other parent is needed as the family earner and remains distant from the day-to-day realities of caring for their shared child. This more distant parent can fast develop a redundant and incompetent stance towards caring for the child and be unwilling to relieve their partner. A 'good cop'/'bad cop' split between the parents may result, relating to deeper injuries within both adults and leaving them isolated from one another.

In the case of Fred and Mary, this competent/incompetent split added further pressure to their relationship. The split became evident in session as Fred confidently and concretely knew what the best thing for Iris was. This air of absolute certainty was a collusion between the couple and I began to understand that the illusion of 'knowing', even if only located in one, was perhaps preferable to acknowledging their shared 'not knowing' what to do. If a couple can admit their anxieties around parenting to each other, a more creative tolerance of 'not knowing' but working together to feel their way forward may help them create a more shared parenting stance. Left unexamined, this competent/incompetent split can trigger unprocessed feelings linked to Oedipal transitions, where one parent is seeking to compensate for feelings of being lesser or rejected in their own childhoods. Such replaying of vulnerabilities, created in the past, are evidenced in this clinical vignette, with the 'maternally incompetent' and defeated Mary feeling left out and rejected, while the 'expert', Fred, temporarily triumphs.

In conclusion, in exploring the parenting relationship in therapy, there is a good chance that material becomes available that can help to understand aspects of the couple's intimate relationship. In addition, in perhaps understanding and moving towards developing as a couple away from this difficulty, there is fresh hope that their parenting relationship will develop in parallel. Both roles, as partners and as parents, are co-dependent and react in a bi-directional relationship with one another, as both conscious and unconscious drives between parents and couples develop and change.

Note

1 Throughout I refer to couples and parents and wish the reader to know that these descriptions mean two adults in a relationship that may encompass lesbian, gay male, straight, queer, neurodivergent, or gender fluid couples of different cultures, religions, and ethnicities.

References

Bion, W. R. (1962) *Learning from Experience*. London: Heinemann (Reprinted London: Karnak Books, 1984).

Connolly, C. (1938) Enemies of promise (Chapter 14) London: Routledge. In '*The New Penguin Dictionary of Modern Quotations*' (Eds) Andrews, R. & Hughes, K. London: Penguin. (p. 86). ISBN 0140293078 – via Internet Archive

Fisher, J. (1999) *The Uninvited Guest: Emerging from narcissism towards marriage*. New York: Routledge. (pp. 5 & 1).

McCann, D. (2024) All change! All change! Couples responding to the transition to parenthood. In '*Couples as Parents*' (Eds.) Thompson, K. & McCann, D. London: Routledge (p. 15).

Morgan, M. (2024) Being a couple and developing the capacity for creative parenting. In '*Couples as Parents*' (Eds.) Thompson, K. & McCann, D. London: Routledge (p. 23).

Reid, M. (2007) The loss of a baby and the birth of the next infant. *The Mother's Experience. Journal of Child Psychotherapy*, 33(2): 181–201.

Chapter 20

Making space for a third

A family case study

Alejandra Perez

This chapter will describe parent-infant psychotherapy work with a mother, father, and their 2½-month-old baby boy, as each struggled to relate to one another and find their place in the family[1]. As discussed in my previous chapters, both the experience of parenthood and the quality of parenting that a parent provides are affected by a complex interplay of unconsciously repeated early experiences, unconscious phantasies, and identifications—all of which are joined and modified by current life circumstances and relations. Parent-infant psychotherapy (PIP) was developed in response to a lack of an early treatment intervention that could help parents with their difficulties, address their infants' needs, and also support the parent-infant relationship at this crucial life stage. In supporting this relationship, PIP aims to facilitate the infants' development. One focus is on enabling parents' reflection on their baby's different states of mind, and how these manifest in various ways. Another aim is to facilitate the baby's age-appropriate degree of dependency and gradual movement towards separation (see Baradon and Joyce, 2005, for a full list and description of the aims of PIP work). Through an understanding of the parents' and baby's affective experiences and representations in relation to one another (Baradon, 2005), and by explaining and supporting the baby's experience, the PIP therapist creates a space for the baby, both within the parent-baby relationship, and internally within the parents' minds.

Meeting the family: A restricted contact

The family was referred to PIP due to the mother's borderline personality disorder and postnatal depression. More specifically, their health visitor had expressed concern about the fact that she did not want anybody apart from herself to hold the baby.

I was hardly able to see baby Oliver in the first few sessions, as his mother, Celia, kept him covered and attached to her in a baby sling throughout. When I met them for the first time in the waiting room, Oliver seemed to respond to my voice. He wriggled around in the sling, craning his neck away from his mother's body and trying to see his surroundings, his face red from the effort. However, Celia quickly and firmly put a hand to his head, turning him back towards her. This continued for

DOI: 10.4324/9781003530473-25

the first few sessions: Oliver making attempts to turn around but then seeming to give up, eventually lying quietly in the sling and falling asleep.

Initially Oliver's father, Alan, would not speak unless I spoke to him, and then would only reply that he felt tired and sleepy. He was a warm but absent presence in the first few months of therapy, and would usually lie down quietly on the floor in the corner of the room. Celia, on the other hand, claimed most of the attention, describing her difficulties and displaying great anxiety, anger, frustration, and fear of not being understood. Both Alan and the baby seemed to disappear into the background when the mother spoke, as if they were not there.

Celia talked about her difficult feelings: she felt angry, anxious, and burdened by the thought of other people wanting to see and hold Oliver. She also experienced a sense of catastrophe whenever she became aware of Oliver's separateness. For example, when Oliver smiled at the father, when he crawled away towards toys, or when other people held his attention, there was behind the mother's angry responses an intense sadness: she described feeling empty and without anything of value. She experienced others as intruding into her space and wanting to control her—to "*take over*". She felt anger and panic around most people with whom she came into contact, except for her own mother and, to a lesser extent, her partner. They lived an isolated life. Given Celia's difficulties, her partner had stopped seeing his family and friends. Neither of them worked, so they spent much of their time at home. At times, this isolation troubled Celia. At other times it was a great relief, and she felt convinced that others had nothing of value to offer her. She seemed troubled by not really understanding other people, and belittled them out of apparent defensiveness.

At times, his mother seemed to deny Oliver's curiosity, and his wish to interact with his father and me, by physically holding him back, claiming he was about to fall or hurt himself. She would put her face intrusively close to him and smile as he tried to get away. At other times, she would burst into anger. However, at other moments she seemed confused as to what Oliver might be feeling or wanting to do, especially in moments of distress. His cries were at times heard by her as coughing; his attempts to hug her were sometimes interpreted as him wanting to reach the wall behind her; when a toy fell from his grasp, she would pick a different one to give back to him. More and more, Oliver became withdrawn, growing more interested in toys and objects than people. He often slept or looked out of the window. His movements were uncoordinated and awkward, and he continually crashed into toys and furniture. It was as though, because of his mother's denial and misunderstanding of his experience, he was unable to develop a sense of himself, his body, and the world around him.

I saw glimpses of Alan's sensitivity and connection with the baby from the start. However, he seemed to be in a predicament: when he engaged fully with Oliver, Celia felt worthless and angry. Struggling with guilt, Alan had become passive, withdrawn, and trapped in an enmeshed relationship with Celia. He had given up his studies and contact with his friends and family, and had relinquished any sense of himself as a father.

Maternal and paternal functions; mothers and fathers

Psychoanalytic literature includes many explorations and descriptions of different parental functions. These have been broadly grouped into 'maternal' and 'paternal' functions: the 'maternal' includes those that closely identify with the child's state in order to understand and contain their experiences (Bion, 1970), while the 'paternal' encompasses aspects of a separating 'third', and the provision of psychic safety (Davies and Eagle, 2013). However, this broad distinction oversimplifies the complexity of these different functions. Also important are a passive permeability on the part of the parent (for example, the concept of maternal metabolisation by Miller, 2019 and Perris-Myttas, 2021)—through which they can understand their child's experience—and the active, transformational elements in the maternal function (Bollas, 1979; Kristeva, 2014). Davies and Eagle (2013) describe four dimensions of the term 'paternal function', as used in psychoanalysis: a 'separating third'; a facilitator of mental structure and the capacity to think; a facilitator of affect management; and a provider of psychic safety. All of these functions are important for a child's development. These functions and their descriptions have been, at times, mistakenly used to refer to the functionary themselves, i.e. actual mothers and fathers. It is true that the terms originated in the observation that the different maternal functions were more commonly seen in the primary caregiver (typically the mother in previous generations), given the need for close contact and identification, and that paternal functions were more commonly observed in the secondary caregiver (most often the father in previous generations), given the need for a certain psychic distance from which to enter and triangulate the dyad. However, the value of these psychoanalytic concepts lies in the description of the functions, which can be—and are—adopted and identified in various family configurations, and at different stages in psychoanalytic clinical work.

In the case of this family, it is likely that Celia experienced a sense of being understood and closely identified with by her mother, yet this experience could not be transformed and could only be contained through her withdrawing from the world. She had probably not had the experience of a 'separating third', which could have given her a sense of the value of becoming independent. Now, she not only lacked these capacities, she also rejected them in Alan. Oliver's internal world was likely dominated by a primary maternal object that did not allow difference or separation, and an ineffectual paternal object that could not helpfully come between them and provide psychic safety. This appeared to be leading to Oliver's withdrawal from the world of people into one of toys and objects.

'Ghosts in the nursery' – an enmeshed mother and a rejected, absent father

Fraiberg, Adelson, and Shapiro (1975) coined the term 'ghosts in the nursery' to describe how people's unresolved traumatic pasts with their parents may be reawakened when becoming parents themselves, and unconsciously reenacted in the relationship with the new baby. Similarly, Balsam (2000) described how the internalised mother may become manifest in the new mother's mothering behaviours, without her complete awareness.

Both Celia and Alan had suffered painful childhoods of early trauma and neglect, which they had tried to put behind them. Celia's father had died by suicide when she was four years old, and her uncle had been physically abusive. Her parents had, in different ways, suffered abuse from their own parents. School life for Celia had also been grim, as she was bullied from early on. However, in our sessions Celia talked mostly about her childhood relationship with her mother. In glowing terms, she described what seemed a symbiotic, merged relationship that made her feel *"special"*. She said that her mother knew Celia's mind, and was able to *"say to others what* [Celia] *wanted, without* [her] *having to say anything"*. Celia greatly valued this, as it made her feel protected, and that she did not have to think about her feelings or interact with others whom she experienced, from a young age, as threatening. In contrast, when asked about her father, Celia not only struggled to remember anything about him or her relationship with him, but also seemed to lack any interest in thinking about him. An ongoing and important theme in our PIP work was her idealised view of a merged mother-baby dyad, in which there is no need for a separate point of view—a father (or third)—and no space to think about her own individual experience, or that of Oliver. Celia's traumatic childhood brought to the fore her defensive, idealised view of symbiosis, which she now attempted to recreate with Oliver.

Alan's childhood had been one without much contact with his parents: his father had worked abroad and his mother had spent much of her time taking care of Alan's elder brother, who was severely disabled. It seemed that Alan's parents had little mental space to think about him. Alan had been sent to boarding school aged seven, which he said had allowed him to escape his family situation. In therapy, we explored the mixed feelings he had towards his brother and mother. On the one hand, he felt extremely guilty that he had been spared both his brother's terrible disability and the responsibility of taking care of him. On the other hand, he felt resentful that he had been excluded from his mother's attention and, with sadness, wondered what it would have been like had he had more time with her. He described his father as a calm person, and also felt sad about his lack of contact with him. We explored how Alan had made great efforts to be present in Oliver's life, quitting his job and moving in with Celia, because he wanted to avoid being absent for Oliver in the way that his own parents had been. However, in many ways he was repeating the pattern of the absent parent: wanting to escape the pain and anger he felt towards Celia, and feeling confused and at a loss as to what to do in his role as father. He would then become withdrawn, reenacting the role of the absent parents that he had experienced as a child.

'Giving voice' to baby

Understanding what the baby is experiencing is a challenging process that takes time. A parent gets to know their baby slowly; the process cannot be rushed along, especially since infants' pre-verbal experiences and feelings are often experienced as quite intense and 'raw' by both parents and babies. Putting into words what a baby might be feeling and saying it out loud to the baby (who is non-verbal) is one way for parents to try to make sense of their child's experience, while also communicating to the baby that they are being thought about. Speaking in this way— 'giving voice' to the baby—is intuitive for some parents and encouraged in some cultures. In others, parents do not speak to babies. 'Giving voice' to a baby in PIP is at times a process of co-creating meaning, which is an important part of the parent-infant relationship, and helps parents to understand both their baby and themselves.

Of great concern in this case was that Oliver was beginning to show signs of moving into an autistic-like state: he would often look out of the window during stressful moments in a session, either when his mother was describing her distress or when his parents were arguing. During one session I noticed Alan look at Oliver while he was looking out of the window. Oliver had a dazed, absent look on his face as Celia talked anxiously about her ongoing low mood. I leaned over to Oliver and asked him whether he was looking out of the window because he found it very difficult to hear mummy so upset. I wondered out loud whether he felt that it was all too much and was trying to escape, if only with his eyes and his mind. Alan turned to me and asked, *"Do you think that's what he is doing? I've noticed he does that a lot at home too. At first I thought that he was interested in windows ..."* I said to Oliver that I did not think that he looked interested in the window, or in anything at all. Instead, he looked rather absent, as though he wished that he was not there. Alan nodded and was deep in thought for a moment. Celia joined in by saying that Oliver often did that. We talked about how difficult it was for Oliver to see Celia upset and to see his parents arguing. By then Alan had sat up, and he asked me what they could do. He was beginning to 'wake up', so to speak, as though he had recognised in himself a similar concern that he had not given voice to. I pointed out that, as soon as we had started to think about Oliver, Oliver had turned back to us, and was now looking at us with interest. As I spoke to Oliver, he smiled and reached out his hand. I touched him, and Celia reached out and held his other hand. He smiled, and Celia moved his hand up and down playfully. Alan smiled and commented that he could see the change in Oliver.

My work involved keeping a space in my mind for observing, thinking about, and reflecting on Oliver—a thinking third position. In therapy, my attempts at understanding each family member's experience had the effect of making them more aware of their separateness from one another. My work with the mother indirectly created more space for Alan to interact with Oliver. Alan began wanting more: more time with Oliver; more time to focus on his studies; more time with his extended family. In relation to Oliver, the more Alan interacted with him, the more his fear and guilt about the possible damage that he might cause Oliver came to the fore. My work with the father involved making him aware of his tendency to withdraw, as a defence against this fear, and the impact his withdrawal could have on Oliver.

Oliver gradually had more space to move around independently, and we began to explore how his mother understood, and felt about, Oliver's developments. This physical separation allowed Celia to experience Oliver as different, and she became more aware of how helpless and empty she felt without him. She also expressed her resentment that he wanted to get away from her, and grew more open about her anger towards him. She began to describe him as strong, mischievous, and rebellious, and at times felt afraid that he might grow up to be a violent person. Being more open about her anger made Celia more congruent in her reactions to Oliver. She also began to recognise how much he enjoyed moving on his own; she noticed him smiling and becoming much more energetic. In time, Oliver would not only crawl away from her but would also turn back, smile, and seek comfort with her.

Note

1 This case has been written also in Perez, A. (2018). From pathological merger to a reflective, triangular space: Parent-infant psychotherapy with a mother with borderline personality disorder. *Journal of Infant, Child, and Adolescent Psychotherapy*, 17(1):15–27.

References

Balsam, R.H. (2000). The mother within the mother. *The Psychoanalytic Quarterly*, 69(3): 465–492.

Baradon, T. (2005). What is genuine maternal love?: Clinical considerations and technique in psychoanalytic parent-infant psychotherapy. *The Psychoanalytic Study of the Child*, 60:47–71.

Baradon, T. & Joyce, A. (2005). The theory of psychoanalytic parent-infant psychotherapy. In T. Baradon, C. Broughton, I. Gibbs, J. James, A. Joyce, and J. Woodhead (Eds.), *The practice of psychoanalytic parent-infant psychotherapy* (pp. 25–40). London, England: Routledge.

Bion, W.R. (1970). Ch 7. Container and contained. *Attention and Interpretation: A Scientific Approach to Insight in Psycho-Analysis and Groups*, 2:72–82.

Bollas, C. (1979). The transformational object. *The International Journal of Psychoanalysis*, 60:97–107.

Davies, N. & Eagle, G. (2013). Conceptualizing the paternal function: Maleness, masculinity, or thirdness? *Contemporary Psychoanalysis*, 49(4):559–585.

Fraiberg, S., Adelson, E. & Shapiro, V. (1975). Ghosts in the nursery: A psychoanalytic approach to the problems of impaired infant-mother relationships. *Journal of American Academy of Child Psychiatry*, 14(3):387–421.

Kristeva, J. (2014). Reliance, or maternal eroticism. *Journal of the American Psychoanalytic Association*, 62(1):69–85.

Miller, P. (2019). Working through the body-ego in the analytic process. *European Psychoanalytical Federation*, 73:134–142.

Perez, A. (2018). From pathological merger to a reflective, triangular space: Parent-infant psychotherapy with a mother with borderline personality disorder. *Journal of Infant, Child, and Adolescent Psychotherapy*, 17(1):15–27.

Perris-Myttas, M. (2021). The Soma and the body: Navigating through the countertransference. In K. Robinson and J. Schachter (Eds.) *The contemporary Freudian tradition. Past and present* (pp. 155–173). London, England: Routledge.

Chapter 21

Neurobiological changes in early parenthood

Helena Rutherford

There is an increasing acknowledgement that the transition to parenthood is a key period of development in adulthood. Despite decades of research evidencing neurobiological changes underscoring maternal behaviour in animals (Pawluski et al., 2021), neuroscience studies of human parents are more recent (Mayes et al., 2012). Not only is a neurobiological understanding of early parenthood theoretically interesting, but there is considerable clinical value to this approach. Specifically, the transition to parenthood has been conceptualised as an inflection point for mental (and physical) health concerns (Saxbe et al., 2018). Therefore, a neurobiological understanding of early parenthood may provide significant insight into the mechanisms that underscore the transition to parenthood and provide novel directions for intervention.

Structural brain changes during early parenthood

Neuroimaging methods examine the structure and the function (or activity) of the brain. There have been several compelling studies that have evidenced structural brain changes in response to pregnancy. Using magnetic resonance imaging (MRI), Hoekzema and colleagues (2017) scanned women before and after their pregnancy, finding grey matter (GM) volume reductions over this period. Brain regions evidencing GM reductions included those in the anterior and posterior midline, and the prefrontal and temporal cortex. Similar observations of brain volume reductions in participants scanned during and after pregnancy have been reported (Oatridge et al., 2002). Pritschet and colleagues (2024) further dived into neuroanatomical changes of the maternal brain by scanning a single individual repeatedly from preconception, across pregnancy, and over two years postpartum (26 MRI scans). GM volume reductions were again observed alongside decreased cortical thickness during the transition to parenthood. Furthermore, during the first and second trimester, increased white matter integrity was noted. Sex hormones were also collected, with findings suggesting that the structural brain changes observed were tied to changing levels of these hormones.

Postpartum studies have also evidenced changes in maternal brain structure. Kim et al. (2010) scanned mothers at 2–4 weeks and 3–4 months postpartum finding

DOI: 10.4324/9781003530473-26

GM volume increases during this period, including in the parietal lobes, prefrontal cortex, and the midbrain. GM volume increases have also been observed in multiple brain regions in mothers with varying early to mid-postpartum scanning timepoints (Lisofsky et al., 2019; Luders et al., 2020). Notably, structural brain changes in response to parenthood appear long-lasting: in a follow-up study of a subset of participants enrolled by Hoekzema et al. (2017), GM volume reductions were still apparent at six years postpartum (Martínez-García et al., 2021). Additional investigations of the impact of parenthood on maternal brain structure have been conducted later in life. Orchard and colleagues (2020) demonstrated that cortical thickness measured in late-life was associated with parity (i.e. number of children) in women, with differences in cortical thickness also noted between fathers and non-parent men. Another study reported that in middle-age, mothers evidenced less structural brain indicators of ageing than nulliparous women (de Lange et al., 2019), again suggesting a lasting impact of parenthood on the brain.

Together, these studies suggest structural changes in the maternal brain in response to pregnancy. Although GM volume reductions may imply a detrimental consequence of pregnancy to brain structure, it has been argued that GM volume reductions are beneficial and reflect synaptic pruning that leads to the "fine tuning" of the maternal brain in preparation for caregiving (Pawluski et al., 2022). In support of this, structural brain changes have been associated with a number of caregiving outcomes, including attachment, bonding, and positive perceptions of the child (Hoekzema et al., 2017; Kim et al., 2010; Spalek et al., 2024). Therefore, volumetric changes in the maternal brain, both decreases and increases, may have adaptive significance for the mother-child relationship.

Functional brain changes during early parenthood

Numerous studies have examined functional changes to the maternal brain during early parenthood. These studies typically examine brain activity using functional MRI (fMRI) and event-related potentials (ERPs) in response to salient infant cues (e.g., photographs of infant faces, audio recordings of infant cries). A handful of studies have examined differences between participants identifying as mothers and fathers as compared to non-parent females and males finding convergence in heightened responding to infant distress in the parent sample (e.g., Proverbio et al., 2006; Seifritz et al., 2003). Building on this work, Feldman (2015) laid out the evidence to suggest the existence of several "parental brain networks" (p. 391) activated by exposure to infant cues that include brain regions implicated in mentalisation, empathy, and emotion regulation. Given the number of neuroimaging studies probing the parental brain, several meta-analyses have been conducted to provide insight into the reliability of parental brain findings (Kuzava et al., 2020; Rigo et al., 2019; Paul et al., 2019).

Increasingly it is recognised that there is not a uniform response to infant cues in the brain during early parenthood but there are meaningful individual differences. ERP research has shown that primiparous (i.e., first-time) mothers have a larger

P300 response to infant faces than multiparous mothers at two and seven months postpartum (Bunderson et al., 2020; Maupin et al., 2018). Given the P300 is implicated in attention allocation, these findings suggested greater attentional processing of infant faces in first-time parenthood. Interestingly, a heightened P300 response to infant faces, as well as adult faces and houses, has also been observed in women pregnant for the first-time, in contrast to their multiparous pregnant counterparts (Rutherford et al., 2019).

Other normative factors that have been implicated in the neural response to infant stimuli include whether mothers are breastfeeding or formula feeding (Kim et al., 2011) and whether mothers had a vaginal delivery or caesarean section (Swain et al., 2008). Early life experiences related to attachment and unresolved trauma may also contribute to maternal neural processing of infant cues (e.g., Groh & Haydon, 2018; Kim et al., 2014; Lowell et al., 2021; Strathearn et al., 2009) alongside experiences of poverty and exposures to stress (Kim et al., 2016; Kim et al., 2020). Consequently, these findings at a normative level suggest there is significant variability in maternal brain responses when engaged with infant cues.

Given that the transition to parenthood can be a period of vulnerability for maternal mental health, a number of studies have examined the intersection of clinical symptomatology and maternal brain responses to infant cues. In the presence of postpartum depression, recent mothers evidence a decreased neural response to infant cry stimuli, as compared to mothers not currently depressed (Laurent & Ablow, 2011), with depression-related alterations in the neural processing of infant stimuli apparent before birth (Rutherford et al., 2016). Maternal anxiety has been reliably associated with more pronounced neural processing of neutral infant faces during pregnancy (Rutherford et al., 2017), postpartum (Malak et al., 2015), and in middle childhood (Kungl et al., 2020). A number of studies have also showcased differential maternal neural responding to infant stimuli in the presence of substance use (see Rutherford et al., 2021, for review). More recent efforts have utilised data-driven approaches to examine profiles of psychological risk in postpartum mothers and resultant differences in the neural processing of infant stimuli (Wall et al., 2024). The inherent value of understanding the neurobiology of early parenthood in the context of clinical risk can reveal underlying mechanisms that might affect maternal responding and signpost new opportunities for interventions. Leveraging this approach during pregnancy is particularly valuable in providing early indicators of risk, and intervention implications, before birth.

Multiple studies have evidenced links between maternal neural responses to infant signals and concurrent or future caregiving, including maternal sensitivity (e.g., Bernard et al., 2018; Endendijk et al., 2018; Kim et al., 2011; Kuzava et al., 2019; Musser et al., 2012). Of note, Dudek et al. (2020) examined ERPs elicited by infant faces during pregnancy and postpartum, finding that the change in the neural response over time was associated with maternal self-reported bonding with her child—further highlighting the value of assessing the maternal brain before birth. Several studies have also shown links between maternal neural response to infant cues and measures related to mentalisation (Hipwell et al., 2015; Rutherford,

Bunderson, et al., 2021; Rutherford et al., 2018). In bridging maternal brain assessments to child outcomes, Laurent and Ablow (2012) evidenced maternal neural reactivity to infant cries predicted their child's attachment security. Preliminary ERP research has also linked maternal neural responses to their own infant's face to an assessment of their child's socio-emotional development (Wall et al., under review). Together, these studies extend the validity of the neurobiology of early parenthood to informing child developmental outcomes.

Conclusion

In this chapter, evidence has been discussed showcasing structural changes in the maternal brain in response to pregnancy and variability in maternal brain responses to salient infant cues in low-risk and clinical contexts. Importantly, most research has enrolled pregnant or postpartum individuals identifying as women, leaving open questions regarding the neurobiology of early parenthood for other birthing and non-birthing identities. Existing research studying the paternal brain has shown some functional overlap with maternal brain networks (Feldman, 2015), which may be driven by caregiving experience (Abraham et al., 2014) necessitating parallel lines of longitudinal research. Furthermore, there is a great need to understand the generalisability of maternal brain findings, given the often limited racial and ethnic diversity of these samples (Penner et al., 2023). Finally, exciting lines of research have showcased the value of examining the maternal brain during pregnancy that may have implications for future caregiving.

References

Abraham, E., Hendler, T., Shapira-Lichter, I., Kanat-Maymon, Y., Zagoory-Sharon, O., & Feldman, R. (2014). Father's brain is sensitive to childcare experiences. *Proceedings of the National Academy of Sciences, 111*(27), 9792–9797.

Bernard, K., Kuzava, S., Simons, R., & Dozier, M. (2018). CPS-referred mothers' psychophysiological responses to own versus other child predict sensitivity to child distress. *Developmental Psychology, 54*(7), 1255.

Bunderson, M., Diaz, D., Maupin, A., Landi, N., Potenza, M. N., Mayes, L. C., & Rutherford, H. J. (2020). Prior reproductive experience modulates neural responses to infant faces across the postpartum period. *Social Neuroscience, 15*(6), 650–654.

de Lange, A.-M. G., Kaufmann, T., van der Meer, D., Maglanoc, L. A., Alnæs, D., Moberget, T., ... & Westlye, L. T. (2019). Population-based neuroimaging reveals traces of childbirth in the maternal brain. *Proceedings of the National Academy of Sciences, 116*(44), 22341–22346.

Dudek, J., Colasante, T., Zuffianò, A., & Haley, D. W. (2020). Changes in cortical sensitivity to infant facial cues from pregnancy to motherhood predict mother–infant bonding. *Child Development, 91*(1), e198–e217.

Endendijk, J. J., Spencer, H., van Baar, A. L., & Bos, P. A. (2018). Mothers' neural responses to infant faces are associated with activation of the maternal care system and observed intrusiveness with their own child. *Cognitive, Affective, & Behavioral Neuroscience, 18*, 609–621.

Feldman, R. (2015). The adaptive human parental brain: Implications for children's social development. *Trends in Neurosciences, 38*(6), 387–399.

Groh, A. M., & Haydon, K. C. (2018). Mothers' neural and behavioral responses to their infants' distress cues: The role of secure base script knowledge. *Psychological Science, 29*(2), 242–253.

Hipwell, A. E., Guo, C., Phillips, M. L., Swain, J. E., & Moses-Kolko, E. L. (2015). Right frontoinsular cortex and subcortical activity to infant cry is associated with maternal mental state talk. *The Journal of Neuroscience, 35*(37), 12725–12732.

Hoekzema, E., Barba-Müller, E., Pozzobon, C., Picado, M., Lucco, F., García-García, D., ... & Crone, E. A. (2017). Pregnancy leads to long-lasting changes in human brain structure. *Nature Neuroscience, 20*(2), 287–296.

Kim, P., Capistrano, C., & Congleton, C. (2016). Socioeconomic disadvantages and neural sensitivity to infant cry: Role of maternal distress. *Social Cognitive and Affective Neuroscience, 11*(10), 1597–1607.

Kim, P., Feldman, R., Mayes, L. C., Eicher, V., Thompson, N., Leckman, J. F., & Swain, J. E. (2011). Breastfeeding, brain activation to own infant cry, and maternal sensitivity. *Journal of Child Psychology and Psychiatry, 52*(8), 907–915.

Kim, P., Leckman, J. F., Mayes, L. C., Feldman, R., Wang, X., & Swain, J. E. (2010). The plasticity of human maternal brain: Longitudinal changes in brain anatomy during the early postpartum period. *Behaviour Neuroscience, 124*(5), 695–700.

Kim, P., Tribble, R., Olsavsky, A. K., Dufford, A. J., Erhart, A., Hansen, M., ... & Gonzalez, D. M. (2020). Associations between stress exposure and new mothers' brain responses to infant cry sounds. *Neuroimage, 223*, 117360.

Kim, S., Fonagy, P., Allen, J., & Strathearn, L. (2014). Mothers' unresolved trauma blunts amygdala response to infant distress. *Social Neuroscience, 9*(4), 352–363.

Kungl, M. T., Rutherford, H. J., Heinisch, C., Beckmann, M. W., Fasching, P. A., & Spangler, G. (2020). Does anxiety impact the neural processing of child faces in mothers of school-aged children? An ERP study using an emotional Go/NoGo task. *Social Neuroscience, 15*(5), 530–543.

Kuzava, S., Frost, A., Perrone, L., Kang, E., Lindhiem, O., & Bernard, K. (2020). Adult processing of child emotional expressions: A meta-analysis of ERP studies. *Developmental Psychology, 56*(6), 1170.

Kuzava, S., Nissim, G., Frost, A., Nelson, B., & Bernard, K. (2019). Latent profiles of maternal neural response to infant emotional stimuli: Associations with maternal sensitivity. *Biological Psychology, 143*, 113–120.

Laurent, H. K., & Ablow, J. C. (2011). A cry in the dark: Depressed mothers show reduced neural activation to their own infant's cry. *Social Cognitive and Affective Neuroscience, 7*(2), 125–134.

Laurent, H. K., & Ablow, J. C. (2012). The missing link: Mothers' neural response to infant cry related to infant attachment behaviors. *Infant Behavior and Development, 35*(4), 761–772.

Lisofsky, N., Gallinat, J., Lindenberger, U., & Kühn, S. (2019). Postpartal neural plasticity of the maternal brain: Early renormalization of pregnancy-related decreases? *Neurosignals, 27*, 12–24.

Lowell, A. F., Dell, J., Potenza, M. N., Strathearn, L., Mayes, L. C., & Rutherford, H. J. (2021). Adult attachment is related to maternal neural response to infant cues: An ERP study. *Attachment & Human Development, 25*(1), 71–88.

Luders, E., Kurth, F., Gingnell, M., Engman, J., Yong, E.-L., Poromaa, I. S., & Gaser, C. (2020). From baby brain to mommy brain: Widespread gray matter gain after giving birth. *Cortex*, *126*, 334–342.

Malak, S. M., Crowley, M. J., Mayes, L. C., & Rutherford, H. (2015). Maternal anxiety and neural responses to infant faces. *Journal of Affective Disorders*, *172*, 324–330.

Martínez-García, M., Paternina-Die, M., Barba-Müller, E., Martín de Blas, D., Beumala, L., Cortizo, R., ... & Picado, M. (2021). Do pregnancy-induced brain changes reverse? The brain of a mother six years after parturition. *Brain Sciences*, *11*(2), 168.

Maupin, A. N., Rutherford, H. J., Landi, N., Potenza, M. N., & Mayes, L. C. (2018). Investigating the association between parity and the maternal neural response to infant cues. *Social Neuroscience*, 14(2), 214–225.

Mayes, L., Rutherford, H. J. V., Suchman, N., & Close, N. (2012). The neural and psychological dynamics of adults' transition to parenthood. *Zero to Three*, *33*(2), 83.

Musser, E. D., Kaiser-Laurent, H., & Ablow, J. C. (2012). The neural correlates of maternal sensitivity: An fMRI study. *Developmental Cognitive Neuroscience*, *2*(4), 428–436.

Oatridge, A., Holdcroft, A., Saeed, N., Hajnal, J. V., Puri, B. K., Fusi, L., & Bydder, G. M. (2002). Change in brain size during and after pregnancy: Study in healthy women and women with preeclampsia. *American Journal of Neuroradiology*, *23*(1), 19–26.

Orchard, E. R., Ward, P. G., Sforazzini, F., Storey, E., Egan, G. F., & Jamadar, S. D. (2020). Relationship between parenthood and cortical thickness in late adulthood. *PLoS ONE*, *15*(7), e0236031.

Paul, S., Austin, J., Elliott, R., Ellison-Wright, I., Wan, M. W., Drake, R., Downey, D., Elmadih, A., Mukherjee, I., Heaney, L., Williams, S., & Abel, K. M. (2019). Neural pathways of maternal responding: Systematic review and meta-analysis. *Archives of Women's Mental Health*, *22*(2), 179–187

Pawluski, J. L., Hoekzema, E., Leuner, B., & Lonstein, J. S. (2022). Less can be more: Fine tuning the maternal brain. *Neuroscience & Biobehavioral Reviews*, *133*, 104475.

Penner, F., Wall, K. M., Guan, K. W., Huang, H. J., Richardson, L., Dunbar, A. S., ... & Rutherford, H. J. (2023). Racial disparities in EEG research and their implications for our understanding of the maternal brain. *Cognitive, Affective, & Behavioral Neuroscience*, *23*(1), 1–16.

Pritschet, L., Taylor, C. M., Cossio, D., Faskowitz, J., Santander, T., Handwerker, D. A., ... & Jacobs, E. G. (2024). Neuroanatomical changes observed over the course of a human pregnancy. *Nature Neuroscience*, 27(11), 2253–2260.

Proverbio, A. M., Brignone, V., Matarazzo, S., Del Zotto, M., & Zani, A. (2006). Gender and parental status affect the visual cortical response to infant facial expression. *Neuropsychologia*, *44*(14), 2987–2999.

Rigo, P., Kim, P., Esposito, G., Putnick, D. L., Venuti, P., & Bornstein, M. H. (2019). Specific maternal brain responses to their own child's face: An fMRI meta-analysis. *Developmental Review*, *51*, 58–69.

Rutherford, H. J., Bunderson, M., Bartz, C., Haitsuka, H., Meins, E., Groh, A. M., & Milligan, K. (2021). Imagining the baby: Neural reactivity to infant distress and mind-mindedness in expectant parents. *Biological Psychology*, *161*, 108057.

Rutherford, H. J., Crowley, M. J., Gao, L., Francis, B., Schultheis, A., & Mayes, L. C. (2018). Prenatal neural responses to infant faces predict postpartum reflective functioning. *Infant Behavior and Development*, *53*, 43–48.

Rutherford, H. J., Kim, S., Yip, S. W., Potenza, M. N., Mayes, L. C., & Strathearn, L. (2021). Parenting and addictions: Current insights from human neuroscience. *Current Addiction Reports*, *8*, 380–388.

Rutherford, H. J., Maupin, A. N., & Mayes, L. C. (2019). Parity and neural responses to social and non-social stimuli in pregnancy. *Social Neuroscience*, *14*(5), 545–548.

Rutherford, H. J. V., Byrne, S. P., Austin, G. M., Lee, J. D., Crowley, M. J., & Mayes, L. C. (2017). Anxiety and neural responses to infant and adult faces during pregnancy. *Biological Psychology*, *125*, 115–120.

Rutherford, H. J. V., Graber, K. M., & Mayes, L. C. (2016). Depression symptomatology and the neural correlates of infant face and cry perception during pregnancy. *Social Neuroscience*, *11*(4), 467–474.

Saxbe, D., Rossin-Slater, M., & Goldenberg, D. (2018). The transition to parenthood as a critical window for adult health. *American Psychologist*, *73*(9), 1190.

Seifritz, E., Esposito, F., Neuhoff, J. G., Luthi, A., Mustovic, H., Dammann, G., ... & Tedeschi, G. (2003). Differential sex-independent amygdala response to infant crying and laughing in parents versus nonparents. *Biological Psychiatry*, *54*(12), 1367–1375.

Spalek, K., Straathof, M., Koyuncu, L., Grydeland, H., van der Geest, A., van't Hof, S. R., ... & Denys, D. (2024). Pregnancy renders anatomical changes in hypothalamic substructures of the human brain that relate to aspects of maternal behavior. *Psychoneuroendocrinology*, *164*, 107021.

Strathearn, L., Fonagy, P., Amico, J., & Montague, P. R. (2009). Adult attachment predicts maternal brain and oxytocin response to infant cues. *Neuropsychopharmacology*, *34*(13), 2655–2666.

Swain, J. E., Tasgin, E., Mayes, L. C., Feldman, R., Todd Constable, R., & Leckman, J. F. (2008). Maternal brain response to own baby-cry is affected by cesarean section delivery. *Journal of Child Psychology and Psychiatry*, *49*(10), 1042–1052.

Wall, K. M., Penner, F., Armstrong, K., Lowell, A., MN, P., Mayes, L., & HJV, R. (under review). Investigating associations between maternal neural responsivity and infant developmental outcomes.

Wall, K. M., Penner, F., Dell, J., Lowell, A., Potenza, M. N., Mayes, L. C., & Rutherford, H. J. (2024). Maternal psychological risk and the neural correlates of infant face processing: A latent profile analysis. *Development Psychobiology*, *66*(1), e22445.

Chapter 22

The bodily self after birth

Elena Panagiotopoulou

The postpartum period is perhaps the most critical period in the lives of mothers, yet it tends to be the most neglected (WHO et al., 2013). This period is character- ised by significant biological, psychological, and social changes for women, with the maternal body at the core of these transformations. Postpartum bodily changes are complex and interconnected, facilitating recovery from childbirth, breast- feeding, and infant caregiving (Brunton & Russell, 2008). Post-birth, the uterus shrinks, breasts lactate, and hormones shift, causing stretch marks, hair shedding, and weight changes. Equally significant is the emotional and symbolic transition that accompanies these bodily changes. The 'two-in-one' experience of carrying the baby within the mother's body, described in our previous chapter (9), gives way to a sense of separation as the baby enters the world, outside the mother's body. Many mothers grapple with the physical absence of their baby from their body while simultaneously embracing a new relationship with their own body and with the baby, centred on bodily caregiving.

Bonding through the body

Following the abrupt bodily separation during childbirth, where body boundaries break (Draper, 2003), bodily interactions between mother and infant are key for their bonding. Qualitative research conducted by the editors of this book has shown that the experience of meeting the baby for the first time after birth is emotionally complex, with some mothers feeling exhausted or numb, trying to recover from labour and feeling disconnected from their babies (Perez et al., 2025; Stumpfögger & Panagiotopoulou, 2021). However, we also found that holding the baby for the first time and having extensive skin-to-skin contact after birth appears to be an important milestone for mothers' bonding with their babies, allowing many of them to start connecting with their baby (Stumpfögger & Panagiotopoulou, 2021).

Skin-to-skin contact is not only important for this initial connection, but, mostly through holding and breastfeeding, it plays a crucial role in strengthening the ongoing bond between mother and baby throughout the postpartum period. During skin-to-skin contact, oxytocin levels significantly elevate in infants, moth- ers, as well as fathers, and parents with higher oxytocin levels demonstrate greater

DOI: 10.4324/9781003530473-27

synchrony and responsiveness in their interactions with their infants (for a review see Scatliffe et al., 2019). Moreover, although not all mothers find breastfeeding highly pleasurable, and it is important to recognise individual differences and subjective experiences (Schmied & Lupton, 2001), qualitative research has shown that, for many mothers, breastfeeding is often experienced as a special moment of closeness, evoking feelings of connectedness and intimacy (Stumpfögger & Panagiotopoulou, 2021; Schmied & Lupton, 2001). On the whole, a large body of literature suggests that the mother's body serves as a vital medium for connection with the baby.

Blurred body boundaries

As discussed in our previous chapter (9), pregnancy (and birth) blurs the boundaries between self and other for women, as their body becomes a shared space with the baby. After birth, while the physical separation of mother and baby resolves this shared bodily experience, a sense of oneness often continues, highlighting the ongoing bond between mother and child (Draper, 2003). Breastfeeding fosters a sense of interconnectedness, with many mothers reporting feelings of merging, continuity, or oneness with their baby (Ammaniti et al., 2014; Schmied & Lupton, 2001). Importantly, this blurriness of body boundaries has also been noted in the context of infant distress, that is when the baby cries or is in pain. In our qualitative study in 2021, mothers expressed that their baby's cry "*hurts*" and induces a sense of "*panic*", as if they are personally experiencing their distress (Stumpfögger & Panagiotopoulou, 2021). Brain imaging evidence supports these reports, showing that parental worries and mood are related to specific brain activations in response to their own baby-cry, thus pointing to a neurological basis for the perceived lack of distinction between the mother's and baby's needs and experiences (Swain et al., 2008). Numerous studies comparing parents and non-parents have found heightened responding to infant distress among the parent group (e.g., Proverbio et al., 2006), suggesting the existence of parental brain networks activated by exposure to infant cues (Feldman, 2015).

Panksepp and Biven (2012) identified the CARE system as one of the primary emotional systems rooted in mammalian brains, which is activated when a baby is in need, thus, enhancing the mother's sensitivity to the baby's needs and fostering protective and nurturing behaviours. From a psychoanalytic lens, a mother's strong reaction to her baby's distress could reflect what Winnicott (1956) described as 'primary maternal preoccupation', a time-limited psychic state of heightened identification with the infant and, consequently, sensitivity to the infant's needs (Winnicott, 1956 [1975]). The visceral feeling of experiencing their baby's distress that many mothers describe could also be thought about in the context of 'containment', a process where the infant not only gets rid of unbearable feelings into the mother in an unconscious phantasy, but the mother receives, digests and processes this communication in an attempt to help the infant take it back, while allowing herself to by affected by the infant's primitive emotional states (Bion, 1962; 1967).

Taken together, the concept of blurred body boundaries after birth is supported by psychological and neurobiological evidence, as well as psychoanalytic theories, highlighting its adaptive role in facilitating bodily and emotional caregiving (see Stumpfögger & Panagiotopoulou, 2021).

Rebuilding the relationship with mother's own body

Mothers' bodily transitions after birth require a negotiation of roles and identities. The embodied experiences of pregnancy and childbirth shape their new "I-as-mother" position, forming the basis of their maternal identity and connection to the child (Uriko & Bartels, 2023). However, the immediate separation of mother and child after birth disrupts not only the emotional and psychological continuity but also physical continuity and it is physical closeness that helps restore a sense of coherence in the maternal identity, supporting their psychological adaptation (Uriko & Bartels, 2023). This highlights the critical role of the maternal body both as a site and a medium for these processes. Importantly, during these processes of reorganisation of the sense of self and coherence, mothers face a challenging task: finding a balance between meeting the baby's needs mostly through bodily caregiving and reclaiming their own body; between connecting with the baby and re-connecting with themselves.

In addition to navigating the blurred body boundaries between self and baby described above, another aspect of the bodily self that is significantly affected is body image. Mothers' body satisfaction has been reported to significantly worsen over the first nine months postpartum and this is associated with non-Black race, non-breastfeeding status, fewer immediate family relationships, and worse mental health (e.g. Gjerdingen et al., 2009; Rallis et al., 2007). Although women recognise the functionality of their bodies for caregiving, they often feel heightened pressure in the postpartum period to restore their bodies to a pre-pregnancy state (Clark et al., 2009). This pressure, influenced by societal expectations, is frequently more intense than what they experienced before pregnancy (Upton & Han, 2003), and affects both primiparous and multiparous women. Many women hold unrealistic-ally high expectations for their postpartum bodies (Hodkinson et al., 2014), shaped by social comparisons and appearance ideals influenced by societal factors, such as media. Over the past decade, social media platforms like Instagram, Twitter, and Facebook have become prevailing forms of communication, with around 90% of mothers actively using them (Tang et al., 2022). Evidence suggests that exposure to body-focused social media posts has a negative impact on postpartum body sat-isfaction (Tang et al., 2022).

Apart from the important repercussions on both a newborn's and mother's phys-ical and mental health discussed in Chapter 9, body dissatisfaction also impacts women's sexual self-efficacy and self-confidence (Shoraka et al., 2019), in turn influencing social and marital relationships. Numerous studies highlight a high prevalence of low sexual interest or desire among first-time mothers, ranging from 61% at three months postpartum to 40–51% at 12 months after childbirth (e.g.

O'Malley et al., 2018). Hormonal fluctuations following childbirth can also affect sexual function, including desire and arousal, while breastfeeding may further impact a woman's sexual experience (Szablewska et al., 2023). Also contributing to this decreased sexual desire and interest is women's sense that their postpartum bodies embody a beauty linked to their identity as mothers, rather than conforming to the socially accepted standards of sexual attractiveness (Bailey, 1999).

Overall, in the midst of postpartum transformative demands, mothers encounter the complex challenge of rebuilding their relationship with their own bodies, striving to regain a positive body image and sense of ownership, while simultaneously attending to the constant demands of their baby's care.

Fostering an empowering postpartum journey

The postpartum period represents a multifaceted journey of transformation for mothers, on a physical, emotional, and social level. The maternal body emerges as both a medium and a symbol of connection, fostering the bond between mother and baby through bodily caregiving. This period, however, also challenges mothers' sense of self, as they navigate the blurred boundaries between self and baby. The tension between fulfilling caregiving roles and reclaiming their bodies highlights the complexities of this transition. Societal pressures, shaped by unattainable beauty standards and the influence of social media, often heighten body dissatisfaction, affecting mental health, sexual desire and confidence, and intimate relationships. Yet, amid these challenges, many mothers find a new appreciation for their bodies as vessels of life and caregiving in ways that resonate with their new maternal role. By recognising and supporting these unique and diverse experiences, healthcare providers, families, and society at large can contribute to fostering a positive and empowering postpartum journey for mothers.

References

Ammaniti, M., Tambelli, R., Odorisio, F., Lucarelli, L., & Vismara, L. (2014). Breastfeeding and mother–infant interaction at 3 months. *Infant Behavior and Development*, *37*(2), 132–141.

Bailey, L. (1999). Refracted selves? A study of changes in self-identity in the transition to motherhood. *Sociology*, *33*(2), 335–352.

Bion, W. R. (1962). *Learning from experience*. Heinemann.

Bion, W. R. (1967). A theory of thinking. In *Second thoughts* (pp. 110–119). Heinemann.

Brunton, P. J., & Russell, J. A. (2008). The expectant brain: Adapting for motherhood. *Nature Reviews Neuroscience*, *9*, 11–25.

Clark, A., Skouteris, H., Wertheim, E. H., Paxton, S. J., & Milgrom, J. (2009). My baby body: A qualitative insight into women's body-related experiences and mood during pregnancy and the postpartum. *Journal of Reproductive and Infant Psychology*, *27*(4), 330–345.

Draper, J. (2003). Blurring, moving and broken boundaries: Men's encounters with the pregnant body. *Sociology of Health and Illness*, *25*, 743–767.

Feldman, R. (2015). The adaptive human parental brain: Implications for children's social development. *Trends in Neurosciences*, *38*(6), 387–399.

Gjerdingen, D., Fontaine, P., Crow, S., McGovern, P., Center, B., & Miner, M. (2009). Predictors of mothers' postpartum body dissatisfaction. *Women & Health*, *49*(6–7), 491–504.

Hodgkinson, E. L., Smith, D. M., & Wittkowski, A. (2014). Women's experiences of their pregnancy and postpartum body image: A systematic review and meta-synthesis. *BMC Pregnancy and Childbirth*, *14*, 330.

O'Malley, D., Higgins, A., Begley, C., et al. (2018). Prevalence of and risk factors associated with sexual health issues in primiparous women at 6 and 12 months postpartum: A longitudinal prospective cohort study (the MAMMI study). *BMC Pregnancy and Childbirth*, *18*, 196.

Panksepp, J., & Biven, L. (2012). *The archeology of mind: Neuroevolutionary origins of human emotions*. W.W. Norton.

Perez, A., Panagiotopoulou, E., Vourda, M. C., Pereira, M., McCrory, E., & Roberts, R. (2025). Trajectories of change in mothers' parenting confidence and relationship with baby: A 15-month qualitative longitudinal study. *BMC Pregnancy and Childbirth*, *25*, 709.

Proverbio, A. M., Brignone, V., Matarazzo, S., Del Zotto, M., & Zani, A. (2006). Gender and parental status affect the visual cortical response to infant facial expression. *Neuropsychologia*, *44*(14), 2987–2999.

Rallis, S., Skouteris, H., Wertheim, E. H., & Paxton, S. J. (2007). Predictors of body image during the first year postpartum: A prospective study. *Women & Health*, *45*(1), 87–104.

Scatliffe, N., Casavant, S., Vittner, D., & Cong, X. (2019). Oxytocin and early parent-infant interactions: A systematic review. *International Journal of Nursing Sciences*, *6*(4), 445–453.

Schmied, V., & Lupton, D. (2001). Blurring the boundaries: Breastfeeding and maternal subjectivity. *Sociology of Health & Illness*, *23*, 234–250.

Shoraka, H., Amirkafi, A., & Garrusi, B. J. I. (2019). Review of body image and some contributing factors in the Iranian population. *International Journal of Preventive Medicine*, *10*, 19.

Stumpfögger, N., & Panagiotopoulou, E. (2021). Blurred body boundaries of first-time mothers: An interpretative phenomenological analysis. *Neuropsychoanalysis*, *23*(2), 97–109.

Swain, J. E., Tasgin, E., Mayes, L. C., Feldman, R., Constable, R. T., & Leckman, J. F. (2008). Maternal brain response to own baby-cry is affected by cesarean section delivery. *Journal of Child Psychology and Psychiatry, and Allied Disciplines*, *49*(10), 1042–1052.

Szablewska, A. W., Michalik, A., Czerwińska-Osipiak, A., Zdończyk, S. A., Śniadecki, M., Bukato, K., & Kwiatkowska, W. (2023). Breastfeeding vs. formula feeding and maternal sexuality among Polish women: A preliminary report. *Healthcare (Basel, Switzerland)*, *12*(1), 38. https://doi.org/10.3390/healthcare12010038

Tang, L., Tiggemann, M., & Haines, J. (2022). #Fitmom: an experimental investigation of the effect of social media on body dissatisfaction and eating and physical activity intentions, attitudes, and behaviours among postpartum mothers. *BMC Pregnancy and Childbirth*, *22*(1), 766.

Upton, R. L., & Han, S. S. (2003). Maternity and its discontents: "Getting the body back" after pregnancy. *Journal of Contemporary Ethnography*, *32*(6), 670–692.

Uriko, K., & Bartels, I. (2023). Separation in unity: Dialogical transformation of maternal bond. *Integrative Psychological & Behavioral Science*, *57*(2), 590–606.

Winnicott, D. W. (1956 [1975]). *Primary maternal preoccupation*. Brunner/Mazel.

World Health Organization. (2013). *WHO recommendations on postnatal care of the mother and newborn*. World Health Organization.

Chapter 23

Parenthood readiness education in Japan

Akira Kanazawa

The low birth rates in Japan. Why are young people not transitioning into parenthood?

The declining birth rate has been a serious issue in Japan. According to the National Institute of Population and Social Security Research in Japan (2016), the Total Fertility Rate (TFR) has been under 1.5 since 1994. Issues with marriage are considered to be a major factor (Atou, 2017). The average age of marriage, and the number of people remaining single, are both on the rise. According to the national census (National Statistics Centre in Japan, 2025), the lifetime single rate for males rose to 28.3% and for females to 17.8% and the average age of marriage for males was 31.0 years old and for females 29.4 in 2020. Compared to the data from 1995, it has increased by three years. As a result, the average age of first child delivery has risen to 30.9 years old in 2021 compared to 26.4 years old in 1980. Conversely, more than 80% of both young males and females hope to get married and have more than two children (Yamanishi, 2016). Financial, political, and cultural issues are behind this gap. Financially, non-regular employment and social inequality have been issues. The rate of non-regular employment was at 15% in the mid-1980s, increasing to 38% in 2015 and causing income disparity (Ministry of Health, Labor and Welfare, 2023). As a result, young people live with their parents even after they have reached adulthood to maintain their standard of living, being labelled "Parasite Singles" (Yamada,1999). Politically, there has not been sufficient government expenditure for child raising and education. Regarding the expenditure for education, it was about 4% of GDP in 2021, being ranked 26th out of the 36 Organisation for Economic Co-Operation and Development countries (OECD, 2024). On top of that, people of marriageable age after 2000 had wealthy childhood lives during high economic growth with fathers as breadwinners and mothers as homemakers. Yamada points out that those of marriageable age do not want their children to live poorer lives than they did, which has resulted in unwillingness to get married and have children.

There are also other significant factors such as high education levels and growing economic independence of women. Culturally, there have been strong traditional family values in Japan that cause severe gender divisions in labour (Atou,

DOI: 10.4324/9781003530473-28

2017). It is still females who have to take care of children and elderly parents while working. In addition, there is no public support for children born outside of marriage to protect their rights.

On the whole, young people are not transitioning into parenthood; not because they don't want to, but because of the social difficulties in Japan such as economic decline, poor public support for child raising, and conservative family traditions.

Parenthood readiness education

There are existing programmes for young people in Japan that teach 'parenthood readiness education'. 'Parenthood readiness' is defined as the ability and readiness for child raising (Kanazawa, 2024). Programmes focus on interaction with babies and young children, which aim to enhance affection for infants and increase interest in parenting. The ministry of Education and Science has started a 'contact with infant and toddlers programme', which involves playing with toddlers as a part of home economics lessons (Ministry of Education and Science, 2019).

A literature review (Kanazawa, 2024) found several issues in its effectiveness. Negative feelings towards infants and toddlers sometimes remain flat or even increase. Motivation for child raising is not necessarily enhanced. Qualitative research focusing on the internal experiences of programme participants is needed to further understand effectiveness because most previous research has only been quantitative. Additionally, previous research has examined the physical care components of programmes such as holding, changing diapers, and playing; less research has focused on participants' experiences. Okamoto and Okada (2021) suggest that it is important for young people to not only interact with children, but to have experiences that will help them develop their ideas of parenting.

To address these research limitations, this chapter shares novel research by the author examining young people's feelings and ideas about children and parenting as they attend a parenting readiness programme in Japan.

Experience before and after taking part in a parenthood readiness programme

Six women, aged 21 to 22, participated in a parenthood readiness programme at a childcare facility, completing six one-hour sessions. They selected a specific child, aged 2–5, as the subject of their observation, and the same child was observed every time.

Participants were asked to complete semi-structured interviews asking them to describe their feelings about young children as well as their feelings about raising young children before and after they completed sessions. They were also asked to describe their experience in a group facilitated by the author, a psychoanalytic clinician.

The interviews were analysed using the KJ method, which was invented by Japanese Anthropologist Kawakita Jiro (1967) as a way to sort ideas, categorise, and name them. This method was applied to clarify the nature of experiences through interactions with children. Three main themes were found: 1) ideas about children, 2) ideas about child raising, and 3) thoughts on group discussion. These were compared in relation to pre- and post-programme participation.

Ideas about children

When asked to describe their ideas about children before taking part in this programme, statements could be broadly grouped into two categories: 1) 'feelings towards children', and 2) 'characteristics of children'. 'Feelings towards children' had two sub-categories, where children were described with: 1) 'affection' (e.g., "children are pretty"), and/or 2) 'aversion' (e.g., "children are noisy and emotional"). Participants described 'characteristics of children' broadly in two categories: children having 1) 'curiosity' and 2) 'innocence'.

After taking part in the programme, responses about 'feelings towards children' expanded into four sub-categories. Participants described 1) 'joy at children's attachment' (e.g., happiness with children's innocent attention seeking from participants), 2) 'confidence' (e.g., initial apprehension moving to natural engagement with children), 3) 'increased affection' (e.g., aversive feelings changing to positive feelings) and 4) 'feelings of strain' (e.g., difficulty in maintaining positive feeling due to fatigue by continuous responding to children). Participants described positive and negative feelings both before and after the programme, but there exists a mixture of feelings and more detailed descriptions after.

Similarly, after taking part in the programme, responses about 'characteristics of children' expanded into four sub-categories. Participants described 1) 'diversity and individuality' (e.g., children having their own personalities), 2) 'competent children' (e.g., children are curious about learning from interactions), 3) 'communication skills' (e.g., children listen, understand, and communicate effectively), and 4) 'the healing power of children' (e.g., feeling energised and empowered by children's honesty and innocence). In short, participants' descriptions of children expanded, with children being described as diverse, having individual personalities and competencies, being effective communicators, and having a healing influence on participants.

After participating in the programme, participants' responses regarding ideas about children yielded an additional category, 'reminiscing about childhood experience'. This consisted of two sub-categories: 1) 'overlapping childhood experiences with children observed' (e.g., being reminded of experiences with their own parents, feeling not only a sense of happiness and familiarity but also pain), and 2) 'distinguish childhood experiences from children observed' (e.g., remembering their own childhood, comparing it with children observed, and recognising differences between them). Participation in the programme allowed participants to explore their past experiences in relation to the children they were observing.

Ideas about child raising

Participants were also asked to describe their feelings about child raising before participating in the programme. Their descriptions divided into two categories: 1) 'anxiety about child raising', and 2) 'expectations of child raising'. 'Anxiety about child raising' consisted of three sub-categories: 1) 'self-sacrifice' (e.g., not being able to do things for oneself), 2) 'mental and physical strain' (e.g., drain on strength), and 3) 'strains on emotional care' (e.g., difficulty in dealing with children's emotions and needs). Overall, participants demonstrated negative views on child raising as being difficult and stressful. 'Expectations of child raising' had two sub-categories: 1) 'fulfilling days' (e.g., children's growth refreshes parents), and 2) 'vicarious living' (e.g., parents' expectations of children; use of children to satisfy their ego). Participants shared both positive and negative views of their expectations about raising a child.

After participating in the programme, participants still described 'anxieties about child raising'. The sub-category, 'mental and physical strain' still contained the presumption that child raising is a mental and a physical burden, with participants recognising that the programme was different to actual parenting. The sub-category 'self-sacrifice' contained the new expectation that parenting would be manageable with support from others. 'Strain on emotional care' was replaced with a new sub-category 'sense of responsibility as a parent'. Participants described their worries about leaving their children with someone else such as nursery teachers. Interestingly, they reported that their worries about this had existed before they participated in this programme, although they did not mention it at the first interview. Moreover, they described how the programme reduced their worries about this. Overall, there is anxiety in parenting even after participating in this programme, but the programme also encourages participants to feel that they can cope with child raising with the support of those around them.

The category 'expectations of child raising' still contained the 'fulfilling days' sub-category after participants took part in the programme, with participants now feeling that having children is a probable option. The sub-category 'vicarious living' was replaced with 'expectations for children', with participants realising that children could be independent, which seemed to alleviate some stress. After the programme, participants' expectations became more positive and realistic.

Thoughts on group discussion

Regarding the group discussion aspect of the programme, two categories emerged: 1) 'satisfaction with interaction', and 2) 'better understanding of themselves'. 'Satisfaction with interaction' contained two sub-categories: 1) 'comfort and joy by sharing' (e.g., sharing experiences brings feelings of relief and connection), and 2) 'growing interest in children' (e.g., interest and satisfaction in hearing about different children). Participating in group discussion brought feelings of satisfaction to participants, both in interacting with others and in their thinking about children. 'Better understanding of themselves' also contained two sub-categories: 1) 'comparison' (e.g., the realisation of different perspectives and ways of thinking than one's own by hearing others' opinions), and 2) 'remembering past experiences' (e.g., being reminded of similar experiences to other participants). Participants were able to reflect on others' views and consider similarity of experiences.

Discussion

Ideas about children

Generally, participation in a parenting readiness programme tended to broaden and deepen participants' 'ideas about children' rather than change them. For example, basic descriptions of children's characteristics such as 'innocence' and 'curiosity' shifted into thoughts about 'competent children' and 'the healing power of children'. This suggests that, after taking part in the programme, participants came to recognise children's 'curiosity' as something that leads to learning and growth, and their 'innocence' as something that gives participants energy and vitality.

'Feelings toward children' became more complex and specific after programme participation. Although 'affection' increased and included a new 'sense of joy at children's attachment' and 'confidence', 'feelings of strain' were also aroused. It suggests that negative feelings towards children reported in previous research (Kanazawa, 2024) may not be a sort of aversion but rather feelings of strain that come from wanting to meet the demands of children.

Additionally, participation in the programme allowed participants to 'reminisce about childhood experience' and explore their own past experiences in the context of interacting with children.

Ideas about child raising

Changes in participants' thoughts about child raising were also found. After participating in the programme, participants still described 'anxieties about child raising', including 'mental and physical strain'. However, there were positive aspects attributed to programme participation. 'Self-sacrifice' changed to reflect the importance of support systems in making parenting manageable. These findings are consistent with findings from previous research (Kanazawa, 2024), which found that motivation for child raising is not necessarily enhanced through interaction with children. Participants may think child raising is tough, as was anticipated, which causes motivation for child raising to remain flat or decrease. However, participants also learned about the importance of support, as is shown in the change within 'self-sacrifice'. 'Sense of responsibility' was included in 'anxieties about child raising' after programme participation. It described difficulties in imagining the child with a caregiver, but also how the programme made this process easier to think about. As was reported by participants after programme participation, this anxiety existed at unconscious level prior to participation. This may have become apparent after taking part in the programme because interacting with children makes responsibilities more salient or it may be that speaking with others provided an opportunity to explore this anxiety. Changes to 'expectations of child raising' were also noted after participants took part in the programme. Participants still reported 'fulfilling days' but participants interestingly reported new recognition of having children as a realistic life event. New 'expectations for children' were reported with participants realising that parenting might not be as difficult once children became more independent. Participants' expectations of child raising became more favourable and informed.

Group work as a way of helping child raising

Generally, there were positive feelings about the opportunity for group discussion, which provided an opportunity to share similar experiences, notice different ways of thinking about things, and learn about themselves. Although the focus has only been on the interaction between children and young adults in previous research, this research highlights the importance of connections among participants, in terms of coping with anxiety and negative feelings. According to Okamoto and Okada (2021), it is only after becoming a parent that they realise that helpful local networks for child raising exist. Participating in parenting readiness programmes may help young people to recognise the importance of social networks for child raising.

Conclusion

This chapter explored the author's research about experiences of parenting readiness programmes in Japan. After taking part in a parenting programme, participants had greater capacity to discuss their ideas about children and child raising. Participants were able to describe more positive child attributes and characteristics. While anxieties and feelings of strain remained, participants had more favourable and realistic expectations about child raising. Some of the positive aspects of programme participation stemmed from the opportunity to speak with other participants and share experiences.

References

Atou, M. (2017). Shoushika Mondai wo Kangaeru [Thinking about very low fertility in Japan]. *Iryo to Shakai [Journal of Medicine and Health]*, *27*(1), 5–20.

Kanazawa, A. (2024). Daigakusei wo Taishouto shita Nyuyouji Fureai Taiken Niyoru Oyasei Junbisei Kyouiku no Doukou [Research trends on the parenthood education through infant care]. *Gaidai Ronsou [Journal of Kobe City University of Foreign Studies]*, *77*, 89–106.

Kawakita, J. (1967). *Hassouhou* [Idea creation]. Chukou Shinsho.

Ministry of Education and Science. (2019). Gakushu Shidou Youryou [Curriculum guideline]. Retrieved February 6, 2025, from www.mext.go.jp/a_menu/shotou/new-cs/1384661

Ministry of Health, Labor and Welfare. (2023). Hiseikikoyou no Genjou to Kadai [Current status and challenges of non-regular employment]. Retrieved February 6, 2025, from www.mhlw.go.jp/content/11601000/001062550.pdf

National Institute of Population and Social Security Research. (2016). Jinkou Toukei Shiryoshu 2016 [Population statistics of Japan 2016].

National Statistics Center in Japan. (2025). *Heikin Konin Nenrei [The average age to get married]*. Retrieved February 6, 2025, from www.e-stat.go.jp/dbview?sid=0003411844

OECD. (2024). *Education at a glance 2024 sources, methodologies and technical notes.* https://doi.org/10.1787/e7d20315-en

Okamoto, C., & Okada, M. (2021). Daigakusei to Hagaoyani okeru Kosodate Image ni Kansuru Kenkyu [A comparative study of image on child caring between university students and mothers]. *Hokkaido Kyoiku Daigaku Kiyou [Journal of Hokkaido University of Education], 72*(1), 367–375.

Yamada, M. (1999). Kodomoni Tsurai Omoi wo Sasetaku Nai [Japanese parents do not want to make children feel miserable]. *Iryo to Shakai [Journal of Medicine and Health], 27*(1), 41–51.

Yamanishi, Y., Itou, Y., & Degawa, S. (2016). Chihou no Jinkougenshou to Shoushika taisaku ni taisuru torikumi ni tuite no ichikousatu [Consideration on the measures for population decline and low birth rate in rural areas]. *Shakai Fukushi Kenkyujo Hou [Journal of Social Welfare Institution], 44*(1), 19–47.

Chapter 24

Transition to parenthood

A discussion

Alejandra Perez and Elena Panagiotopoulou

The chapters in this section explore important aspects of becoming a parent, from the biological (neurobiological and hormonal, and structural and functional brain changes in early parenthood); societal and cultural (one's identity as a parent); family dynamics (changes in the couple's relationship when starting a family); to the intrapsychic and interpsychic, conscious and unconscious elements. In Chapter 18, Salomonsson draws on psychoanalytic theory and his own clinical and research work to discuss some of the psychological challenges of parenthood, emphasising the importance of therapeutic support for the parent-infant dyad. In Chapter 19, Thompson explains the conscious and unconscious pressures placed on the couple relationship in the transition to parenthood and the importance of maintaining a flexible and secure boundary between partner and parental roles. In Chapter 20, Perez presents a clinical case study of a family, and explains how parent-infant psychotherapy can act as a facilitating third, helping parental couples understand the impact of their own childhood experiences on their parenting and, ultimately, make space for their baby. In Chapter 21, Rutherford, drawing on neuro-imaging data, discusses structural and functional brain changes in the transition to parenthood and their implications for caregiving and mental health. In Chapter 22, Panagiotopoulou explores empirical research demonstrating the complex and inter-connected postpartum bodily changes and their psychological impact, and how the maternal body becomes a site for connection with the baby while mothers navigate reclaiming a new relationship with it. Finally, in Chapter 23, Kanazawa offers a socio-cultural perspective on low birth rates in Japan and presents findings from a parenthood readiness education intervention, revealing how the programme helps participants cultivate a more positive and realistic view of child-rearing.

Changes and challenges in the transition to parenthood

Becoming a parent entails various physical, socio-emotional, psychological, and financial changes. Many of these changes support the transition to parenthood, helping the new parent to become more attuned and receptive to, and focused on the care of, their new baby. However, these changes also place great psychological demands on the new parent.

DOI: 10.4324/9781003530473-29

From a psychoanalytic perspective, parents may unconsciously draw on their own early experiences of being a baby and being parented, as well as their identifications with their own parents, in order to understand and parent their new baby. However, as the chapters by Salomonsson, Thompson, and Perez lay out, various challenges can emerge out of these unconscious processes. Salomonsson refers to Donna, a new mother struggling to bond with and understand her baby daughter while in the grip of an unconscious identification with a 'non-mothering mother'. Donna's recollection of her own mother powerfully captures the struggles that many new mothers face when their internalised mother is one who does not give much thought to their baby self. Having such an internal figure makes it very difficult for them to get in touch with their own baby's experience, since they did not experience being held and understood in this way when they were a baby. This internalisation of a 'non-mothering mother' is a process that can be transmitted across generations. For some people, as for Donna, it serves them to become emotionally distant but autonomous, allowing them to focus on their work and career, yet they can then feel intense loss and anxiety when faced with the task of trying to understand their baby's cues for care.

Both chapters by Thompson and Perez describe the anxiety of being excluded that arises for each parent upon the arrival of their baby. Thompson's couple psychotherapy work with new parents Mary and Fred shows how their initial 'couple fit'—based on the differences that they saw in each other and needed—came under great strain at the arrival of their baby, a new, third member of the group. Transitioning from a couple to a family triad provoked for Mary a deep anxiety about being excluded, while for Fred it created new meaning in his life, as he came to occupy the place of both parents. Mary became depressed, feeling unable to understand or bond with her daughter, and Fred grew convinced that he knew everything about the baby. Thompson explains how many couples struggle to take an open, flexible approach as they become parents, and to create psychic space for both their new baby and themselves in their new roles. Instead, unconscious fears and anxieties come to the surface, leading to splitting within the couple, whereby one is experienced as the good and the other as the bad parent.

The chapter by Perez sketches a period of parent-infant psychotherapy work with a family in which the mother, Celia, in contrast to Salomonsson's case of Donna, felt convinced that her baby would be protected only if she took sole charge of him and excluded everyone else. Perez describes the importance of exploring parents' beliefs and experiences, as they often indicate complex unconscious dynamics. Both parents, Alan and Celia, had suffered painful childhoods marked by early trauma and neglect. Celia had internalised a merged relationship with her mother, which was intended to protect her from the harm that came from others. By contrast, Alan had grown up without his parents' attention and had come to admire and identify with both his father's calmness and his distance. Becoming a parent brings fear of the unknown: what will this baby be like? What will I be like as a parent? For many parents, drawing on their own internalised parents is a bridge by which to get to know their baby. For others, like Donna, Mary and Fred, and Celia and Alan, becoming parents stirs up deep anxieties, leading them to hold on to their internalised parents too rigidly, and so to miss forming real contact with and understanding each other and their baby.

The chapters by Rutherford and Panagiotopoulou explain how the physiological changes involved in the transition to parenthood, despite having adaptive significance for caregiving outcomes, also represent a complex adjustment for parents. In her chapter, Rutherford discusses neurobiological changes during the perinatal period, such as hormonal shifts and volumetric changes in the maternal brain, which are long-lasting. Functional brain changes during early parenthood are also noted in this chapter, such as heightened responding to infant distress, although there is considerable individual variability influenced by factors such as mental health or whether the parent is a first-time or experienced parent. This heightened sensitivity to infant cues is also discussed by Panagiotopoulou, who draws on qualitative data to describe mothers' experiences of blurred body boundaries in the context of infant distress. In her chapter, Panagiotopoulou explains how the rapid and significant postpartum bodily transitions require mothers to negotiate roles and identities, while navigating societal pressures, for example around body image, which can impact their mental health, self-confidence, and relationships. Both of these chapters highlight the challenges faced by parents, particularly pregnant/birthing individuals, as they adapt to such significant brain and body alterations and simultaneously adjust to their new roles.

In addition to the physical and psychological challenges involved in the transition to parenthood, Kanazawa's chapter describes the social, cultural, and financial changes that new parents face in Japan, and how these have deterred people from becoming parents. Kanazawa has introduced a 'parenting readiness programme' and presents findings from his study that explored young women's views on children and child-rearing before and after this parenting programme. The programme involves giving young people more exposure to toddlers and providing a discussion group, led by Kanazawa, to talk about their experiences. The aim of the programme seems to be to encourage a real relationship with a child, perhaps to help them connect to the emotional aspect of having a baby and have a counterpoint to the social, cultural, and financial struggles of becoming a parent. Before completing the programme, some of the women described motherhood as self-sacrificing, while afterwards they were more aware of the support systems that can make motherhood less difficult and self-sacrificial.

Parental functions and roles, gender, the body, and contemporary culture

Recent times have seen a growth in different family configurations, an expansion of gender identities, and changing cultural views on parental roles. There is more awareness of the importance of early relationships for children's development. In many countries, parents are spending more time with their infants, and while studies show that mothers still spend more time with their children than their partners do, fathers are more involved now than fathers were in the 1950s and 1960s (Oritz-Ospina et al., 2020). There is now an abundance of parenting information online, which is accessible to most parents—although, given that the information is frequently opinion-based, and can be contradictory, this proliferation of material also presents new challenges for parents. Certainly, the landscape of parenthood has changed; it has become more diverse and complex. So, what effect does this have on our understanding of what it means to be a mother or father? Are the very concepts of 'mother' and 'father' irrelevant in today's world?

The chapter by Perez helpfully describes the psychoanalytic concepts of maternal and paternal *functions*—as distinct from particular individuals who are mothers or fathers. In fact, these two parental functions cannot be fully understood without another psychoanalytic concept: that of 'psychic bisexuality' (see Perelberg, 2018 for more on this). This idea emphasises the movement within each person between these functions and the associated unconscious mental *positions*. These two functions are important insofar as they relate to the infant's various needs: on one hand, the baby needs to be understood at a mental, bodily, and experiential level, which requires a deep, often unconscious identification. On the other hand, the baby needs to be helped to separate from the parents, to develop greater awareness, and to adapt to their environment. There are multiple psychoanalytic accounts of maternal and paternal functions—which Perez summarises—and each conveys the different levels of identification and separation in the parent-infant relationship. There is further complication in that these terms are commonly used to refer to particular, clearly defined qualities: 'maternal' is often used to describe someone warm, nurturing, and sympathetic, while 'paternal' is frequently used to describe a protective and vigilant figure. Moreover, Perez introduces a further layer of complexity; that is, the diversity of descriptions of the parental functions within the psychoanalytic literature. There are many psychoanalytic accounts of these different functions, each exploring the various elements in the early parent-infant relationship that help in the structuring of the baby's mind and their development.

The chapters by Salomonsson, Thompson, and Perez describe cases where unconscious conflicts hinder the parents from fulfilling these important parental functions: such conflicts can cause parents to repeat an unthinking, insensitive stance towards the baby (see the case of Donna, in Salomonsson's chapter), or impose on them an idealised, symbiotic manner of relating that fails to recognise the baby as different (see Celia, in Perez' chapter). These conflicts can also provoke individual parents to try to occupy both parental roles at once, so as to compensate for their own feelings of exclusion and not knowing (see Fred, in Thompson's chapter). In these instances, parents have not been able to closely identify with or understand their baby's individual needs and so support their development.

While psychoanalysis does not place gendered limits on the two parental roles, it does place great importance on the body. At this stage of early parenthood, much of an individual's identification, self-regulation, and understanding occurs at an unconscious, bodily level. The concept of 'maternal metabolisation', as described by psychosomatic psychoanalysts Miller (2019) and Perris-Myttas (2021), explains how the mother must be penetrable by the baby at a somatic level; how she must herself experience the baby's earliest bodily experiences at a bodily level, and then also suffer the demands that this places on the psyche. Winnicott (1956) had stressed the importance of a mother's capacity to experience her baby's body needs and imaginatively elaborate for her baby their somatic parts, feelings, and functions, in order that the baby could then internally integrate these experiences.

As Rutherford explains in her chapter, the hormonal and brain-level changes to the mother's body during pregnancy, birth, and the post-partum period are believed to help her become sensitised to the baby's needs and to develop caregiving behaviours, such as attachment, bonding, and positive perceptions of the child. Similarly, Panagiotopoulou elucidates how bonding with a newborn baby is done through the mother's body, in skin-to-skin contact and breastfeeding. Various authors in this section highlight that most research and clinical work has been done with women, and so their references are mostly to women. However, there is a need to understand how physical, bodily changes, subjective experiences, and bodily metabolisation of a baby's early experiences manifest among a more inclusive range of birthing people, including transgender men and non-binary individuals.

Establishing a parental identity is a very important process for a new parent, yet it is a complex one. For example, in her chapter, Panagiotopoulou outlines the difficult situation faced by new mothers, whereby they must separate from the baby and reclaim their own self and body, while simultaneously bonding intensely with the baby. The chapters by Thompson and Perez demonstrate how some parents' identities and roles become fixed early on, and are characterised by a defensive 'knowing', resulting in the exclusion of others including their partners. These chapters show how the parenthood journey of several such individuals was supported by psychotherapy, which allowed for an exploration of roles, identities, fears and anxieties, and family dynamics. Crucially, this psychotherapeutic work enabled the parents to develop a necessary understanding of their baby's individual needs.

While many countries and cultures have seen a broadening of attitudes to parenting, and, in particular, challenges to traditionally gendered parenting roles, various difficulties remain. Kanazawa's chapter describes the struggle that young Japanese women currently face, as their rising levels of education and economic independence clash with their country's traditional view of women as the primary caregivers for both children and elderly parents. The financial difficulties that young people face there are similar in many other countries. However, Kanazawa explains that, in Japan, it is the contrast with their own wealthy childhoods that deters many young people from becoming parents: they do not want their children to have a lower economic status than themselves. For many, parenthood seems to be associated with a regression from their adult development: it means a loss of control and less financial power.

Narcissism (self-love) vs object-love (baby-love), and a facilitating third

Freud's paper 'On Narcissism' (1914) introduced the idea, among many others, that a person can treat him- or herself as a love object (self-love). This paper marked a significant development in psychoanalysis not least because it paved the way for a dynamic, structural model of the mind (which is beyond the scope of this chapter to discuss). A key aspect of this paper, which is of particular relevance here, is Freud's idea that we have a natural impulse to love, care for, and protect ourselves, and that, in moments of illness or stress, we may withdraw our libidinal investment in our loved ones and redirect it toward ourselves (or our ego). Freud sees this withdrawal and redirection as a process of rebalancing (this is an economic model based on the idea of quantities of libidinal and emotional energy). Another important psychoanalytic contribution relevant here is Anna Freud's (1963) description of the normal trajectory, progression, and regressions in development. The mother's care for the baby can begin as an extension of her narcissism (self-love), as she perceives the baby as being part of herself. The mother and baby have to then begin to separate. The mother needs to understand the baby with unique, individual needs and invest in him or her (object-love). The child has then to begin to understand him- or herself as well as others, separating from the mother and creating new relationships, what Anna Freud termed the developmental line from dependency to emotional self-reliance and adult object relationships.

These conceptualisations of narcissism shed light on the parents' effort to get to know and love their child (object-love), and then their rebalancing of their energy, at times, via a more narcissistic investment in themselves (self-love). What helps the infant to develop towards more sophisticated relationships is an experience of being understood, and a feeling that their parent has survived the baby's strong needs, desires, and loving and hateful feelings. These experiences help the infant to internalise the parental containing capacity and move towards forging new relationships. However, what is it that helps the parent in this process? At times the parent feels taken over by this pull to withdraw, to reinvest in themselves as an act of self-love or self-care. A facilitating third in the form of psychoanalytic psychotherapy is one possible form of support in this. Supportive groups, online information, partners, friends, and family are other possibilities. The crucial point is that the parent needs help when they feel emptied from the investment in their baby. Once the parent feels rebalanced, they are better able to understand, bear, and contain the needs of the baby, so that the baby can in turn experience him- or herself being understood. The baby needs the parent's containment as their internal capacity for containment is insufficient (see Part 6: The early parent-infant relationship for more on this). These movements from self-love to baby-love and back again are a normal part of parenthood; when these become rigid and stuck in one or the other, there is a need for a facilitating third.

These concepts of 'narcissism' are also relevant for parental couples as described in the chapter by Thompson, who explains how the challenges of parenthood can lead one or both parents to unconsciously exclude the other partner by becoming the narcissistically 'better' parent with the child. Again, a facilitating third is needed, and this can take the shape of a 'creative couple' state of mind. This is described as a third space co-created by the couple where each individual identity and development can thrive, and feelings of separateness and togetherness co-exist. This third position, separate from the partners' two individual selves, represents the couple they have created together and can help keep their relationship secure and navigate the challenges of parenthood.

Finally, Panagiotopoulou also addresses the parenthood challenge surrounding the tension between self-love and baby-love. She explains that mothers face a demanding task: balancing the need to connect with and meet the baby's needs while also reconnecting with and reclaiming their own bodies. During the process of negotiating roles and identities, the mother's body serves the baby by providing nourishment, comfort, and care (baby-love), while simultaneously she strives to regain a positive body image and a sense of ownership (a more narcissistic investment in the self). Striking a balance between these two aspects is crucial, as a mother's mental vulnerability can impact her ability to offer consistent emotional and physical care to her baby. This further highlights how the flexible movement between self-love and baby-love is an essential part of parenthood.

The chapters in this section describe how the physical, socio-emotional, psychological, and financial changes involved in the transition to parenthood can be overwhelming and challenging without adequate support. The transition to parenthood, therefore, represents another critical period for mental health vulnerability and recognising and supporting these diverse experiences and adjustments is key to promoting a positive postpartum journey for parents and babies.

References

Freud, A. (1963) The Concept of Developmental Lines. *Psychoanalytic Study of the Child* 18:245–265.

Freud, S. (1914). On Narcissism: An Introduction. In J. Strachey (Ed. & Trans.), The Standard Edition of the Complete Psychological Works of Sigmund Freud 14:67–102. London: Vintage, The Hogarth Press.

Miller, P. (2019). Working Through the Body-Ego in the Analytic Process. *European Psychoanalytical Federation* 73:134–142.

Ortiz-Ospina, E., Giattino, C., & Roser, M. (2020). "Time Use" Published online at OurWorldinData.org. Retrieved from: https://ourworldindata.org/time-use

Perelberg, R.J. (2018) *Psychic Bisexuality; A British-French Dialogue.* London: Routledge and The New Library of Psychoanalysis.

Perris-Myttas, M. (2021). The Soma and the Body: Navigating through the Countertransference. In K. Robinson & J. Schachter (Eds.), *The Contemporary Freudian Tradition. Past and Present* (pp. 155–173). London, England: Routledge.

Winnicott, D.W. (1975). Chapter XXIV. Primary Maternal Preoccupation. *Through Paediatrics to Psycho-Analysis (International Psycho-Analytical Library)* (No. 100, pp. 300–306). London: Hogarth Press & Institute of Psycho-Analysis.

Part V

Infancy

Chapter 25

Psychoanalytic and attachment perspectives on the infant's inner world

Alejandra Perez

In trying to understand infants' experience and development, it is important to consider both their internal and external worlds. The internal, or inner world has been broadly defined as the mind's organisation, structures, and functioning (Renn, 2010). It encompasses one's thoughts and feelings, which are individual and subjective, and is distinguished from the external, or outer world that is broadly defined as the objective reality in which we live. However, there are many and various conceptualisations of the inner world. Psychoanalytic theories place significant emphasis on unconscious thoughts, feelings, and phantasies, as well as early bodily and unrepresented experiences. Meanwhile, attachment theory and research posit the internalised attachment relationship as a core organising schema.

The development of the inner world in psychoanalysis

We cannot conceptualise an internal world without an external reality to demarcate it, and we cannot perceive external reality without an internal world to meet it. The internal and external worlds are constantly influencing and shaping each other. The outer reality is perceived and taken in, or internalised, but not as a mirror image; instead, it is continually transformed in accordance with the inner world that perceives it. And the inner world of an infant is greatly influenced by the quality of the environment in which they live.

Psychoanalytic theories have postulated that the infant's inner world emerges as they try to comprehend themselves and the world around them. This inner world has the function of containing the infant's emerging thoughts and feelings, both conscious and unconscious. In Freud's (1923) formulation of a structural model of the mind, he argued that the ego comes into being in order to understand and differentiate different stimuli (i.e. bodily sensations, the external world, and internal responses to this external world). This is dependent on both innate characteristics and a primary caregiver/environment that supports this development.

Klein (1930) posited that the internal world is formed from experiences in the external world, the intense feelings evoked by these, and the phantasies resulting from this encounter. She believed that unconscious phantasising starts from birth (it might even be argued that it begins in utero) and is a foundational mental

DOI: 10.4324/9781003530473-31

activity, indeed one essential to mental growth. She believed that the infant initially only perceives parts or individual functions of the parent (what she termed 'part-objects') and that these are invested with the infant's drives. The part-object is therefore experienced as 'good' if drives are gratified, generating loving feelings, or as 'bad' if these are frustrated, creating hateful feelings.

Sandler and Rosenblatt (1962) also conceptualised the inner world (which they termed the 'representational world') as an internalisation of the external, and as influenced by the infant's subjectivity. However, very differently from Klein, they considered the aim of the inner world to be the achievement of a sense of safety and wellbeing, in turn helping the infant to organise diverse stimuli in meaningful ways, and to make better predictions about the outside world.

For Laplanche (1992), the infant's interiority and subjectivity are built through their efforts to understand communications from the parent, such as gestures, actions, and words. These are experienced by the baby as enigmatic, and they stimulate creative activity in the baby's mind, whereby the baby breaks, shapes, and reshapes these stimuli in order to comprehend the other, ultimately resulting in the formation of their inner world.

Winnicott (1956) introduced the concept of transitional phenomena as constituting an intermediate area between inner and outer reality, and between infant and parent. This transitional area is important for the baby's development in that it allows the baby a space to imagine and perceive the world at their own pace.

Presence, absence, internalisation, and symbolisation

The capacity to symbolise is an integral part of being human. As a mental function it is essential for socio-emotional and cognitive development, since it plays a central role in thinking, communicating with others, and understanding the world. Infants begin to use symbols early on to indicate objects, actions, and events (Namy and Waxman, 1998).

The presence, availability, and understanding of an external other (e.g., a primary caregiver) is needed at the very beginning of life as a foundational source of support. This can then be internalised by the baby, before being separated from as a normal part of development. Psychoanalytic theories also describe this internalising process within the baby: how the infant must first inhabit the parent's physical and mental space, and then, in moments of separation, imagine, invoke, or represent the absent parent. This is the beginning of symbolisation. Winnicott's (1956) transitional space is an intermediate state where imagination, incipient symbolic representation, and reality coincide.

Unconscious phantasies

The concept of unconscious phantasy is important in psychoanalytic theories of development and mental life. Psychoanalytic literature often uses the English spelling of 'unconscious phantasy' with a 'ph', to further distinguish it from the more commonly used concept of 'fantasy', which refers to conscious imaginations or daydreams. Freud (1911) defined two types of unconscious phantasies: those formed in the very early stages of development, which never reach consciousness, or which have a mental representation and remain unconscious; and those which were once conscious fantasies (daydreams and thoughts), and which were defensively repressed because they were felt to be unbearable or too full of conflict. It is the first of these definitions of unconscious phantasy that is relevant when considering the infant's internal world.

While it is beyond the scope of this chapter to give a detailed account of Freud's models of the mind, it is important to note the distinguishing characteristics of what Freud termed the 'System Unconscious', to which the infant's early unconscious phantasies belong. As the earliest-forming structure of the mind, Freud believed that it was imbued with free and uninhibited psychic energy (which he termed 'primary process'). Slowly a regulatory process (which he termed 'secondary process') gets underway, to bind this energy and organise it under rules of logic and reality. Initially, however, the infant's mind operates mainly in the realm of this primary process, which is not governed by rules of time, space, and logic, but is greatly influenced by bodily sensations and needs, affect, and psychic drives. Freud postulated that, during earliest infancy, the baby both creates and is populated by these sensorially rich, affect-laden, at times illogical images and phantasies. These will remain unconscious and will never be fully accessed, as no verbal, mental representation of secondary processing has transformed them. Elements of these unconscious phantasies are continually transferred or projected onto others, and can be understood, reconstructed, or given meaning by a containing other—such as a parent—or by a psychoanalyst in the process of analysis. Most notably, Klein took on with deep interest the task of trying to understand early unconscious phantasies in her analytic work with children.

Internal working models of attachment

The internal world as conceptualised in attachment theory and research includes the baby's mental representations of the parent, the self, and the attachment relationship, drawn from their continual day-to-day interactions with the caregiver. These repeated encounters establish a set of interactional schemas. The baby's attachment behaviours, of seeking proximity or avoiding the attachment figure, are guided by these underlying cognitive structures, which also include sensorimotor and affective components (Fearon et al., 2016).

Bowlby's attachment theory was intended by him as a model to help explain psychosocial difficulties. While Bowlby was a psychoanalyst and his views on attachment originated in his clinical work with children and adolescents, he became increasingly interested in understanding the impact of the real environment on children's development, in particular the effects of separation and loss. He criticised the psychoanalytic views of his time, which emphasised the infant's unconscious phantasies and drives, at the expense of exploring more rigorously the impact of the environment. Drawing from ideas in ethology, psychoanalysis, and developmental psychology, Bowlby (1969) proposed that there is a universal human need to form close affectional bonds.

Bowlby (1979) described the seeking of proximity and psychological availability in others as part of a behavioural and motivational system that develops from infancy. An attachment figure serves as a secure base from which children feel supported and motivated to explore the outside world. Therefore, attachment theory does not only describe children's need to be close to their attachment figure, it also explains how this feeling of security promotes children's competent exploration away from that caregiver.

Bowlby (1969) explained that internal working models grow out of children's need to regulate, interpret, and predict their caregiver's behaviour, thoughts, and feelings, and thus permit a closer, multi-layered relationship. Bowlby (1982) also emphasised that internal working models consist of "higher processes of integration and control of behavioural systems" (p.80). He explained that, in order for these models to be adaptive, they would need to be built with reference to relevant data, to be generative (in new situations), and to be continuously checked for consistency. These internal working models, once organised, tend both to operate outside conscious awareness and to influence future relationships. Fearon et al. (2016) explain how Bowlby's concept of internal working models has been understood by Bretherton (1990, in Fearon et al., 2016) in more recent theories of infant cognition and event representation.

Measuring attachment behaviours and representations

The attachment behavioural system works in conjunction with the exploratory and fear behavioural systems. Exploration is needed for social, physical, and cognitive development. However, there are always risks in the environment during exploration. Fear increases proximity-seeking with the attachment figure, in order to secure protection from potentially dangerous situations. The relationship between infant and caregiver should contain a balance between these systems while maintaining a certain degree of proximity. This proximity ensures a feeling of security, which, in turn, allows for further exploration.

Ainsworth, Blehar, Waters, and Wall (1978) empirically tested the concepts of attachment theory, thereby both expanding the theory and guiding the direction of subsequent research. The concept of the attachment figure as a secure base is a contribution by Ainsworth. She defined the notion of maternal sensitivity to infant signals, and its role in the development of attachment patterns between infants and their mothers.

An important development in attachment research was its move away from only exploring attachment behaviour to also studying internal attachment representations. Main, Kaplan, and Cassidy (1985) made such a shift by investigating the relationship between adults' attachment representations, their own early attachment experiences, and their children's attachment patterns. They found continuity between children's attachment patterns at twelve months and at six years, and concluded that individual differences in attachment patterns are actually differences in mental representations, which not only influence behaviour and feelings, but also attention, memory, and cognition. As children develop more complex cognitive understanding of relationships and the environment, their internal working models of attachment are modified and transformed as functions of this cognitive development. Main et al.'s paper was a seminal contribution to attachment theory because it demonstrated that attachment could be examined at a representational level, and not only by observing behaviours. The stability of these internal attachment representations has been shown to be consistent over time (Steele et al., 2025).

Points of convergence and divergence between psychoanalysis and attachment theories

Both psychoanalytic and attachment theories of the inner world include a conceptualisation of the internalisation of the infant's relationship with their primary caregiver. This internalised relationship begins to take shape in the form of affect-laden representations of the self, the parent/caregiver, and the external relationship, which in turn help the infant to organise various stimuli, namely sensations and perceptions arising from interactions with the parent. In both theories, these internalised representations are thought to function largely or entirely outside of conscious awareness.

However, there are also important differences between these two perspectives. Psychoanalytic theories draw on psychoanalytic clinical work (with adults, and with parents and babies), elucidating individuals' intricate, complex unconscious phantasies, and how these then shape, and manifest in, their mental lives and relationships. It is therefore not only affect, cognition, and real experiences that are understood as building the internal world: bodily experiences, primary-process thinking, and phantasies—transmitted unconsciously—also underpin more conscious mental processes. While the real external environment and its impact on the baby's inner world is recognised, psychoanalysis considers also the creative activity of the infant; how they shape and create an inner world, given their circumstances.

Attachment theory, on the other hand, was able to attest to the impact of the environment on the infant's development—more specifically the impact of early loss and separation—given our innate need to form close attachments. Arguably the most significant contribution of attachment theory has been, through its operationalisation of attachment behaviours and mental representations, to empirically test these ideas, establishing a strong body of evidence. Attachment research has been able to test, confirm, and clarify its theoretical positions; in particular, the long-term socio-emotional impact of the infant's early relationships.

Clinical vignette: A wobbly inner world

Ava was eight months old when her mother came with her to parent-infant psychotherapy. Her mother felt worried about their bonding, and she felt that her baby rarely smiled or looked at her. Ava, on her mother's lap, looked away when her mother spoke, and looked limp and motionless, her eyes fixed on the wall. I remember feeling concerned for both of them. Mother looked pained and desperate, exuding a growing sense of anxiety as she spoke, and she seemed to spiral into her various worries. Looking at Ava, I imagined holding a shield over her, as if wanting to protect her from what I felt was the crushing weight of her mother's anxiety. After a moment, Ava squirmed, and her mother distractedly released her hold. Ava slowly but determinedly crawled to the corner of the mat, towards some toy blocks that were laid out for her. She sat with her back to her mother. I could see that she was placing one block on top of another, building a tower. However, each block was placed, not directly above the last so as to have sufficient support, but somewhat precariously. As she placed the third block, the tower wobbled and collapsed. I leaned over and said to Ava that this was a very wobbly tower, and I wondered out loud whether this was how she felt at times, especially when things felt so wobbly for her mother too. Ava seemed curious when I spoke, looking intently at me. Ava's mother was teary. Later on in this consultation, mother recounted a humorous incident on the tube where a passenger had been kind and helpful. Ava looked at her mother as she spoke, and smiled. I pointed out to the mother that, when she herself felt helped, her daughter seemed to feel it too—hence her smiling. Mother leaned over and smiled back at Ava. She began to play with her and build the block tower.

From an attachment perspective, Ava was not seeking reassurance from her mother; in fact, she was turning away from her while exploring toys. Gaze avoidance was one way in which she was self-regulating. Yet, her limpness and fixed gaze on the wall signalled something more concerning, as though her attachment patterns were becoming disorganised—that her attachment figure was not one Ava felt secure with. From a psychoanalytic perspective, it seemed that my emotional reaction of concern, and my imagining a protective shield, helped me to develop an assumption about Ava's inner world and the difficulties in her relationship with her mother. It is conceivable that the collapsing tower captured something of Ava's experience—perhaps not yet as symbolic play, but with some elements of unconscious phantasy. It was my use of imagination that seemed to stimulate Ava's curiosity and her mother's sensitivity. More than fully understanding the content of Ava's inner world, I think that it was my effort to understand that helped both mother and Ava feel that their inner experiences could be thought about, imagined, symbolised, and, importantly, shared.

References

Ainsworth, M., Blehar, M., Waters, E., & Wall, S. (1978). *Patterns of attachment: A psychological study of the Strange Situation*. Hillsdale, NJ: Erlbaum.

Bowlby, J. (1969). *Attachment and loss* (Vol. 1: Attachment). New York: Basic Books.

Bowlby, J. (1979). *The making and breaking of affectional bonds*. London: Tavistock.

Bowlby, J. (1982). *Attachment* (2nd ed. Vol. 1: Attachment and loss). London: Hogarth Press.

Fearon, R. M. P., Groh, A. M., Bakermans-Kranenburg, M. J., van Ijzendoorn, M. H., & Roisman, G. I. (2016). Attachment and developmental psychopathology. In D. Cicchetti (Ed.), *Developmental psychopathology: Theory and method* (3rd ed., pp. 325–384). New York: John Wiley.

Freud, S. (1911). Formulations on the two principles of mental functioning. In J. Strachey (Ed. & Trans.), The Standard Edition of the Complete Psychological Works of Sigmund Freud, 12:213–226. London: Vintage, The Hogarth Press.

Freud, S. (1923). The ego and the id. In J. Strachey (Ed. & Trans.), The Standard Edition of the Complete Psychological Works of Sigmund Freud, 19:1–66. London: Vintage, The Hogarth Press.

Klein, M. (1930). The importance of symbol formation in the development of the ego. In *The Writings of Melanie Klein* (Vol. 1). London: Hogarth Press.

LaPlanche, J. (1992). Interpretation between determinism and hermeneutics: A restatement of the problem. *The International Journal of Psychoanalysis* 73:429–445.

Main, M., Kaplan, N., & Cassidy, J. (1985). Security in infancy, childhood and adulthood: A move to the level of representation. In I. Bretherton & E. Waters (Eds.), *Growing points of attachment theory and research. Monographs of the Society for Research in Child Development* (Vol. 50, 1-2, Serial No. 209, pp. 66–104).

Namy, L. L., & Waxman, S. R. (1998). Words and gestures: Infants' interpretations of different forms of symbolic reference. *Child Development* 69(2):295–308.

Renn, P. (2010). Psychoanalysis, attachment theory and the inner world: How different theories understand the concept of mind and the implications for clinical work. *Attachment: New Directions in Relational Psychoanalysis Psychotherapy* 4(2):146–168.

Sandler, J., & Rosenblatt, B. (1962). The concept of the representational world. *Psychoanalytic Study of the Child* 17:128–145.

Steele, M., Perez, A., Segal, F., Fearon, P., Fonagy, P., & Steele, H. (2025). Transition to motherhood: Stability and change in attachment representations from pregnancy to 5+ years later. *Attachment and Human Development*, 27(2):330–347. DOI: 10.1080/14616734.2025.2484923

Winnicott, D. W. (1956)[1975]. Chapter XVIII. Transitional objects and transitional phenomena. *Through Paediatrics to Psycho-Analysis (International Psycho-Analytical Library* (No. 100, pp. 229–242). London: Hogarth Press & Institute of Psycho-Analysis.

Chapter 26

Biological basis of attachment[1]

Paula Oliveira and Ana Mesquita

Introduction

Attachment, defined as the deep emotional bond formed between an infant and their primary caregiver(s), represents one of the most fundamental aspects of early development. Present from birth and increasingly complex as the infant develops, proximity-seeking behaviours protect the infant from danger while providing a relational context in which social, emotional, and cognitive capacities can flourish across the lifespan.

From its conception by John Bowlby (1969/1982), attachment theory integrated psychoanalytic thinking with ethological principles to propose attachment as a biologically-based behavioural system with evolutionary significance. Drawing on clinical work with homeless and delinquent children and on ethological studies of animal caregiving, Bowlby argued that attachment is a primary, biologically-based motivational system selected through evolution because it promotes survival by keeping the infant close to protective adults. Thus, although often viewed as a social phenomenon, attachment is, at its core, also profoundly biological (Fraley et al., 2005; Simpson & Belsky, 2008).

In recent decades, developments in neuroimaging, genetic analyses, and neuroendocrine studies have provided unprecedented insights into how attachment relationships become biologically embedded, influencing neural architecture and physiological functioning from infancy onward.

Understanding the biological bases of attachment offers several advantages for both researchers and clinicians: it provides mechanistic explanations for how early experiences 'get under the skin' to influence development; it bridges traditional disciplinary boundaries, creating a comprehensive framework encompassing multiple levels of analysis; and it informs intervention approaches by identifying biological markers of attachment security and potential targets for preventive and therapeutic efforts.

This chapter explores the biological mechanisms underlying attachment during infancy and early childhood. We begin by examining attachment from an evolutionary perspective, highlighting its adaptive value across species. We then explore the neurobiological foundations, identifying key brain structures and circuits

DOI: 10.4324/9781003530473-32

involved in attachment formation. Next, we explore the neurochemical and hormonal regulation of attachment behaviours. We then discuss emerging approaches, including epigenetics and the role of tactile stimulation. Finally, we consider translational perspectives that connect biological findings with clinical practice and cultural contexts.

Evolutionary and neurobiological foundations of attachment

Attachment as an evolutionarily adaptive behaviour

Evidence for attachment as an evolutionarily adaptive behavioural system that enhances offspring survival can be seen across mammalian species. Human infants, in particular, are born in a state of significant neurological immaturity, necessitating prolonged dependency on caregivers. This extended period of vulnerability creates selective pressure for robust attachment mechanisms that maximise caregiver investment and protection (Simpson & Belsky, 2008). Despite the limitations of cross-species comparisons, studies with other mammalian species illuminate the biological basis of attachment and the mechanisms involved.

A classical animal model comes from research on prairie voles. Unlike their closely related montane vole cousins, prairie voles form monogamous pair bonds and exhibit biparental care. Influential research by Insel and Shapiro (1992) demonstrated that these species' differences in social bonding correlate with differential distribution of oxytocin receptors in reward-related brain regions. Young and Wang (2004) expanded on these findings, explaining that when prairie voles mate, the release of oxytocin and vasopressin in conjunction with dopamine facilitates partner preferences—a process that can be experimentally manipulated. These studies provided some of the first clear demonstrations of neurobiological mechanisms underlying selective social attachment, offering important parallels to human bonding processes. Animal models are still used to enhance our understanding of attachment-relevant biological systems and will be drawn upon throughout the chapter.

Key brain structures in attachment

The neurobiology of attachment involves multiple interconnected brain systems that process social information, generate emotional responses, and regulate approach/avoidance behaviours. Several key pathways and structures support the infant's motivation and capacity to seek out and maintain attachment relationships. Particular importance is attributed to the amygdala and hippocampus, two limbic structures that mature significantly during infancy and remain highly sensitive to early relational experiences.

The amygdala serves as a critical hub for emotional processing, salience, and threat detection. It is highly responsive to others' emotional expressions, particularly those signalling potential threat (Tottenham & Sheridan, 2010), and helps children differentiate the face of their caregiver from that of a stranger (Olsavsky et al., 2013). Adverse early caregiving affects the amygdala's development, for example by making it hyper-responsive to angry faces (Teicher et al., 2016). In parents, particularly mothers and especially in the post-partum period, the amygdala's capacity for salience detection contributes to vigilance toward their own infant, such as being more responsive to their own baby's cry (cf. Swain et al., 2014).

The hippocampus, with its central role in memory formation, contributes to attachment by supporting the infant's recognition of caregivers and the formation of association memories linking caregivers with comfort and security. Animal studies demonstrate that early maternal care affects hippocampal development through epigenetic mechanisms that influence stress reactivity throughout life (Weaver et al., 2004), consistent with human studies showing effects on hippocampal volume following poor or absent maternal care (cf. Tottenham & Sheridan, 2010).

Top-down modulation of these limbic structures is provided by medial and orbitofrontal sectors of the prefrontal cortex (PFC), and an effective limbic-PFC coupling is associated with better emotional regulation. Though the PFC develops gradually over the first decades of life, early attachment relationships lay the foundation for its functional organisation. For example, activations in the orbitofrontal cortex (OFC) have been reported in infants as young as 12 months specifically when looking at their own mother's smiling expression (Minagawa-Kawai et al., 2009). Secure attachment relationships provide external regulation that scaffolds the development of the PFC's self-regulatory capacities (Schore, 2001), while disrupted early attachment can alter prefrontal development, potentially compromising later emotional regulation abilities.

The motivational aspect of attachment is supported by the mesolimbic pathway connecting the ventral tegmental area (VTA) with the nucleus accumbens (NAcc). These regions are rich in dopaminergic neurons and become activated during positive caregiver-infant interactions. While evidence for the reward network in infants is more indirect, infants show a preference for their mother's face and voice from the first few months of life, indicating that maternal cues carry rewarding value. This reward circuitry, extending from the VTA to the NAcc, as well as OFC and amygdala, forms an integrated network that assigns emotional value to caregiver cues, reinforcing proximity-seeking and supporting the development of early attachments.

Neurochemical and hormonal regulation

The formation of early attachments is governed by neurochemical and hormonal systems that coordinate emotional attunement, motivational salience, and physiological regulation. While the brain structures mentioned earlier provide the anatomical substrates for attachment, specific neurochemical systems—particularly oxytocin, vasopressin, dopamine, and the hypothalamic-pituitary-adrenal (HPA) axis—modulate the functional dynamics of relational experience.

Oxytocin, often referred to as the bonding hormone, plays a pivotal role in the development of trust, reciprocity, and caregiver-infant synchrony. Released during birth, lactation, and physical proximity, oxytocin facilitates sensitive caregiving and promotes affective regulation between parent and child (Feldman, 2016). Research has shown that maternal oxytocin levels during pregnancy and early postpartum are predictive of maternal sensitivity and affectionate behaviour (Levine et al., 2007). Moreover, interactions between parent and infant can lead to synchronised oxytocin release in both, supporting a biobehavioural feedback loop fundamental to secure attachment (Weisman et al., 2012).

Vasopressin, a structurally similar neuropeptide, is more closely associated with protective and paternal behaviours, particularly in males. It contributes to social vigilance and territorial bonding, often enhancing responsiveness to social cues related to safety and caregiving (Hiura et al., 2023).

Dopamine, a key component of the mesolimbic reward system, underlies the motivational dimensions of attachment. It reinforces proximity-seeking behaviour and caregiving through the association of social interaction with reward. Notably, oxytocin and dopamine systems interact synergistically: oxytocin can enhance dopaminergic responses to social cues, strengthening positive reinforcement and learning in relational contexts (Baskerville & Douglas, 2010; Atzil et al., 2011). This interaction is crucial during early development when the infant learns to associate the caregiver with comfort and security.

The HPA axis regulates the stress response and is highly sensitive to relational contexts. In the presence of consistent and responsive caregiving, the infant's stress system is buffered, resulting in lower baseline cortisol and more adaptive stress reactivity (Gunnar & Donzella, 2002). However, in the context of early adversity—such as neglect or abuse—chronic activation of the HPA axis may occur, resulting in elevated cortisol levels, neurotoxic effects, and disruptions in the circadian rhythm of cortisol production. Dysregulated cortisol patterns, where initially elevated levels give way to flatter diurnal slopes and lower morning cortisol, have been linked to adverse socio-emotional developmental outcomes (Gunnar & Fisher, 2006).

These neurochemical systems exhibit reciprocal regulation rather than functioning independently. Oxytocin attenuates HPA axis activity, promoting calm states conducive to social engagement, while elevated cortisol may suppress oxytocin release, compromising attachment processes (Heinrichs et al., 2003). Such interdependencies highlight the system's sensitivity to early relational experiences.

Dysregulation in these neurobiological systems—particularly due to early adversity—can result in insecure attachment, affective instability, and increased vulnerability to psychopathology (Sullivan, 2013).

Emerging approaches

Recent advances in developmental neuroscience and molecular biology have significantly deepened our understanding of how caregiving becomes biologically embedded in early life. Two particularly promising lines of inquiry—epigenetic modulation and the neurobiology of affective touch—highlight the diverse pathways through which relational environments shape long-term emotional and physiological outcomes.

The neurobiology of touch

A renewed interest in the neurobiology of touch led to a growing body of research uncovering the role of somatosensory-affective channels in the co-regulation and formation of attachment bonds. A class of unmyelinated low-threshold mechano-receptors has been identified—C-tactile (CT) afferents—specifically responsive to the slow, gentle stroking characteristic of nurturing physical contact (McGlone et al., 2014). These afferents project to brain regions such as the posterior insular cortex, where affective and interoceptive signals are integrated, thus shaping the perception of touch as emotionally salient and socially affiliative. In the context of early development, such forms of contact not only foster proximity and emotional attunement but also promote mutual regulation of physiological arousal—core processes underpinning secure attachment.

Building on these findings, research on embodied caregiving practices has further clarified the autonomic benefits of physical contact. Skin-to-skin care and infant massage have been shown to enhance vagal tone and parasympathetic regulation, thereby supporting the development of early self-regulatory capacities (Field, 2010). Moreover, evidence suggests that both the frequency and emotional quality of these interactions predict socio-emotional outcomes in childhood (Stack & Muir, 1992).

Epigenetic mechanisms

The field of epigenetics has opened a molecular window into how early relational experiences leave enduring biological imprints by influencing gene expression. Seminal work in animal models by Meaney and colleagues demonstrated that variations in rats' maternal tactile behaviour—particularly licking and grooming—can modulate DNA methylation at the promoter region of the NR3C1 gene, which encodes the glucocorticoid receptor (Weaver et al., 2004). These epigenetic changes were associated with enhanced receptor expression in the hippocampus and more adaptive HPA axis regulation, pointing to a clear link between caregiving quality and stress physiology.

Such findings have since been echoed in human studies. For instance, Provenzi et al. (2020) reported that maternal affectionate touch in early infancy was associated with differential methylation of genes implicated in affect regulation and immune function. These results support the view that tactile caregiving constitutes a biologically potent signal, capable of influencing developmental pathways via epigenetic mechanisms.

Together, these research strands reveal how affective touch operates as a primary channel through which emotional availability and safety are communicated, while epigenetic processes function as molecular 'record-keepers' of caregiving quality. This convergence not only deepens our understanding of how attachment relationships are biologically embedded but also sheds light on the intergenerational transmission of caregiving patterns. It highlights the potential of early relational interventions—particularly those grounded in physical and emotional attunement—to foster resilience and promote long-term wellbeing.

Translational perspectives: Clinical and cultural considerations

Clinical applications of neurobiological findings

Understanding the biological bases of attachment has significant implications for clinical practice, offering insights into how caregiving quality affects children's neurodevelopment and informing interventions targeting parent-infant relationships.

Attachment experiences become biologically embedded, influencing neural circuitry, stress regulation, and neurochemical functioning across development. Studies of children exposed to institutional care or maltreatment show reduced volumes in stress-sensitive brain regions, diminished electrical brain activity, and altered hemispheric asymmetry trajectories (for a review of the evidence in maltreated and looked-after children, see Oliveira, 2024). These effects likely stem from the absence of expected environmental input necessary for typical neural development to unfold, with studies consistently showing reduced activation in reward-related circuits and heightened activity in threat-processing pathways among these children.

Neurophysiological studies using electroencephalography (EEG) demonstrate that children reared in institutions or foster care show blunted neural responses to faces, although their ability to distinguish the face of caregivers from strangers at the neural level is preserved. Variations in neural responses correlate with the level of caregiver deprivation, highlighting the importance of consistent, individualised caregiving.

Brain alterations following caregiving adversity, such as reduced EEG power, blunted neural activation in response to viewing faces, and compromised white matter integrity, are associated with poorer attachment outcomes and socioemotional difficulties. However, secure attachments, even when formed after early adversity, show a buffering effect against adversity's negative impact on these neural systems, pointing to the possibility of recovery through relational interventions.

Several neurobiologically-informed interventions address attachment disruptions by targeting underlying biological mechanisms. Touch-based interventions leverage the power of tactile stimulation for oxytocin release and physiological regulation. For example, infant massage and skin-to-skin 'kangaroo care' for premature infants induce maternal oxytocin release and sensitivity, decrease infant stress reactivity, and improve developmental outcomes (Feldman et al., 2002).

Trauma-focused interventions for children who have experienced early adversity implicitly or explicitly address the neurobiological impact of those experiences on attachment systems. These interventions help parents provide co-regulation by enhancing their ability to recognise and respond appropriately to infant distress signals. The Attachment and Biobehavioral Catch-up (ABC) intervention exemplifies the integration of attachment theory with neurobiological research. ABC helps caregivers provide nurturing care during distress, follow children's lead during play, and reduce frightening behaviours. Research shows that infants receiving ABC demonstrate normalised cortisol patterns, improved behavioural regulation, and higher rates of secure attachment, with effects persisting years after intervention (Bernard et al., 2015).

Biological markers increasingly complement observational assessments in treatment evaluation. Measures of cortisol patterns, autonomic regulation, and parent-child physiological synchrony provide objective indicators of attachment processes, allowing us to track biological changes that may precede observable behavioural improvements.

Cultural influences on attachment biology

Attachment is at once a conserved biological adaptation and an experience-dependent process. While neurobiological approaches offer valuable insights, they have limitations that require integration with other perspectives to avoid reductionism—viewing attachment purely through the lens of brain structures or hormone levels.

While attachment is a universal phenomenon with biological foundations, its expression and development are shaped by cultural contexts that influence caregiving practices. Cross-cultural research reveals both invariant aspects of attachment and culturally-specific patterns, challenging simplistic notions of universal norms (Mesman et al., 2016).

Different cultural practices related to infant care—such as sleeping arrangements, feeding practices, and carrying methods—may influence the biological processes underlying attachment formation. For example, cultures that practice extensive carrying of infants and co-sleeping may facilitate different patterns of oxytocin release and autonomic regulation compared to cultures emphasising independent sleeping and scheduled feeding.

Interpreting biological markers of attachment requires cultural sensitivity. What constitutes 'optimal' levels of stress reactivity or parent-infant synchrony may vary across cultural contexts, reflecting different adaptive strategies. Future research examining how cultural practices modulate biological aspects of attachment could contribute to our understanding of both universal and culturally-specific dimensions of early relationships.

Note

1 The work developed by P. Oliveira and A. Mesquita at ProChild CoLAB was supported by Mission Interface Programme from the Resilience and Recuperation Plan, notice number 01/C05-i02 /2022, approved by ANI—Agência Nacional de Inovação, SA.

References

Atzil, S., Hendler, T., & Feldman, R. (2011). Specifying the neurobiological basis of human attachment: Brain–oxytocin–affiliation interface. *Psychoneuroendocrinology*, *36*(9), 1510–1522.

Baskerville, T., & Douglas, A. (2010). Dopamine and oxytocin interactions underlying behaviors: Potential contributions to behavioral disorders. *CNS Neuroscience & Therapeutics*, *16*(3), e92–e123.

Bernard, K., Dozier, M., Bick, J., & Gordon, M. (2015). Intervening to enhance cortisol regulation among children at risk for neglect: Results of a randomized clinical trial. *Development and Psychopathology*, *27*(3), 829–841.

Bowlby, J. (1969). *Attachment and loss: Vol. 1. Attachment* (2nd ed.). Basic Books.

Feldman R. (2016). The neurobiology of human attachments. *Trends in Cognition Sciences*, *21*(2), 80–99.

Feldman, R., Eidelman, A., Sirota, L., & Weller, A. (2002). Comparison of skin-to-skin (kangaroo) and traditional care: Parenting outcomes and preterm infant development. *Pediatrics*, *110*(1), 16–26.

Field, T. (2010). Touch for socioemotional and physical well-being: A review. *Developmental Review*, *30*(4), 367–383.

Fraley, R., Brumbaugh, C., & Marks, M. (2005). The evolution and function of adult attachment: A comparative and phylogenetic analysis. *Journal of Personality and Social Psychology*, *89*(5), 731–746.

Gunnar, M., & Donzella, B. (2002). Social regulation of cortisol levels in early human development. *Psychoneuroendocrinology*, *27*(1–2), 199–220.

Gunnar, M. R., & Fisher, P. A. (2006). Bringing basic research on early experience and stress neurobiology to bear on preventive interventions for neglected and maltreated children. *Development and Psychopathology*, *18*(3), 651–677.

Heinrichs, M., Baumgartner, T., Kirschbaum, C., & Ehlert, U. (2003). Social support and oxytocin interact to suppress cortisol and subjective responses to psychosocial stress. *Biological Psychiatry*, *54*(12), 1389–1398.

Hiura, L. C., Lazaro, V. A., & Ophir, A. G. (2023). Plasticity in parental behavior and vasopressin: Responses to co-parenting, pup age, and an acute stressor are experience-dependent. *Frontiers in Behavioral Neuroscience*, *17*, 1172845.

Insel, T., & Shapiro, L. (1992). Oxytocin receptor distribution reflects social organization in monogamous and polygamous voles. *Proceedings of the National Academy of Sciences*, *89*(13), 5981–5985.

Levine, A., Zagoory-Sharon, O., Feldman, R., & Weller, A. (2007). Oxytocin during pregnancy and early postpartum: Individual patterns and maternal–fetal attachment. *Peptides*, *28*(6), 1162–1169.

McGlone, F., Wessberg, J., & Olausson, H. (2014). Discriminative and affective touch: Sensing and feeling. *Neuron*, *82*(4), 737–755.

Mesman, J., van IJzendoorn, M., & Sagi-Schwartz, A. (2016). Cross-cultural patterns of attachment: Universal and contextual dimensions. In J. Cassidy & P. R. Shaver (Eds.), *Handbook of attachment: Theory, research, and clinical applications* (3rd ed., pp. 852–877). Guilford Press.

Minagawa-Kawai, Y., Matsuoka, S., Dan, I., Naoi, N., Nakamura, K., & Kojima, S. (2009). Prefrontal activation associated with social attachment: Facial-emotion recognition in mothers and infants. *Cerebral Cortex*, *19*(2), 284–292.

Oliveira, P. (2024). The impact of out-of-home care on brain development: A brief review of the neuroscientific evidence informing our understanding of children's attachment outcomes. *Frontiers in Behavioral Neuroscience, 18*, 1332898.

Olsavsky, A., Telzer, E., Shapiro, M., Humphreys, K., Flannery, J., Goff, B., et al. (2013). Indiscriminate amygdala response to mothers and strangers after early maternal deprivation. *Biological Psychiatry, 74*(11), 853–860.

Provenzi, L., Brambilla, M., Scotto di Minico, G., Montirosso, R., & Borgatti, R. (2020). Maternal caregiving and DNA methylation in human infants and children: Systematic review. *Genes Brain Behaviour, 19*(3), e12616. doi: 10.1111/gbb.12616

Schore, A. (2001). Effects of a secure attachment relationship on right brain development, affect regulation, and infant mental health. *Infant Mental Health Journal, 22*(1–2), 7–66.

Simpson, J., & Belsky, J. (2008). Attachment theory within a modern evolutionary framework. In J. Cassidy & P. R. Shaver (Eds.), *Handbook of attachment: Theory, research, and clinical applications* (2nd ed., pp. 131–157). Guilford Press.

Stack, D., & Muir, D. (1992). Adult tactile stimulation during face-to-face interactions modulates five-month-olds' affect and attention. *Child Development, 63*(6), 1509–1525.

Sullivan, R. (2013). The neurobiology of attachment to nurturing and abusive caregivers. *Hastings Law Journal, 64*(6), 1475–1490.

Swain, J., Kim, P., Spicer, J., Ho, S., Dayton, C., Elmadih, A., & Abel, K. (2014). Approaching the biology of human parental attachment: Brain imaging, oxytocin and coordinated assessments of mothers and fathers. *Brain Research, 1580*, 78–101.

Teicher, M., Samson, J., Anderson, C., & Ohashi, K. (2016). The effects of childhood maltreatment on brain structure, function, and connectivity. *Nature Reviews Neuroscience, 17*(10), 652–666.

Tottenham, N., & Sheridan, M. (2010). A review of adversity, the amygdala and the hippocampus: A consideration of developmental timing. *Frontiers in Human Neuroscience, 3*, 68.

Weaver, I., Cervoni, N., Champagne, F., D'Alessio, A., Sharma, S., Seckl, J., ... & Meaney, M. (2004). Epigenetic programming by maternal behavior. *Nature Neuroscience, 7*(8), 847–854.

Weisman, O., Zagoory-Sharon, O., & Feldman, R. (2012). Oxytocin administration to parent enhances infant physiological and behavioral readiness for social engagement. *Biological Psychiatry, 72*(12), 982–989.

Young, L., & Wang, Z. (2004). The neurobiology of pair bonding. *Nature Neuroscience, 7*(10), 1048–1054.

Chapter 27

The role of individual factors in infant development

Jodi Swanson and Dan Erickson

Introduction

With this chapter, we examine how infants' individual innate characteristics—genetics, temperament, resilience, and their interplay—are directly linked to infants' experiences, health, and developmental trajectories. Bioecological perspectives, attachment theory, and a social cognitive framework guide this line of study.

Biological beginnings

Genetics and heritability

Infants' *phenotypic*—the visible, outward—features are only a small portion of their *genotypic* makeup: the 23 chromosomes, or individual strands of DNA, provided by each biological parent. Within the 46 total DNA strands are millions of other contributions that directly and indirectly shape development beginning at conception. These remain permanent fixtures of the developing baby after birth, including the way genes are expressed and interact with the environment, the steering of genetic predispositions, and so forth. During pregnancy, an individual's genetic blueprint interacts with itself and the prenatal environment to contribute to each infant's uniqueness (Ramesar, 2019).

Despite the short time in utero, prenatal conditions are indelibly linked to long-term developmental trajectories. The DNA in sperm and egg provides the blueprint for physical traits (e.g., eye shape/colour, hair texture, growth patterns, cardiovascular health) and less visible traits (e.g., emotional reactivity, metabolism, health susceptibility). Similar to preparing a physical stage for a theatrical production, what is, or is not, present during the setting of the prenatal stage necessarily affects what is possible for the performance in life—the infant's temperament, proclivity for particular skills, and more.

Heritability is the amount of variability in a given trait, such as intelligence, that can be attributed to genetic factors. Heritability statistics are estimated from twin studies or adoption studies, and range from 0 (i.e., this trait is completely due to environmental influences—*nurture*) to 1 (i.e., this trait is completely due to

DOI: 10.4324/9781003530473-33

genetics—*nature*). For example, compared to lower heritability estimates for body composition, indicating stronger environmental influences (Brener et al., 2021), heritability for human height is estimated around .80, indicating that about 80% of height can be attributed to genetics (Jelenkovic et al., 2016).

Environmental effects on genetic development

The prenatal environment itself also influences infant development. Prenatal providers emphasise exercise and nutritious foods during pregnancy, because the pregnant parent's endocrine system, including hormonal levels and imbalances, directly affects the developing infant (e.g., neurodevelopment, handedness; Richards et al., 2021). Exposure to endocrine-disrupting chemicals disrupts pregnant caregivers' thyroid functionality and can lead to foetuses' cognitive impairment and neurotransmitter imbalance (Salazar et al., 2021). The influence of *teratogens* (i.e. agents responsible for birth defects), such as smoking or drinking alcohol during pregnancy, is especially evident (Gómez-Roig et al., 2021). Effects depend on the timing, dosage, and length of exposure; the first trimester is typically riskiest during the embryonic period when organs form.

Later, the pregnant parent's anxiety during and after pregnancy can affect the infants' emotion regulation problems, social engagement, stress, fear regulation, and autonomic nervous system functioning after birth (Mueller et al., 2021). Caregivers' elevated cortisol levels likely affect the developing foetus's brain, HPA-axis, or immune system, increasing infants' susceptibility to even mild stresses.

Epigenetics

Epigenetics is the interaction of genetics and environment, a dynamic, synergistic interplay that can amplify developmental outcomes beyond either independently. Environmental influences can rearrange chemical markers known as *epigenomes*, modulating genetic expression: The genetic code may outline the propensity of a particular trait, but the environment can determine whether and how much is actually expressed. Analogously, identically manufactured computers have the same hard-wiring, but the individual family that takes home a given computer will determine its operation and how much of the hard-wiring is utilised.

Epigenetic interventions may be temporary or permanent. For example, early childhood trauma, neglect, or toxic stress can substantially alter individual infants' typical brain development. Moreover, widespread cohort effects are possible: In 1944 Nazi-occupied Netherlands, widespread famine and malnourishment resulted in almost universally immediate (i.e. low birthweight) and long-term (i.e., increased risk of disease later in life) consequences for Dutch infants conceived during this time (Ramesar, 2019).

Malleability principles of epigenetics address universal questions of *nature versus nurture* (it's both!), offering insight to those contributing to infants' genetic or environmental circumstances. Caregivers can aim for healthy environments and genes (as much as possible) and work to limit genetic restructuring, such as specialised early diets to reverse epigenetic modifications linked to prenatal malnutrition and responsive caregiving for neglected or abused infants to mitigate epigenetic stress markers.

Individual temperament

Temperament is a set of biologically based differences in reactivity (i.e. how individuals respond to changes in the environment) and regulation (i.e. how individuals manage their reactivity). Clinical child psychologists Thomas and Chess (1977) introduced the modern study of temperament when they observed some child clients exhibiting adjustment difficulties despite a normative, healthy environment and others able to thrive even after extreme hardship. They categorised infants into three temperament types: *difficult* (negative mood, withdrawing), *easy* (positive mood, adaptable), or *slow-to-warm-up* (initially withdrawing, low activity level). Rothbart and colleagues integrated developmental, personality, and animal research models, proposing three broad dimensions of temperament (Putnam et al., 2001; Rothbart & Bates, 2006). *Surgency*, similar to the personality construct 'extraversion', involves activity level, impulsivity, and positivity when encountering novelty. *Negative Affectivity*, similar to 'neuroticism', involves frustration, sadness, and trouble bouncing back when distressed. *Effortful Control* (*Orienting* in infancy), similar to *'conscientiousness'*, includes focusing attention and self-control. Based in genetics (Saudino & Wang, 2012), but malleable to changes across the life span, temperament is the foundation of personality in humans and other social animals, constantly adapting to changes across developmental periods and in the environment (Rothbart, 2011).

Neural network origins

Human central and peripheral nervous systems, including cardiothoracic system responses when experiencing intense emotions, demonstrate individual behaviour differences resulting from genetic differences. Porges and others (1994) began contemporary investigations of how cardiac vagal tone, the changes in heartrate with changes in breathing, can affect emotional reactivity and regulation. Around the same time, neuroscientists began measuring how neural activity explains individual differences in negative emotions and approach/withdrawal (Fox, 1994).

Neural networks responsible for reactivity processing and regulation develop at different rates, and children are more or less susceptible to influences at particular times (Rothbart, 2011). Likewise, environmental influences affecting the developing child, including relationships with caregivers and peers, are constantly shifting. For example, in the first year of a baby's life, the executive attention network in the midprefrontal cortex develops substantially. Early in life, infants and caregivers must work together to control the infant's distress; caregivers first tend to hold and rock the infant, gradually next using visual stimulation to control distress, and eventually redirecting the infant's attention to activities to minimise distress. These types of early parenting behaviours may develop the midprefrontal area as a regulation system for negative emotion. This network undergoes rapid upgrades during preschool and early elementary years, when children are particularly susceptible to emotion-related socialisation.

The environment's influence on temperament and goodness-of-fit

Caregivers and important others in the baby's environment (e.g., other trusted adults, siblings, teachers) play a critical role in helping infants understand what emotions are, and how and when to express them (Propper & Moore, 2006), modelling and instructing optimal regulation of reactivity especially until babies can self-regulate. Children whose caregivers are sensitive and responsive to their emotional needs benefit in the short term (e.g., less likely to be emotionally overwhelmed or act out; Eisenberg et al., 2005) and long term (e.g., academic achievement; Swanson et al., 2014).

How well an infant's temperament aligns with the environment, including social relationships, household demands, expectations, or routines (including sleep schedules), is termed *goodness-of-fit* (Thomas & Chess, 1977). A good fit between the baby and the environment is expected to propel best-possible developmental outcomes, whereas chronically poor fits beget poor outcomes for all parties, particularly if individuals feel there is nothing about the situation they can change to improve the fit. Often, situations are hardest when children whose temperaments are high in reactivity/low in regulation have caregivers who are dysfunctional and unsupportive (Rothbart & Bates, 2006).

Factors contributing to infant adaptability

Resilience is the ability to withstand, adapt, and recover afterward from adversity. A key aspect of individual infant resilience is *neuroplasticity*, the brain's ability to reorganise synaptic connections. Neuroplasticity, in concert with epigenetics, affects vulnerability and susceptibility to the environment. Developmentalists have theorised infants may vary in resilience because certain individuals are simply more susceptible to environmental influences than others—termed *differential susceptibility* (Ellis et al., 2011).

Resilient physical development

Based in mammalian neuroscience, caregivers can help infants develop strong physical health, which can promote greater resilience. Touch and sensory stimulation, such as skin-to-skin contact, promotes physiological and cardio-respiratory stability (Moore et al., 2016), as well as overall cognitive, socio-emotional, and motor development (Figueiredo et al., 2024). Breastfeeding, chestfeeding, or comparable nutritional support, too, is imperative for infants' physical health (Wallenborn et al., 2021). Finally, adequate and efficient sleep prompts infants' emotional and physical functioning (McLaughlin et al., 2022), and meeting early motor milestone windows (e.g., rolling over, crawling) are also associated with overall physical health and subsequent resilience (de Silva et al., 2021).

Failure to thrive describes instances when infants, who are surviving physically, experience delays or fall short of developmental milestone windows. For example, infants of caregivers with postnatal depression can exhibit stunting, decreased motor level, or low weight-for-length (Asare et al., 2022; Wang et al., 2024). Often a result of physical deficiencies (e.g., inadequate caloric intake; Goodwin et al., 2023), failure to thrive can also result from attachment issues and other environmental factors (Chatoor et al., 1998). Early Head Start and similar programmes aim to intervene for these situations.

Differential susceptibility

Stress response systems are critical to navigate the environment; however, some children's oversensitivity to stress may be a leftover trait from human evolution, prioritising the genes of humans most aware of survival threats as fittest. Scholars investigating this phenomenon categorised children as *maskrosbarn* or *orkidebarn*, a Swedish neologism for "dandelion children" and "orchid children", respectively (Ellis & Boyce, 2008, p.184). Despite that dandelions and orchids are capable of growth and bloom, what is necessary for their individual survival—and indeed, thriving—is exceedingly different. Whereas dandelions can grow in abundance almost anywhere, despite otherwise unfavourable circumstances, orchids require meticulous care and attention to their growth, but when they grow healthily they can be exquisite. Similarly, some "dandelion" children may thrive in almost any circumstance, whereas "orchid" children flourish only in specific and distinct circumstances.

Recognising that some children are differentially positioned for successful development is crucial in harnessing epigenetic power. Caregivers can aim to provide environments that nurture children positioned differently to thrive by ensuring physical and emotional safety, structure, and routine (for all children), and emotional sensitivity (catered to each child). Supportive peers, siblings, and neighbours, as well as flexible community- and school-district policies, can offer multi-system buffers for "orchid" children (see Bronfenbrenner, 2000).

Risk versus protective factors

Unfortunately, young children in unsupportive contexts may experience accumulating risks. For instance, Adverse Childhood Experiences (ACEs) have been associated with lifelong poor physical, emotional, and psychological adjustment. Individuals with four or more ACEs, such as exposure to domestic violence, parental substance abuse, neighbourhood crime, or imprisoned family members, were at significantly greater risk for poor health or death before age 50 compared to those with no ACEs (Hughes et al., 2017).

Caregivers are best-positioned to bolster their own resilience by developing consistent caregiving strategies, providing consistent emotional responsiveness, and reinforcing that infants' needs are legitimate and valid (Noroña-Zhou & Tung, 2021). These protective practices provide the foundation for infants' physical and emotional wellbeing, including developmental milestone windows across domains, and promote resiliency throughout the infants' lifetimes.

Conclusion

Humans' genetic blueprints underlying their biology and their temperament are outlined at conception and stable across time and developmental situations, yet individuals' choices and interaction with the environment determine how the blueprint manifests itself. Although proneness to reactivity or regulation may be partly heritable, the environment can significantly foster or bar the expression and behavioural manifestation of this proneness, and some children are simply better at thriving across contexts, whereas others can only thrive in supportive contexts.

Armed with this knowledge, how can caregivers promote babies' healthiest outcomes? Early on, infants and caregivers work jointly to soothe the infant and control distress initially. Caregivers model calming, distress-management methods; over time, infants learn regulatory skills (e.g., deep breathing, distraction) to master their distress. In childhood, socialisers (e.g., caregivers, siblings, teachers, coaches) help children to accept and express emotions healthfully, provide responsive environments, and demonstrate respect for children's autonomy. Caregivers can encourage opportunities to practice self-regulation and self-acceptance after mistakes or unexpected challenges with creative tasks, executive and planning tasks, and resolving conflict tasks. When caregivers understandably feel overwhelmed or unsure of their abilities, it may be helpful to consider infants' own resilience as motivation: Despite having no agency over their environment, infants inspire with their continued engagement, exploration, and remarkable capacity to find joy despite their circumstances.

References

Asare, H., Rosi, A., Scazzina, F., Faber, M., Smuts, C.M., & Ricci, C. (2022). Maternal postpartum depression in relation to child undernutrition in low-and middle-income countries: A systematic review and meta-analysis. *European Journal of Pediatrics, 181*(3), 979–989. https://doi.org/10.1007/s00431-021-04289-4

Brener, A., Waksman, Y., Rosenfeld, T., Levy, S., Peleg, I., Raviv, A., ... & Lebenthal, Y. (2021). The heritability of body composition. *BMC Pediatrics, 21*, 225.

Bronfenbrenner, U. (2000). *Ecological systems theory.* American Psychological Association.

Chatoor, I., Ganiban, J., Colin, V., Plummer, N., & Harmon, R.J. (1998). Attachment and feeding problems: A reexamination of nonorganic failure to thrive and attachment insecurity. *Journal of the American Academy of Child & Adolescent Psychiatry, 37*(11), 1217–1224.

de Silva, A., Neel, M.L., Maitre, N., Busch, T., & Taylor, H.G. (2021). Resilience and vulnerability in very preterm 4-year-olds. *The Clinical Neuropsychologist, 35*(5), 904–924.

Eisenberg, N., Zhou, Q., Spinrad, T.L., Valiente, C., Fabes, R.A., & Liew, J. (2005). Relations among positive parenting, children's effortful control, and externalizing problems: A three-wave longitudinal study. *Child Development, 76*, 1055–1071.

Ellis, B.J., & Boyce, W.T. (2008). Biological sensitivity to context. *Current Directions in Psychological Science, 17*(3), 183–187.

Ellis, B.J., Boyce, W.T., Belsky, J., Bakermans-Kranenburg, M.J., & Van Ijzendoorn, M.H. (2011). Differential susceptibility to the environment: An evolutionary–neurodevelopmental theory. *Development and Psychopathology, 23*(1), 7–28.

Figueiredo, A.R., Moniz, P., & Laureano, M. (2024). Touch: A review of the infant-caregiver relationship in the neonatal field. *International Journal of Psychiatric Trainees, 3*(1), 1–7.

Fox, N.A. (1994). Dynamic cerebral processes underlying emotion regulation. In N.A. Fox (Ed.), *Emotion regulation: Behavioral and biological considerations*. Monographs of the Society for Research in Child Development. Chicago, IL: University of Chicago Press.

Gómez-Roig, M.D., Pascal, R., Cahuana, M.J., García-Algar, O., Sebastiani, G., Andreu-Fernández, V., ... & Vento, M. (2021). Environmental exposure during pregnancy: Influence on prenatal development and early life: A comprehensive review. *Fetal Diagnosis and Therapy, 48*(4), 245–257.

Goodwin, E.T., Buel, K.L., & Cantrell, L.D. (2023). Growth faltering and failure to thrive in children. *American Family Physician, 107*(6), 597–603.

Hughes, K., Bellis, M.A., Hardcastle, K.A., Sethi, D., Butchart, A., Mikton, C., ... & Dunne, M.P. (2017). The effect of multiple adverse childhood experiences on health: A systematic review and meta-analysis. *The Lancet Public Health, 2*(8), e356–e366.

Jelenkovic, A., Sund, R., Hur, Y.-M., Yokoyama, Y., Hjelmborg, H.v.B., Möller,, S., ... & Silventoinen, K. (2016). Genetic and environmental influences on height from infancy to early adulthood: An individual-based pooled analysis of 45 twin cohorts. *Scientific Reports, 6*, 28496.

McLaughlin, K., Chandra, A., Camerota, M., & Propper, C. (2022). Relations between infant sleep quality, physiological reactivity, and emotional reactivity to stress at 3 and 6 months. *Infant Behavior and Development, 67*, 101702.

Moore, E.R., Bergman, N., Anderson, G.C., & Medley, N. (2016). Early skin-to-skin contact for mothers and their healthy newborn infants. *Cochrane database of systematic Reviews*, (11).

Mueller, I., Snidman, N., DiCorcia, J.A., & Tronick, E. (2021). Acute maternal stress disrupts infant regulation of the autonomic nervous system and behavior: A CASP study. *Frontiers in Psychiatry, 12*, 714664.

Noroña-Zhou, A.N., & Tung, I. (2021). Developmental patterns of emotion regulation in toddlerhood: Examining predictors of change and long-term resilience. *Infant Mental Health Journal, 42*(1), 5–20.

Porges, S.W., Doussard-Roosevelt, J.A., & Maiti, A.K. (1994). Vagal tone and the physiological regulation of emotion. In N.A. Fox (Ed.), *The development of emotion regulation: Biological and behavioral considerations*. Monographs of the Society for Research in Child Development (Vol. 59, Serial no. 240, pp. 167–186). Hoboken, NJ: Wiley-Blackwell.

Propper, C., & Moore, G.A. (2006). The influence of parenting on infant emotionality: A multi-level psychobiological perspective. *Developmental Review, 26*, 427–460.

Putnam, S.P., Ellis, L.K., & Rothbart, M.K. (2001). The structure of temperament from infancy through adolescence. In A. Eliasz & A. Angleitner (Eds.), *Advances/Proceedings in research on temperament* (pp. 165–182). Germany: Pabst Scientist Publisher.

Ramesar, R.S. (2019). Epigenetics-an introductory overview. *South African Medical Journal, 109*(6), 371–374.

Richards, G., Beking, T., Kreukels, B.P., Geuze, R.H., Beaton, A.A., & Groothuis, T. (2021). An examination of the influence of prenatal sex hormones on handedness: Literature review and amniotic fluid data. *Hormones and Behavior, 129*, 104929.

Rothbart, M. (2011). *Becoming who we are: Temperament and personality in development.* New York: Guilford Press.

Rothbart, M.K., & Bates, J.E. (2006). Temperament. In W. Damon (Series Ed.) & N. Eisenberg (Vol. Ed.) (Eds.), *Handbook of child psychology. Vol 3. Social, emotional, personality development* (6th ed., pp. 99–166). New York: Wiley.

Salazar, P., Villaseca, P., Cisternas, P., & Inestrosa, N.C. (2021). Neurodevelopmental impact of the offspring by thyroid hormone system-disrupting environmental chemicals during pregnancy. *Environmental Research, 200*, 111345.

Saudino, K.J., & Wang, M. (2012). Quantitative and molecular genetic studies of temperament. In M. Zentner & R.L. Shiner (Eds.), *Handbook of temperament* (pp. 315–346). New York: Guilford Press.

Swanson, J., Valiente, C., Lemery-Chalfant, K., Bradley, R.H., & Eggum-Wilkens, N.D. (2014). Longitudinal relations among caregivers' reactions to children's negative emotions, effortful control, and math achievement in early elementary school. *Child Development, 85*, 1932–1947.

Thomas, A., & Chess, S. (1977). *Temperament and development.* Brunner/Mazel.

Wallenborn, J.T., Levine, G.A., Carreira dos Santos, A., Grisi, S., Brentani, A., & Fink, G. (2021). Breastfeeding, physical growth, and cognitive development. *Pediatrics, 147*(5), 1–10.

Wang, M., Bai, T., Zhang, J., Liu, H., Wu, L., & Zhang, F. (2024). Relationship between maternal postpartum depression, fatigue, sleep quality and infant growth: A cross-sectional study. *Japan Journal of Nursing Science, 21*(4), e12614.

Chapter 28

The development of self-awareness in infancy

Andrew J. Bremner and Victoria Southgate

Introduction

At last, it feels like we are making some progress in understanding the origins of our capacity for self-awareness. While this particular focus of developmental science has somewhat stagnated in recent years, new progress—which we will illustrate in this short chapter—has emerged from interdisciplinary dialogue, particularly between developmental psychology, cognitive neuroscience, and philosophy. The progress arises, in part, because of recognition that established accounts of the early origins of self-awareness in developmental psychology are incompatible with what we understand of the mechanistic basis of the self in cognitive neuroscience.

If you were to consult a developmental psychology textbook regarding the origins of self-awareness in infancy, our guess is that this would yield something like: 'Humans are born with a sensory self-awareness, able to differentiate their own bodies from the world around them. More conceptual forms of self-awareness, such as the development of an ability to represent the self as first person, likely develop later but are difficult to study partly as it is difficult to define and operationalise what self-awareness is.' (We have no definitive measures of self-awareness and are entirely reliant on indirect measures, like the classic mirror self-recognition (MSR) test. Consequently, researchers have spent more time disagreeing about whether these properly operationalise the phenomena of interest than studying the development of the conceptual self.)

Ask a cognitive neuroscientist on the other hand and they are more likely to say: 'Body representations arise from complex multisensory brain networks which are largely dependent on sensory experience. Conceptual self-awareness is supported by functional connectivity in the Default Mode Network (DMN) between sensory inputs regarding the body and other sources of neural information regarding affect, motivation etc. By the way, the DMN is functional in newborn infants.'

So developmentalists tend to think bodily self-awareness is available at birth (or innate) and the conceptual self develops through early postnatal life. At least some positions in cognitive neuroscience give us the exact opposite impression (e.g., Bayne et al., 2023). Here we argue that progress can be made in understanding the development of self-awareness, by confronting the challenge that these conflicting

DOI: 10.4324/9781003530473-34

accounts present, and validating methods. We illustrate this with brief reviews of our respective programmes of developmental cognitive neuroscience research in bodily (Bremner) and conceptual (Southgate) self-awareness.

The development of bodily self-awareness in infancy

Rochat (2010) has it that humans are born with an innate sense of the 'ecological self' (or what we might refer to as the bodily self). This claim rests on two key sources of evidence. First, Rochat and Hespos's (1997) report of newborns' rooting responses to perioral touches initiated by themselves or others claims greater rooting in response to other-touch in newborns, and greater rooting in response to self-touch in 1-month-olds. The conclusion is that newborn infants represent the position of their limbs in relation to their mouth, and the postural spatial origin of the 'double touch' sensation. But on closer inspection Rochat and Hespos report no statistically reliable differentiation in newborns. Furthermore, differentiated responses in 1-month-olds could easily be due to learned manual-oral interactions scaffolded by learned interactions of these somatosensory surfaces that come into frequent contact *in utero* (De Vries et al., 1984; see Bremner, 2017, for discussion).

The second key to Rochat's claim is early sensitivity to crossmodal synchrony between visual/auditory and somatosensory stimuli occurring on the body. Bahrick and Watson's (1985) study, followed up and developed by Rochat (2010), shows that young (5-month-old) infants discriminate between visual displays of the movements of their legs, which are synchronous vs asynchronous with their own leg movements, demonstrated via preferential looking towards visually asynchronous displays. Bremner and colleagues (see Bremner, 2022) demonstrate something quite similar in 4-month-old infants concerning visual-tactile events on the hands and feet, and Filippetti et al. (2013) even find evidence that newborn infants of a few days of age differentiate synchronous from asynchronous visual-tactile touch to the face. In both of these scenarios, young infants demonstrate visual preferences for synchronous/co-located visual-tactile displays.

Demonstrations of a sensitivity to spatiotemporal contingencies between somatosensory and visual cues to the limbs are suggestive that the multisensory basis of body representations is available early in multisensory development. However, a number of other sources of evidence demonstrate that there are substantial limitations in these multisensory interactions in early life. Bremner and colleagues (Begum Ali et al., 2015; Rigato et al., 2014; see Bremner, 2022), inspired by neuroscientific models of the experiential origins of multisensory body representations (e.g., Röder et al., 2004; Stein, 2012), demonstrate that behavioural orienting responses and sensory feed-forward neural processing of cutaneous touches on the hands/feet are limited to crude anatomical spatial coding, making no reference to external spatial coordinates in the first six postnatal months of life. Accurate visual orienting to touches presented without concurrent visual stimuli does not emerge until ten months of age.

Together, these findings indicate that early sensitivity to crossmodal contingencies between visual and tactile/proprioceptive bodily cues (Bahrick & Watson, 1985; Begum Ali et al., 2021; Filippetti et al., 2013; Rochat, 2010) are not sufficient to support the unified multisensory body representations required to coordinate action in external space. Contrary to one recent account (De Klerk et al., 2021), it may be that simple spatiotemporal associations between visual and tactile sensory cues are not sufficient to combine the senses into common spatial and temporal representation of the body and the external environment. Interestingly, and in contrast to claims of innate body representations (Rochat, 2010), recent data from comparisons of sighted and congenitally blind infants clarify that visual experience in early postnatal infancy is required for the normative developmental integration of somatosensory with external (auditory) sensory cues into a common bodily frame of reference (Gori et al., 2021).

In sum, recent studies into the developmental origins of bodily self-awareness indicate that, although there is early postnatal sensitivity to crossmodal associations between the senses, electrophysiological findings and measures of behavioural orienting responses show that a unitary multisensory representation of the body develops gradually through the first postnatal years of life as a result of sensory experience. Of course, given the scale of physical development in infancy, this seems unsurprising. Because of the altricial nature of human newborns, the shape, size, and proportions of the infant body, not to mention the postural movements that it is capable of, change dramatically in early life. The gradual construction of a bodily self may help avoid integrating the senses in such a way as to create a body representation that is unsuitable for underpinning the repertoire of controlled actions, which infants build increasingly rapidly across the first year of life.

The development of conceptual self-awareness in infancy

Historically, the capacity to take oneself as the object of attention—or to think "I thoughts" (Musholt, 2015) has been argued to be evident in young children's capacity to recognise themselves in a mirror, emerging between 18 and 24 months of age in Western societies. While some have challenged the idea that mirror self-recognition indicates anything about a child's ability to think about the self (Heyes, 1994; Suddendorf & Butler, 2013), there is extensive evidence that this ability is associated with other behaviours that could indicate the capacity to think about the self. For example, children who pass the mirror self-recognition measure are more likely to show self-conscious emotions (Lewis & Ramsay, 2004), to use personal pronouns (Lewis et al., 1989), and to show empathic behaviours (Bischof-Kohler, 2012). Nevertheless, these associations could reflect a general cognitive development and do not necessarily imply that a development of self-awareness underpins these associations. What is needed is both a theoretical account that makes systematic predictions concerning the absence and presence of self-awareness in a unitary framework, and empirical means to control more general cognitive developmental factors that are not expected to differ with respect to self-awareness status. Southgate (2020) proposed just such an account of the development of early perspective taking. Under this model:

i)   An initial absence of the capacity to think about the self facilitates infants' early demonstrated ability to track the targets of others' attention due to the absence of interference from their own perspective. This hypothesis was based on ample findings that, when adults have to track another person's perspective that differs from their own, they have to engage regions of the prefrontal cortex implicated in inhibitory control.

ii)   The emergence of a conceptual self-representation in the second year of life generates a challenge for infants: Because now they have to manage two conflicting perspectives, the tracking of others' perspectives becomes more difficult. This account therefore predicts that, as infants develop self-awareness, we should see the recruitment of brain regions involved in inhibitory control.

iii) If there is a genuine change in the capacity for self-representation in the second year of life, we should also see indicators of self-prioritised cognition appearing, like the classic self-reference memory effect that is well-documented in adults.

Manea et al. (2023) have recently demonstrated support for hypothesis (i). They showed that infants better remember objects when they are the targets of others' attention than if they are merely the target of the infant's attention. This effect is clearly present in 8-month-olds but disappears by 12 months of age. Importantly, multiple abilities change between 8 and 12 months of age and we cannot yet link the disappearance of this altercentric bias to the emergence of a conceptual self-representation.

In line with prediction (ii), Yeung et al. (2022; 2024 preprinted) showed that mirror self-recognising infants, when faced with a context in which their own and another agent's perspectives were in conflict, exhibited greater pupil dilation (a measure of cognitive effort), as well as greater activation of the right prefrontal cortex (a region overlapping with that implicated in inhibition of the self-perspective in adults). These studies indicate that only those infants who have developed a self-representation experience a conflict when self and another perspective is in conflict.

Grosse Wiesmann et al. (2025) find support for prediction (iii). They show that the onset of the self-reference effect is linked to the emergence of a self-representation, again indexed by MSR. The self-reference effect describes the tendency in adults to better remember items that can be related to the self, and is logically dependent on the pre-existence of a conceptual representation of the self. Eighteen-month-old infants took part in a test of mirror self-recognition, as well as a memory paradigm that measured memory for novel objects that had previously been assigned to the infant or to a puppet. As we predicted, only those infants who passed the MSR test showed evidence of better memory for the self-assigned objects, suggesting that, like adults, they show a self-reference effect. However, infants who did not show MSR actually remembered better the objects assigned to the puppet, suggesting an *other*-reference effect, which we interpret as a manifestation of the altercentric bias, already documented by Manea et al. (2023).

But what of the Default Mode Network (DMN), the marker of self-awareness in adults, which has been observed to be functional in newborn infants? Finally, despite evidence that the DMN functions at birth (Scheinost et al., 2024), perhaps supporting claims of a very early self-other distinction, Bulgarelli et al. (2019) demonstrate significant changes in DMN function in the second year of life. They found significantly greater resting-state functional connectivity in brain areas comprising the DMN in mirror recognisers than mirror non-recognisers. Given the important role of the DMN in the adult inclination to think about the self, these findings point to profound changes in infants' capacity for self-representation in the second year of life that is captured by the MSR test.

The studies discussed above together indicate profound changes in infants' capacity for conceptual self-representation in the second year of life, and validate the MSR as an important indicator of this capacity. In both Yeung et al. (2022, 2024 preprinted), and Grosse Wiesmann et al. (2025), additional measures of more general cognitive development like inhibitory control were taken, but did not differ between 18-month-olds who recognised themselves in the mirror and those who did not, allowing the isolation of effects specific to the development of self-representation. Rather than continuing to debate the usefulness of MSR, we can now be confident that it measures a genuine change in self-awareness and we can proceed with trying to understand why there is such a change between 18 and 24 months of age, and what inputs and mechanisms give rise to this change.

Summary

We started this chapter by making the observation that developmental evidence has tended to be marshalled in favour of an account that bodily self-awareness is innate and conceptual self-awareness more slow to develop, while cognitive neuroscience offers the converse perspective. The work we have reviewed here shows that both sensory and conceptual self-awareness appears to undergo significant postnatal development, even to the extent of excluding infants' own perspectives from their encoding of objects in memory. A fascinating possibility is raised here. Perhaps self-awareness in both bodily and conceptual domains develop concurrently. Indeed, if as we have argued here, coherent multisensory body representations are gradually constructed across the first year of life, it may be that the gradual development of a bodily frame of reference in sensory processing constrains the emergence of infants' ability to understand and encode the world according to their own perspectives.

What must it be like to sense the world without perspective? If John Campbell is right, then it must be very different phenomenologically from what we would recognise as our self-aware experiences in adulthood:

The idea of absolute space ... can seem dizzying ... What is dizzying is the kind of complete objectivity, the degree of abstraction from one's own busy concerns, that is required. A first interpretation of what is wanted is a kind of top-down view, so that we think in terms of a kind of aerial photograph ... But that would not be enough, for it would only give the viewpoint of the photographer, and we need a picture of the world that is objective in that it is not from any viewpoint at all ... What would you expect to be able to discern from nowhere?

(Campbell, 1994, p.6)

References

Bahrick, L. E., & Watson, J. S. (1985). Detection of intermodal proprioceptive-visual contingency as a potential basis of self-perception in infancy. *Developmental Psychology*, *21*(6), 963–973.

Bayne, T., Frohlich, J., Cusack, R., Moser, J., & Naci, L. (2023). Consciousness in the cradle: On the emergence of infant experience. *Trends in Cognitive Sciences*, *27*, 1135–1149.

Begum Ali, J., Thomas, R. L., Mullen Raymond, S., & Bremner, A. J. (2021). Sensitivity to visual-tactile colocation on the body prior to skilled reaching in early infancy. *Child Development*, *92*(1), 21–34.

Begum Ali, J., Spence, C., & Bremner, A. J. (2015). Human infants' ability to perceive touch in external space develops postnatally. *Current Biology*, *25*(20), R978–R979.

Bischof-Köhler, D. (2012). Empathy and self-recognition in phylogenetic and ontogenetic perspective. *Emotion Review*, *4*(1), 40–48.

Bremner, A. J. (2017). The origins of body representations in early life. In F. de Vignemont & A. J. T. Alsmith (Eds.), *The subject's matter: Self-consciousness and the body* (pp. 3–31). Cambridge, MA: MIT Press.

Bremner, A. J. (2022). Developmental origins of bodily awareness. In A. J. T. Alsmith & M. R. Longo (Eds.), *The Routledge handbook of bodily awareness.* Oxford, UK: Taylor & Francis.

Bulgarelli, C., Blasi, A., de Klerk, C. C., Richards, J. E., Hamilton, A., & Southgate, V. (2019). Fronto-temporoparietal connectivity and self-awareness in 18-month-olds: A resting state fNIRS study. *Developmental Cognitive Neuroscience*, *38*, 100676.

Campbell, J. (1994). *Past, space, and self.* Cambridge, MA: MIT Press.

de Klerk, C. C. J. M., Filippetti, M. L., & Rigato, S. (2021). The development of body representations: An associative learning account. *Proceedings of the Royal Society B: Biological Sciences*, *288*(1949), 20210070.

de Vries, J. I. P., Visser, G. H. A., & Prechtl, H. F. R. (1984). Fetal motility in the first half of pregnancy. *Clinics in Developmental Medicine*, *94*, 46–64.

Filippetti, M. L., Johnson, M. H., Lloyd-Fox, S., Dragovic, D., & Farroni, T. (2013). Body perception in newborns. *Current Biology*, *23*(23), 2413–2416.

Gori, M., Campus, C., Signorini, S., Rivara, E., & Bremner, A. J. (2021). Multisensory spatial perception in visually impaired infants. *Current Biology*, *31*(22), 5093–5101.e5.

Grosse Wiesmann, C., Rothmaler, K., Habdank, K., Hasan, E., Yang, C., Yeung, E., & Southgate, V. (2025). The self-reference memory bias is preceded by an other-reference bias in infancy. *Nature Communications*, *16*(1), 6311.

Heyes, C. M. (1994). Reflections on self-recognition in primates. *Animal Behaviour, 47*(4), 909–919.

Lewis, M., & Ramsay, D. (2004). Development of self-recognition, personal pronoun use, and pretend play during the 2nd year. *Child Development, 75*(6), 1821–1831.

Lewis, M., Sullivan, M. W., Stanger, C., & Weiss, M. (1989). Self development and self-conscious emotions. *Child Development, 60*(1), 146–156.

Manea, V., Kampis, D., Grosse Wiesmann, C., Revencu, B., & Southgate, V. (2023). An initial but receding altercentric bias in preverbal infants' memory. *Proceedings of the Royal Society B, 290*(2000), 20230738.

Musholt, K. (2015). *Thinking about oneself: From nonconceptual content to the concept of a self.* Cambridge, MA: MIT Press.

Rigato, S., Begum Ali, J., van Velzen, J., & Bremner, A. J. (2014). The neural basis of somatosensory remapping develops in human infancy. *Current Biology, 24*(11), 1222–1226.

Rochat, P., & Hespos, S. J. (1997). Differential rooting response by neonates: Evidence for an early sense of self. *Early Development and Parenting, 6*(3–4), 105–112.

Rochat, P. (2010). The innate sense of the body develops to become a public affair by 2–3 years. *Neuropsychologia, 48*(3), 738–745.

Röder, B., Rösler, F., & Spence, C. (2004). Early vision impairs tactile perception in the blind. *Current Biology, 14*(2), 121–124.

Scheinost, D., Changc, J., Brennan-Wydrad, E., Lacadiea, C., Constablea, R. T., Chawarskac, K., & Mentf, L. R. (2024). Developmental trajectories of the default mode, frontoparietal, and salience networks from the third trimester through the newborn period. *Imaging Neuroscience, 2*, Article 201.

Southgate, V. (2020). Are infants altercentric? The other and the self in early social cognition. *Psychological Review, 127*(4), 505–523.

Stein, B. E. (2012). *The new handbook of multisensory processing.* MIT Press.

Suddendorf, T., & Butler, D. L. (2013). The nature of visual self-recognition. *Trends in Cognitive Sciences, 17*(3), 121–127.

Yeung, E., Askitis, D., Manea, V., & Southgate, V. (2022). Emerging self-representation presents a challenge when perspectives conflict. *Open Mind, 6*, 232–249.

Yeung, E., Askitis, D., & Southgate, V. (2024). Developing self-awareness generates perspective conflict: Evidence in the infant brain. https://osf.io/6ytfw/download.

Chapter 29

Faith identity and psychological therapies with Muslim families

Rachel Abedi

In the UK there has been little research into the scope and impact of psychological therapies with young children of Muslim heritage. This is for a range of reasons, not least that CAMHS[1] services rarely collect data about the faith identity of the children referred. While ethnicity data is sometimes considered important in understanding whether services are accessible and relevant to the communities in which we work, faith identity is not. In part due to the secular origins and context of most of our trainings, Muslim faith is (at best) seen as a sub-set of culture, at worst as a risk factor. This means that we have little idea whether or not our services are accessible to the Muslim families in our communities (and if not why not), let alone whether the therapies we offer have meaningful outcomes for Muslim children and families. The absence by omission of faith identity in our thinking and training has an impact on populations to whom faith is an important part of their identity, including many Muslims.

However, faith identity is not disregarded entirely, as it features consciously and unconsciously in underlying assumptions and judgements about families (Abedi 2021; Fleming, 2020) and in clinical decision-making (Kam and Midgley 2006). Thinking about Muslim patients is often characterised by anxiety on the part of the clinician (Abedi 2021), whether in relation to the socio-political context (e.g. Prevent), unfamiliarity with Muslim beliefs and practices, or fear of causing offence, and is often intersectional with assumptions about culture, race, and class. This has a significant impact both on how clinicians work with Muslims, including parents, and whether the patients and parents feel they can trust the clinician. This in turn influences what they feel able to share with the clinician (Maynard 2023).

The longstanding level of wider societal prejudice against Muslims is also significant (Jones and Unsworth 2022, Tell Mama Report 2023), as demonstrated in the riots of summer 2024. "The sense that Muslim people are a threat to Britain has become overt and direct" (Runnymede Trust 2024).

Poverty, with its well-documented impact on mental health, exacerbates the situation for many Muslims. 40% of England's Muslim families live in the most deprived wards (Woolf Institute Factsheet 2023), and deprivation levels are often hugely disproportionate compared to the size of local populations.[2] Together, these

DOI: 10.4324/9781003530473-35

factors contribute to systemic disadvantage for Muslims in the UK affecting every stage of their lives (Stevenson et al. 2017).

Research has shown that the vast majority of young Muslims do not seek professional help when experiencing mental health problems. Only 13% accessed professional help, and of these, 90% said they would prefer faith-sensitive support (Bunglawala et al. 2019). Practitioners should be aware that Muslims often use alternative interventions and coping strategies, such as turning to the Quran and *Hadith* as primary sources for comfort and guidance, or seeking the advice of a trusted religious scholar or *imam*. Often, the family also plays an important role in managing difficulties (Ahmed and Amer 2012). Sadly, this can be judged by non-Muslim practitioners as avoidance of (what they regard as) appropriate support, often with prejudicial consequences.

Parenting in Islam

Parenting is a sacred responsibility in Islam. "The family is the foundation of Islamic society" (Winter 2002 p.23), with the stability of the family unit seen as essential for the spiritual growth of its members. Traditionally, children are treasured, and the approach to their upbringing is "both serious and caring, stressing respect for parents and teachers, personal modesty and cleanliness, and the memorisation of the Quran and other sacred texts" (p.55). According to the Quran, children are born without sin, and it is the parents' duty to protect their children from making bad choices. For this reason, Muslim parents often feel a sense of personal responsibility for their children's wrongdoing, made all the more weighty by their understanding of eternal consequences of being held to account.

Faith and culture

It is important to understand the difference between beliefs and practices prescribed by Islam and those by the family's culture. The conflation of culture and religion is a result of ignorance, secularism (particularly in the theoretical underpinning of Western psychological therapies), and a manifestation in the global north of the echoes of colonialism. For example, while some Muslim societies prefer sons to daughters (as do some non-Muslim societies), this is a cultural influence. In fact, the Quran condemns those who are dissatisfied with the birth of a girl.[3] Similarly, forced marriage is a cultural practice, as "unmarried young Muslims have the right to decline any partner who may be suggested by their parents or guardians" (Winter, 2002, p.42). In Muslim families, it is common for parenting to be shared by members of the extended family who might also share the family home. This is regarded as a valuable resource, despite the tensions that might also arise depending on individual relationships. However, it can be viewed by those unfamiliar with extended family households as inevitably negative.

If a marriage breaks down, there is a variety of practice in terms of custody of children. Very young children usually remain with the mother, but from the age of 7 (according to some schools of Islamic law) boys are brought up by their fathers while girls remain with their mothers until puberty. Other schools of Islamic law recommend that boys and girls choose between their parents when old enough to do so (Winter 2002). While some Muslim families in the UK might want to align their decisions with such positions, they might also decide to align with British law on such matters, and individual circumstances will always be important. They might also be influenced by family cultural (rather than religious) practice.

Challenges for Muslim parents in the UK

The racism and Islamophobia that are part of many Muslims' daily experience (especially if visibly Muslim), the resulting fear of judgement and wish to protect their children, inevitably affect the parenting choices of Muslims. Non-Muslim clinicians often attribute reticence to engage with services to 'cultural stigma', without being aware of the impact of prejudice, which creates an anticipation of attack/judgement leading to further marginalisation. In psychoanalytic terms, the unwanted aspects of self (stigma/shame) are projected by the majority into the minoritised 'other' and effectively disowned (Davids 2011).

Furthermore, the pressure on minoritised families not to appear to conform to this negative view can create a sense of shame that prevents some from seeking professional help. More significant perhaps is the expectation that, even if help is sought, it will not value or even acknowledge their faith identity, or worse will make it a cause for concern.

Clinicians should be aware of the extent to which stigma around mental health affects access to mental health support which is not offered in a faith- and culture-sensitive manner. For example, in some Muslim communities even the term 'mental health' is laden with terrifying connotations of chains and being locked away, and so phrases such as 'emotional wellbeing' are preferred. Similarly, the term 'counselling' might be preferred to 'therapy', although in the profession we see these as different approaches.

Meanwhile, the challenges for Muslim parents raising children in the UK are significant. For many 'practising' Muslim families, the values and religious observance that are foundational aspects of family life at home are often in contrast to the secular context of school and other features of British children's lives such as social media. This creates significant challenges in terms of identity for young British Muslims to navigate as they grow up, and the resulting tensions are often evident in conflict with parents, especially during adolescence. Depending on the diversity of the area, Muslim parents might not have access to the peer support enjoyed by some at the school gates, and can feel isolated, embattled, ashamed, and fearful for their children's future. The problem is often framed in the media as the Muslim's problem with integration—'fit in or get out'—which itself is a manifestation of prejudice. Therapists might sympathise with their young patients/clients, even affirm their attempts to defy family expectations, without fully appreciating the faith and cultural context and therefore the consequences for the young person, unintentionally colluding with a society that positions Islam as the bad object. As we know, it is hard for us to maintain an awareness of the influence of our own upbringing.

The problems for refugee parents, many of whom are of Muslim heritage,[4] are even more complex. They are more likely to experience poor mental health than the general population (Woolf Institute, 2023). Many will have experienced significant trauma associated with displacement and immigration, and are likely to face multiple social problems in addition to poverty and prejudice, including poor housing and difficulty accessing services. Many refugees feel that these difficulties prevent them from being good parents (Alayarian 2017). "Specifically, depression amongst mothers, caused by social distress and isolation, increases the worry for their children" (Alayarian 2017, p.16). They might lack support networks yet also feel uncomfortable leaving their children in nursery where no-one speaks their language. They can also be worried about how social services perceive their parenting skills (p.16). With more under-fives than the general population, refugee parents might need earlier provision of services, yet the lack of training for service providers prevents healthcare workers from meeting their emotional needs (Alayarian 2017, p.17).

Parenting infants

In Islam, an individual's timeline goes far beyond the 'birth until death' span of secular approaches, as every person is regarded as being known by God beyond time—certainly before conception and after death. In Islamic tradition, the foetus has its soul breathed into it at around 120 days post-conception, thereby actualising its humanity.[5] A baby is not only a blessing from God to love and treasure, but a sacred responsibility. This idea (and associated expectations), combined with isolation, unacknowledged birth trauma, and the experience for many of discrimination when giving birth in hospital (Shaikh 2023), might make it all the more difficult to seek help when struggling during pregnancy or experiencing postnatal depression. Additionally, many Muslim mothers experience cultural stigma around mental health from within their communities, making it hard to discuss any emerging concerns (for example about child neuro-developmental issues), and removing the ordinary peer support that can be so helpful.

Examples of faith-sensitive work with parents (TRP)

The challenges described above are a common feature in work with Muslim parents. Here, I will outline examples of work in an innovative faith- and culture-sensitive psychotherapy service for Muslim families, The Reflection Project (TRP), which operates in areas with significant Muslim populations. Settings vary, and include mosques, community centres, schools, and council-run children's centres. The first two examples describe the perspective of Muslim parents, and the third example demonstrates some of the challenges for non-Muslim practitioners.

1. Parent work in various TRP settings, including groups. Frequently occurring themes include fear of being stereotyped, not being believed by practitioners from outside the community, fear of judgement from within the community, worry about the negative influence of secular culture on their children, wish to protect the faith identity of their children, and being unsure how to communicate with their teenaged children who are growing up with cultural norms and pressures often different to the parents' own experience.
2. Perinatal wellbeing workshops at an East African community centre. The workshops were designed to provide a space where parents could discuss their children's mental and emotional health with experts in the field and with each other. The intention was to support non-judgemental conversations about how these issues affect families' lives, and to develop faith- and culture-sensitive responses. The discussion was wide-ranging and included: the difficulty of having conversations about mental health and SEN within their community, isolation, pressure of expectations as mothers, experiences of discrimination when giving birth,[6] and the importance of postnatal services yet fear of asking for help. Participants wanted more opportunities to discuss issues that are not openly discussed in the community, and requested a regular local class for new mothers.
3. Reflective spaces for adoption and LAC social workers working with Muslims. Participants expressed their need for spaces like this to allow them to develop their understanding, ask difficult questions, tackle complexities, and challenge their own biases and assumptions without fear of causing offence. For example, understanding the potential significance to a Muslim foster carer of being pressured by services to allow a fostered child to eat pork in her home— not just a matter of a simple 'choice' but one of considering consequences beyond this life and the foster carer's responsibility for decisions made on behalf of a child.

Summary

A recent report recommended the provision of religiously sensitive mental health care for Muslim communities, and religious literacy training for practitioners, particularly in areas with significant Muslim populations, "to ensure a deeper understanding of the nuanced needs of Muslim patients" (Hekmoun and Abrar, 2024, p. 3). These would certainly go a long way to improving accessibility and quality of support for Muslim parents. Such recommendations are sometimes accused of not being 'inclusive', which disingenuously uses the language of EDI to advocate for the status quo. Yet treating all minorities the same, disregarding the intersectional contexts that create multiple barriers to accessing support, further marginalises Muslim communities and perpetuates health inequalities.

Notes

1 NHS Child and Adolescent Mental Health Services.
2 For example, while 16% of children in Barnet are Muslim, they represent 43% of the borough's most deprived children (Insight and Intelligence Unit, 2023).
3 Surah 15 verse 68 referenced in Winter 2002 p.41.
4 In 2024, the five most common countries of origin of people seeking asylum in the UK were Muslim: Pakistan, Afghanistan, Iran, Bangladesh, Syria (Walsh and Jorgensen 2025). While not all refugees from these countries were Muslim, a significant percentage of refugees to the UK identify as Muslim.
5 As the soul is considered an essential part of being human. As such, if the foetus dies after 120 days it should be given a proper burial and funeral prayers.
6 Such as expectation of pain tolerance, concerns not being taken seriously by professionals. Also see Shaikh, A. (2023) *British Muslims' experiences of pregnancy and birth*.

References

Abedi, R. (2021). *How do clinicians respond to the faith identity of young Muslims in a London Child and Adolescent Mental Health Service (CAMHS) clinical context? An interpretative phenomenological analysis.* Other Thesis, University of Essex & Tavistock and Portman NHS Trust.

Ahmed, S., & Amer, M. M. (Eds.). (2012). *Counseling Muslims: Handbook of mental health issues and interventions.* Routledge/Taylor & Francis Group.

Alayarian, A. (2017). *Children of refugees: Torture, human rights, and psychological consequences.* Karnac Books.

Bunglawala, S., Meha, A., & Tunariu, A. (2019). *Hidden survivors: Uncovering the mental health needs of British Muslims.* BCBN, University of East London, Inspirited Minds, The Muslim Network.

Davids, M. F. (2011). *Internal racism: A psychoanalytic approach to race and difference.* Palgrave Macmillan.

Fleming, A. (2020). Child psychotherapists' fantasies about working with 'cultural difference'. *Journal of Child Psychotherapy, 46*(2), 168–190..

Hekmoun, J., & Abrar, S. (2024). *Faith in mental health.* Woolf Institute, Cambridge.

Insight and Intelligence Unit. (2023). Data set sent on request [October 2023]. London Borough of Barnet Council.

Jones, S. H., & Unsworth, A. (2022). *The dinner table prejudice: Islamophobia in contemporary Britain.* University of Birmingham, The British Academy, and YouGov.

Kam, S.-E., & Midgley, N. (2006). Exploring clinical judgement: How do child and adolescent mental health professionals decide whether a young person needs individual psychotherapy? *Clinical Child Psychology and Psychiatry, 11*, 27.

Maynard, S. A. (2023). The racism you know is not the racism we experience: A perspective on Islamophobia and racism concerning the therapeutic frame—What Muslims bring and what they leave behind. *Psychotherapy and Politics International, 21*(3–4), 1–14.

Runnymede Trust Perspectives Paper. (2024). *Islamophobia: the Intensification of racism against Muslim communities in the UK.* Retrieved on 26 January 2025 from www.run nymedetrust.org/publications/islamophobia-the-intensification-of-racism-against-mus lim-communities-in-the-uk

Shaikh, A. (2023). *British Muslims' experiences of pregnancy and birth.* University of London.

Stevenson, J., Demack, S., Stiell, B., Abdi, M., Clarkson, L., Ghaffar, F., & Hassan, S. (2017). *The social mobility challenges faced by young Muslims.* Social Mobility Commission and Sheffield Hallam University.

Tell Mama Report. (2023). *A decade of anti-Muslim hate.* Faith Matters.

Walsh, P.W., & Jorgensen, N. (2025) *Briefing: Asylum and refugee resettlement in the UK.* [Table 1: Nationality of people seeking asylum in the UK: the top 10 most common in 2024. Page 10]. The Migration Observatory at the University of Oxford. https://migra-tionobservatory.ox.ac.uk/wp-content/uploads/2025/08/2025-Briefing-Asylum-and-refu-gee-resettlement-in-the-UK.pdf

Winter, T. J. (2002). *Understanding Islam and the Muslims.* Fons Vitae.

Woolf Institute. (2023). *Fasctsheet on Muslim mental health.* Retrieved on 26 January 2025 from www.woolf.cam.ac.uk/whats-on/news/fact-sheet-muslim-mental-health

Chapter 30

Infancy

A discussion

Alejandra Perez and Elena Panagiotopoulou

It is important to note that, in this section on infancy, all of the authors explore the importance of the environment and/or the parent for the infant's development and inner world. This centrality of the environment/parent attests to the enduring observation made by Winnicott in the 1940s that, "there is no such thing as an infant, meaning, of course, that whenever one finds an infant one finds maternal care, and without maternal care there would be no infant" (Winnicott, 1965 p.39).

In Chapter 25, Perez explores different conceptualisations of the baby's inner world. The chapter draws on psychoanalytic and attachment theories, exploring points of convergence, such as the internalisation of the infant's relationship with their primary caregiver, but also divergence, such as the important role of unconscious phantasy and individual forms of internalisation across psychoanalytic theories and of the environment for attachment theory. The clinical use of these theories is exemplified with a parent-infant psychotherapy case. In Chapter 26, Oliveira and Mesquita draw on evolutionary, neurobiological, neurochemical, clinical, and cultural perspectives to explore the biological mechanisms of attachment during infancy and early parenthood, therefore illustrating why this phenomenon, which if often viewed as social, is, at its core, profoundly biological. In Chapter 27, Swanson and Erickson, drawing on bioecological perspectives, attachment theory, and a social cognitive framework, examine how genetic blueprints underlying biology and temperament are present at conception, yet interactions with the environment determine how these will manifest themselves, thus exploring the role of individual factors in developmental trajectories. In Chapter 28, Bremner and Southgate discuss conflicting accounts between developmental psychology and cognitive neuroscience regarding the development of self-awareness, and, inspired by techniques and findings from cognitive neuroscience, explain why both sensory and conceptual forms of self-awareness develop gradually throughout infancy. In Chapter 29, Abedi examines the lack of faith-sensitive psychological support for young Muslim children in the UK, affecting access, trust, and outcomes for Muslim families. The chapter also discusses the challenges Muslim parents face, including racism, isolation, and cultural tensions, and calls for faith- and culture-sensitive services and religious literacy training for practitioners to improve accessibility.

DOI: 10.4324/9781003530473-36

The complex interplay between the internal and the external

The various authors of this section present different conceptualisations of our internal and external worlds, and different permutations of their interrelatedness. In her chapter, Perez describes the internal or inner world as the collection of one's individual, subjective thoughts and feelings. The external world is defined generally by Perez as the objective reality in which we live. However, the specific manifestation of the external world that forms the focus of her chapter is the parent and the care that they give the infant; it is predominantly this aspect of reality that helps or hinders the infant's development, and that plays such a powerful role in shaping their inner world. Similarly to Perez, in their respective chapters Swanson and Erickson, as well as Oliveira and Mesquita, consider the parent to be the aspect of the external world most relevant to their thinking about the infant. However, instead of focusing on the infant's internal world, these authors focus on the infant's individual innate characteristics—their genetics, physiology, and brain mechanisms. Bremner and Southgate contribute to this dialogue by showing that both bodily and conceptual self-awareness are neither purely innate nor purely environmental but emerge through an intricate interplay between early neural systems and sensory experience. Abedi's chapter, on the other hand, considers the interplay between the external world of society and culture, and the internal world of the parents' faith identity; that is, the ways in which the parents' personal beliefs and traditions are perceived by the wider society.

The interplay between innate predispositions and environmental influences

One way to conceptualise the distinction between an infant's internal and external worlds is to view the internal world as what is innate, and the external world as what is shaped by environmental influences. In their chapter, Swanson and Erickson explain that genes serve as a blueprint for both visible traits (e.g., eye shape, hair texture, cardiovascular health) and less visible traits (e.g., emotional reactivity, metabolism, health vulnerabilities). However, the environment plays a crucial role in how these genetic blueprints are expressed. For instance, while tendencies toward emotional reactivity or regulation may be partially inherited, temperament is also shaped by environmental factors that either encourage or inhibit the expression of these traits. The authors highlight how caregivers and other socialisers—such as siblings, teachers, and coaches—can model healthy emotion regulation, provide supportive environments, and promote respect for children's autonomy. This dynamic interaction, referred to as the "goodness-of-fit" (Thomas & Chess, 1977), suggests that optimal developmental outcomes are fostered when temperament and environment align well. In their chapter, Oliveira and Mesquita explain that attachment is at once a conserved biological adaptation and an experience-dependent process. In other words, while multiple interconnected brain systems provide anatomical substrates for attachment, specific neurochemical systems, like oxytocin, dopamine, and the HPA axis, modulate the functional dynamics of relational experience. Such neurochemical systems are highly sensitive to environmental influences, for example responsive caregiving or early adversity. Therefore, caregiving becomes biologically embedded in the early years of life, shaping long-term emotional and physiological outcomes and, thus, highlighting the dynamic and complex interplay between the internal and the external. Similarly, Bremner and Southgate emphasise that the development of self-awareness cannot be explained solely by innate mechanisms, but rather sensory and conceptual forms of self-awareness develop gradually through infancy. Specifically, they explain that, while there is early postnatal sensitivity to cross-modal associations between the senses, hence suggesting an innate basis, the development of a unified multisensory body representation occurs gradually over the first few years of life through sensory experience. Moreover, they suggest that infants' capacity for conceptual self-representation also undergoes significant changes in the second year of life, explaining that despite the Default Mode Network (DMN) being active at birth (a neural basis for self-related thought), its functional connectivity changes significantly during the second year, aligning with the emergence of conceptual self-awareness. Therefore, developmental trajectories of the self appear to be actively and dynamically constructed across infancy.

Overall, these chapters demonstrate that the interplay between innate predispositions and the environment underscores the complexity of human development. The internal world, guided by biological predispositions, and the external world, shaped by interactions with caregivers and surroundings, constantly influence each other in a dynamic process, driving development in profound ways. This highlights the importance of a supportive, responsive environment in enabling the full expression and flourishing of inherent capacities.

The infant's creative role in forming their inner world in the context of the parental environment

In her chapter, Perez describes the points of convergence and divergence between the inner worlds described in psychoanalytic and attachment theories. It is important to tease out these differences further. Each person's inner world starts to develop from infancy (perhaps even, as some psychoanalysts have argued, from in utero, e.g. Piontelli, 1992), and psychoanalytic and attachment theories alike emphasise the significant impact that the environment has in the early formation of this inner world. However, broadly speaking, these theoretical perspectives differ with regards to their particular areas of focus.

In psychoanalytic theorising and exploration, what take centre stage are the individual, subjective inner world, and the mechanisms and creativity that the infant employs in shaping it. As Perez lays out, among the greatest contributions made by Klein were her rich descriptions of infants' deep and complex unconscious fantasies. These fantasies do not only encompass the parent and their behaviour towards the infant, but they also begin to capture the complex emotions arising from the infant's needs being met—or not. In addition, the infant's initial defence mechanism of splitting also colours their internal world and helps explain their early experiences. Sandler and Rosenblatt's concept of the representational world shares similarities with attachment theory's internal world, in that it is seen as forming out of a need to predict, adapt to, and feel safe with the parent. Both LaPlanche and Winnicott, in their different theories, focus on the gap between the infant and the parent, and how the infant creatively shapes that gap: for LaPlanche, the infant is striving to understand the parent, while, for Winnicott, they are seeking a way of 'going-on-being'.

Attachment research, on the other hand, has paid close attention to the different external environments and how these affect the infant's development and attachment behaviours, and the shaping of their internal working models. In the chapter by Perez, she draws attention to the significance of continual, day-to-day interactions, and how these bring about particular internal working models. These models, which guide attachment behaviours and are experienced emotionally, help orient the infant, enabling them to predict the environment, and to seek or avoid proximity to the attachment figure.

Navigating socio-cultural views and practices

Parents and infants relate to one another not in a vacuum but rather within complex and diverse socio-cultural contexts. Their relationship and respective experiences are shaped and influenced by many external factors, such as culture, religion, social norms, community values, economic conditions, etc.

In her chapter, Abedi focuses on parents' faith identity—their beliefs and practices—and of wider society's perceptions of that faith identity. The chapter explains how clinicians' conscious and unconscious perceptions of parents' faith identities constitute a significant part of their underlying assumptions about families, and also affect their clinical decision-making. First, Abedi explains that faith is an important aspect of the identity of many Muslims. Parenting is given the highest priority within Islam, and Muslim parents often feel the weight of this responsibility. They are seen within their faith to be the figures responsible for protecting their children from sin and wrongdoing, and for ensuring that they follow the Quran. Second, Muslim families are regularly confronted with prejudice and Islamophobia, in the UK and elsewhere, and this hostile environment often deters them from looking for help (outside of their faith) with parenting or mental health. Within some Muslim communities exists a fear around the very term 'mental health', which can have connotations of being taken away and locked up, contributing to a lack of trust in mental health clinicians. To add to these challenges, Abedi explains that there is a widespread conflation and confusion of Islamic faith and culture, where certain families' or communities' preferences are attributed to the faith as a whole (for example, preference for sons over daughters). Abedi gives the example of 'The Reflection Project', which undertakes faith-sensitive work with parents, allowing many such issues to be discussed alongside parents' concerns and difficulties around parenthood. This type of work recognises the differences in faith practices, acknow-ledges the experience of being minoritised and treated with prejudice by the wider society, and allows space for parents to discuss their own individual experience with their babies. Furthermore, in their chapter, Oliveira and Mesquita explain that, while attachment is a universal phenomenon with biological foundations, its expression and development are shaped by cultural contexts that influence caregiving practices. For example, cultures that involve frequent infant carrying and co-sleeping may promote distinct patterns of oxytocin release and autonomic system regulation com-pared to those that prioritise solitary sleep and structured feeding routines.

On the whole, parents navigate complex socio-cultural contexts shaped by their faith identities, cultural practices, and societal perceptions, which influence their parenting roles and practices, access to support, and development of attachment patterns, thus further highlighting the complex interplay between the internal and the external.

The importance of the body from infancy to parenthood

One thread of this book explores the importance of the body—from the infant's developing sense of self and growing relationship with others, to the birthing par-ent's experiences of separation and subsequent connection with their baby, and parents' affect on regulation, containment, and metabolisation of their baby's experience—the body of the parent and of the baby are the sites where these important processes occur.

A developing sense of self

Psychoanalysis, neuroscience, and developmental psychology have explained how the body is the first 'place' from which babies begin to build a sense of self. Freud's famous statement that "the ego is first and foremost a bodily ego" (1923, p.26) refers to a developing mind arising from a need to make sense of bodily sensations and to regulate tensions and energy from internal and external stimuli. Winnicott described the developmental achievement of what he termed, the 'in-dwelling' of the mind in the body (1962), explaining the process of integration to establish a sense of self and the body as a place to live. Bremner and Southgate (in chapter 28), bringing together rich empirical evidence, describe how the devel-opment of conceptual self-awareness during infancy is constrained by the gradual emergence of multisensory body representations. In other words, a baby cannot fully develop a deeper awareness of themselves as a person until they achieve a stable, integrated sense of their body—through touch, sight, movement, and spatial awareness. Apart from the importance of the body for infants' developing sense of self, Panagiotopoulou (in Chapter 22) explains how the prepartum and postpartum body acts as a dynamic site of identity transformation, where parents' sense of self is reshaped and enriched with new layers of meaning.

Symbiosis and separation

From conception to pregnancy and birth, the expectant parent goes through various bodily changes to prepare for the baby. Perez (in Chapter 7) explains how these changes are extensive as they affect every organ system in the body: the respiratory, musculoskeletal, reproductive, endocrine, cardiovascular, neurological, gastrointestinal, and immunological systems. From neuroscientific and neurobiological perspectives, Barba-Müller (Chapter 8), Dahan (Chapter 14), Veale, Munns, and Preston (Chapter 15), and Rutherford (Chapter 21) explain how the various neural, hormonal, structural, and functional brain changes occurring during pregnancy may specifically occur to prepare the body for birth and caregiving. Panagiotopoulou and Preston (Chapter 9) further explain that bodily changes during pregnancy may be underpinned by neural changes, which rebalance the weighting of bodily information away from informing about emotional state in favour of foetal well-being. These studies support Winnicott's concept of 'primary maternal preoccupation' where the expectant mother orients herself to the infant and develops a heightened sensitivity to her changing body, and then of the infant's when born.

Importantly, pregnancy entails the sharing of the birthing parent's body—a symbiosis. Perez (in Chapter 7) presents clinical examples to explain the varied experiences of bodily changes in expectant women—some rejoice at the changes that will accommodate their baby and others become psychically destabilised with claustrophobic panic and feelings of disintegration. Panagiotopoulou and Preston explain that, during pregnancy, there is a surge in bodily awareness—pregnant individuals become attuned to internal signals like the baby's kicking, which can deepen bonding. Jones and Thackeray's (Chapter 10) qualitative study of a transgender pregnant man also describes the importance of bodily changes and how these are experienced.

Birth marks the physical separation of the baby from the birthing parent's body and how this is experienced, understood, and symbolised also varies among parents. For some, it can be experienced as traumatic, where the body feels—as Goulder (Chapter 13) describes from a parent in her postnatal group—"torn in two". Perez (Chapter 12) explains that the ongoing separations and coming-together of parents and baby form an essential part in the development of parental life. However, because labour always entails a risk to the birthing parent and their baby, it can become unconsciously associated with death.

At the other end of the experiential spectrum, Dahan (in Chapter 14) describes 'birthing consciousness', which is a heightened awareness of bodily sensations during birth, accompanied by a diminished sense of time and space, and intense emotional experiences ranging from euphoria to profound peace. Dahan, as well as Veale, Munns, and Preston, advocate for maternity services that enhance birthing parents' connection to their bodies during birth.

Connection and metabolisation

The heightened bodily awareness and sensitivity continues in the postpartum period as parents connect and attune to their baby's experiences. Panagiotopoulou (Chapter 22) describes that this attunement comes through embodied experiences, like touch and breastfeeding. Therefore, the maternal body emerges as both a medium and a symbol of connection, embodying the bond between mother and baby through bodily caregiving. Although during birth, the physical separation of mother and baby resolves this shared bodily experience, a sense of oneness often continues after birth, thus challenging mothers' sense of self, as they navigate the blurred boundaries between self and baby.

Looking ahead to Part VI, the baby's capacity to regulate their affects and bodily experiences is developed through the parent-infant relationship, and the parent's capacity to metabolise, contain, and regulate these intense bodily experiences is crucial. Clinical examples in Chapters 19 and 25 demonstrate the impact of failures of these capacities manifesting in babies' bodies becoming frozen, limp, or unstable. Furthermore, in Chapter 26, Oliveira and Mesquita present evidence that, in the context of early development, affective touch, that is gentle touch of the skin, not only fosters closeness and emotional attunement but also promotes mutual regulation of physiological arousal—core processes underpinning secure attachment. This highlights that embodied caregiving practices play a crucial role in supporting infants' physiological regulation and emotional development, with long-term implications for their social and emotional well-being. In line, in their interdisciplinary target article, Fotopoulou and Tsakiris (2017) put forward the claim that the feeling qualities associated with being an embodied subject (that is, the understanding that our experiences, thoughts, and feelings are shaped by our physical body and our interactions with the world) are primarily formed through body-to-body interactions with others, starting in early infancy and continuing over time. The authors explain that embodied interactions between infants and caregivers, such as affective touch, directly influence infants' physiological arousal and integration of bodily experiences, effectively 'binding' internal feelings about the body's state with external perceptions of the body and the world. This process plays a unique developmental role in shaping the infant's sense of self—establishing the physical boundaries of the psychological self—and in supporting emotional regulation. A similar observation was made by Winnicott in 1956 (described in Perez Chapter 7), when, based on his clinical work with mothers and infants, he described how the primary caregiver's capacity to imaginatively elaborate the baby's somatic parts, feelings, and functions supports the infant's development of a sense of self, while also providing physical and emotional holding. There is a parallel between the infants' bodily experiences mediated and shaped by the environment, and the parents' bodily changes and experiences also socially mediated and shaped by cultural norms, medical systems, and interpersonal interactions, all of which influence how individuals perceive their bodies and, ultimately, themselves.

These diverse perspectives illustrate how, across early parenthood and infancy, the body emerges not only as the foundation of the sense of self but also as a site of profound transformation—shaped by neural change, experience, and the parent-infant relationship. These recurring themes across the chapters illustrate how the bodily self is a dynamic, evolving construct at the heart of development.

References

Fotopoulou, A., & Tsakiris, M. (2017). Mentalizing homeostasis: The social origins of interoceptive inference. *Neuropsychoanalysis, 19*(1), 3–28.

Freud, S. (1923). The ego and the id. In J. Strachey (Ed. & Trans.), The Standard Edition of the Complete Psychological Works of Sigmund Freud, 19:1–66. London: Vintage, The Hogarth Press.

Piontelli, A. (1992). *From fetus to child: An observational and psychoanalytic study. The New Library of Psychoanalysis*. London: Routledge.

Thomas, A., & Chess, S. (1977). *Temperament and development*. Brunner/Mazel.

Winnicott, D.W. (1956)[1975]. Chapter XXIV. Primary maternal preoccupation. *Through Paediatrics to Psycho-Analysis (International Psycho-Analytical Library)* (No. 100, pp. 300–305). London: Hogarth Press & Institute of Psycho-Analysis.

Winnicott, D.W. (1965). The theory of the parent-infant relationship. *Int Psycho-Anal Lib, 64*, 37–55.

Winnicott, D.W. (1962)[1965]. Providing for the child in health and in crisis. *Int Psycho-Anal Lib, 64*, 64–72.

Part VI

The early parent-infant relationship

Chapter 31

Holding, containment, and regulation of early experiences

Alejandra Perez

The importance of the parent-infant relationship in the infant's socio-emotional development is widely accepted. There are various theories about the mechanisms by which the parent helps the infant foster a capacity to regulate their affects, organise and understand their early experiences, and develop a sense of self. These theories differ in how they understand the infant's early capacities and gradients of awareness of being separate from the parent. It is beyond the scope of this chapter to give a comprehensive overview of these different theories and the growing infant research in this area. The chapter will instead focus on a few of these theories, and illustrate them with clinical material.

The intensity of early, pre-verbal experiences

Human babies' long period of dependency on the parent, compared to other animals, is thought to be adaptive as it allows complex social learning (such as language acquisition, and development of morality, theory of mind, and empathy) (Faust et al., 2020). While there is still much to learn about infants' early experiences, clinical and research work have shown that they sense and are aware of a range of different stimuli, and that these create particular affective experiences in them. Infants have been shown to have rudimentary instinctive means of regulating some of their affective experience, such as through gaze avoidance, turning away, or self-soothing behaviours. However, it is widely agreed that babies cannot rely solely on these rudimentary strategies without risking a negative impact on their development. Bion (1962) described how raw sensory and emotional information from the external world (rapid and aggressive changes in their caregivers' emotional state) and from inside their bodies (such as intense hunger or pain) can be experienced as overwhelming, and how such information needs processing by another to make it more bearable for the baby.

Affect regulation or emotion regulation refers to the capacity to modulate (most often by decreasing) our emotional experiences (emotions, feelings, affects, and moods) and to control our expressions of these. This capacity is considered to be essential in building relationships and mental wellbeing (Fonagy et al., 2004). However, as indicated above, infants' affective regulation is initially immature and

DOI: 10.4324/9781003530473-38

undeveloped, and so must be supported and developed by the other, usually the parent(s) (Schore, 2003; Taipale, 2016). Affect regulation is a complex skill that grows and develops throughout life. An important shift in the study of early affect regulation was away from an initial focus on the infant's self-regulatory capacity, and toward considering it as a mechanism that forms between the parent and infant, with the parent's own capacity acting as a driving force in the infant's development (Taipale, 2016). Parental affect regulation involves the parent keeping their own affective state regulated while also facilitating their baby's regulation (Rutherford et al., 2015).

The parent's permeability to their infant's experience

Rutherford and colleagues (2015) argue for a particular definition—and investigation—of parental affect regulation, stressing that it is unique insofar as it involves simultaneously regulating one's own and one's infant's emotions. They propose that such investigations should consider the neurobiological, hormonal, and behavioural shifts that occur during the transition to parenthood, as they consider these to be key in enabling parental regulation in response to infant cues.

However, a question remains: Is it only affect that needs attending to, and is it only a matter of regulation? Psychoanalytic theories have explored how bodily needs, raw sensory phenomena, and emotional experiences are processed, as well as how the parent-infant relationship allows communication, a deep, pre-verbal understanding, and growth and transformation of these experiences. For example, in his formulation of 'primary maternal preoccupation', or a mother's heightened sensitivity towards the baby, Winnicott (1956) describes an unconscious identification with the infant's bodily needs and experience of complete dependence.

Clinical vignette: Whose body?

A first-time mother recounted to me her stress and intense focus when cutting her newborn son's fingernails for the first time. She had not imagined that she would find it such a struggle. Seeing her son squirm as she tried to cut his delicate nails on his tiny fingers felt dangerous. She was confronted with his fragility. However, she proudly told me, she managed to do it. He seemed to relax and fall asleep in the process. Moments later in the session, as the mother was talking about something else, she looked down at her hands and saw her long fingernails and said, "That's strange, I could have sworn that I cut my fingernails this morning." She was confused for a few seconds until she realised that it was her son's fingernails that she had trimmed. She was struck by this momentary confusion, and by how powerfully she felt that her son's body, in those moments, was her own. Winnicott had postulated that this confusion, or intense identification, allowed the parent to understand the baby's pre-verbal early experiences and bodily needs, but also that it required a certain somatic permeability. This mother experienced only a brief state of confusion, yet, for other mothers, such identification with experiences of intense dependence and bodily needs can become overwhelming and dysregulating, thus rendering them unable to support their child.

Modulating and transforming the infant's early experience

The proposed mechanisms through which the parent helps the infant with their early experiences are varied. For example, attachment research posits that attachment security is developed through repeated experiences with a caregiver who responds sensitively to the infant's affects (Cassidy, 1994; Fonagy et al., 2004). From a neurobiological perspective, an important study by Feldman and colleagues (2010) found that a mother's affective touch regulates the infant's behavioural and physiological reactivity to stress. Gergely and Watson (1996) assert that babies learn about their own emotions through a social biofeedback model with the caregiver. They believe that the baby has an innate capacity to make connections (a 'contingency-detection mechanism'), whereby they examine the environment for connections between events in the external world and internal states. However, the baby does not understand their emotions at first. Parents instinctively mirror the baby's emotions through an exaggerated expression of those same emotions (called 'marked mirroring'). This allows the baby to feel understood, yet also reassured that the parent is not overcome by the emotion, which in turn enables the baby to understand and locate the feeling in him- or herself. Fonagy and Bateman (2007) explain that an early disorganisation of the parent-infant attachment relationship leads to impairment of the child's social-cognitive capacities, or 'mentalisation', which is the integration of cognition and affect (Luyten, Mayes, Nijssens, and Fonagy, 2017). Failure to develop the capacity to mentalise leads a person to remain fixed in their own subjective states, with pre-mentalisation modes of representing them, such as concrete (psychic equivalence) and dissociated (pretend mode) thinking, and with teleological (outcome and action oriented) modes of functioning (Bateman and Fonagy, 2013). Parental reflective functioning refers to the parent's capacity to conceive of their child as being motivated by internal mental states, including emotions, wishes, and desires, as well as the ability to think about their own mental experiences and the bi-directional channel of influence between them and their child (Luyten, Mayes, Nijssens, and Fonagy, 2017).

Gergely and Watson (1996) describe two different forms of pathological parental affect-mirroring. In one of these, the parent's mirroring is incongruent with the emotion felt by the child. In the other, the emotion displayed by the parent is congruent yet lacks 'marking'; that is, it loses its 'as if' quality, thereby giving the infant the experience of their parent feeling the emotion as intensely as they do. Bion (1962) had explained why parents might not be able to contain their child's experience (nor respond congruently or markedly): that experience might be felt by the parent to be unbearable. Bion extended Klein's (1930) view of the infant relating to part-objects in an active and continuous way from the start by getting rid of unbearable, unintelligible, unprocessed experiences (what Bion termed 'beta-elements') through projection, and taking in experiences from the part-objects by introjection. Bion introduced the idea that projection is also a form of communication, not only a method of expelling negative experiences. The baby hopes that the other can understand through experiencing the same feeling, and can then process it for the baby. In other words, the parent identifies with what the baby projects, then detoxifies, digests, and transforms these raw experiences into what Bion termed 'alpha-elements', thus providing containment. Moreover, the baby not only internalises the now detoxified, digested information, but also begins to internalise this containing ('alpha') function.

Clinical vignette: An escalating, violent nightmare

Some parents are not able to contain their child's experiences because they themselves become too identified with, and disturbed by, those experiences. For example, a six-year-old boy wakes up in the middle of the night from a nightmare and screams for his mother. When she arrives, he is quite shaken, and still not fully awake. He tells her between sobs and gasps that he saw a growling dog chasing him. His mother is reminded of frightening repetitive nightmares she had as a young girl, and tells him about them: she was chased by a pack of hungry wolves that would catch her, their teeth tearing into her skin. In that moment, neither of them is able to bear this frightening experience. The mother cannot contain the child's fear and instead becomes identified with it, augmenting it by linking it to her past experiences. The child feels disturbed and overwhelmed, now not only by his own nightmare, but by the experience of his fear growing, infecting his mother, and taking an even more frightening shape. This leaves the child feeling that his fears cannot be thought about, and that they might disturb his mother, who, in turn, has to rid herself of her fears by putting them into him. While this example is of a six-year-old child, not an infant, it helps to describe something that can also be seen in parent-infant exchanges at the pre-verbal level; for example, a baby's cries intensifying their parent's fear, anger, or despair.

A containing parental function

Frightening and disturbing as these nightmares were for this child and mother, in psychoanalysis dreams are thought to be a way of representing our experiences, and so are also an attempt to process these experiences in the mind. Psychoanalysts Sara and Cesar Botellas (2005) focused on instances where trauma was so intense or occurred so early that the mind was unable to represent it. Unrepresented trauma leaves a trace of emotional memory, but eludes conscious recollection. The Botellas' work involves facilitating figuration, or representation, in the patient's mind, so as to allow the processing of such kinds of traumatic experience.

These examples highlight the various functions of, and demands on, the parent. Psychoanalytic literature describes the important parental function of stillness, or passive permeability, on the part of the parent: this allows them to form an intense identification with their child's internal state, and thereby understand the infant's experience. Winnicott (1960) stressed the importance of the infant's developing sense of self—their 'going-on-being'—which is enabled by the mother's 'holding'. Holding includes both the physical handling and psychological protection of the baby, so that the baby can remain in an unperturbed, undifferentiated state (giving special importance to meeting the baby's bodily needs). 'Good enough' parenting includes this holding, but also a gradually increasing failure to meet the baby's needs, allowing the baby a manageable way of understanding and adapting to their own feelings and external reality.

However, psychoanalysts have also stressed the importance of the maternal function to involve an active, transformational element (Bollas, 1979; Kristeva, 2014). Bion (1962) believed that it is the mother's function of containment that is, importantly, internalised. Similarly, Bollas (1979) described the infant's first experience of the parent (or internal object) as a process of transformation; the parent is not initially 'known' or represented, but is rather experienced as the process of transforming their self-experience.

Clinical vignette:[1] A misunderstood, dysregulating infant's approach

From early on, Celia found it difficult to understand her son's feelings, intentions, or behaviour, especially in moments of excitement or distress. His cries were at times heard as coughing; his attempts to hug her were repeatedly interpreted as him wanting to reach the wall behind her; when a toy fell out of his grasp, she picked up a different one to give back to him. More and more, Oliver had become withdrawn, growing more attracted to toys and objects than to people. He often slept or looked out of the window. His movements were uncoordinated and awkward, and he continually crashed into toys and furniture. It was as though, because of his mother's denial and misunderstanding of his experience, he was unable to develop a sense of himself, his body, and the world around him. During one session, when Oliver was nine months old, he stood up holding a toy that he had been playing with. He seemed eager to show it to his mother and, though unsteady on his feet, he appeared determined to get to her. He began to babble excitedly. As he walked closer, Celia suddenly looked away and began telling me about her difficulties on the tube that morning. Oliver stumbled on the small rug and fell, hitting his shoulder and head. Celia let out a loud laugh, while the father gasped but stood motionless. Celia stood up quickly and picked him up. Oliver looked stunned and confused. Celia did not say anything, but continued with her story about the tube while carrying Oliver.

It seemed to me that Celia had become emotionally overwhelmed when seeing her son approach her with intent. Celia's difficult childhood meant that she often misunderstood her son's excitement, energy, and difference from her as a threat. I think that she unconsciously diverted her attention as a way of defending herself from what she felt was dangerous. I think that Oliver, on the other hand, felt abruptly 'dropped' from his mother's mind when she turned her attention away from him and into the emotional atmosphere of the difficult tube ride. When Oliver fell, it seemed as though what had been holding him was suddenly retracted. I understood mother's laugh to be the result of conflicting feelings of anger and fear, which she felt towards her son. Whenever he appeared independent and energetic, Celia feared that he would grow up to be a violent man like the people who had abused her as a child, and this fear made her hate him. His fall, however, also reawakened feelings in Celia of having been hurt and un-held in her childhood. During these moments, she was quite dysregulated and in turn became a dysregulating figure for Oliver: she was unable to think about Oliver's own individual experience.

I tried to give voice to some of these feelings, starting with the shared experience of shock and confusion. I said to Oliver that his fall had made his mum very scared and confused about what had happened. She was laughing, I thought, because she was nervous and did not know what to do when she felt that Oliver had been hurt. I then said that, before he fell, Oliver had seemed to me very excited to show mum something. *"What was it?"* Celia asked, a little loudly—I think because she was still nervous. I said that maybe it had been frightening not to know what Oliver was doing. I looked down at the fallen toy and picked it up. I waited for Oliver to make eye contact with me, and then asked him if he had wanted to share this with his mother. Celia reached for the toy more calmly and held it, at first turning it over in her hand, then giving it back to Oliver. Oliver seemed engaged with our conversation and took the toy.

In this short excerpt from this session, I want to show how certain experiences might reawaken difficult feelings for the parent, some of which cannot be processed on their own in the moment. I also want to show how the child might be left feeling in such a situation, namely, as though their feelings are unbearable to the other, which then creates a confusing gap in their mind that hinders development.

Note

1 The parent-infant psychotherapy work with this family has also been described in Chapter 20 in this book.

References

Bateman, A. W. & Fonagy, P. (2013). Mentalization-based treatment. *Psychoanalytic Inquiry*, 33(6):595–613.

Bion, W. R. (1962). A theory of thinking. *The International Journal of Psychoanalysis*, 43:306–310.

Bollas, C. (1979). The transformational object. *The International Journal of Psychoanalysis*, 60:97–107.

Botellas, S. & Botellas, C. (2005). *The work of psychic figurability: Mental states without representation*. London: Routledge.

Cassidy J. (1994). Emotion regulation: Influences of attachment relationships. *Monographs of the Society for Research in Child Development*, 59(2–3):228–283.

Faust, K.M., Carouso-Peck, S., Elson, M.R. & Goldstein, M.H. (2020). The origins of social knowledge in altricial species. *Annual Review of Developmental Psychology*, 2:225–246.

Feldman, R., Singer, M., & Zagoory, O. (2010). Touch attenuates infants' physiological reactivity to stress. *Developmental Science*, 13(2):271–278.

Fonagy, P., & Bateman, A. W. (2007). Mentalizing and borderline disorder. *Journal of Mental Health*, 16(1):83–101.

Fonagy, P., Gergely, G., Jurist, E. L., & Target, M. (2004). *Affect regulation, mentalization and the development of the self.* London: Karnac Books.

Gergely, G., & Watson, J. S. (1996). The social biofeedback theory of parental affect-mirroring: The development of emotional self-awareness and self-control in infancy. *International Journal of Psychoanalysis*, 77(6):1181–1212.

Klein, M. (1930). The importance of symbol formation in the development of the ego. In *The Writings of Melanie Klein* (Vol. 1). London: Hogarth Press.

Kristeva, J. (2014). Reliance, or maternal eroticism. *Journal of the American Psychoanalytic Association*, 62(1):69–85.

Luyten, P., Mayes, L. C., Nijssens, L., & Fonagy, P. (2017). The parental reflective function-ing questionnaire: Development and preliminary validation. *PLoS ONE*, 12(5):1–28.

Rutherford, H.J.V., Wallace, N.S., Laurent, H.K. & Mayes, L.C. (2015). Emotion regulation in parenthood. *Developmental Review*, 36:1–14.

Schore, A.N. (2003). *Affect regulation and the repair of the self.* New York: W. W. Norton.

Taipale, J. (2016). Self-regulation and beyond: Affect regulation and the infant-caregiver dyad. *Frontiers in Psychology*, 7(889):1–13.

Winnicott, D. W. (1956)[1975]. Chapter XXIV. Primary maternal preoccupation. *Through Paediatrics to Psycho-Analysis (International Psycho-Analytical Library)* (No. 100, pp. 300–305). London: Hogarth Press & Institute of Psycho-Analysis.

Winnicott, D. W. (1960). The theory of the parent-infant relationship. *International Journal of Psychoanalysis*, 41:585–595.

Chapter 32

Internal experiences of separations

Weaning, feeding, and sleeping

Alexandra de Rementeria

The way that carers and babies negotiate ordinary early separations shapes our relationship to others, the emergence of thought, and our relationship to reality itself. In the beginning, 'internal experience' is a collection of sensory perceptions and affect. It will be argued that it is the stress of separation that demands a shift to creating '*internal representations*', which afford thought and all that comes with it. The psychoanalytic theoretical frame I will draw on is in the Kleinian tradition and includes Bion's (1962) theory of thinking, and its links to Freud's (1900) hallucinatory wish-fulfilment and Isaac's (1952) work on the importance of primitive unconscious fears and desires in the emergence of symbolic thought. In describing internal experiences of everyday separations such as feeding, weaning, and sleeping, this chapter will explore how our unique human intelligence is shaped, with all its impressive power and its particular frailty.

Birth, the first separation

The cord is cut, creating a gap that must be bridged. A new connection between mouth and nipple, or teat, must be formed if the infant is to survive. For the first time, from this moment of birth, what is needed can be absent, the lifeline can be lost, and every subsequent separation demands a working through of this original and seismic loss.

In a rare foray into infant observation, Freud (1900) noticed that, before crying out for a feed, hungry infants sometimes seem to content themselves with behaving as though they were already having a feed as observed by their sucking at thin air. He postulated that they were hallucinating what they wished for. Bion (1962) elaborated that, when present, the breast, or any desired thing, does not need to be conceived of. It will be registering at some level as a collection of percepts but this sort of perception process is not likely to be at the cutting edge of the latest in the infant's cognitive capacities, because it is not motivated by need. When what we need is absent, our mind gropes for it and in so doing creates the idea of the missing thing or experience. These representations, these building blocks of thought, then, are born of desire. They are pulled into existence by our passions rather than because the cognitive apparatus for thought spontaneously comes online and

DOI: 10.4324/9781003530473-39

enables us to represent what we directly perceive. This is an important point that we will return to.

Sleeping, and not sleeping

Sleep involves a separation for the baby. Separation from consciousness and, with that, his conscious awareness of his proximity to his attachment figure. He must trust that, as he falls asleep and his awareness of his carer slips from his mental grasp, that neither she nor life itself will be lost. He must trust that she has not actually vanished, that they both continue to go on being, even if he can't feel her or himself anymore. To do this, the infant will need to create and call on an internal representation of the carer.

Many parents describe as 'blissful' the state of a baby slipping into sleep while feeding, and this pleasure for baby and parent is important. However, like most pleasurable things in life, there is a tipping point when you know you are doing it to avoid feelings that are difficult, rather than straightforwardly for pleasure (Daws and Sutton, 2022). The difficult feelings in this situation are the anxiety around separation, which will require the baby to do the cognitively and emotionally challenging work of creating an internal representation of what is desired and making use of that representation to sustain him until the desire can be sated. He needs an idea to believe in, an idea of the warm, gentle pressure of holding arms, the pleasurable fit of a latch on the nipple or teat, the smell of the carer and the sense of safety all this brings. However, he would prefer to have the real thing and so the carer has to face the baby's protest, which might escalate to panic or rage. But, if Bion is right, the baby needs the gap in order to discover that he can bridge it. The gaps must be timely and tolerable, though, so as not to overwhelm these emerging capacities.

For a carer, knowing how to judge what is tolerable and when is a delicate business. Surprisingly often, when a baby is not sleeping, we find that there has been a bereavement or another serious loss or separation in the parents' lives. Then, an ordinary small separation, like putting the baby down to sleep, can feel as though it is unbearable. When this happens the internal experience of separations for parents inevitably gets into how they manage those separations, which in turn starts to shape the baby's internal experiences of these separations. If the carer feels it is unsafe to leave the baby in their cot, then the baby will sense this and feel frightened and confused by attempts to do so. However, it is always important to be aware that there is huge diversity across cultures in practices around babies and sleep. An anecdote shared by Asha Phillips illustrates this rather well. An English woman who had been working at a children's charity in India was approached by an Indian colleague who said: "*We've been working together for some time now, and I see how lovely you are with the children, tell me, it can't be true what they say about English women can it? That you keep your babies in cages at night?*" Perhaps the point is that, when we diverge from the cultural norms where we are, it is worth being curious about why. It is not that any one practice is better than others or that divergence from common practice where you are always indicates pathology, but that it behoves us to be curious about such divergence.

Older babies have more say in negotiations around separation but, paradoxically, this can make it even more anxiety provoking. As they grow more independent, crawl and walk away from their parents, they may also worry whether their parents will be there for them to come back to. This new independence brings with it a quite normal period of insecurity and many babies wake in the night at this time. Also, the excitement of new achievements may keep a baby of this age awake: after a triumphant day of learning to stand up, it can be quite difficult to calm down enough to go to sleep. Teething can wake babies, perhaps not just the simplistic explanation of feeling pain—the teeth may also represent newly found aggressive feelings, the pleasures of biting, which also bring worries about hurting others.

Feeding

Feeding might seem to be about a connection, a coming together, and of course it is. However, as discussed, it is also only made necessary after birth because of the loss of the umbilical connection of intrauterine life. If we think of the experience of the baby as she comes to know about her own life drives—her instinct to root and suck and the feeling of being sated after being hungry—we can imagine the pleasure. However, we also know that, when something in that process goes awry, in the ordinary way that it will sometimes—be it too long a wait, too little or too much milk when it comes, or difficulty with making a latch—then what is wanted, in its absence or failure to satisfy, might be experienced as no good. In this way, hunger is understood to be experienced, as something done unto the infant, the discomfort in his stomach to be experienced as a motivated attack. The internal representation, then, might be benign and sustaining or persecuting (Isaacs, 1952).

Herein lies the frailty of our thinking minds. Thought starts with representation, not a direct perception of a thing itself but an approximated version of it, necessarily coloured by our emotional experience at the moment of creating the representation. However, when we are supported to develop our tolerance for frustration and a capacity to bear loss, we are less prone to creating persecuting or idealised internal representations. So, our susceptibility to persecuted states of mind and our valency for avoidance and denial of reality are all written into the way our thinking minds are constructed. Support to bear the frustrations and mourn the losses of separation are what ameliorate this susceptibility.

Weaning

Weaning is much more obviously about loss and separation, but it is important to keep in mind that, if carer and baby have had a good experience of breast or bottle feeding, then they will both be better resourced to do the work of mourning the loss. Also, a baby is not weaned from the breast to starvation but to the delights of a whole new world of flavours and textures, to the prospect of choosing food and picking it up in her hand and putting it in her mouth. This can be a messy business and mothers might have to adjust to allowing the baby to have some control. It may have felt that the baby was quite passive before but, especially with breastfeeding, the baby has to be quite active in pulling the nipple right into the mouth and sucking and swallowing at the pace they choose. It can feel to the baby that they have lost some of this agency when a carer starts to insert a spoon of gloop at the rate they deem appropriate.

I am going to share some material from my infant observation, conducted nearly twenty years ago as part of my clinical training. It is a naturalistic observation conducted during weekly visits to the home throughout the first two years of a baby's life. In the following excerpt, Ruben, aged 8 months, could be said to be fulfilling a wish but there seems to be a more complex unconscious phantasy at play that both avoids the pain of loss and exacts the satisfaction of punishing whomever is causing that loss. He was the first child of a stable and happy enough couple who delighted in him, offered appropriate boundaries, and were well attuned to his needs. At around this time his mother was preparing to return to work and was, in various ways, beginning to create some emotional distance between them. My seminar leader, Dilys Daws, suggested that this was a way of preparing them for, or even an attempt to inoculate them from, the anticipated pain of loss with coming separation.

> Mother leaves the room to prepare his bottle. He is holding a mouse-doll, which is made of stuffed fabric. It has long floppy ears and a sausage-like snout with spindly arms and legs that hang limply. He puts the nose in his mouth. I imagine that it gives a satisfying amount of resistance. He bites harder into it, wrinkling his nose and shutting his eyes with the effort. Taking an ear in each hand, in order to get a better purchase on it, he pulls the mouse away from him while holding the nose fast in his mouth so that he is yanking it so hard in two directions that he starts to wobble. The mouse arms and legs swing violently until eventually he topples over and cries.

His mother returns and scoops him up to comfort him and moments later the feed begins. Mother's role in creating distance during feeding becomes evident, as does his anger about it.

> Mother sits cross-legged on the floor opposite me and lifts him into her lap but facing out towards me. She puts the bottle to his mouth and he takes in the teat and sucks and swallows at a fast rate taking half the bottle without a pause. Then he begins to slow the pace and, as he does so, he turns a little so that he is facing side-on and can glance up at her face. He also begins to reach up her body with his left arm so that the back of it gently rubs her breast as he feeds. His face relaxes, as his eye lids flutter and close momentarily. All this is lost when she suddenly props him up again. The arm that had been against her body he now brings round to cup the bottle. Soon he begins to tap the bottle, at first

in the distracted and sensual way he had moved it up and down her body but increasingly the tapping gets harder and faster until it is more like hitting. He is no longer drinking the milk but holding the bottle in place by biting down on the teat while he hits it from side to side.

Once his hunger is sated, Ruben attempts to bring the couple together again through his positioning and caresses. However, when she returns him to his outward-facing disconnected place, the bottle becomes the recipient of a punitive attack on the withholding mother/breast. Likierman (2001) describes Klein's observation about feeding and weaning: "When the object becomes available again the infant is simultaneously relieved yet vengeful ... these two contradictory impulses are united in the single phantasy of a vengeful devouring" (p.104). Ruben's play with the mouse-doll seems to betray just such an unconscious phantasy.

As an older baby, Ruben might be said to have developed some symbolic functioning. However, if it is posited that his experience went something like: 'I have a feeling state—the combined wish to punish and to possess. To give this expression, I will act out the composite "devouring" with this toy pretending that it is the breast.' This would involve the capacity to make one thing stand in for another while it is known that it is not actually that thing. This would involve suspending disbelief in order to behave 'as if' it were the same thing. That is not what I felt I saw. To me it felt that the unprocessed or undischarged devouring urge was awakened by the feeling of the mouse-doll snout in his mouth and he imbued it with, or projected onto it, the intention of 'withholding' because withholding was the relational antecedent to his sensori-affective state. I did not believe that he was making a distinction between breast and doll. Indeed, it was not really a categorical item that he had an internal representation of but an embodied representation of a relational procedure—that is to say, the urge to suck and the suckable thing are not distinguished either. He was relating to the live intention to withhold, which in that moment he felt to be located in the doll. This is not 'as if' symbolic thinking but an unconscious phantasy distortion that starts with the sensori-affective state and this, often, profoundly distorts our perception of reality. According to Bion (1962), this is why our species is vulnerable to psychosis, at the extreme end, and explains our more ordinary valency to denying reality. However, the centrality of unconscious phantasy in the construction of our thinking minds is also a strength. It is through this partly imagined relational experience that Ruben works through the coming separation with his mother. He is exploring his rage and wish for control, in his 'vengeful devouring', but also his loss and the work of mourning, as is felt so profoundly when his manic control gives way to sorrow when he topples and cries.

It is interesting to note that neuroscience seems to be finding compelling evidence that might support these theories. What is being proposed by Bion (1962) and Isaacs (1952) assumes that the experience of an-other-with-whom-one-is-in-relationship precedes the conception or perception of real, whole people. This ill-defined other could be a 'part-object' like the breast (or mouse-doll) but is thought to be experienced as having relational motivations like vengeance or benevolence.

When it is claimed that relational motivations can be attributed by the very young infant, what is being claimed is that these sensori-affective-motor representations can be attributed. This has been rejected, by many, on the grounds that young infants lack the cognitive complexity to manage propositional thought. However, developments in neuroscience do support the notion that through 'simulation' (Gallese, 2011), sensori-affective-motor representations can be attributed directly without need for a fully formed conception of self, other, or Theory of Mind. 'Simulation' is a phenomenon that is similar to, but also different from, Rizzolatti's mirror neurons (2004). Importantly this capacity precedes the capacity for propositional thought.

Concluding comments

I have argued that separations are what spur the mind to create the first thought in the form of an idea that represents what is missing. This means that our first thoughts are wishful, rather than reality facing. The sequalae of this are both our capacity for symbolic thought, having something stand for another thing that is not being directly perceived, and our loose relationship to reality. Well-negotiated separations help us to tolerate frustrations and losses in relation to others. We need to be supported to be in touch with loss and build the capacity to mourn so that we don't become too dependent on denial and avoidance as the organising principles of our minds. To bring this back to the practical, this might manifest as a carer tolerating her infant's protest around a separation, to show him that he can tolerate his distress and she can register his loss and make space for his feelings about it. If we always act to replace what is lost, we collude with the phantasy that we can avoid loss and frustration, which increases our vulnerability to mental illness.

References

Bion, W.R. (1962). A theory of thinking. In *Second Thoughts* (pp. 110–119). New York: Aronson, 1967.

Daws, D., & Sutton, S. (2020). *Parent-Infant Psychotherapy for Sleep Problems: Through the Night* (1st ed.). London: Routledge. https://doi.org/10.4324/9780429198212

Freud, S. (1900) *The Interpretation of Dreams* (3rd ed.). Trans. by A. A. Brill. New York: The Macmillan Company, 1913; Bartleby.com, 2010.www.bartleby.com/285/. (accessed 11/09/17)

Gallese, V. and Sinigaglia, C., 2011. What is so special about embodied simulation?. *Trends in Cognitive Sciences*, *15*(11), 512–519.

Isaacs, S. (1952). The nature and function of phantasy. In J. Riviere (Ed.), *Developments in Psychoanalysis* (pp. 67–121). London: Hogarth Press.

Likierman, M. (2001) *Melanie Klein: Her work in context.* New York, NY, US: Continuum.

Rizzolatti, G., & Craighero, L. (2004). The mirror-neuron system. *Annual Review of Neuroscience*, *27*, 169–192. https://doi.org/10.1146/annurev.neuro.27.070203.144230

Chapter 33

The neurobiological basis of infant-parent attachment

Amanda Lucas and Pascal Vrtička

In this chapter we illustrate how infant-parent attachment is formed in early life through the lens of our functional neuro-anatomical model of human attachment (*NAMA*; Long et al., 2020). Specifically, we demonstrate how two aspects of parent-infant communication—sensitivity and synchrony—impact four developing neural *NAMA* networks to depict the inner workings of a securely attached brain.

Four neural networks

In the interests of compatible language use across disciplines, we describe *NAMA* as we have translated it for new parents. Figure 33.1 depicts the four neural networks that are in constant dialogue with one another during *Connection, Stress-Fear-Pain, Emotion Regulation* and perceiving *Self and Others*.

Parental sensitivity to infant cues is one of the most widely tested and robust predictors of secure attachment (Madigan et al., 2024). Differential patterns of parent-infant synchrony are also associated with infant attachment classification (Barbosa et al., 2021). The focus of sensitivity is on parental responsiveness at the global level, whereas, for synchrony, the emphasis is on the interactive relationship at the micro-level of communicative exchange. Both impact the development of the four *NAMA* networks and the way in which they 'speak' to each other.

Stress-Fear-Pain Network

The *Stress-Fear-Pain Network*, incorporating the hypothalamic-pituitary-adrenal (HPA) axis, mobilises energy and bodily resources for infants to respond to stress. HPA axis sensitivity is calibrated to a 'just right' (not too reactive or under-reactive) level in accordance with how safe infants perceive their environment to be and how supported they are. Timely, sensitive parental responses to infant cues—involving soothing distress, being physically and psychologically available, exhibiting a positive and affirming regard, and following infant lead and interest—longitudinally predict the size of limbic structures involved in detecting and learning about threats (Bernier et al., 2019; Rifkin-Graboi et al., 2015). Variations in parenting sensitivity during infancy are associated with *Stress-Fear-Pain Network* activation at

DOI: 10.4324/9781003530473-40

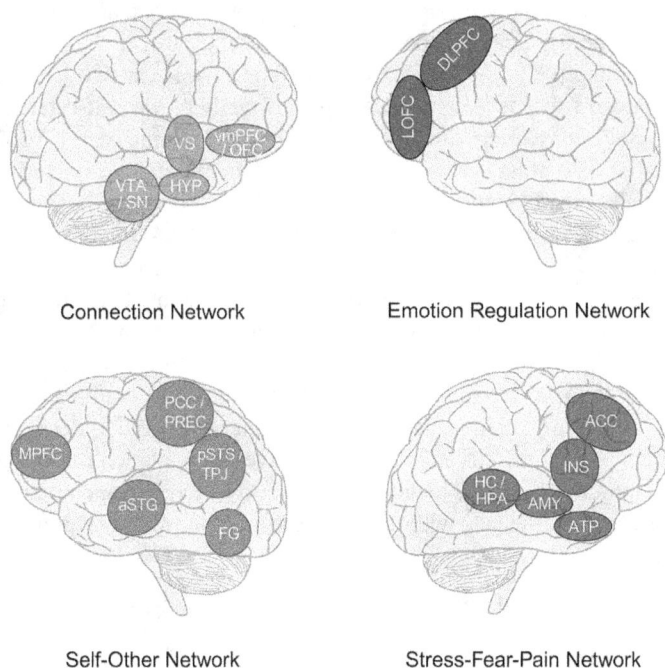

Connection Network   Emotion Regulation Network

Self-Other Network   Stress-Fear-Pain Network

Figure 33.1

Note: Adapted from Long et al. (2020). Connection Network: HYP = hypothalamus; vmPFC/OFC = ventromedial prefrontal/orbitofrontal cortex; VS = ventral striatum; VTA/SN = ventral tegmental area/substantia nigra. Emotion Regulation Network: DLPFC = dorsolateral prefrontal cortex; LOFC = lateral orbitofrontal cortex. Self–Other Network: aSTG = anterior superior temporal gyrus; FG = fusiform gyrus; MPFC = medial prefrontal cortex; PCC/PREC = posterior cingulate cortex/precuneus; pSTS/TPJ = posterior superior temporal sulcus/temporo-parietal junction. Stress–Fear–Pain Network: ACC = anterior cingulate cortex; AMY = amygdala; ATP = anterior temporal pole; HC/HPA = hippocampus/hypothalamic–pituitary–adrenal axis; INS = insula.

cross-sectional time points (e.g., cortisol recovery after taking an infant out of the bath; Albers et al., 2008) and longitudinally (e.g., predicting electrodermal reactivity in adulthood when arguing with a romantic partner; Raby et al., 2015).

The quality of synchronous interactions between mothers and their infants—characterised by sensitive contingency of facial, vocal, and gestural affect—is also associated with attenuated activity of the infant HPA axis (Thompson & White, 2022; Provenzi et al., 2017). One route to this association may be through reduced methylation of genes involved in the stress response (Conradt et al., 2016).

Beyond the HPA axis, the *Stress-Fear-Pain Network* is more broadly responsible for prioritising and orientating to salient stimuli—within the body or in the environment—to guide behaviour. Increased connectivity between anterior areas (e.g., the anterior cingulate cortex and the insula) in adults is associated with: a) higher respiratory sinus arrhythmia (RSA), a measure of heart rate and respiration indicating increased parasympathetic control over arousal (Sturm et al., 2018); and b) the capacity to adaptively 'switch' between different *NAMA* network 'modes' (i.e., effortful, outward-focused *Regulation Network* activity vs. self-referential, inward-focused *Self-Other* Network activity; Schimmelpfennig et al., 2023). Regarding the latter, parenting styles that support autonomy and are reflective of infant emotional and mental states predict anti-correlations between connectivity in anterior areas of the *Stress-Fear-Pain Network* and the *Self-Other Network* at age 10 (Dégeilh et al., 2018). This inverse coupling may be interpreted as a sign of brain maturity and is associated in adults with efficient 'switching' to deploy cognition, resources, and attention to internal and external events. Regarding the former, maternal sensitivity in infancy is associated with higher resting RSA, as well as steeper lowering of RSA in response to stressful or challenging situations (such as arm restraint or jointly solving a puzzle—Köhler-Dauner et al., 2022; Perry et al., 2016). These findings suggest that infants who receive more attuned responses to their cues and communications are better able to employ energetic and attentional resources to overcome challenges, without over-recruiting the stress response.

Emotion Regulation Network

Caregiver sensitivity tunes connections between limbic structures and the *Emotion Regulation Network*. For instance, normative variations in responsiveness to babies' cues predicts functional connectivity at age 4 between the hippocampus and prefrontal cortices, whereby activity in one yields decreased activity in the other (Wang et al., 2019).

Parental sensitivity may have differential benefits in promoting regulation of withdrawal behaviours on one hand, and approach behaviours on the other. Infants of mothers observed to be low in maternal sensitivity or high in intrusiveness (i.e. overly directive in their infants' play, feeding, and care) are more likely to show a resting profile of right frontal asymmetry (Diego et al., 2006). This refers to brain activity in the alpha range being relatively increased on the right (vs. the left) side of the prefrontal cortex, and is associated with withdrawal and inhibition. These infants display fewer positive emotions when interacting with their caregiver and more fear and escape behaviour in stressful situations (e.g., confronted with scary masks; Hane & Fox, 2006). The opposite profile—left frontal asymmetry—is linked with approach behaviours, surgency, and displays of emotion (positive and sometimes anger). While predictive of more optimal outcomes, it is also a risk factor for externalising symptoms. A surgent baby's curiosity can turn to anger if their goals are often thwarted (He et al., 2010), and sensitive parenting has been shown to moderate the relationship between surgency and externalising symptoms (McDoniel & Buss, 2020).

Self-regulatory capacities are fostered through the co-regulation that synchrony affords. For instance, infants' ability to calm themselves by looking away from an unpredictable toy (e.g., a shaking 'bumble ball') is augmented by parents' contingent responsiveness to their looking away from it (Crockenberg & Leerkes, 2004).

Infants who engage in emotionally positive exchange with their mothers, and for whom ruptures in communication are swiftly repaired, make more attempts at re-engagement during stressful 'still-face' episodes (in which mothers are asked to be unresponsive to their infants). They are also more likely to self-soothe when re-engagement attempts fail and recover more quickly—indexed by a return to posi-tive affect and heart rate returning to baseline—during reunions. Such recovery is associated with increased regional cerebral blood flow (rCBF) in infants' orbito-frontal cortex, indicating relatively increased maturation of functional connected-ness in the *Emotion Regulation Network* (Catalina Camacho et al., 2020).

This effect of increased rCBF is more pronounced for infants who present more negative emotionality, aligning with the findings of Pratt et al. (2015) that more reactive babies benefit differently from parent-infant synchrony than those who are less so. While slower to develop self-regulatory skills, their inclination to dis-engage when stressed is countered by countless instances of being scaffolded back to positive emotion by the parent. This results in more negative infants relying on co-regulation, rather than withdrawal, when stressed.

Connection Network

Soothing holds, contingent eye-contact, and nurturing touch stimulate dopamine and oxytocin receptors in the ventral tegmental area and ventral striatum, tuning the infant reward system to become increasingly social in nature (Feldman, 2017). Accordingly, infants of sensitive parents may derive more *Connection Network* activation—or reward—from interaction with their caregivers. While all infants' brains give high precedence to processing threatening social stimuli (like fear-ful faces), infants of more sensitive mothers increasingly prioritise happy faces (Taylor-Colls & Pasco Fearon, 2015) and may even up-regulate the reward derived from doing so (as indexed by activation in the *Emotion Regulation Network*; Stern et al., 2024).

Connection Network activity is considered to motivate social 'approach' behav-iour (Izaki et al., 2024), and correspondingly preferential neural processing of mother's (vs. a stranger's) face is associated with six-month-olds' distress and proximity seeking behaviour during separation from their mother (Swingler et al., 2010). Caregiver responsiveness signals to infants the extent to which they can expect to access social support when under stress, hence infants from synchronous and sensitive dyads attempt to engage their mother more during 'still-face' epi-sodes (Barbosa et al., 2021) or when their arms are restrained (Perry et al., 2016).

As well as fostering the *seeking* of caregiver support and connection, synchrony and sensitivity additionally influence the extent to which babies *benefit* from it. Body contact and nurturing touch are associated with lower cortisol responses and physiological arousal in infants (Feldman et al., 2014; Field, 2010). However, infants who are touched intrusively by their caregiver (e.g., when infant gaze is averted) exhibit higher cortisol than those who are touched synchronously (Feldman et al., 2010). In an extended version of the 'still-face' experiment encompassing two 'still-face' episodes, only infants of parents who scored higher on a measure of contingent responsiveness were able to benefit from their mother's support and recover in the final reunion (as indexed by positive affect and their heartrate returning to baseline). In contrast, infants of parents with lower scores were unable to benefit. Their heart rates continued to rise, and they displayed increasingly negative affect (Haley & Stansbury, 2003). People less able to benefit from social support over the lifetime use up extra bodily resources and are at risk of stress-related physical and mental health issues (Sterling, 2020). Indeed, a longitudinal assessment of maternal sensitivity throughout infancy and childhood indicates that it buffers the relationship between life-stress and later health outcomes (Farrell et al., 2017). This is an indication that infants who are unused to eliciting consistent support are more susceptible to the ill effects of stress in later-life.

Self-Other Network

In a longitudinal study lasting more than 20 years, Ulmer Yaniv et al. (2021) demonstrated that parent-infant synchrony retains its character throughout the lifetime. Those who experience to-and-fro interactions that adapt to the other, and are low in tension, proceed as teenagers to better see their parent's perspective and find solutions to issues of contention. These capacities, in turn, predict their *Self-Other Network* activity as young adults, in response to the joy, sadness, and distress of others. This work illustrates how early parent-infant synchrony attunes babies, at the micro-level of communicative exchange, to adapt to and align with others' perspectives.

Recent hyperscanning studies simultaneously measure the brain activities of parents and infants while they interact, revealing how 'brain-to-brain' synchrony may underpin dyadic social interactions. These studies show that neural synchrony during face-to-face interactions increases when behavioural synchrony is more optimal (i.e. when mothers adapt emotionally to their infant, engage in appropriate affectionate touch, and are low in intrusiveness; Endevelt-Shapira & Feldman, 2023; Nguyen et al., 2021). Such inter-brain synchrony involves parents' and babies' prefrontal and temporo-parietal cortices whose functions are related to the *Self-Other Network* (and also the *Emotion Regulation Network*). We may interpret that, through reciprocal exchange, a parent's mature brain externally scaffolds, engages, and develops the *Self-Other* (and *Emotion Regulation*) *Network(s)* in their infant.

Maternal sensitivity is associated with increased connectivity in the *Self-Other Network* in 5-month-old infants (Chajes et al., 2022), and such connectivity is associated with developing mental state representations and social understanding. Additionally, the *Self-Other Network* is thought to underpin *attachment representations* or infant expectations regarding caregiver availability and attachment-related behaviours. Zhao et al. (2019), using functional near-infrared spectroscopy, revealed that more directive/intrusive parenting was associated with stronger activation in 6-month-old infants' temporal cortex to angry than happy speech sounds, and that this effect was reversed for less intrusive parenting. This finding may suggest that infants are learning to expect and pay attention to different aspects of infant-directed speech. When intrusiveness is high, infants may be prepared to attend to negatively valenced language that implies compliance or prohibition. When low, expectations may be for positive affirming language that supports exploration and joint attention.

Indeed, maternal sensitivity (and low intrusiveness) is associated with infants initiating joint attention (IJA), e.g., pointing at an exciting toy (Hane & Fox, 2006). IJA may be viewed as an informative index of an infant's attachment representations, signalling their expectancy of an adult's motivation to share emotion, attitudes, interest, and information about objects in the world (Tomasello et al., 2007). IJA in infancy is linked to functional connectivity between areas associated with the *Self-Other Network* (Eggebrecht et al., 2017), as well as predictive of emerging social-emotional competence (Vaughan Van Hecke et al., 2007).

Thus, both synchrony and maternal sensitivity can be viewed as driving neural pathways in the *Self-Other Network* that underpin a suite of social-emotional capacities. These capacities may be further enforced through attachment representations, which not only foster expectations of security, but also anticipations of positive experiences of sharing and learning about the world.

Conclusion

Micro- and macro-aspects of parent-infant communication likely impact the development of four neural networks in the developing brain and how they 'speak' to each other, as reflected in our functional neuro-anatomical model of human attachment (known as *NAMA*). When babies experience sensitive, supportive, and timely responses to their cues and communications on the macro-level, and responsive, to-and-fro, emotional contingency and exchange on the micro-level, their *Stress-Fear-Pain Network* becomes tuned to be 'optimally reactive', influencing a proportional response to stress throughout the lifetime. Furthermore, functional connectivity is optimised within and between the *Emotion Regulation Network*, enabling inhibition of both withdrawal responses and excessive surgency, while also fostering the development of a suite of differential self-regulatory skills—in accordance with infant temperament—through co-regulation. In addition, *Connection Network* activation with familiar caregivers may be experienced as more rewarding and associated with more support seeking. Such support from significant others is more effective in reducing stress. Finally, the *Self-Other Network* is tuned to align with, adopt, and share the perspectives of others, and caregivers are viewed both as a source of support and benefactors who share enthusiasm and inform on points of interest in the world, scaffolding curiosity and autonomy.

References

Albers, E. M., Marianne Riksen-Walraven, J., Sweep, F. C., & Weerth, C. D. (2008). Maternal behavior predicts infant cortisol recovery from a mild everyday stressor. *Journal of Child Psychology and Psychiatry, 49*(1), 97–103.

Barbosa, M., Beeghly, M., Moreira, J., Tronick, E., & Fuertes, M. (2021). Emerging patterns of infant regulatory behavior in the Still-Face paradigm at 3 and 9 months predict mother-infant attachment at 12 months. *Attachment & Human Development, 23*(6), 814–830.

Bernier, A., Dégeilh, F., Leblanc, É., Daneault, V., Bailey, H. N., & Beauchamp, M. H. (2019). Mother–infant interaction and child brain morphology: A multidimensional approach to maternal sensitivity. *Infancy, 24*(2), 120–138.

Catalina Camacho, M., King, L. S., Ojha, A., Garcia, C. M., Sisk, L. M., Cichocki, A. C., ... & Gotlib, I. H.(2020). Cerebral blood flow in 5-to 8-month-olds: Regional tissue maturity is associated with infant affect. *Developmental Science, 23*(5), e12928.

Chajes, J. R., Stern, J. A., Kelsey, C. M., & Grossmann, T. (2022). Examining the role of socioeconomic status and maternal sensitivity in predicting functional brain network connectivity in 5-month-old infants. *Frontiers in Neuroscience, 16*, 892482.

Conradt, E., Hawes, K., Guerin, D., Armstrong, D. A., Marsit, C. J., Tronick, E., & Lester, B. M. (2016). The contributions of maternal sensitivity and maternal depressive symptoms to epigenetic processes and neuroendocrine functioning. *Child Development, 87*(1), 73–85.

Crockenberg, S. C., & Leerkes, E. M. (2004). Infant and maternal behaviors regulate infant reactivity to novelty at 6 months. *Developmental Psychology, 40*(6), 1123.

Dégeilh, F., Bernier, A., Leblanc, É., Daneault, V., & Beauchamp, M. H. (2018). Quality of maternal behaviour during infancy predicts functional connectivity between default mode network and salience network 9 years later. *Developmental Cognitive Neuroscience, 34*, 53–62.

Diego, M. A., Field, T., Jones, N. A., & Hernandez-Reif, M. (2006). Withdrawn and intrusive maternal interaction style and infant frontal EEG asymmetry shifts in infants of depressed and non-depressed mothers. *Infant Behavior and Development, 29*(2), 220–229.

Eggebrecht, A. T., Elison, J. T., Feczko, E., Todorov, A., Wolff, J. J., Kandala, S., Adams, C. M., Snyder, A. Z., Lewis, J. D., Estes, A. M., Zwaigenbaum, L., Botteron, K. N., McKinstry, R. C., Constantino, J. N., Evans, A., Hazlett, H. C., Dager, S., Paterson, S. J., Schultz, R. T., Styner, M. A., ... & Pruett, J. R., Jr (2017). Joint attention and brain functional connectivity in infants and toddlers. *Cerebral Cortex, 27*(3), 1709–1720.

Endevelt-Shapira, Y., & Feldman, R. (2023). Mother–infant brain-to-brain synchrony patterns reflect caregiving profiles. *Biology, 12*(2), 284.

Farrell, A. K., Simpson, J. A., Carlson, E. A., Englund, M. M., & Sung, S. (2017). The impact of stress at different life stages on physical health and the buffering effects of maternal sensitivity. *Health Psychology, 36*(1), 35.

Feldman, R. (2017). The neurobiology of human attachments. *Trends in Cognitive Sciences, 21*(2), 80–99.

Feldman, R., Rosenthal, Z., & Eidelman, A. I. (2014). Maternal-preterm skin-to-skin contact enhances child physiologic organization and cognitive control across the first 10 years of life. *Biological Psychiatry, 75*(1), 56–64.

Feldman, R., Singer, M., & Zagoory, O. (2010). Touch attenuates infants' physiological reactivity to stress. *Developmental Science, 13*(2), 271–278.

Field, T. (2010). Touch for socioemotional and physical well-being: A review. *Developmental Review, 30*(4), 367–383.

Haley, D. W., & Stansbury, K. (2003). Infant stress and parent responsiveness: Regulation of physiology and behavior during still-face and reunion. *Child Development, 74*(5), 1534–1546.

Hane, A. A., & Fox, N. A. (2006). Ordinary variations in maternal caregiving influence human infants' stress reactivity. *Psychological Science, 17*(6), 550–556.

He, J., Degnan, K. A., McDermott, J. M., Henderson, H. A., Hane, A. A., Xu, Q., & Fox, N. A. (2010). Anger and approach motivation in infancy: Relations to early childhood inhibitory control and behavior problems. *Infancy*, *15*(3), 246–269.

Izaki, A., Verbeke, W. J., Vrticka, P., & Ein-Dor, T. (2024). A narrative on the neurobiological roots of attachment-system functioning. *Communications Psychology*, *2*(1), 96.

Köhler-Dauner, F., Roder, E., Gulde, M., Mayer, I., Fegert, J. M., Ziegenhain, U., & Waller, C. (2022). Maternal sensitivity modulates child's parasympathetic mode and buffers sympathetic activity in a free play situation. *Frontiers in Psychology*, *13*, 868848.

Long, M., Verbeke, W., Ein-Dor, T., & Vrtička, P. (2020). A functional neuro-anatomical model of human attachment (NAMA): Insights from first-and second-person social neuroscience. *Cortex*, *126*, 281–321.

Madigan, S., Deneault, A. A., Duschinsky, R., Bakermans-Kranenburg, M. J., Schuengel, C., van IJzendoorn, M. H., & Verhage, M. L. (2024). Maternal and paternal sensitivity: Key determinants of child attachment security examined through meta-analysis. *Psychological Bulletin*, *150*(7), 839–872.

McDoniel, M. E., & Buss, K. A. (2020). Maternal responsiveness protects exuberant toddlers from experiencing behavior problems in kindergarten. In C. L. Smith & D. J. Bridgett (Eds.), *Moving forward in the study of temperament and early education outcomes* (pp. 98–111). Routledge.

Nguyen, T., Abney, D. H., Salamander, D., Bertenthal, B. I., & Hoehl, S. (2021). Proximity and touch are associated with neural but not physiological synchrony in naturalistic mother-infant interactions. *NeuroImage*, *244*, 118599.

Perry, N. B., Calkins, S. D., & Bell, M. A. (2016). Indirect effects of maternal sensitivity on infant emotion regulation behaviors: The role of vagal withdrawal. *Infancy*, *21*(2), 128–153.

Pratt, M., Singer, M., Kanat-Maymon, Y., & Feldman, R. (2015). Infant negative reactivity defines the effects of parent–child synchrony on physiological and behavioral regulation of social stress. *Development and Psychopathology*, *27*(4pt1), 1191–1204.

Provenzi, L., Fumagalli, M., Giorda, R., Morandi, F., Sirgiovanni, I., Pozzoli, U., ... & Montirosso, R. (2017). Maternal sensitivity buffers the association between SLC6A4 methylation and socio-emotional stress response in 3-month-old full term, but not very preterm infants. *Frontiers in Psychiatry*, *8*, 171.

Raby, K. L., Roisman, G. I., Simpson, J. A., Collins, W. A., & Steele, R. D. (2015). Greater maternal insensitivity in childhood predicts greater electrodermal reactivity during conflict discussions with romantic partners in adulthood. *Psychological Science*, *26*(3), 348–353.

Rifkin-Graboi, A., Kong, L., Sim, L. W., Sanmugam, S., Broekman, B. F. P., Chen, H., ... & Qiu, A. (2015). Maternal sensitivity, infant limbic structure volume and functional connectivity: A preliminary study. *Translational Psychiatry*, *5*(10), e668–e668.

Thompson, L. A., & White, B. L. (2022). Social network and behavioral synchrony influences on maternal and infant cortisol response. *Journal of Human Behavior in the Social Environment*, *32*(5), 574–590.

Tomasello, M., Carpenter, M., & Liszkowski, U. (2007). A new look at infant pointing. *Child Development*, *78*(3), 705–722.

Schimmelpfennig, J., Topczewski, J., Zajkowski, W., & Jankowiak-Siuda, K. (2023). The role of the salience network in cognitive and affective deficits. *Frontiers in Human Neuroscience*, *17*, 1133367.

Sterling, P. (2020). *What is health?: Allostasis and the evolution of human design*. MIT Press.

Stern, J. A., Kelsey, C. M., Yancey, H., & Grossmann, T. (2024). Love on the developing brain: Maternal sensitivity and infants' neural responses to emotion in the dorsolateral prefrontal cortex. *Developmental Science, 27*(6), e13497.

Sturm, V. E., Brown, J. A., Hua, A. Y., Lwi, S. J., Zhou, J., Kurth, F., ... & Seeley, W. W. (2018). Network architecture underlying basal autonomic outflow: Evidence from fronto-temporal dementia. *Journal of Neuroscience, 38*(42), 8943–8955.

Swingler, M. M., Sweet, M. A., & Carver, L. J. (2010). Brain–behavior correlations: Relationships between mother–stranger face processing and infants' behavioral responses to a separation from mother. *Developmental Psychology, 46*(3), 669.

Taylor-Colls, S., & Pasco Fearon, R. M. (2015). The effects of parental behavior on infants' neural processing of emotion expressions. *Child Development, 86*(3), 877–888.

Ulmer Yaniv, A., Salomon, R., Waidergoren, S., Shimon-Raz, O., Djalovski, A., & Feldman, R. (2021). Synchronous caregiving from birth to adulthood tunes humans' social brain. *Proceedings of the National Academy of Sciences, 118*(14), e2012900118.

Vaughan Van Hecke, A., Mundy, P. C., Acra, C. F., Block, J. J., Delgado, C. E., Parlade, M. V., ... & Pomares, Y. B. (2007). Infant joint attention, temperament, and social competence in preschool children. *Child Development, 78*(1), 53–69.

Wang, Q., Zhang, H., Wee, C. Y., Lee, A., Poh, J. S., Chong, Y. S., ... & Qiu, A. (2019). Maternal sensitivity predicts anterior hippocampal functional networks in early childhood. *Brain Structure and Function, 224*, 1885–1895.

Zhao, C., Chronaki, G., Schiessl, I., Wan, M. W., & Abel, K. M. (2019). Is infant neural sensitivity to vocal emotion associated with mother-infant relational experience? *PLoS One, 14*(2), e0212205.

Chapter 34

Tuning in to baby

The importance of parental mentalising

Ruth Roberts

What is mentalising?

Mentalising is the ability to understand one's own mental states and the mental states of others. This includes recognising needs, desires, feelings, goals, and purposes that underlie behaviour (Fonagy et al., 1991; Luyten et al., 2020). Mentalising involves consideration of the intention behind behaviour, which helps one to make sense of their social world (Luyten et al., 2020). Mentalising is central to understanding, regulating, and communicating emotions and feelings. When one feels like their desires and goals are not understood or not being met, they may feel threatened or frustrated. Conversely, when they are being met, they are likely to feel secure and able to connect with others (Fonagy & Allison, 2012; Slade 2005).

Mentalising in the first year of life

The origins of mentalising begins in the first year of life. Newborns are sensitive to communication signals (Csibra & Gergely, 2009) and rely on basic sensory and emotional signals to interact with their caregivers. Newborns can detect when communication is intended for them, as shown by a preference for mothers reading stories in infant directed speech rather than adult-directed speech (Saito et al., 2007). By around five months, infants prefer eyes with direct gaze rather than averted gaze (Farroni et al., 2002) and can detect when their gaze is followed (Grossmann, Lloyd-Fox, & Johnson, 2013). This leads to the development of joint attention and sharing of experiences. By nine months infants look longer at objects following a joint attention interaction vs a non-joint attention interaction (Striano et al., 2006), which shows increases in attention to things that are most salient. In all these cases, infants are utilising information from another person to make sense of their social world.

Parent mentalising—four ways of examining parental mentalising during infancy

Mentalising ability does not develop in isolation. As seen above, the ability to mentalise requires interaction with others, and in the first year of life this is most often

DOI: 10.4324/9781003530473-41

with parents (Fonagy & Allison, 2012; Luyten et al., 2020). One important aspect of parental interaction is a parent's ability to consider the mental states of their infant.

Four methods are commonly used to measure different aspects about parents' ability to mentalise about their infant: parental reflective functioning, parental mind-mindedness, parental insightfulness, and parental embodied mentalising. The first three focus on comments parents make about their infant's mental state and the last focuses on bodily interactions between the parent and the infant.

Parental reflective functioning describes the parent's ability to consider both their own and their child's mental states, including thoughts, feelings, and intentions (Fonagy et al., 1991). Often assessed via interview or questionnaire, it involves understanding the reasons behind the infant's and the parent's own behaviours and emotions. This reflection helps parents to respond sensitively to the infant's needs and allows the infant to regulate their emotions (Slade, 2005).

Parental mind-mindedness involves parents' tendency to view their infant as having their own mind, with their own unique mental states (Meins et al., 2003). Usually examined through observation of the parent and infant interacting with one another, it focuses on parents' spontaneous interactions with their infant and the parents' ability to accurately interpret and describe the infant's thoughts and feelings. A parental comment would be coded as *appropriate* if the caregiver's comment was congruent with the infant's internal state (e.g., the parent says 'You like the blue one', while the infant is focused on a blue block) or *non-attuned* if it was not aligned with the infant's internal state (e.g., 'You want to play with the car', while the child is still actively playing with a doll) (Meins & Fernyhough, 2015).

Parental insightfulness involves parents' understanding of the thoughts and feelings that drive infants' behaviours (Koren-Karie & Oppenheim, 2018). Parental insightfulness is assessed via parents reviewing a previously unseen video of an interaction with their infant. Parents are asked to share their views of the infant's mental states as well as their own during this interaction. It focuses on parents' tendency to provide a comprehensive, positively accepting, and child-focused description of the child's behaviour and motives within the context of the interaction and considers how parents update their views of the infant in line with the review of the interaction (Oppenheim & Koren-Karie, 2002; Koren-Karie et al., 2002).

Parental embodied mentalising involves parents' implicit ability to identify, understand, and respond to their infant's emotions, thoughts, and intentions through bodily movements and shared kinaesthetic interactions (Shai & Belsky, 2011). This form of mentalising is particularly useful in early parent-infant interactions, where communication is mostly non-verbal and reliant on bodily expressions. Parent-infant interactions are video recorded and cycles of interaction, which include clear moments of metal connection, are coded to assess a range of movement qualities of both the parent and the infant, including parents' ability to adjust their movements in response to their infant's signals (Shai & Belsky, 2017).

It is worth mentioning that Zeegers *et al.* (2017), in their meta-analysis of parental mentalising, noted that little research has been done to assess the similarities and differences of different mentalising constructs.

Why is parental mentalising so important?

Attachment security and maternal sensitivity

Even before the child is born, parental mentalising is important as evidenced by Fonagy *et al.* (1991), who found that antenatal parental mentalising predicted child attachment, 12–18 months after birth. Parents who more readily described their unborn child later made more mind-related comments about the infant (McMahon et al., 2017).

A meta-analysis across different assessments of parent mentalising found that parents' ability to mentalise about their child's mental states predicted child attachment security and parental sensitivity, and sensitivity mediated the association between mentalising and child attachment (Zeegers et al., 2017).

McMahon *et al.* (2017) found that several studies have reported correlations between the proportion or frequency of attuned mind-related comments and maternal sensitivity and attachment security. Mothers' ability to understand their infant's mental state and provide a timely and sensitive response in the moment may be an important driver behind the association between mind-mindedness and maternal sensitivity. However, the authors also note some studies reporting null findings and challenges with methodology and highlight a need for more empirical research and replication in this area (McMahon et al., 2017).

In a study with 12–17-month-old infants, mothers who were positively insightful had higher maternal sensitivity scores and were more likely to have infants with secure attachment than mothers who were not positively insightful (Koren-Karie et al., 2002). Interestingly, insightfulness accounted for variation in attachment beyond variance explained by maternal sensitivity, which the authors propose may be due to the fact insightfulness into the child's mental state may sometimes result in parental actions that would not be deemed to be outwardly sensitive, such as setting boundaries and limits (Koren-Karie et al., 2002).

Higher parental embodied mentalising reduced the likelihood of insecure attachment at 15 and 36 months, even after controlling for maternal sensitivity (Shai & Belsky, 2017).

Emotional regulation and behaviour

Parental mind-related comments are thought to provide feedback and support regulation for their child's emotions and behaviour (McMahon et al., 2017). Several studies have found mind-mindedness was related to children's executive functioning skills, including effortful and inhibitory control (McMahon et al., 2017). Parental insightfulness is thought to encourage children to discuss their behaviours and feelings openly and help children to cope with emotional experiences (Koren-Karie & Oppenheim, 2018). Parental increases in insightfulness following intervention were associated with reduction in preschool children's externalising and internalising problems (Koren-Karie & Oppenheim, 2018).

Higher levels of parental embodied mentalising predicted lower levels of internalising and externalising problems and better social skills and peer relationships at 54 months (Shai & Belsky, 2017).

Language, communication, and cognitive abilities

Additionally, parental mind-mindedness has been found to scaffold language skills and cognitive abilities. Several studies have found that appropriate mind-related comments predicted children's later language skills and school readiness (McMahon et al., 2017).

Higher levels of parental embodied mentalising predicted advanced language abilities and better academic performance at 54 months even after controlling for maternal sensitivity (Shai & Belsky, 2017).

Child mentalising ability

Parents who interpret and understand their child's mental states provide meaning to their child's behaviour and conversations about emotions helps to facilitate the child's developing awareness of self and others as mental agents (McMahon et al., 2017). Several studies have found that attuned mind-related comments during infancy predict children's later theory of mind ability (McMahon et al., 2017).

Factors affecting parental mentalising

It is important to note that mentalising is thought to develop within the attachment relationship. Parental experiences of early attachment either help or hinder their ability to mentalise about their own and their child's mental states. Securely attached parents tend to have high levels of mentalising owing to their experience of responsive and attuned caregiving. They are able to respond contingently to the child, which allows the child to feel recognised and understood, and fosters secure attachment and mentalising ability in the child (Luyten et al., 2020). Parents who are insecurely attached may not have experienced optimal mentalising early on—possibly owing to difficulty in sharing a mental space with their parent or experiencing an absence of mirroring of experience—and this impairs their capacity to mentalise later on (Lutyen et al., 2020; Slade et al., 2005).

Parental mental health difficulties may reduce/impair a parent's capacity to understand and respond to their infant's mental states (Luyten et al., 2020; Koren-Karie & Oppenheim, 2018). Similarly, high levels of stress, including financial difficulties, lack of social support, may cause difficulties with a parent's capacity to consider their infant's mind. Having a strong support network that provides emotional and practical support may help to alleviate stress and improve parents' abilities to focus on their infant.

Parents who have experienced trauma may have impaired capacity to mentalise (Koren-Karie & Oppenheim, 2018), however high levels of parental reflective functioning about their traumatic experiences may protect against attachment difficulties in their child (Luyten et al., 2020). Interventions to support parental mentalising may support parents who have experienced trauma and adversity.

Interestingly, the influence of cultural factors on mentalising is still less known. Different cultures have varying norms regarding the expression of emotions and caregiving practices, which may influence mentalising. However, a recent study examined mind-mindedness in Korean parents, where the mother-infant dyad is considered to be a single unit (which is thought to afford Korean parents a unique and highly accurate insight into the mind of the infant), as compared to British parents, and found no differences in overall levels of mind-mindedness (Lee, Meins & Larkin, 2025).

Summary

Tuning in to what infants may be thinking or feeling well before they can verbalise it is important for infant development across a range of factors. Parents are optimally positioned to do this given the closeness of the parent-infant relationship. Although there are variations in how parental mentalising is conceptualised and assessed, it is an important aspect of parent-infant interaction. Parents who may have difficulties with mentalising may benefit from additional support.

References

Csibra, G., & Gergely, G. (2009). Natural pedagogy. *Trends in Cognitive Sciences*, *13*(4), 148–153. https://doi.org/10.1016/j.tics.2009.01.005

Farroni, T., Csibra, G., Simion, F., & Johnson, M. H. (2002). Eye contact detection in humans from birth. *Proceedings of the National Academy of Sciences of the United States of America*, *99*(14), 9602–9605. https://doi.org/10.1073/pnas.152159999

Fonagy, P., Steele, M., Steele, H., Moran, G. S., & Higgitt, A. C. (1991). The capacity for understanding mental states: The reflective self in parent and child and its significance for security of attachment. *Infant Mental Health Journal*, *12*(3), 201–218. https://doi.org/10.1002/1097-0355(199123)12:3<201::AID-IMHJ2280120307>3.0.CO;2-7

Fonagy, P., & Allison, E. (2012). What is mentalization?: The concept and its foundations in developmental research. In N. Midgley & I. Vrouva (Eds.), *Minding the child: Mentalization-based interventions with children, young people and their families* (pp. 11–34). London: Routledge/Taylor & Francis Group.

Grossmann, T., Lloyd-Fox, S., & Johnson, M. H. (2013). Brain responses reveal young infants' sensitivity to when a social partner follows their gaze. *Developmental Cognitive Neuroscience*, *6*, 155–161. https://doi.org/10.1016/j.dcn.2013.09.004

Koren-Karie, N., Oppenheim, D., Dolev, S., Sher, E., & Etzion-Carasso, A. (2002). Mothers' insightfulness regarding their infants' internal experience: Relations with maternal sensitivity and infant attachment. *Developmental psychology*, *38*(4), 534–542. https://doi.org/10.1037//0012-1649.38.4.534

Koren-Karie, N., Oppenheim, D. (2018). Parental insightfulness: Retrospect and prospect. *Attachment & Human Development*, *20*(3), 223–236. 10.1080/14616734.2018.1446741

Lee, Y., Meins, E., & Larkin, F. (2025). Parental mentalization across cultures: Mind-mindedness and parental reflective functioning in British and South Korean mothers. *Infant Mental Health Journal, 46*(2), 133–147. https://doi.org/10.1002/imhj.22151

Luyten, P., Campbell, C., Allison, E., & Fonagy, P. (2020). The mentalising approach to psychopathology: State of the art and future directions. *Annual Review of Clinical Psychology, 16*, 297–325. https://doi.org/10.1146/annurev-clinpsy-071919-015355

McMahon, C., & Bernier, A. (2017). Twenty years of research on parental mind-mindedness: Empirical findings, theoretical and methodological challenges, and new directions. *Developmental Review, 46*, 54–80. https://doi.org/10.1016/j.dr.2017.07.001

Meins, E., Fernyhough, C., Wainwright, R., Clark-Carter, D., Das Gupta, M., Fradley, E., & Tuckey, M. (2003). Pathways to understanding mind: Construct validity and predictive validity of maternal mind-mindedness. *Child Development, 74*(4), 1194–1211. https://doi.org/10.1111/1467-8624.00601

Meins, E., & Fernyhough, C. (2015). Mind-mindedness coding manual, Version 2.2. *Unpublished manuscript.* New York, UK: University of York.

Oppenheim, D., & Koren-Karie, N. (2002). Mothers' insightfulness regarding their children's internal worlds: The capacity underlying secure child-mother relationships. *Infant Mental Health Journal, 23*(6), 593–605. https://doi.org/10.1002/imhj.10035

Saito, Y., Aoyama, S., Kondo, T., Fukumoto, R., Konishi, N., Nakamura, K., Kobayashi, M., & Toshima, T. (2007). Frontal cerebral blood flow change associated with infant-directed speech. *Archives of Disease in Childhood. Fetal and Neonatal Edition, 92*(2), F113–F116. https://doi.org/10.1136/adc.2006.097949

Shai, D., & J. Belsky. 2011. When words just won't do: Introducing parental embodied mentalizing. *Child Development Perspectives, 5*(3), 173–180. https://doi.org/10.1111/j.1750-8606.2011.00181.x.

Shai, D., & Belsky, J. (2017). Parental embodied mentalizing: How the nonverbal dance between parents and infants predicts children's socio-emotional functioning. *Attachment & Human Development, 19*(2), 191–219. https://doi.org/10.1080/14616734.2016.1255653

Slade, A. (2005). Parental reflective functioning: An introduction. *Attachment & Human Development, 7*, 269–281. https://doi.org/10.1080/14616730500245906]

Striano, T., Reid, V. M., & Hoehl, S. (2006). Neural mechanisms of joint attention in infancy. *European Journal of Neuroscience, 23*, 2819–2823. https://doi.org/10.1111/j.1460-9568.2006.04822.x

Zeegers, M. A. J., Colonnesi, C., Stams, G. J. M., & Meins, E. (2017). Mind matters: A meta-analysis on parental mentalization and sensitivity as predictors of infant-parent attachment. *Psychological Bulletin, 143*(12), 1245–1272. https://doi.org/10.1037/bul0000114

Chapter 35

Psychoanalytic parent-infant psychotherapy as preventative work

Coretta Ogbuagu

Psychoanalytic parent-infant psychotherapy (PPIP) is a treatment focused on the improvement of the relationship of the parent and their baby. It is underpinned by a psychoanalytic model that privileges the exploration of unconscious processes at work in our lives, and is informed by other developmental models such as neuroscience and developmental psychology to understand human emotional, biological, and physiological life. The aim is to intervene where there is evidence of patterns of behaviour and interactions that are deemed to pose a risk to the baby's and parents' development (Baradon et al., 2016, p.30). As the baby is growing and learning, so is/are the parent(s)—even if it is not their first child. This makes for a pertinent time to intervene and offer support, especially as we know early intervention has better long-term outcomes.

Where possible, I like to meet parents while they are expecting. In my experience, anything from 12 weeks gestation onwards is usually when parents are more receptive to thinking with a professional about their dreams, wishes, anxieties, and concerns about the new baby and how their life will change. Parents may need support as together we explore fantasies, expectations, dreams, worries, and I think it is helpful for a parent to know before giving birth that they will have therapeutic support as soon as possible following delivery.

Setting up

A first encounter is always important. In PPIP work, I usually 'meet' a parent on a telephone call before the first in-person meeting. During the initial telephone contact, I try to explain who I am, what I do, and what we will think about in the first meeting as well as, very briefly, what I have understood about their referral to me from their health professional (usually perinatal psychiatrist or health visitor)—giving them the chance to expand if they wish. I see this as a very important part of the engagement process. Trust is important and feeling psychologically held in safe hands is paramount. I want parents to get a sense of my voice, my way of thinking and listening to them, and also pay attention to anything about them that stands out. If meeting parents who have already given birth, I also listen out for the baby. Most times, I will hear the baby's voice and comment on hearing the baby to the parent.

DOI: 10.4324/9781003530473-42

It helps to bring the baby into the setting and again gives me a sense of how the parent may talk about their baby or indicate current levels of stress/coping. I talk about the baby as a little person if they are still pregnant—again, making it known that we will think about the baby growing inside the parent and the relationship they have to them, even at this stage.

I like to let mothers know that their partner may also attend if they wish and that we can also talk about this more when we meet so I can hear their views.

Assessment and treatment

PPIP treatment, like other therapies, has a beginning, middle, and end. It begins with an assessment. First, I discuss with parents the reasons that parent-infant work may be useful in pregnancy and beyond; second, I explain the PPIP setting, where we sit on the floor with the baby and age-appropriate toys to help us play and think together. Third, but not always, I request permission to video-record the sessions, to assist my own thinking about our work outside of the session during supervision, but also at times to watch back some of the material with them during sessions; finally, I explain the fact that I would not suggest a time-limit to our work together, although our NHS PPIP service caters for families until the child's second birthday.

We tend to meet weekly. The room and time are usually kept the same, creating a consistent routine. I think this helps parents to set a rhythm to the week for them and their baby—*on a Wednesday, we see Coretta*. By the end of the assessment, which is usually three sessions, we would have made some therapy goals and I have a sense of a formulation of the presenting needs and areas for focus.

Discovering the voice of the pre-verbal baby

I previously wrote about Bianca and her baby son Peter in an article (Ogbuagu, 2019) where I described the process of PPIP. I would like to revisit parts of this work to illustrate how powerful a tool this modality is in assisting the development of the pre-verbal baby and their parents in becoming attuned to their baby.

I would like to focus on two examples: one when Peter was a few weeks old and the other when he was nine months old. In the early example, Peter was drinking from the bottle as we discussed the difficult feelings Bianca had around breast feeding. I made a very premature comment about this perhaps being tied up with earlier sexual trauma (although this is likely to have been plausible, it was definitely too raw to have said to her at this point).

> In the session, Bianca cried as she fed Peter. She turned away as she did not want him to see her cry. At this point, Peter seemed to fix his gaze on his mother. Apart from his sucking from the bottle, his whole face and body were frozen. Once the bottle was complete, he grizzled a little and Bianca offered him the dummy.
>
> (Ogbuagu, 2019, p.264)

This was a time when Bianca's vulnerabilities were at the surface. She was recovering from a traumatic c-section, she was a young mother who was quite isolated. She was more or less a single parent. The approach of PPIP is not to move away from difficult topics, but to sensitively and skillfully hold them for both baby and parent while looking for the best moment to bring them into the light for reflection on both perspectives.

For Peter, he would have felt the heartbeat of his mother—perhaps a change in its pace or rhythm as he fed while closely nestled into her body. He looked to her and held her gaze until he finished the bottle. Observing him and the stillness and stiffness of his body helped me to see that there was more going on for his mother. Bianca tried to protect him by turning away as her tears dropped. This seemed to only command Peter's attention all the more. In moments like these, I tend to be silent; preferring to hold the space and allow for the tears and the feelings that come with them until I feel that I can ask about the tears or give my own words to what I see is happening for both baby and mum. What is interesting here is that both mum and baby are non-verbal in this moment, but, despite this, so much is being communicated. By offering my own suggestions about what might be going on for Bianca and for Peter, I model a way of reading the non-verbal that she can then adopt to apply to reading the communications of her baby. This is especially helpful if I get it 'wrong' as this also shows that, despite being a skilled clinician, I am human and have moments where I don't get it right, but I use our therapeutic relationship and trust built so far, which includes my authenticity and realness, to attempt a repair. If there is enough trust, most parents will manage to forgive and move forward from the faux pas. This offers hope: that in a trusting relationship from mum to son, if Bianca sometimes doesn't quite 'get it right' with Peter, all is not lost. They will both survive it and even reinforce the strength of their relationship.

In the second example when Peter was about six months old, he and his mother were playing at the doll's house—at his request:

Bianca and Peter played a game of peekaboo. I thought this was interesting, given that another break for Christmas was approaching. This was also something Peter had experienced – seeing less of his mother now that she was at university. Soon, he would see even less of her, as she was due to return to work a few months later, when Peter would be nine months old.

Peter was eager today; he went for all the toys around him with great voracity. He wanted to look in the doll's house and Bianca explored this with him – even setting up the furniture. She seemed to be playing just as much as he. She'd never had a doll's house and as a child never knew they existed … Bianca played a teasing game of peekaboo with a toy Peter was using. I pointed out how crestfallen he was when the toy disappeared. She followed this and when she went too far, she stopped the game.

(Ogbuagu, 2019 p.268)

This moment of play between Bianca and Peter is initiated by Peter showing an interest in the doll's house and Bianca responding positively to this by following his lead. She joins in, in a way that allows me to access the child in her: the child who never had this experience of play or even knew it was available. As a therapist, I feel I am holding different versions of the mother-baby relationship. I am holding a past version before Peter was born; a current version of the here and now; and a future version—a hopeful projection of how they might occupy space together when both are older and further along the developmental trajectory.

Being with her baby in this way allows Bianca to be in touch with a former version of herself. I wonder if Peter feels like he is with a different version of his mother in this moment? Also, when I point out that Peter is really affected by the missing object in the adapted peekaboo game, Bianca takes this seriously. Again, she understands the remit of PPIP that I provide Peter's view and potential unconscious phenomena for him and for her allowing more to be potentially seen, accepted, and worked through in the safety of the consulting room.

It is a challenge to the therapist to amplify the baby's voice when the mother has a diagnosis of PTSD or has other mental health needs of her own. Space needs to be allowed for both. I believe you cannot attend to one without the other. However, there is a danger of the baby's voice not being heard because mum can easily dominate the space as she has language and it is challenging as a therapist not to respond to this verbally. I find it helpful to remind parents of this at times so they remember this is a shared space with their baby—something they have to adjust to in many areas of their life in this new normal.

Discussion

These two examples indicate that when there are difficult transitions to charter for parent and baby, the PPIP setting allows for sensitive intervention to facilitate thinking about these, thus supporting the relationship to manage through the challenging events and also look back and see how they worked through things last time and what they can take into future transitions. Being able to review in a non-judgemental environment with or without the use of video-recording is incredibly useful. Often parents do not realise what they have learned and accomplished until it is pointed out. This builds confidence and resilience, which is helpful for the parent to see they can manage, especially when they are no longer in treatment and it is just them and their baby working things out.

There is a strong tradition across many cultures of storytelling to inform and guide the next generation. In PPIP work, I always hold in mind the new mother's own mothering/early bonding experience. Graham Music talks about the gains of intergenerational cultural and spiritual transmission for the nervous system of both foetus and mother (Music, 2024, p.8).

In his self-described guide book, *Womb Life*, Music (2024, p.40) points out that it takes time for a human adult to bond with a baby—it does not happen immediately. This is welcome news for those many parents whom I have helped in my consulting room, where their baby could not be placed on the chest for skin-to-skin immediately after birth, leaving mothers especially feeling that all was lost because that moment had passed due to the baby or them needing urgent medical care. Music goes on to point out that, historically, we humans have always raised babies and children in groups, which again is at odds with the parents and babies I have met over the last decade in PPIP treatment—struggling to raise their children in the most challenging, austere, and isolating circumstances, often in a country far away from their cultural home of origin (p.41). I often think about the importance of the baby seeing me regularly for a significant period of their new post-uterine life and connecting with someone outside the family being so important for these babies who are often not in multi-family environments. Peter and his mother, Bianca, were one such family, not least because Bianca was a university student and her peers were not having babies at the same time.

We know that when there is good prenatal bonding, evidently there will be good postnatal bonding (Tichelman et al., 2019). In my paper I talk about how advantageous it was to meet Bianca in late pregnancy. She had prepared Dr Seuss stories and read and talked with Peter inside the womb as she prepared to welcome him to my consulting room: "a place to think and play" as she described it. I suspect that some of what I observed between them in the room postnatally may have been familiar to the dyad in the prenatal stages of their developing relationship. With this in mind, it can be said that the PPIP therapist arrives late to the party and our work is to get to know how this dyad have been getting on and help put this into words and symbols that both mum and baby can understand and appreciate. Understanding the status of one's relationship is key to knowing the direction in which it is headed.

As a therapist, I tend to speak to the baby bump too—which may seem crackers to some parents (some have even told me so!), but helps break down any embarrassment parents may have in doing so. Speaking to the baby is an important part of the process of eliciting the voice of the baby; connecting emotionally and perhaps spiritually to 'listen out' for what the baby needs and wants. When Bianca closed the door of her bedroom on my first post-birth visit, she gave me Peter to hold. I took the precious little bundle of life and whispered to him that it was good to finally meet him and that I was looking after him and mummy for the time being. He slept soundly and managed to settle in my arms—hardly uncurling from his comfortable positioning.

Knowing what we do about intergenerational influences passed unconsciously and consciously to the newborn, we can conclude that the baby's voice is its own plus the influences of its ancestors. How do we pay attention to this in PPIP? As the baby's voice is concerned, does this mean that we are inclined to hear some things and ignore others, as we do of our elders at times? The parent-child relationship is imbued with tensions, conflict, joy, and everything in between but how do we tune into the voice of the baby? I like to think of what baby is 'saying' as an ongoing conversation we are having with the baby. I think that sometimes parents can feel that they are at the mercy of what their baby is 'saying', that the voice is rather critical and persecutory, which would of course tell us more about the parent's state of mind than that of the baby's. Helping parents to develop this more nuanced understanding of the baby's communications is crucial to helping them develop a more balanced experience of their baby and hopefully be more open to their baby's communications, whatever they may be.

During the PPIP assessment, I find using the AAI (Main et al., 1985) helps parents connect to the voice of their baby as they reflect on their younger selves and are reminded of how they felt and experienced being brought up by their own caregivers. I have recently adapted my use of this tool and added my own questions to include remembering how their parents managed their own experiences of racism and prejudice and those of my patients when they were little. This helps to get a sense of how global majority parents and those who are not white British may manage and unfortunately have to talk through, on some level, the racist experiences they will encounter with their baby and toddler.

It is clear that PPIP offers hope. Families I see may have many odds stacked against them: trauma, ACEs, racism, poverty, and so on. However, even in the direst circumstances, PPIP offers a chance for a healthier relationship to develop between a baby and their parents, which has powerful long-term effects for the family and society. I provide scaffolding and model a way of being open to the baby's distress to show that, even here, meeting the baby's needs is so important despite it feeling overwhelming or unmanageable at times.

References

Baradon, T., Biseo, M., Broughton, C., James, J., & Joyce, A. (2016). *The practice of psychoanalytic parent-infant psychotherapy, claiming the baby* (2nd ed.). London: Routledge.

George, C., Kaplan, N., & Main, M. (1985). *Adult attachment interview* (3rd ed.). Berkeley: University of California.

Music, G. (2024). *Womb Life, Mind-Nurturing Books*. London: Mind-Nurturing Books.

Ogbuagu, C. (2019). "I don't want to die die, I want to feel better': Finding hope through psychoanalytic parent-infant psychotherapy. *Journal of Child Psychotherapy*, 45(3), 257–273. doi: 10.1080/0075417X.2019.1703786.

Tichelman, E., Westerneng, M., Witteveen, A.B., van Baar, A.L., van der Horst, H.E., de Jonge A., et al. (2019, September 24). Correlates of prenatal and postnatal mother-to-infant bonding quality: A systematic review. *PLOS ONE*, 14(9), e0222998.

Chapter 36

Parent-infant dynamics in an observant Jewish context

Sue Schraer

Introduction

Arising from the specific need for specialist perinatal mental health practitioners with in-depth cultural knowledge and understanding, Menucha (*meaning in Hebrew 'ease'; 'rest'; 'calm'*), the Perinatal Mental Health Charity was born in 2019.

The charity was set up by Rivki Dwek and her co-founder, who had suffered significant mood disorders in the perinatal period themselves. They experienced a dearth of culturally-appropriate help to serve the specific needs of their religious community: The highly observant element of the Jewish spectrum in an overall Jewish population of 56,000 in London, (often referred to by others as Orthodox or Ultra-Orthodox), concentrated in the London Borough of Barnet (out of a total UK Jewish population of over 290,000) (Schraer, 2024).

A few years prior to the launch, in-depth consultation with leading institutions, for example, the Tavistock and Portman Clinic and the Parent-Infant Project at the Anna Freud Centre, had taken place. The founders of Menucha were determined to offer the community a highly professional, joined-up service with close liaison with local National Health Service (NHS) Perinatal Mental Health Services, local general practitioners (GPs), psychiatrists, and NHS midwives. Referrals come from all these sources as well as from rabbis and rebbetzins (rabbis' wives who are pastoral leaders and educationalists in the community) and self-referrals. Their mission is to offer support; valuable resources; specialist therapy and comprehensive assistance to individuals and families navigating post-natal depression and perinatal mental health issues, and to address the stigma around these issues. Menucha aims to foster an environment of empathy, acceptance, and non-judgement where everyone is heard and valued. The team of therapists are all registrants of either UKCP (UK Council for Psychotherapy), BACP (British Association for Counselling and Psychotherapy), or BPC (British Psychoanalytic Council), and supervised by an NHS specialist psychologist in perinatal mental health. The Menucha team has, in addition to their primary training, undertaken a bespoke Tavistock and Portman course in perinatal mental health. A range of modalities are available to clients and assiduous effort is made to match appropriately: Psychoanalytic/dynamic, integrative, family systems therapy, and compassion-focused therapy, parent-infant psychotherapy (PIP), and

DOI: 10.4324/9781003530473-43

birth trauma resolution work by a specialist practitioner. Clients are seen once per week and blocks of work are offered and then reviewed. Their babies are sometimes brought to the sessions and, of course, are central if the work is PIP.

The following chapter will attempt to illustrate, using clinical work as a vehicle, how these cultural practices, which affect every aspect of daily life, might impact parents, infant, and child-rearing. As Graham Music posited (2017, p.86), "There is extraordinary richness of cultural diversity, and a danger of assuming one's own practices are right or best." He writes that cultures frame our thoughts, physiology, and brain. This is the central ethos and cornerstone of the clinical and support work the team at Menucha aims to offer.

Context

This community lives a life devoted utterly to faith in one God, highly observant of, and adherent to, the laws taken from sacred texts, primarily, the *Torah* (Five Biblical Books of Moses or Old Testament) and the accompanying rabbinical interpretations throughout the generations. The Sabbath (*Shabbat),* the seventh day (from sunset on Friday to sunset on Saturday), is a sacred and ring-fenced day of rest and prayer where workaday activities cease. It involves much preparation week-on-week and perhaps makes Friday afternoon a less-than-optimal time to offer an appointment.

It is in this perinatal domain of life, in particular, where shame and guilt can be mobilised if difficulties emerge. Given the centrality of large families and the continuity of the faith and culture, one of the very *raisons d'etre* of Jewish life, it can add a further layer of reluctance to disclose when there are issues.

Much of the material will be drawn from the author's experience of working in Menucha's therapeutic team.

Modesty (Laws of *Tzniut*)

To maintain modesty and discretion, girls are educated with other girls and largely mix only with boys to whom they are related: Brothers and cousins.

Reproducing is a holy endeavour, viewed as the central life-project. It is the fulfilment of the commandment set out in Genesis 1:28: "Be fruitful and multiply". The community takes fulsome delight in family life. Infants are welcomed with great celebration and joy (*simcha)* by family, friends, and community.

It is important for those treating women from this community to understand the importance and value of modesty, the laws of *Tzniut* that maintain the dignity of the human body. Girls are protected from harm by being encouraged to dress modestly as womanhood approaches and married women cover their heads with hats, scarves, or wigs to preserve the beauty of their natural hair for the special and sacred relationship of marriage. In spite of the intimacy of the marital relationship, men do not directly observe their wife while she is immodestly exposed (as in childbirth), maintaining her privacy and dignity.

Menstruating and post-partum women must separate from men and become *niddah*, meaning separate (Leviticus 11:1–15) and are not allowed to touch males, for example, shaking hands, or have any form of intimate touch with husbands at this time. Following menstruation, a woman has to be completely free from menstrual blood in order to resume physical relations with her spouse and, before doing so, will visit and be immersed in the *mikvah* (ritual bath), which marks the return from being *niddah* to being once again available for intimacy within the sanctity of her marriage.

Menstruating and post-partum women sleep separately from husbands. In the mix of a possible mood disorder or post-natal depression could be the difficulty of not being able to receive the reassuring touch or physical holding by the spouse. Professionals benefit from this cultural knowledge and will know the wife cannot go to her husband for physical reassurance, although he can, of course, comfort, encourage, and reassure in other ways like eye-contact, kind deeds, words, and prayer. This cultural knowledge is likely to prevent a professional misinterpreting, as illustrated below in a report by a labour and delivery nurse in the USA of a newly-delivered primigravida. The nurse suspected marital discord and a potential attachment problem, rather than what was culturally and religiously appropriate to this Orthodox couple:

I have some real concerns about this couple. Although they attended childbirth preparation classes, the father wasn't physically supportive of his wife ... he would not touch her at all, not hand-holding or back-rubbing. Any time we checked his wife ... he left the room and didn't return until we called him back. He refused to enter the delivery room too! He stayed in the labour room reading [praying]. In the recovery room he kept his distance. None of the hugging and kissing we usually see after birth. They both say they're happy with the baby and yet they won't call her by name.

(Lutwak, Ney, White, 1988, p.45)

Baby girls are named in synagogue and boys are named at the circumcision occurring eight days after birth if the baby is well. No names are, therefore, revealed until these rituals have taken place.

To address similar misunderstandings, Menucha has made significant progress in disseminating information to local statutory services about the community's particular cultural needs. The founder attends the weekly multi-disciplinary meeting of the local NHS Perinatal Mental Health Service; liaises closely with NHS midwives who work in the community, and has enlisted the help of a specialist female doctor who gives invaluable information regarding *niddah* and contraception (which is now used more widely in the community). Menucha has been featured in a Ted Talk, rolls out monthly Podcasts, has a website, a magazine, and runs events and talks. All practitioners attend a cultural information seminar before becoming part of the team.

Perinatal mood disorders

Since its launch, Menucha has provided 205 women with therapeutic help out of a total of 600 who have been supported with other forms of assistance during the perinatal period (to include fathers). Menucha's figures suggest one in four of this population in London suffers from perinatal mental health issues.

There can sometimes be pressure to suppress any less than joyous feelings around the life events or to have agency in slowing down the speed with which they are happening at times of overwhelm (as illustrated in the vignette below). It is well understood—and extensively researched—that maternal mental health issues can compromise the mother-infant relationship, including the work of Gerhardt, Music, Beebe, Slade, Baradon. The early affectionate bond between caregiver and infant is known to influence the very architecture of the developing brain (Gerhardt, 2004).

Clinical vignette

Shira, aged twenty, a primigravida, was demonstrating difficulty adjusting to all that had happened. A large number of considerable life events occurred in Shira's life within 18 months when she was between the ages of 18½ and 20 years old. Not only the significant life events of meeting a life-partner (in the community, the process starts via an introduction and marriage happens fairly quickly after an agreement); the cultural context of the onset of head-covering; laws of *niddah*; going to *mikveh;* leading up to childbirth and the arrival of a baby: its raw bodily presence and insistent demands, which she could not always decipher or meet. It seemed to symbolise how much responsibility she had; her overwhelm and how very much had changed for her. Perhaps a crying baby triggered the crying baby in herself that still needed attention and a chance to 'grow up'.

She had hardly come to know her husband before she found herself pregnant and with another identity to adjust to, that of mother, although she described her spouse as very supportive. Whenever possible, he would take her out for a walk and buy her a treat: a waffle or ice cream. The therapist's countertransference was that in the consulting room was a young girl who still needed treats and playtime herself and was overwhelmed by a sense of loss of her younger identity as a carefree self and the onset of responsibility. She wanted to keep therapy very private and brief. She felt shame acutely and a sense she had failed.

Shira's disclosure of having "lost herself", and the therapist's countertransference that she was in the consulting room with a child and a feeling she never quite found Shira in the therapy, seemed to indicate how confused and untethered Shira felt. She had not had the opportunity to self-actualise or to adjust to, imagine, and fantasise about her new roles. Shira's difficulties challenged the capacity to make an attuned connection with a baby. There was a deadness and a sense of loss and 'lost-ness' about her that would inevitably impact her baby. Shira needed her time to 'play' to process all that had happened to her, to slow down and allow liminal space, and thus an opening up in her mind to her baby (Schraer, ibid).

In the mix of her sadness, Shira was having to navigate the conflict and tension between community expectations of joy and the reality of her contrasting feelings. She tended to withdraw from the social opportunities that would amplify her feelings of insufficiency and maintain her comparisons with others whom she perceived as coping well, further isolating her.

The clinical work focused on allowing her confidential space to express the feelings that she experienced as shameful and transgressive. She was helped with normalising them and taking a more realistic approach to her punitive internal critic and possible perfectionism. It helped to illuminate how very much she had gone through in a whirlwind of time with sparse opportunity for processing in between. The desire for quiet, liminal space (Gillman, 2022; Khan, 1983) and to identify her agency and available opportunities for re-charging (and what replenished her) to help her feel less trapped were encouraged and validated and experienced as a source of healing.

The baby in mind

An area that is taking longer to be taken up by this population is that of PIP. At this point in the infancy of Menucha, it is difficult to know the extent to which mothers fully understand what this entails and steps are gradually being taken to disseminate this knowledge.

One speculation is the possible suspicion of 'the other', borne out of a very long history of persecution and the legacy of the Holocaust. Intergenerational trauma is active and appears in the consulting room in diverse guises and can be enacted as fear of letting in professionals (the possibly powerful and persecutory other); fear of social services having the authority to take away babies (with all the historic echoes); and the fear of judgement in a domain that is so prized, that of motherhood. There is often a history of closing down emotions and not talking about past generations' extreme experiences. The community has been identified in the past as a hard-to-reach group by statutory services. The dark history of being a persecuted minority throughout the centuries seems to be burned into the unconscious minds of the community, in spite of many never having experienced persecution first-hand in their own lives. Many *Charedim* (pious Jewish sects) escaped persecution in Eastern Europe and have Holocaust traumata, often transmitted intergenerationally, in their families of origin. Feelings of shame around not bonding with a God-given baby are very painful and the defence of dissociation is frequently present. There may also be an unconscious intergenerational survivors' guilt, which becomes activated by the creation of new infant life in the knowledge of brutal annihilation of previous generations.

A further element to consider when looking at PIP is the kind of mental representations of mothering within the internal world of women who were often the infants themselves of very young mothers who, in turn were mothered by very young mothers, perhaps characterised as the 'children' of 'children'. The author has often observed clinical cases where mothers are competently caring for the physical needs of their infant and often show physical affection but are not narrating; using motherese; mimicking sounds; or engaging in proto-conversations, and sometimes there does not seem to be easily observable signs of mentalising. Large families are the norm, and women often start procreating between the ages of 19 and 23 years.

Some of the women who have sought help from Menucha bring to the therapeutic situation an awakened needy infant in themselves (see the above case of Shira) and sometimes it appears that the space with the therapist is not something the mother wants to share with her baby. This can sometimes be overtly expressed as a time they desire without their baby (where mothers can be given attention). Some mothers may unconsciously long for a kind of primary maternal preoccupation from the therapist, which perhaps did not fully occur in their own infancy.

Conclusion

To give optimal support to this population, who have highly specific cultural needs and a strict code of living, a depth of knowledge, sensitivity, and understanding by professionals is necessary to guard against misinterpreting, misunderstanding, or misjudging. It is also important to recognise, in the context of a society that so fulsomely and publicly celebrates procreation, women who struggle at this time with feelings of depression, low mood, and anxiety activated by the very *raison d'etre* of Jewish life, may find it harder to disclose and reach out for help, compounding and maintaining their condition and isolation. In the words of two Menucha clients:

Menucha made me realise I was not crazy for what I was experiencing and that it is actually quite common. (anonymous, 2021)

This is the first time I have asked for help and not felt judged. (anonymous, 2022)

References

Gerhardt, S. (2004). *Why love matters.* Routledge.

Gillman, C. (2022). *Learning to love the spaces between: Discover the power of liminal spaces.* Welbeck.

Khan, M. M. (1983). On lying fallow. In M. M. Khan (Ed.), *Hidden selves* (pp. 183–188). Routledge.

Lutwak, R. A., Ney, A. M., & White, J. E. (1988). Maternity nursing and Jewish law. *MCN American Journal of Child Nursing, 13*(1), 44–46.

Music, G. (2017). *Nurturing natures* (2nd ed.). Routledge.

Schraer, S. (2024). The silence between: The role of transitional time and space to adjust to key life events in the Orthodox Jewish community. In Wayne, D. (ed.) *Attachment: New directions in psychotherapy and relational psychoanalysis.* Phoenix.

Chapter 37

The early parent-infant relationship

A discussion

Alejandra Perez and Ruth Roberts

The chapters in this section use a range of perspectives to explore the parent-infant relationship, including how it supports infant development and the different ways in which this relationship can be supported. In Chapter 31, Perez draws on psychoanalytic theories and illustrative clinical vignettes to explore the ways in which parents help infants to develop capacity for affect regulation and how this experience can be dysregulating for parents who must work to keep their own affect regulated during this process. In Chapter 32, de Rementeria uses psychoanalytic theories and reflections from infant observation to examine how parents and infants negotiate various separations that happen in the early parent-infant relationship, including birth, sleeping, and weaning. In Chapter 33, Lucas and Vrticka draw on empirical evidence to give insight into how sensitivity and synchrony impact the neuro-anatomical model of human attachment. In Chapter 34, Roberts draws on developmental research to discuss parental mentalising and how it shapes infants' ability to understand and navigate the complexities of their social world. In Chapter 35, Ogbuagu draws on her clinical expertise to explain how parent-infant psychotherapy works to improve the parent-infant relationship. The chapter provides a clinical vignette to illustrate how this intervention can give voice to the non-verbal baby and offer support to both the parent and the infant. Finally, in Chapter 36, Schraer offers a socio-cultural perspective on the parent-infant relationship, using religious text, psychoanalytic theories as well as clinical vignettes to describe the experiences of observant Jewish families and the importance of culturally-appropriate intervention.

The infant's developing capacities through the parent-infant relationship

The infant's developing capacities through the parent-infant relationship as described in this book are various, so it is important to first enumerate them. Perez, in her chapter in this section, thinks about the development of the infant's capacity for affect or emotion regulation, and the resultant modulation of behavioural and physiological reactivity; for the forging of connections between events; for the organisation, understanding, and mental representation of early experiences;

DOI: 10.4324/9781003530473-44

for the development of a sense of self; for complex social learning (such as language acquisition, and development of morality, theory of mind, and empathy); for the processing of raw sensory and emotional information, coming both from the external world and from inside their body (containment); for the development of a secure emotional bond or attachment and the consequent feeling of security; for projective forms of communication; and, finally, for transforming their self-experience (at least, beginning to do so). Perez also describes the baby's emerging capacity to psychically integrate different body parts and bodily experiences: what Winnicott (1962) termed the 'in-dwelling' of the mind in the body.

The chapter by de Rementeria offers a description of the infant's emerging capacity to think, form internal representations, and fantasise, as well as to relate to reality. She also touches on the infant's developing capacity to wait—to 'bridge the gap' between a present need and the moment when that need is me—and to mourn the loss entailed by the weaning process. Meanwhile, in her chapter Roberts details the infant's capacity to make use of joint attention with their caregiver, and to deploy information from another to make sense of their social world. Roberts also sets out how the parents' ability to mentalise forms the building blocks for the development of the infant's own capacity for mentalisation, and for emotional and behavioural regulation.

The oscillating closeness and distance needed to understand baby

Throughout this book, the different authors have highlighted the various parental capacities, functions, and positions required to understand, respond to, and help the infant develop the aforementioned capacities. We can broadly (albeit reductively) group all of the parental capacities and functions into two large groups: those that relate to closeness with the baby, and those that necessitate distance from the baby. Closeness here refers to the ability 'to put oneself in the shoes' of the baby; to become closely identified and to experience the baby's experience. This identification and experiencing can occur at different levels: emotional, bodily, unconscious phantasies, and conscious thinking. The chapters by Barba-Müller (Chapter 8), Dahan (Chapter 14), and Rutherford (Chapter 21) describe the physical changes (neurobiological, hormonal, and at a structural and functional brain level) that occur during pregnancy and early parenthood, and that allow a sensitivity to infant's cues that is not seen in non-parents nor at other stages in life. In Chapter 31, Perez outlines Winnicott's (1956) concept of unconscious identification, and demonstrates what such close identification looks like by way of a clinical vignette. In this vignette, a mother is momentarily confused about what is her body and what is her baby son's body, after having cut his fingernails. As Winnicott explained, in order to reach this level of identification with her baby, the mother needs to be somatically permeable, and Perez' clinical example illustrates clearly how a mother might, at times, feel that her son's body is her own.

Approaching from a different angle, in Chapter 22 Panagiotopoulou outlines brain imaging and qualitative research that shows how, for mothers in the early post-partum period, there is a lack of distinction between their baby's distress and their own needs; a blurring of bodily boundaries, where the mother's body becomes a shared space with the baby. Much as in Winnicott's (1956) description of the concept of 'primary maternal preoccupation', this psychic and bodily 'closeness' at any other stage in life, or within any other relationship, would raise concerns about psychological illness, precisely because of the lack of distinction and distance between self and other, and the concomitant loss of reality. But when nurturing a newborn or very young infant, the mother needs this lack of distinction—the intense closeness necessary to grasp what her baby might be experiencing.

However, crucially, the parent not only needs to achieve close identification with the baby—this 'living' of the baby's experience—they must also process this experience on behalf of the baby, which conversely demands a certain distance. The parent must 'step back' from their immersion in the baby's experience in order to access their own capacity to make sense of, and help transform, that experience into a form that the baby can tolerate. Perez (in Chapter 31) and Roberts (in Chapter 34) explain how the baby, with a still very limited capacity to regulate emotions and experience, requires support from another; the baby cannot manage this task on its own. The authors of this book examine the different levels on which this experiential processing takes place: the bodily level (that is, maternal metabolisation, a kind of digestion of somatic experiences); raw sensorial perception (where the parent gives psychic figuration to sensorial perceptions, transforming them into thoughts); unconscious phantasy (where the parent contains and processes intense emotions and drives and allows the development of a good internal object); the emotional level (emotion regulation and marked mirroring); sensitive attunement to an infant's attachment needs (helping develop a secure attachment relationship); and conscious thought (considering the baby's mental states). All of the instances mentioned here belong to a process in which the parent takes in information from the infant, then transforms it into something that they give back to the baby in a way that makes the baby feel understood and safe, and can then begin to make sense of the world. Building on these ideas, in Chapter 32 de Rementeria explores the importance of separation and distance for the baby's development, revealing how they foster the baby's capacity for symbolic thinking.

The challenge for many parents consists not only in the various capacities that they need to hold, but also in the ongoing oscillating movement between closeness and distance that they must negotiate. This sustained flexibility and responsiveness entail great psychic demands on the parent, and the presence of vulnerabilities, whether in the parent, the infant, or the environment, can lead to difficulties in the parent-infant relationship.

Getting it 'wrong' and getting to know parents and baby

The numerous clinical vignettes in these chapters show how parents' mental health vulnerabilities, early trauma, or unconscious conflicts, and lack of support and understanding from others (friends, family, medical professionals, and clinicians) might impede their ability to move between these close and distant ways of being with their baby, and thus hinder their understanding and support of their baby.

Though the vignettes are short, they are not meant merely to represent isolated moments. Rather, they capture an ongoing, stuck aspect in either the parent or environment that the clinician believes has begun to pervade the parent-infant relationship. This is important to emphasise because parents can at times feel persecuted by the need to 'get it right' with their baby all the time; the demand that they know their baby's needs from the very start. In fact, attachment research has shown that caregivers need only to 'get it right' in responding to their baby's needs approximately 50% of the time, in order to develop secure attachment (Woodhouse et al., 2020). Winnicott (1956) underscored the importance for the baby's development of the inevitable, regular failures in the environment (as long as they are not too impairing or intense)—what he termed 'good-enough' mothering. In his view, this imperfect, good-enough parenting helps the baby to gradually adapt to reality. However, while these ordinary failures are important for a baby's development, it should be emphasised that they are also unavoidable. Getting to know a baby inevitably entails getting it wrong at times (indeed, many times), as the individuality of the baby is largely unknown to the parent. The physical changes in the post-partum period and close identification with the baby help the parent to become more sensitive to their baby's needs, yet each baby is different (and each parent is different), and each parent will have to get to know their baby, and their particular way of experiencing the world, over time. Sometimes, it is only after 'getting it wrong' that a parent can understand what 'right' (at that particular moment) might be for their baby.

Similarly, clinicians and health professionals working with parents and babies also need to get to know and understand the parents and babies they are working with. In interactions with clinicians and health professionals, parents can at times have the experience of not being listened to, understood, or helped.

Psychoanalytic practice involves ongoing reflection about instances where the analyst or therapist 'gets it wrong', and why that might be. For example, as in Schraer's example of the nurse, it may be that misunderstandings arise due to a lack of knowledge of the cultural practices of the parents. The psychoanalytic clinician will have to consider how much their own anxieties about needing 'to know' or 'to get it right' stem from their own difficulties, and how much these anxieties might be signalling more subtle, complex, unconscious dynamics at play within the family that they are treating. It is of great importance that the clinician can remain in this unknowing state, and from there help the parents to explore their relationship with their baby. Work with parents and babies comes with a particular anxiety, as the baby's fragility, dependence, and highly time-sensitive development process bring a particular urgency to the work. In Chapter 35, Ogbuagu demonstrates the importance of getting it wrong in her work with parents: her modelling being imperfect and making mistakes offers a deep, authentic hope to the parents, showing them that this is all part of being with a baby. Moreover, and just as importantly, this 'realness' is what allows for sincere and repeated attempts at repair when one gets it 'wrong'.

Socio-cultural perspectives on parent-infant interactions

Cultural differences

The importance of understanding cultural variations in parent-infant relationships and parenting practices is also important and was noted by several authors. de Rementeria uses an example of how cultural differences can result in misunderstandings—an Indian colleague observed how an English colleague was lovely with the children she was working, which was at odds with her understanding that English women put their babies in cages to sleep at night. de Rementeria uses this example to highlight that when there is a divergence in cultural norms it is important to have curiosity about why there is a difference and not assume that one way of doing things is superior or inferior to the other.

Schraer also notes an important cultural difference in observant Jewish families that can be misunderstood for marital discord. Even with the intimacy of marriage, observant Jewish men do not directly observe their wives when they are immodestly exposed, so they are not normally present during childbirth. Not calling the baby by its name, which happens during cultural rituals after the birth, may be misinterpreted as attachment difficulty if there is not awareness of cultural practice.

It is also important to note that, although notions about parenting vary across cultures, there are also similarities in parent-infant interactions. Roberts notes research that finds that, although Korean parents have a unique view of the mother-infant dyad as being a single entity, allowing mothers to have a deep and accurate understanding of the infants' thoughts and feelings, Korean parents do not differ from British mothers on mentalising ability.

Cultural awareness

The section also highlighted that professionals and practitioners who work with parents and infants should consider the role of culture as part of their practice. Ogbuagu discusses how many families she sees clinically are raising their children in difficult circumstances, often far away from their cultural home of origin. She discusses the importance of the baby connecting with someone outside of the family when other family members are not present and how she often holds that role as part of therapy. She mentions how many cultures share stories to teach and guide the next generation and considers the importance of thinking about what may have been intergenerationally transmitted to the mother and baby, both consciously and unconsciously. She encourages parents to reflect on how their own parent managed experiences of racism and discrimination, which then helps them to think about how they will navigate similar encounters of prejudice with their own infant.

Schraer similarly highlights the importance of thinking about the experiences of previous generations. In the case of Jewish families, past generations have experienced extreme persecutory situations, which may intergenerationally transmit fear and suspicion of professionals, who have the power to make judgements and remove babies from the mother. This may also unconsciously manifest as survivor guilt in being able to create life where previous generations were robbed of theirs. Abedi (in Chapter 29) raised similar calls for awareness for Muslim families in the UK, where stigma around mental health prevents many from accessing help. This is in addition to the racism and prejudice they face from society.

Schraer also notes that many Jewish women become wives and mothers at an early age. This creates considerable change in the mother's life and can create feelings of overwhelm with all of the new responsibilities. They themselves might also have been a child of a young mother and therefore may want to use the therapeutic space to have time where the focus is just on them, without the baby, where the therapist can be highly sensitive and responsive to their needs.

Clashes between cultural expectations and individual experiences

Schraer noted the importance of recognising that individuals may, at times, feel at odds with their culture, which can cause feelings of discord. In Jewish culture, having children is part of religious commandments and the community derives great joy from the arrival of new infants. However, when difficulties emerge during the perinatal period, this may create feelings of shame and guilt in the new mother, particularly if her feelings and experience contrast with the expectations of the delight in the new baby. Having culturally-appropriate intervention allows parents the space to explore and express feelings that they may be viewed as transgressive by others in the community.

The various forms of support needed from conception to early parenthood

One aspect of the work of Lucas and Vrticka has been to explain to parents the importance of parental sensitivity and synchrony for their child's attachment. Their work has involved translating their research findings into accessible forms of communication so that this reaches not only parents, but also practitioners and organisations. Their chapter describes their findings. In sum, they explain how sensitive caregiving aids the child's stress response and emotion regulation. Nurturing touch and synchronous communication fosters emotional bonding and the infant's resilience.

A common thread from various authors throughout this book has been on the importance of support during these life stages. From family planning and conception, Grace (in Chapter 2) had emphasised the growing need for education to provide clear, destigmatising information, tailored to specific audiences. Chapters that have touched on psychoanalytic psychotherapy and supportive groups for expectant parents, parents, and parents and baby have highlighted the importance of a space where parents can explore, process, and understand their intense feelings and thoughts (conscious and unconscious) and be able to bond with their baby. The work of Lucas and Vrticka brings another element—the importance of psychoeducation and science communication more broadly. Translating complex theories and research into accessible language is crucial, building bridges between what is known and what is applied, and hopefully helping parents feel strengthened in their relationship to their baby.

Bringing it all together

This final discussion chapter does not aim to integrate or provide a definitive conclusion to all the varied and important material presented by the authors in this book. Instead, similarly to previous discussion chapters, it aims to bring together some arguments that have stood out to the editors. The value of placing some of these different perspectives side by side is that they generate, quite organically, new ways of thinking about the material.

It seems fitting that the discussion chapters have been the most difficult to write, yet also the most intriguing; within each section of this book is an abundance of rich, complex, diverse material that is difficult to tie together. In many respects, the various ideas and theoretical positions presented here feel very familiar, and yet they are surprising: it would seem that, despite the familiarity of the individual perspectives, when placed side by side they form an engaging and truly productive dialogue. Certainly, this has provoked much thought in us as editors, enabling and encouraging us to think about the many ideas that we need to better understand. We hope that this book provides a similar experience for readers; that it helps them to build an understanding of the complexity of early parenthood and infancy from various perspectives, and encourages them to explore even more widely in this field of study.

References

Winnicott, D.W. (1956)[1975]. Chapter XXIV. Primary maternal preoccupation. *Through Paediatrics to Psycho-Analysis (International Psycho-Analytical Library)* (No. 100, pp. 300–305). London: Hogarth Press & Institute of Psycho-Analysis.
Winnicott, D.W. (1962)[1965]. Providing for the child in health and in crisis. *Int Psycho-Anal Lib, 64*: 64–72.
Woodhouse, S.S., Scott, J.R., Hepworth, A.D., & Cassidy, J. (2020) Secure base provision: A new approach to examining links between maternal caregiving and infant attachment. *Child Dev, 91*(1):e249–e265. doi: 10.1111/cdev.13224.

Index

For Product Safety Concerns and Information please contact our EU
representative GPSR@taylorandfrancis.com
Taylor & Francis Verlag GmbH, Kaufingerstraße 24, 80331 München, Germany

www.ingramcontent.com/pod-product-compliance
Lightning Source LLC
Chambersburg PA
CBHW050628280326
41932CB00015B/2569